CRITICAL ACCLAIM FOR

Invisible Eden

"Flook, who wrote powerfully in *My Sister Life* about her own traumatic, tumultuous coming-of-age, proves to be a savvy, meticulous guide through the thicket of lovers, lawyers, police, friends, and family that surround the murder case . . . While wisely resisting any rush to judgment, Flook nevertheless has produced a chilling, compelling drama."

—*Elle*

"A pungent telling of the tale. . . . In Worthington, Flook found her doppelganger—a single mother, a writer, another refugee in Truro. . . . The identification with her subject . . . injects urgency and empathy into the narrative. Flook writes shrewdly and often with exquisite care about the opposite worlds—Cape Cod and fashion—that were both nurturing and destructive to Christa Worthington. She understands the significance of mollusks in one environment and of tulle in the other, as well as the social hierarchies that prevail in each of these domains. Flook has cooked a sultry chowder from the varied ingredients of Christa Worthington's life and death, whose essence is both exotic yet familiar."

—*New York Times Book Review*

"Flook remains, at least on the surface, nonjudgmental; she allows the characters to hang—or exonerate—themselves. She's also very good on Truro's landscape, the remoteness that's kept the town charmed and protected, though it has its share of notorious history. Even her conjectures and color commentary have the grace of authority. A thoughtful, measured tone gives this tale of murder a sense of depth and reach."

—*Kirkus Reviews*

INVISIBLE EDEN

INVISIBLE

MARIA FLOOK

EDEN

A STORY OF LOVE AND MURDER

ON CAPE COD

BROADWAY BOOKS   NEW YORK

Book design by M. Kristen Bearse

The Library of Congress has cataloged the hardcover edition as:
Flook, Maria.
    Invisible Eden : a story of love and murder on Cape Cod / Maria Flook.—1st ed.
        p. cm.
    1. Murder—Massachusetts—Truro—Case studies. 2. Worthington, Christa, 1955– 3. Fashion editors—Crimes against—Massachusetts—Truro—Case studies. 4. Crimes of passion—Massachusetts—Truro—Case studies. 5. Cape Cod (Mass.)—Social life and customs. I. Title.

HV6534.T78F56 2003   364.15'23'0974492—dc21   2003041853

ISBN 0-7679-1376-0

10 9 8 7 6 5 4 3 2 1

AUTHOR'S NOTE

Invisible Eden was written during an ongoing murder investigation on Cape Cod. No arrests have been made. Individuals portrayed here all deny involvement in the crime. The murder investigation is still active as we go to press. The book does not attempt to solve the crime.

PART ONE

PARADISE ICE

Cape and Islands First Assistant District Attorney Michael O'Keefe told me to meet him Saturday night. He had agreed to discuss the recent murder of forty-six-year-old fashion writer Christa Worthington, who was found dead on the kitchen floor of her seaside cottage, her toddler daughter nestled by her side. O'Keefe said, "We'll meet. We'll talk. We'll talk about how we keep our mouths shut." He agreed to sit down, but first he was taking me to the Mashpee Wampanoag Winter Ball at the Sons of Italy Lodge in Cotuit. O'Keefe was running for office and had to show up at these community spectacles. It helped to have a woman along.

O'Keefe had known Chief Vernon "Silent Drum" Lopez and medicine man Earl Cash, Jr., for a long time, but I'd never met the Wampanoag tribe officials. I knew that in 1620, the Pilgrims had their first encounter with Native Americans in Truro, the small town where I live. A group of half-starved English separatists, led by Miles Standish, pilfered the savages' stash of corn that was buried in a sand dune. It was a rustic caper, but I guess you can say it was the first B&E, or "breaking and entering" violation, perpetrated on Cape Cod by white men. Today, the little crime scene is called Corn Hill.

O'Keefe apologized for making me drive all the way up Route 6 on Suicide Alley, a tight two-lane highway that bisects the peninsula, famous for its long chronicle of head-ons. A lot of travelers avoid the bottleneck and turn around. O'Keefe said he didn't know why anyone with free will would choose to live way out on the tip.

The Cape Cod peninsula is like a flexed arm thrust into the sea. Truro is at its "wrist," and is only a mile wide at its most narrow site. The slender hook is the afterthought of the Wisconsin Stage glacier, a monstrous wall of ice ten thousand feet thick that shaped all of New England twenty-five thousand years ago. Today, the Outer Cape is still carved and remastered by tides, storm surges, waves, and wind. The Cape is a river of sand; the shoreline continually shifts and rebuilds its ridges. Backshore lagoons arise and disappear from one year to the next. The finial arm is always roaring and tingling, eroding three to six feet a year. All aspects of life this far out are evoked and controlled, atoned for or punished, by the sea. That's what I like about it.

But the Outer Cape has a chaotic, fiddlehead topography of dunes and swales that curl around in a spiral. Standing on the breakwater at Land's End, you can lose your sense of direction entirely. What is supposed to be due west is actually looking south, and northward could be east. A person living at the inverted tip has to let go of common sense, drop the reins and rely on intuition, especially in sea mists.

"Why do you live way out there, on that clam strip?" O'Keefe said.

"You mean Truro?"

"That wilderness. Why do you people go for that?"

You people could be Truro's movers and shakers, but more likely O'Keefe is referring to the Land's End losers, lost souls and drifters who wash ashore and pile up down here.

"I guess it's not for everybody," I said. O'Keefe's sentiments mirrored those of the Reverend James Freeman, who in 1790 wrote about Truro, "What could induce any person to remain in such a place?" Even today, many people think that the Outer Cape is a "no man's land," "a god-forsaken wasteland," or "a situation so completely removed from the stir of society," as Emily Brontë writes in *Wuthering Heights*. Even Thoreau was appalled by the Outer Cape, and wrote of Truro, "We shuddered at the thought of living there" and "The walker there must soon eat his heart."

But for *us* it's Eden. It's heaven on earth. In fact, at the end of the selectmen's annual report filed in 1982, it was written, "The Board of Selectmen shall continue to make every effort to seek ways to keep Truro the Garden of Eden of Massachusetts." But I wasn't going to try to convert O'Keefe. I was getting used to his jabs.

In the summer, I like to swim in the Pamet River across from Depot Road, Christa's street. I like it when the tide turns and the water seems to percolate with indecision—its crystal surface becomes chaotic and cross-hatched—is it coming or going? From my side of the tidal river, I had often seen young mothers with their kids. On sunny afternoons, a row of beach umbrellas blooms on the beach across the inlet. As the day advances, one by one these tilts are plucked and carried away. One of these gaudy pinwheels might have been Christa's.

Police have estimated that Worthington's body had not been discovered for thirty-six hours. Left unattended all that time, the little girl was found snuggled beside her mother, nursing. The police found evidence that the toddler had tried to help. A bloodied facecloth was neatly folded across the victim's forehead, and beside the body, they found the baby's weighted Tippee Cup that Ava had tried to offer to her mother.

The event of a murder in our small community was never expected. There hadn't been a murder in Truro for thirty years. Truro is renowned for its stunning wilderness, its remoteness, its quiet. In a recent issue of *Men's Journal,* Truro was placed near the top of the list in their survey "Fifty Best Places to Live." The article noted that one reason for its charmed status is that Truro is just about "invisible. And it means to *stay that way.*" No such luck, when, for instance, one summer, Air Force One helicopters swooped in to deliver Vice President Al Gore and his family at a summer retreat. And Hollywood celebrates "invisible" Truro as the ideal bucolic spot in its blockbuster movies *Men in Black* and *Men in Black II.* In both these films, our small town is depicted as home and haven for Tommy Lee Jones' character, who flees violence and alien threats and returns here to become the "Truro postmaster." As absurd as that might be, before Christa's death was discovered on January 6, a murder in our town would have seemed even a further stretch.

Christa Worthington, the onetime *Women's Wear Daily* dynamo turned single mom, was a high-profile victim. Her killing presented instant contradictions; it crossed boundary lines within the small insular society of Truro, which had always seemed charmed and protected, like a village in a snow globe. Incongruent hitches emerged in a hodgepodge. Christa's chic CV, her Yankee credentials, and patrician lifestyle had become enmeshed with the Outer Cape's blue-collar mystique of mariner traditions, rogue sailors, lady-killers, and one local legend in particular.

Secrets, sex, and money.

The principals at the core of the murder were an offbeat triangle.

There was Tony Jackett, a handsome harbormaster/shellfish constable; Tim Arnold, a quiet, sometimes stormy children's book author; and the woman who had entranced them both, Christa Worthington, a fashion writer. Praised by her editors, one of whom had called her a "fashion anthropologist," Christa left the fashion world and had holed up in Truro with her out-of-wedlock "miracle baby."

In addition to Jackett and Arnold, the murder had an unusual cornucopia of possible suspects. "*Suspect* is a TV word," O'Keefe griped, but the list of people "in the orbit of opportunity" was a ragtag patchwork of the American quilt.

The list included the philanderer's jilted wife, Susan, who remained "the undisputed most beautiful girl to ever graduate from Provincetown High School"; Jackett's edgy, Rapunzel-look-alike daughter, Braunwyn; the estranged husband of the edgy daughter, Keith Amato; Jackett's handsome and monastic sons, Luc and Kyle; and Christa's own father, Christopher "Toppy" Worthington, a retired Boston lawyer. Toppy's young girlfriend, Beth Porter, an ex-prostitute with a heroin habit, was also under investigation. A contrapuntal rumor soon began to circulate that Porter wasn't just a shack job but that she was Toppy's love child from an extramarital affair he had had when Christa was growing up.

That's quite a piebald gymkhana and I needed O'Keefe to help me sort through it.

O'Keefe is usually deadpan, with a wicked gleam that surfaces now and then. His stony face, dark hair, and compact physique is an attractive amalgam of two schools: the film noir detective and the all-too-familiar mainstream-TV *Kojak*. His locution is acerbic, clipped. He speaks in monosyllabic crits of whatever falls in front of him. Serious to a fault, his veneer is hard to break through, highly polished, and he doesn't volunteer much. But his introspections sizzle beneath the surface. It's my goal to soften him up. It's going to be tough to penetrate the steely prosecutor coupled with the savvy politician in him.

O'Keefe had told me, "I've stood over every dead body on the Cape for the last eighteen years. Unattended deaths—you have to figure out if it's suicide, accident, or murder. Like that boy killed last week in West Yarmouth—that was a violent crime. That kid lost twelve pints of his fourteen pints of blood."

"Twelve pints?"

"There's a lot of blood in you," he said.

That's almost a river. I imagined him rolling up his trouser cuffs.

"I've got a mortician's sense of humor by now," he said.

I wanted to learn how O'Keefe nosed around "murder world" without it seeping into him. It was taking its toll on me. I see Christa everywhere. If there's a woman with a little curly-topped girl in the A&P, at the ATM at Seamen's Bank, or a woman waving her Mobil speed pass, her back to me, filling her tank at the next pump, she might have Christa's high forehead, pouty lips, or sorrel hair.

Of course, it's a nobody.

The night of the Wampanoag Ball, I had volunteered to tag up with O'Keefe at the commuter lot at Exit 6 on the Mid-Cape Highway. I thought that it was a convenient spot to leave one of our cars. But he told me to go straight to his office in Barnstable. He'd meet me. He explained that his office was in the big white colonial a couple of doors east of the county courthouse, across from the Dolphin Restaurant and the demure little Barnstable post office. I took my first baby steps just up the street at 6A, and I thought I knew by heart the seventeenth-century picture-book village: the courthouse; the Barnstable Tavern; the Dolphin Restaurant; the Cancer Ransack Shop; shake-roofed cottages and Victorian guesthouses; the block-to-block antiques emporiums; and, at one time, there was an aviary that sold budgies and society finches. But I had never been inside the DA's office.

I arrived after sunset to find the building empty, blacked out. Not one light on. I left my car to walk around the footprint, in case there was an entrance on the other side and maybe O'Keefe expected me to find him. The mountain wasn't going to come to me. As I toured outside the building, I saw the Barnstable County House of Corrections perched just up the hill. Originally built to house seventy-five inmates, it now kennels three hundred. The complex was blazing; a modest little compound with an afterthought of concertina wire that twinkled in the floodlights.

As I circled the white colonial that fronted Main Street, I sidestepped a little mess on the sidewalk, a broken jar of jelly. I stared at the sugary tumble of shattered glass and strawberries. It must have jimmied from a shopping bag and exploded right here. Its blood-red pectin stained a deep scallop on the fresh-swept paving stone. Roadside stands all over Cape Cod sell these homemade jellies, watermelon pickle, and corn relish, but none of these kiosks would be in operation yet. It was early March and still the off-season. The little tub didn't have a label. I stooped and poked the weeping blob with a fingertip. I tasted it. Sweet with a sharp aftertaste.

The little treasure upset me. One time I had left a little jam pot in smithereens in a hotel room in Manhattan. Room service had brought croissants and coffee, and I pitched the mini-jar at my visitor's head as he had skulked out the door.

A car purred into the side lot and squeezed beside my Camry. I walked over to the passenger door. Instead of inviting me to sit down beside him, O'Keefe climbed out of the car. His door swung wide open to deliver a powerful blow of astringent cologne. As the car light flicked on, I saw the spray container propped on the console: "Eternity—for Men." I wondered if he brought his aftershave bottle everywhere he went.

O'Keefe was groomed and suited up in an elegant pinstripe. He was wearing the midnight-black camel hair overcoat I'd admired the first time I met him. The Wampanoag Ball was a semiformal affair. I had wanted to wear trousers because I had recently broken my ankle and it was still swollen. My vanity wounded, I sacrificed my pride and wore a little basic black number and a pair of flats. I was just out of a cast and couldn't wear heels. Embarrassed by the infirmity, I explained to O'Keefe that I felt "uneven," kicking one toe out and then the other to show him my lopsided conformation. I might as well admit the deficit and douse any expectations for perfection. He examined the damage and said, "Well, at least you're standing up."

We were just breaking the ice, but the exchange reminded me of James M. Cain's critique about a woman's "legworks" in the first pages of his noir mystery novel *Serenade*. Something about O'Keefe had reminded me of Cain's obsessive reverence for women even as he dismissed them, like a man who fears his addiction might be revealed if he doesn't publicly decry it.

I saw O'Keefe's hair was still damp from a hasty shower. O'Keefe didn't have an extra minute to waste. His law enforcement schedule was dawn to the wee hours, and he was always charging through his tasks full speed. From his morning coffee, he hopped from his offices with DA Phillip Rollins to the courthouse, to the state police barracks, to CPAC meetings for crime prevention and control, to taped-off chambers-of-horror murder scenes, to community soirees with teapots and trays of petits fours. He is a public man. He told me that he'd been up to the state crime lab in Sudbury, "twisting their arms and holding hands" to get them to complete DNA testing for the Worthington case. In the Sudbury lab, DNA capabilities are so limited that each of the state's district attorneys can submit only one case a month, first come, first serve. "They don't have the bodies," O'Keefe said.

"The bodies? Where do they take the bodies?"

He looked at me as if I was a "silly" and he said, "They don't have the resources. This is Massachusetts. We don't, we *do not* invest in the law enforcement infrastructure. We ran out of state police overtime money February ninth. Done. Gone—even in the best of times, this state doesn't spend enough dough on law enforcement. In the end, fingers are going to wag. The press are yapping, like with that Ramsey case in Colorado."

"You mean, in Colorado they didn't have money for their investigation either?"

"No, in that case, the investigators didn't know what they were doing. I'm not going to take that kind of hit here because *we* know what we're doing." O'Keefe maneuvers in and out of these political boondoggles and the investigation proceeds, he says, "with one arm tied behind its back." It was strange to hear him anthropomorphize a law enforcement procedure. But even as he bitches, he's wearing his impenetrable face, and he doesn't wipe it off until he's alone late at night and settles down to watch the Golf Channel. Recently divorced, he says he keeps the TV on to screen out the roaring quiet. But I imagined that even when he's at home, stretched out on the sofa, his face would be affectless.

He walked ahead of me into the dead building. He unlocked the heavy bolt and held the door for me. Once inside, he couldn't find the light. We walked blind through a few twisting hallways until he had me squared at the bottom of a staircase. The creaky risers were muffled beneath carpet treads as we ascended into the pitch. For an instant, I wondered if the blackout was a gimmick, but he said, "Shit. You'd think I should know where the damn switch is. Just bear with me." At the top of the landing, he patted the wall until the fluorescents fluttered and locked on.

I looked around O'Keefe's office. It was orderly, almost too spanking clean, with neatly stacked folders on one corner of his desk, pens, a blotter, and lots of golf-motif bric-a-brac. Before I could drink it in, O'Keefe grabbed an accordion file from a shelf and turned me around in my tracks. "We need the conference table," he said. I saw that the file had "Worthington" scrawled in black felt tip across its wood-grain cover.

He steered me into a different room, an empty oblong with a honey pine table. He pulled out a chair for me, but he didn't sit down. He lit a cigarette.

As he tugged smoke into his lungs, I tore the difficult plastic tab from a piece of Nicorette.

"You don't want a cigarette?" he said.

"No. I do the gum."

"No kidding? Good for you."

"Not exactly. I chain-chew. I'm a user just like you."

"Smoking isn't glamorous."

"I don't know much about glamour. *Women's Wear Daily* puts out an annual issue called 'Fashion Victims.' That's me."

O'Keefe says, "Murder happens for one of two reasons. 'Fashion' isn't one of them."

"What then?"

"Sex or money."

In my experience, all of life's conflicts and injuries seem to originate from these markers.

O'Keefe pulled the elastic loop from the "Worthington" expanding file and let it snap brightly in the empty room.

He upended the file and spilled five packets of three-by-five color glossies onto the table. He opened one of the envelopes and sorted the photos. He slapped the first snapshots on the tabletop in even rows, aligning them in a studious grid as if he were dealing a game of solitaire.

The photos documented each cluttered room of the little house. The decor was a mix of quirky mementos, pedigree antiques, and ordinary refuse. A friend of Christa's had told me that her cluttered Gramercy Park apartment in New York had been "cyclonic in its disorder, like a ransacked Fabergé egg." And here, in the photo of her Cape Cod kitchen, everything is in disarray, with open jars, dirty plates, scummed glasses lined up on the sink. There isn't an inch of available space. Every surface is a mosaic of haphazard items, kitchen utensils, trash, books, and minutiae, relics of exquisite taste jumbled together with evidence of an ordinary untamed life.

The living room is crammed wall to wall with a toddler's play gear: Fisher-Price bikes and Playskool furnishings; dollhouses; stuffed animals; toys-toys-toys. Bright reds and yellows dominate these preschool plastic emporiums. The gaudy tableau seems twice as bright against the black windows with the night seaside beyond.

Next, he shows me a photo of a cell phone left on the kitchen table. Its lighted LED panel displays only one digit, the number nine punched in. O'Keefe said, "She might have been trying to get nine-one-one."

Without narrative, without melodrama, but almost ceremoniously, he finds the series of prints he really wants to show me. He sorts these in an articulated, methodical progression, in a kind of forensic foreplay, as he positions the photographs before me. I sense his conflicted thoughts, his professional awe, excitement, and gravity, a commitment to his lifelong work, but he's giving me access to evidentiary graphics usually reserved for VIPs. I don't know his angle.

I look down at the table.

It's her. The universal *she*.

Here I connect. I forget O'Keefe.

I'm face-to-face with Christa.

She is almost stripped naked. She lies on her back, her legs scissored, one knee bent. A black jersey is pushed up to her throat, hiding part of her tipped face. Her chestnut hair tumbles in a fan, revealing her bruised and swollen temple. Her tan lines are still visible, but faded since summer. I follow the long plain of her high waist and tight belly, that ends with the predictable little pie wedge of dark wool.

A smeared doily of congealed blood rings the floor to the right of her face.

The toddler, left unattended for thirty-six hours, has trekked bloody footprints from the irregular halo. O'Keefe says with matter-of-fact instruction, "This is probably aspirated blood that she vomited in death throes and gurgles."

Her body lies in a tight doorway between two rooms, where she was felled and stabbed once. A single penetration severed through her trunk to puncture the triangular wall of muscle in her back, called the "trapezius."

O'Keefe tells me that the tip of the blade had pierced clear through, deep enough to actually nick the plank floor underneath.

He collects the upsetting rubric, and hunts through the collection for another image to put before me. He centers the photo on the table. For an instant I think, "Is this a joke?"

All of her bikini underpants are lined up across the double bed.

The photograph shows several pairs of skimpy, French-cut panties arranged in lofting rows like a swarm of butterflies. The state police have emptied her bureau drawers to arrange the display, like a pop art installation by feminist artist Judy Chicago or Portia Munson. O'Keefe says, "These are all Victoria's Secret."

Does he think only an adulteress wears these? I say, "They're not Italian lace or anything."

He looks at me. Maybe I was revealing too much. Once, before a tryst, I had shopped for the Italian version.

"So, it's run-of-the-mill. Lots of girls have Victoria's Secret," he says.

"It's a franchise. There's a store in the Cape Cod Mall."

"These were cotton," O'Keefe says.

I don't ask him why the state police took photographs of the victim's panties. I guess it's some kind of profiling technique, as if to document a victim's lingerie could somehow encompass a person's prehistory, her life's goals and expectations. Cotton or satin? They must think there's a connection between these common textiles and the victim's morals and intentions.

I don't want to study her panties lined up across her tousled bed, and I hunt through more photos of her cluttered house, trying to find comfort in the tumble of domestica. A bowl of Cheerios is left on the lip of the kitchen table. Perhaps the little girl had tried to fill a bowl, or Christa herself might have prepared a bedtime snack before she was assaulted. The familiar oat rings are compelling to me; my own kids walked around with cups of Cheerios. Enough toasty *o*'s to fill a silo. The familiar name brand is a staple used in weaning and child-rearing. But O'Keefe doesn't have children. He isn't touched by the same nostalgia. He looks at the messy rooms. "She was really a slob," he says.

Christa might not have polished every doorknob, but he didn't have to call her names. I wonder what he'd think of my spread, overrun by dogs and cats and teenage boys. I feel a soft spot for Christa, maybe since a friend had told me a story that evoked Christa's playfulness. He had said that whenever a stranger annoyed Christa by talking in a booming voice on his cell phone, in a restaurant or at the airport, she would open her book and start reading out loud. As the stranger jabbered, she recited lines from whatever modernist master or dime novel she had at hand. Her method wasn't overtly confrontational, but with an amount of decorum and wit she won control. It was hilarious, he said, and it always seemed to work.

O'Keefe collects another row of photos. "Wait. Give me that one again," I say. Resting on the floor in her bedroom is a giant mirror with a baroque gilt frame. The wood is carved with elaborate crockets and leaves. It takes up the wall floor to ceiling, and looks like a shimmering pass-through to the beyond, a portcullis between heaven and hell.

"That's some mirror," O'Keefe says.

I tell him, "Her friends say she bought that in Paris and she lugged it back and forth across the Atlantic at great expense."

I wonder what O'Keefe thinks. Usually mirrors this size are bolted to the ceiling at sex spas and massage parlors.

I notice a table lamp on the bureau in the bedroom where she slept on a mattress with her baby. The lamp is an antique "running horse" weathervane. The trotting horse in midstride at the center of a crime scene is shockingly beautiful, a piece of realia that bespeaks a wrenching sweetness. Yes, this lamp is charmed. Its romantic whimsy eases the gritty stereoscope before me. There's something uncompromising about beautiful things. In her lonesome belongings, I sense an intimate sisterhood. Cheerios. Fisher-Price toys. The running horse weathervane. The mirror. The broken jelly jar outside on the street.

But the naked female, she's just too familiar. Her legs akimbo. Her little muff of frizz. Killers who do not dispose of bodies will sometimes arrange their victims for a meticulous presentation, arranging arms and legs just so, spread-eagled or knee-to-knee, and smoothing tousled hair, even using a rat-tail comb to part it, only to leave the comb behind as a calling card. It's a way to prolong the exquisite instant, and to extend final control over the victim.

Christa and I lived one mile apart but we had never met.

I look at the glossy photographs under the fluorescent light, a fractured mosaic of ragtag swatches and scraps, simple household treasures, dirty dishes, baby toys, and Christa's "delicates." In the checkerboard of snapshots, I see my face reflected.

SWAMP YANKEES

Things aren't looking good for Churchill," a tourist tells her friend.
"Yeah, Churchill is doomed. Poor thing." The sunburned and bikini-clad exchange the latest updates about the fifty-ton North Atlantic right whale as they stand in line at Parad*Ice*, a seasonal outlet for frozen treats and pick-me-ups.

"Churchill," the biggest story on Cape Cod during the summer of 2001, has become a national headline. Rescue attempts have proved unsuccessful ever since the whale was discovered struggling for its life on Cultivator Shoal, seventy-five miles east of Cape Cod. The Center for Coastal Studies in Provincetown, led by local hero Stormy Mayo, and with the help of the National Marine Fisheries Service, has tracked endangered "right whale #1102" for two months. They had hoped to remove a loop of synthetic fishing line that snagged its upper jaw. The injury has become necrotic. Its skin is peeling and its flesh is infected with "sea lice." Boats have steamed out of Provincetown Harbor several times to locate and sedate right whale #1102 so they might try to extract the entangled line. A drag buoy and transmitter tag have been attached to the whale for seventy-five days with a distance logged of 3,816 miles. By midsummer, the whale had earned its pet name, "Churchill." But each time the whale is sighted, the wound is worse, the sea lice increasing.

Churchill has been the table talk in Truro all summer. Its story is romantic summer fare, rich with sea lore, suspense, government red tape, and the contest between modern man and nature's biggest innocent. The whale's predicament has won the attention of year-rounders and tourists, whether wealthy summer residents with second homes in upscale Shearwater Estates, manses high above the bay, or the working-class families who have one-week rentals at Truro cottage colonies. The most famous bayside string is Day's "flower cottages"; each spartan shack has a different signboard tacked snugly above the door with its botanical name: Wisteria, Peony, Daisy, Lilac. Twenty-two in all. The tight progression of sparkling cottages follows the curve of Shore Road, from Knowles Hill to Beach Point. From across the water, the shacks look like a row of sharp white incisors.

Everyone roots for Churchill. There are only three hundred right whales in existence. Each newsbreak is disheartening. A biopsy was taken, but the seas were too choppy and halted another effort to disentangle the whale. At the post office, at town beaches, and in the long queues at Parad*Ice*, whale talk dominates the chitchat and total strangers commiserate over their cups of shaved ice.

In Shangri-la, people let their guard down. When visitors arrive on Cape Cod, they enter the ethos of leisure and R&R, *retirement* and recreation, of life without work. For some, it's bald-faced liberty. Defiance. Crossing the canal bridge at Sagamore, one can plead instant amnesia. The canal has even earned the nickname "The River of Forgetfulness," like Lethe. On Cape Cod, the two poles of linear time lose definition, the clock is disconnected. Year-rounders can't claim the same privilege. But even locals who hold regular jobs at the fish piers and souvenir shops, the motel maids, taking a break from a busy changeover Saturday, Irish girl houseworkers from cleaning services called Merry Maids and The Furies, everyone welcomes the distraction from their monotonous routines. Churchill doesn't belong only to marine zoologists and privileged summer folk; he's everyone's mascot.

Parad*Ice* is in Truro Center, just off the Route 6 dike that spans the Pamet River. The small snack shack is a summer landmark, nestled between the tiny post office, the Duarte Real Estate office, and Rock Spray Nursery. Two teen girls are behind the counter.

The girls are nice to look at, but their fingertips are stained with ghoulish food dyes. Pink syrups. Blue syrups. As they wipe their hands on their white aprons, it's liver red. The girls are busy, the line is deep. Tourists love the niveous confection that is smooth, sinful, fierce, dense as powdered snow. It's not your typical Coney Island slushie or 7-Eleven Slurpie or hockey puck of Italian Ice, but a rainbow palate of Matisse colors pumped in generous dollops. Maybe Tiger's Blood or Blueberry Blast. The little establishment's clientele soars in August when Truro's population spikes from eighteen hundred to thirty thousand. Today the shack is swarming.

The restless queue is made up of teen boys in wet suit couture; bird enthusiasts with multiple sets of binoculars and zoom cameras dangling from Velcro straps; fair-skinned Nordic nannies with sun poisoning; Casanova college boys, their surfboards tied onto car roofs like fiberglass codpieces; Boston lawyers and Milk Street bankers wearing four-figure prescription sunglasses; dowagers wrapped up, mummied against the ultraviolets; sport fishermen with lures pinned to their hat brims and their city wives shrieking at Styro cups of live bait, sea worms and sand eels writhing; cyclists in bike tights with padded fannies; single chicks in thong bikinis and straw hats flat as cymbals from a drum kit; oldsters with wicker hampers stocked with a kitty of smoked bluefish and sweaty thermoses of Bombay Sapphire, ready to assemble their martinis at the nightly croquet game on the post office green at cocktail hour. Year-rounders call them "Upper Crustaceans." These are the privileged Parad-*Ice* patrons. It's rare to see chambermaids and landscapers, well-diggers or dishwashers. Not too many shellfish constables, but sometimes *he* stops here.

She stands in line. A slender woman in a tank suit, her beach towel knotted low on her hips like a Tahitian sarong. Her oval face, its high forehead and wide eyes, gives her a childlike cameo, although Christa's in her mid-forties. She has an uncanny likeness to a John Singer Sargent society portrait, most particularly to a painting of the pale Victorian beauty Elizabeth Winthrop Chanler. These milky-skinned charmers, from two different centuries, could be twins. But Christa's curly-haired toddler, clinging to the hem of her beach towel, is entirely different. She has her own distinctive Mediterranean coloring, with skin like golden honey. A woman, standing in line beside Christa, says, "Her daddy must really be something."

Then the chatter returns to Churchill. They like sharing scientific jargon and nautical terms they have learned from the "whale reporter," Emily Dooley, in the *Cape Cod Times*.

A mother could lose her patience having to wait so long with a finicky two-year-old who had missed her afternoon nap. A little scoop of blueberry ice, the color of Windex, would do them both good. Christa is used to the lollygagging vacationers, although she isn't one of them. She's not a washashore but has roots here, even if her roots have sometimes tangled and shifted beneath the surface.

Christa's family dug in a hundred years ago. You won't find their name in the Mayflower Compact nor in the *Boston Social Register* with the Adamses, Cabots, Quincys, and Lowells. But they act anointed anyhow. They mythologize their family name and shoot from the hip.

Worthingtons have settled in.

Real Cape Codders call them "swamp Yankees." Velnette and Robert Worthington came to Truro in 1905. But it was their son, Christa's grandfather, John "Pop" Worthington, who was a beloved figure in town. Before settling in Truro, he had worked in oil fields in the Southwest and Mexico, was a pilot and a veteran of both world wars, and he had piloted a Stinson monoplane across the United States as a salesman for Merrimac Chemical Company. In 1934, he returned to revitalize a fish-processing plant in North Truro, Pondville Cold Storage Company, which provided employment for many local residents. Pop Worthington is credited with boosting trap fishing during the Depression, and he also pioneered rod and reel tuna fishing in Cape Cod Bay. Worthington was a town selectman, was on the board of appeals, and he was an original advocate for the Cape Cod National Seashore. He also gave Worthington land to the town for access to the harbor and to public beaches. Local resident Ken Hnis used to shear privet hedges and mow Pop Worthington's lawn, and when he was finished, Pop would drag him inside the house, pour him a drink, and make him sit down to watch final innings of a Red Sox game. Worthington didn't care if Kenny got drunk and missed his dinner, or if he left sweaty grass stains on the linen sofa cover. Pop Worthington was a "regular guy."

John's wife, Ada "Tiny" Worthington, was almost six feet tall. Reared in England, she brought an Anglo-bohemian mystique to life in Truro that would resonate for generations of Worthingtons. Tiny had been an actress, but she started a business of her own, making fashion accessories out of surplus fishnet textiles. Tiny's Fishnet Industries put Truro housewives to work, and her stylish products were sold at Bergdorf Goodman and Bonwit Teller. As a prologue to her granddaughter Christa's career in fashion journalism, Tiny's fishnet scarves, handbags, and turbans were photographed for the covers of leading fashion and teen magazines like *Vogue* and *Mademoiselle*.

The couple's business finesse helped the town survive during difficult times. Yet Pop Worthington acquired much of his land in tax takings. When folks couldn't pay their property taxes, he'd make loans to his struggling neighbors. The deeds reverted to him when they defaulted.

Christa had loved her grandparents and called them "the real deal." Today, Truro residents refer to John and Tiny as "the original Worthingtons," as if the next two generations don't add up to much, although Margaret Worthington and Ansel Chaplin, the son of Lucy Worthington, are noted conservationists, and her aunt Diana Worthington oversees the Truro Historical Museum. But Christa had been most in awe of her grandmother Tiny, whom she and her cousins had called "Titi." Tiny was refined, sometimes raw and cantankerous, but always honest with Christa. She gave Christa free advice about men. The Worthington women had their own code of romance etiquette: rules were supposed to bend and promises were made to be broken. Christa listened to their stories about the opposite sex, even when the story was revealed in small gestures, secret looks, and not a word breathed about it. Tiny had had a romance with the renowned singer and actor Paul Robeson. Her affair with the black actor was a chic bohemian dalliance that set a high bar for other Worthington distractions, and there were many to come. Almost all the Worthington women—Christa, her aunts, and cousins—were "free-spirited" and were known to have bedded fishermen, contractors, flea market barons, bartenders, and local police officers, but there were artists and movie actors among their suitors. Christa's aunt, Lucinda Worthington, divorced and remarried her same husband three times, but she had dated fishermen and had had a fling with actor Kevin McCarthy. Kevin McCarthy, the brother of Mary McCarthy, is famous for his movie role as the leading man in the original *Invasion of the Body Snatchers*. And Christa herself had once had her hands on a Vanderbilt scion.

Yet Christa had always been the odd sheep in the Worthington clan. Her mother, Gloria, had never felt accepted by her in-laws because she wasn't real Yankee. She wasn't even WASP, but was of Italian descent. She tried very hard to fit in. She had changed her maiden name from Santosossa to Sanders to become Gloria *Sanders* Worthington, and she even got her "nose done." Gloria was pregnant when she married Toppy and the Worthington family thought he had been forced to "marry down." Her father's extramarital affairs over the years were further proof to the family that Gloria just didn't cut the mustard. Christa felt her mother's isolation drift over to her. Some of her cousins were icy.

Truro is small. Some might say it's backward, a kind of "Appalachia by the sea." When hordes of retirees invade town meetings it looks like Sun City. Yet many noteworthies have rambled out this far to set up housekeeping at Land's End. Christa felt in good company, at least in a historical sense. Acclaimed painters Edward Hopper, Hans Hofmann, Ben Shahn have lived out here. Writers piled in. Dos Passos, Eugene O'Neill lived in the dunes at Peaked Hills, and Edmund Wilson purchased a Greek Revival in Wellfleet. Edna St. Vincent Millay lived out on Longnook Road. Current residents include Pulitzer Prize–winning poet and leftist Alan Dugan, and, down the street from him, best-seller Sebastian Junger, author of *The Perfect Storm*, who bought poet Waldo Frank's house "lock, stock, and barrel," including its precious library of rare books. Politicos inched in. Clinton's secretary of labor, Robert B. Reich, former finance chair of the Democratic National Committee Alan Solomant, and Marty Peretz, publisher of the *New Republic*, have all built trophy homes. Even the former director of the CIA, John Deutsch, hid away on Longnook Road after he was defamed.

Norman Mailer is still a squatter in Provincetown's East End.

But most arrivals are wannabe artists, dilettantes, losers, pirates and profiteers, eccentrics and misfits. Washashores come to Cape Cod to escape personal failures and fizzled careers on the mainland. Like the best and worst of these, Christa is someone searching for something. She isn't running. She is just trying to stand still.

She steps up to the counter to order a treat for Ava from the girls in their gruesome aprons when she sees his SUV pulling into the lot. She squares her shoulders and straightens her back. She stiffens. Tall and petrified. Stoic and paralyzed. She waits to see him climb down from the cab. His thick black hair in tight, blinding spirals, his angular face and smudged jawline. Each day, almost as soon as he has rinsed his razor, his brimming testosterone gives him a blue chin by lunchtime. With honeyed skin, he's like an island king from a time in history before men wore cloth shirts, Nikes, or Gore-Tex windbreakers. He's dressed in cutoffs and muddy waders. The shellfish constable in the flesh. Ava's father. The married man who blew her off when she was just six months pregnant.

She knows his routine; he's been down at the harbor selling clamming permits or he's out on the flats tending nursery boxes and trays of juvenile oysters called "spat," and checking seed clams nestled in the muck. The clam beds were coming back with new efforts by the Department of Marine Fisheries and entrepreneurs working together. It was his job to see that these little mollusks had a fighting chance. He drives by her place every day at quitting time when he leaves the harbor.

But it isn't him, after all. It's an impostor, another low-tide prowler in neoprene waders. Lots of amateurs have clam rakes and buckets, with or without a license.

Yet she has already turned Ava around by her little shoulders and marched her back to the car. "We've got Popsicles in the freezer," she says when Ava protests. She doesn't want to face him right then, in the blinding sun. Thank goodness. But she's angry at herself for imagining that it was him; she had missed another opportunity to be near him by happenstance. Sometimes she welcomed his surging effect on her again. Being in his presence could knock her down like a tidal wave, but more often she just wanted a chance to snub him. These conflicting fantasies were neverending. As she bends down to strap the baby into her car seat, the late-August sun burns her back until she feels it ignite in her diaphragm, a searing sensation, and she can't get her breath.

Her place, known by its diminutive nickname the "bungalow" or the "Little House" by family members, is on the west end of Depot Road, only three-tenths of a mile from Pamet harbor. Depot Road is almost like a private Worthington compound; it's not gated like the Kennedys' Hyannisport retreat, but it has a sequestered and remote aura of the mythologized, the privileged. Nonresidents who cruise the mile and a quarter that leads to Pamet harbor can feel as if they are driving without sanction onto private property, into a "no trespassing" zone where they have no legitimate reason to be. But it's a public town road and the only access to the harbor. Christa's aunts, uncles, and cousins live in a string of houses leading to the water; it's a virtual counterpane of Worthingtons. Close neighbors are Worthington sycophants, and a few motley nobodies who are happy to ignore them, including the Hollywood actor Ben Affleck's mother, who lives in a historic captain's house her son purchased for her last year.

Buddleia, rose arbors, trellises of wisteria and trumpet vine adorn the Cape Cod dwellings. Kitchen gardens are fenced against cottontails and skunks. The Worthington "compound" stretches all the way down to the Pamet inlet. They live in an array of antique cottages, updated houses, and a captain's manse, all with seaside vistas. Christa's aunts, uncles, cousins are in their own worlds, but it's an ethos of all-in-one and "us against them."

Her complicated relationship to her large family in Truro was an underlying factor in her choice to live in New York after college. From Manhattan, she went to Paris and from Paris she skittered to London. She didn't return home to Massachusetts very often.

In the summer of '97, Christa came back to Truro to live in "Tiny's Hut," a little cottage at Pamet harbor where she met the shellfish constable and part-time harbormaster. The next year in Truro, she fell into his arms again.

When her mother was dying, Christa was pregnant. Her baby's father had taken a powder. And Gloria, too, was virtually abandoned by her husband, who had found a rent-to-own escort to occupy his time. After a lifelong strained relationship, Christa and Gloria were united. They had both been jilted by their men. It was a poignant triangle: the living, the dying, the yet-to-be-born.

Less than a week after Gloria died, Ava arrived.

A person's immediate grasp of the human cycle of life is not often so vivid as Christa's ordeal. But in her wildest dreams, Christa never thought she'd be returning to Truro in her new role as a first and last chance matriarch, raising her own daughter at the bungalow where she spent her childhood summers.

Christa's house, a Victorian cottage, sits hidden at the end of a winding gravel drive, bordered by hummocks of beach plum, wild cherry, sweet fern, and rugosa roses that are still pumping out blooms with just a touch of leaf-edge crinkling in the August heat. Clumps of Russian sage and the droopy yaws of daylilies hang on. A thick wedge of old-fashioned climbers, eight feet high, shoulders the house, and clusters of red rose hips gleam like tiny Christmas balls.

The shingled house is bleached and weathered almost silver. The house, perched above Mill Pond, looks onto the bay, and at night at the twinkling necklace of Provincetown. A decade before, during Hurricane Bob, with winds gusting to 110 miles an hour, seawater sluiced over the barrier dune between Fisher Beach and Mill Pond and the freshwater marsh was killed off. It is slowly transforming to a saltwater estuary, but the changeover takes time. For now, the marshland view beneath her porch is a withered, poisoned scene of dead brush, skeletal sedge, dry plumes of canary grass, chalky husks of horsetails, and burned vine. It looks dead and unwilling, like a Grimms' fairy tale wasteland. Until new marine plants overtake the burned underbrush it will look cursed and forlorn. But switchgrass, marshmallow, glasswort, and sea lavender have begun to invade and the view should green up again. Her naturalist uncle, Ansel Chaplin, would say, "It's one world giving out, another world coming in. It's gradual. Be patient."

She sometimes felt that her own life was in sync with the evolving marsh. She welcomed the transformation. She had left her city life in New York and Paris to return to the untamed setting of her privileged but difficult childhood, but she found her complex family was a parallel ferment, a wilderness of the heart and mind.

Her self-imposed isolation on the windswept ridge was a life both independent and deprived, a hard-won freedom threatened by a piercing longing. She always second-guessed and fretted over her decisions. She overanalyzed everything. When she engaged in a new routine, she could never be sure if it was the means to an end, the end itself, or a move in the *absolutely wrong direction*. When in New York, she missed Paris; when in Paris, she wanted to be back in the States. Not until Ava did she begin to feel grounded, comfortable in her own skin. Ava was her whole world now.

At Vassar in the seventies, at the crest of feminist idealism, Christa and her classmates were told they could have it all: career and family. For Christa, it hadn't materialized. But a fashion writer can avoid looking homeward, or looking at herself; there was always a show going on.

In Paris, writing for *Women's Wear Daily*, she covered couture houses. Haute couture twice a year, and a few months after that, the ready-to-wear collections. She finagled exclusive previews and private sessions with designers, perhaps Karl Lagerfeld, Emanuel Ungaro, Givenchy. Her colleagues said that Christa had "an eye" and could pick out the important silhouette of a new collection. Her mentor, John Fairchild, taught her to decode the *moment,* for instance: "Paris says *short.*" Or "Paris says *bold.*" At the next show, maybe everything has poufs and flounces. Christa sleuthed trends: fluttery chiffons, beaded jackets, the newest decadence and sex-shop accessories, keyhole leather bustiers, snakeskin stilettos. Then, there were always parties to absorb. *WWD* might send her to chronicle a two-day gala thrown by Baroness Hélène de Rothschild at her grand house on Île Saint-Louis to celebrate her son's wedding to a Belgian princess, or Christa might visit Gianni Versace's villa on Lake Como for the launch of his new scent, Versace. In New York, she went to the opening night of Howard Stein's Rock Lounge at West Broadway and Canal Street to report what hip socialites were wearing and just as important what they were sipping, and whom they were kissing. Who slapped whose face.

She connected preshow with Ralph Lauren, scooped the story about a changeover at Chanel, got the skinny from Puffy Combs (how many yards of fabric are employed in those droopy pants?), had a breadboard chat with Martha Stewart.

For the *Independent* in London, she covered auctions at Christie's. Lady Di's dresses went on the block the summer before her car wreck. Or it was the Jackie O. auction where a fake pearl necklace sold for more than $200,000. A photograph showed the goddess at a casual moment as she nibbled the cheap costume strand with her full lips. In that story, Christa wrote, "The gay community was rumored to be most interested in Jackie's saddles." She learned the knack of finding little crinks and blisters, the absurd human frailties within the famous, impenetrable bastions of glamour. John Fairchild nurtured her edgy genius. She once wrote, "He gave me eyes with which to see the grand comedy of personality behind the signatures of style." She had less success seeing clearly through her own camouflage and disguises.

She covered memorial services for Versace. The fashion industry was superficial, empty, blank, but even with its fireworks, insider rows, and set-tos, murder was rare to Seventh Avenue folk. Christa was in that world but not *of it*. On the page, she deconstructed or enforced the shifting criteria behind supermodel or "fashion victim," but these discriminations became more and more ridiculous.

Her book editor, Jeff Stone, who had edited her three Chic Simple guides called *Scarves*, *Accessories*, and *Clothes*, said that Christa had removed herself from the molten core in New York. She was no longer a "comer," and had been passed over. He said Christa came to the office dressed in many layers, and these were self-protective. She wrapped herself in scarves, and often wore three or four sweaters all at once. As she sat at her desk, she gradually peeled these items off and she'd make "a nest for herself" right there in her desk chair.

But it wasn't enough protection and, like a butterfly released from a Lucite paperweight, she migrated back to her family compound. Once there, she found her complicated relations just as stifling. With her beloved grandparents gone, and her mother dead, her difficult clan of cousins, aunts, and uncles on Depot Road remained just as icy to her as they had been in her childhood.

Her main trouble was her father.

When she came back to Truro to set up housekeeping in the charming but spartan bungalow, there was much to be done. It was a summerhouse, uninsulated, but she wanted to stay the winter. She looked in the Yellow Pages under "Foam Insulation" and made an appointment. But without any warning, her father put the Little House on the market. He had contacted Nick Brown, the famous realty king at Thomas Brown Real Estate, an upscale office that handled better properties, quaint antiques, seven-figure houses with water views, and parcels abutting the National Seashore sanctuary. Nick said that Christa's father, Toppy, had signed the contract with the realty office but had not informed his daughter. When he returned the paperwork to Nick, Toppy asked him, "There's one more thing I want you to do. Will you pick up the phone and tell my daughter I'm selling the house?"

Nick asked, "Am I working for her or for you?"

Toppy said, "You're working for me. But we don't get along. So will you tell her?"

"What should I say? Has the house been something she's been promised?"

"Tell her I've signed these contracts. The house is going on the market and you ought to have access."

Nick Brown waited a few days to drop the bomb, but when he needed to take measurements for the multiple listings service, he called Christa to break the news. The first thing out of her mouth was, "You lousy, pillaging motherfucker." She slammed the receiver down. Her remark, of course, was meant for her father.

In forty-eight hours, Toppy took the house off the market and gave it to Christa. If Christa had made him feel guilty, or if her fury and distress were, in fact, the outcome he desired from his little game, Toppy allowed her to stay. Nick Brown had lost a new listing.

Her father was becoming increasingly erratic. Years before, when Christa was in high school, she and her mother had found a snapshot of a chesty blonde in Toppy's wallet. He kept his girlfriend's picture snuggled between his credit cards, a harbinger of what would later unfold. And even before Gloria died, Christa had learned about her father's mistress in Quincy, a prostitute and heroin addict forty years his junior. Her father's secret life exploded at the worst time. Christa was eight months pregnant, abandoned by the shellfish constable, and caring for her ailing mother in Hingham. Toppy sidestepped his responsibilities as his wife grew worse and Christa was nearing full term. He spent time away from home, riding his bicycle on long-distance trips, and bedding his girlfriend Beth Porter at the boardinghouse apartment he leased for her.

Although Christa had kept him from selling the house in Truro, Toppy put the family's waterfront house in Hingham on the market. Brokers showed up unannounced, ringing the doorbell at all hours. Christa ignored the intruders as she sat beside her mother's deathbed.

She walked inside the bungalow with Ava in her arms. The toddler squirmed and Christa let her down. Ava ran to the upright piano and started to bang the keys. On the floor, beside the damper pedal, Christa noticed a plate of sliced peaches and quartered pears furred like rabbits' feet. How had she let that sit so long? But she left it where it was. Laundry in little mounds across the floor, sleeves and pant legs unfurled against baseboards, made the place look like a messy dressing room between the second and third acts of a play. She collected oddball items, but always left them stranded on tabletops or propped against the steep risers of the Yankee staircase.

Christa had always hoarded mementos, art objects, one-of-a-kind gizmos that had meaning to her. A classmate at Vassar, Jody Cohen, recalls a tag sale Christa had organized before her graduation in '77. People swarmed into Christa's rooms to fondle all the eccentric items Christa had accrued during four years in Poughkeepsie, to see what she was willing to part with. Jody bought a lampshade made out of Popsicle sticks.

In Truro, Christa stacked books and magazines in pyramids and leaning towers to remind her that she had a "life of the mind" somewhere, in all this refuse. Every countertop and surface was covered in something unfinished, forgotten, ignored. Since her boyfriend, Tim, had moved out after a short romance, and her nanny, Ellen, had quit, she didn't have to live up to anybody's neatnik standards. She was nobody's wife. Ava banged the piano in the living room as Christa searched the freezer for the Popsicle she had promised. There wasn't one. As she hunted through frosted items, three lipsticks spilled onto the kitchen floor. She had learned the trick of keeping her lipstick in the ice box during summer months. The expensive tubes wouldn't melt in the heat, and she liked the refreshment when she dabbed the frozen emollient on her mouth. But she rarely wore makeup.

She surveyed the formidable clutter, a domestic disaster too big for any one person to remedy. That month, Christa had enrolled in a playwriting workshop at Castle Hill Center for the Arts, taught by septuagenarian

Maria Irene Fornes, the famous doyenne of the Judson Poets Theatre in Greenwich Village. One of her classmates was her friend Berry Berenson, Tony Perkins' widow, who would be killed on September 11, on a flight to LA. Christa liked going to the writing class. After twenty years decoding fashion trends, writing about chic crusaders, decollating pompous social cyclones, interviewing haute couture gurus and society trophy wives, she was trying to write *for real.* Maybe that week Christa had let the housework go a little too far into the neck of squalor and chaos, a progressive dismantling of traditional housekeeping goals and expectations she had initially tried to fulfill.

In front of her baroque mirror, she slowly brushed her hair, pulling sorrel wefts above her head and letting the strands float back to her shoulders. The mirror was floor-to-ceiling, like a sliding glass door or a waterfall. In her studio apartment in Gramercy Park, her friend Steve Radlauer had said, "That mirror belongs in a château, not in a shoe box." It was a behemoth, that's true, a white elephant. When she was in Europe, Christa had purchased the mirror with hopeful foresight; it was her promise of one day attaining a vaulted, ideal life. She was going to have a great house and stay, with that mirror, in one place. She had crated the mirror and moved it from Paris, to London, to New York, and finally to Truro.

The mirror spilled dapples of late-afternoon sun across the bedroom floor. This was the time of day when Tony used to show up. When he left the harbor to go home to his wife, he had to drive right by her house. He had told her, "It's on my way home. I can't resist. But you make sure of that, don't you?" He liked to accuse her of having an encyclopedia of feminine wiles that were far greater than any man's willpower. Because of her destructive genius—he was innocent. He was a victim. "I was a slave to my ego, an addict to my senses," he had told a CBS reporter on national TV.

He walked into the house. If his boots were wet, he left them outside on the stoop. She'd meet him at the door and he'd waltz her backward across the cluttered kitchen to the bedroom. He kissed her as she backstepped. She let him navigate and he captained her onto the pillowy pier of her Posturepedic.

Shoved onto the bed, she sat to watch him peel down his cutoff jeans.

He was sugared with sand like a delicious confection, his tanned forearms crazed with salty watermarks. Before the big mirror, he unbuttoned her blouse. The mirror was a trigger. It enticed and reflected. It scolded and seduced. It was a dreamy partition between their two worlds—between Gramercy Park and the tarry wharf pilings at Pamet harbor—where they met halfway. The mirror flattered them. In fever, it melted and shimmered, until it exploded.

She went to put a tape in the VCR for Ava, a French-language cartoon. After her years in London and Paris, Christa was half Anglo, half Francophile. She wanted Ava to be fully bilingual. Already, her daughter knew duplicate words in French and English and Christa nurtured Ava's exceptional verbal level. As the video bloomed on the screen, Christa heard something banging upstairs. She left Ava before the TV and went to see what was making the racket.

In an upstairs bedroom, she found a barn swallow knocking against a windowpane. Swallows amassed at Corn Hill by the thousands at the end of August before their autumn migration. She saw the swooping birds in the distance like rolling clouds of pepper. She lifted the sash and tried to chase the swallow outside but it crashed back into the room, knocking against the opposite wall. It pumped its wings, flipped its notched tail, darted back and forth until it became entangled in a dress rack.

Christa's dress racks were secreted upstairs where Ava couldn't disturb them. The poles sagged with a miscellany of style movements and glamour eruptions, a souvenir wardrobe she had accrued during her years on the job. Each dress, jacket, or gown was cocooned in plastic, with tissue paper puffing out sleeves and darts, to maintain the garment's contours and architecture. It was a shrine of luxurious textiles, like a museum collection, where couture artifacts are maintained in freeze-frame perpetuity and elegant disuse. Christa once wrote, "Desire itself is hidden in the folds of silk."

Eggheads have book collections.

Hunters collect moose heads and taxidermy.

Her dress rack was more like a résumé.

Wools, jerseys, crepe de chine, raw silks and tulle, busy jacquard, from ready-to-wear collections by Gaultier, Saint Laurent, Dior, Christian Lacroix. Frothy skirts with a swishy bustle or sliced side seams, and at least three dramatic "little black dresses"; Ungaro's bare-shouldered model looked ready to cha-cha. Tight waists, flared skirts or lean string bean shifts. A Chanel suit, frill-free, with a micro-jacket. She had written about "trends that won't quit. Flirty skirts—the pouf has a lot of life in it yet—and girlishly proportioned pleated skirts, gentle shoulders and pearl jewelry." Christa rarely took the clothes off the hangers, but if she wanted to, she could slip into something. After Ava was born, Christa went to Weight Watchers. She could zip herself into any of these dresses. A clingy shift still fit like a splash from a paintball gun: "taut over the hips and pouffed in a brioche at the knee."

Christa found the swallow entangled in the sleeve of a "distressed" leather jacket, and she carefully tugged it out. As she cupped the weightless puff, she felt its heart puttering in the palm of her hand. What a little microcosm of terror. It was in the wrong habitat. Christa had similar palpitations. She went over to the window and leaned out. She opened her hand and watched the bird shoot off in a steep climb, then it dipped, and climbed again.

She went downstairs to check on Ava. The little girl was watching the French cartoon with complete absorption. Christa went into the next room and sat down at her messy desk. In the stacks of loose papers, she looked for the pages she was working on for her class at Castle Hill. She tried to grab a minute any time Ava was settled, amused with her toys or watching TV.

The Castle Hill instructor had assigned dialogue projects for which she offered different "prompts," springboard quotes from which Christa and her classmates were supposed to invent an active exchange: "He didn't come when he said he would—" and "I felt bad about it, but I think I can manage now—" From that point of reference, the writer must choose the next angry assault or beleaguered concession that a character might make at this crossroads.

BOX-O-BACHELORS

At the Mashpee Wampanoag Winter Ball, the mood is bittersweet this year, due to the tribe's ongoing efforts to gain national recognition and official acknowledgment as a historic Indian tribe. In the mid-'90s, the tribe petitioned the Bureau of Indian Affairs, which had had the Mashpee Wampanoags' paperwork for six years without making a decision. Four hundred years after the Pamet Indians greeted the Pilgrims to "the Land of First Light," their Wampanoag descendants are still ignored. According to Glenn Marshall, president of the Mashpee Wampanoag Tribal Council, the tribe has met all seven criteria for federal recognition, including that they have "maintained a continuous community"; "have had leaders within the tribe who have helped shape decisions that reflect tribal values"; and "its members are valid descendants of historic tribes."

At the Sons of Italy Lodge, O'Keefe walks me through crowds of pretty young Native American women dressed in sherbet-colored evening gowns. Young men wear suit pants and shiny loafers. They look like insurance salesmen, except for their long glistening braids swinging halfway down the backs of their sport jackets. Oldsters wear traditional leather headbands and beaded vests. I wait at a table as a young boy folds a program, punches holes in its crease, then loops a ribbon through the pages. He takes a scissors and curls the ends of the ribbon before handing the program to me. For the next guest, he repeats the procedure with complete absorption, with the kind of concentration his ancestors might have applied to traditional beadwork.

I read from the list of the evening's events: Speeches. Awards ceremony. Box-o-Bachelors & Bachelorettes.

I show O'Keefe the last item. "Box-o-Bachelors?"

He says, "After the traditional stuff, they have a DJ spinning records. If you want, you can get hooked up with a handsome brave."

He leads me over to Chief Vernon "Silent Drum" Lopez and introduces me to the Wampanoag leader, who is known as the "sotyum."

I thought that Christa might have been safe if she had attended these organized events, like "Box-o-Bachelors," to find her perfect romance connection, here, where couples meet under the protective supervision of a "sotyum."

O'Keefe turns me around to meet State Senator Robert O'Leary. The two politicos, O'Leary and Silent Drum, are an interesting combo. O'Leary is lean and chiseled, with a tennis-court tan. His hair is sun-washed, his face crinkled from a lifetime in sailboats without slathering on enough zinc oxide; his crow's-feet have crow's-feet. Compared to the "sotyum" and other smooth-skinned Wampanoag partygoers, he looks as if he needs Botox or could use a strip steak of red buffalo meat.

I stand at O'Keefe's elbow as he takes a minute to complain to the senator, a Democrat, about the trouble he's having at the state crime lab.

O'Keefe says, "They are transitioning from a blood lab to a DNA lab. They've been doing DNA for about a year now. They have fifteen hundred samples up there and they only do one per district, *per month*. It doesn't take long to do the DNA process. If it was an emergency, it could be forty-eight hours. If we could get the resources."

I ask, "How many murders happen in the state weekly?"

O'Keefe says, "Plenty."

O'Leary shakes his head in mock-genuine dismay.

O'Keefe whispers against my neckline, "See over there? That's my opponent."

I see Kevin Callahan, the Democratic candidate for Cape and Islands district attorney. A small man without much of a nose on him. O'Keefe tells me that Kennedy money is being funneled to Callahan's campaign, although he has no experience as a prosecuting attorney.

I say, "That guy over there with the button nose? That Smurf? Oh, please." The *Cape Cod Times* ran a column item saying Callahan falsified his credentials. In a radio interview, he had claimed to have had lengthy experience as a prosecutor. The newspaper made Callahan acknowledge that his statement "was a bit of a stretch." The *Times* said, "The Massachusetts Lawyers Diary and Manual, which lists all prosecutors in the state, does not show Callahan's name." Even so, the Kennedy machine was throwing their weight behind him, and O'Keefe looked peeved.

A speaker reads the Mashpee Wampanoag creed. It is "The quest for self-determination in such a way that will retain the Wampanoag history, culture, and the preservation of tribal land." The speaker thanks supporters for funding domestic-violence programs, for the museum committee, for assistance in sponsoring the Wampanoag powwow princess at distant powwows. "They have to put her up at a Budget Inn," O'Keefe says.

The brightly lit ballroom, children in Indian princess costumes, refined older men shuffling in moccasins is a pleasing shift of scene after my hour squinting at forensic photographs. But the gala isn't enough distraction.

I keep seeing her scissored legs.

O'Keefe invites me to join in a traditional event called the round dance. Two men seated in the center of the ballroom floor begin beating skin drums. If not for the polished floor and overhead lighting, it might be what Miles Standish confronted when he tried to sneak up on the Pamet Indians. Everyone joins hands in a circle. O'Keefe signals me to find a spot. He's already been recruited. I nudge between two distinguished gentlemen who take my hands. My busted ankle feels a little wobbly, but I carefully try to imitate my partners. I move backward a step, forward a step, as the wheel rotates slowly, first clockwise then counterclockwise. It's a gently rolling human gear, calm and composed, suggesting an almost prehistoric energy source.

The dance is hypnotic and healing, the drumbeat affirming. As I move in steady sidesteps, forward and backward, I think of Christa and Ava. Ava had liked to dance at every opportunity. In the Cape Cod Mall, if there was a tape loop of Muzak on store speakers in Filene's, she'd start to twirl. And at home, Ava in her fuzzy socks climbed onto the insteps of her mother's feet and Christa waltzed them in dizzy circles around their cluttered living room.

Leaving the Sons of Italy Lodge, I'm thinking about Christa dancing with Ava, but O'Keefe is stewed about the lab in Sudbury.

"Carl Sevalacka, he's good. He's taken the lab from one level to another level, but he's almost single-handed. You want to get some dinner?"

He's already driving in the opposite direction from where I left my car. I say, sure I'd like dinner. I have a lot of questions to ask. I ask him about the shellfish constable's son-in-law, Keith Amato, Tony Jackett's son-in-law. I've heard Keith has some foggy connection to Christa. I say, "What do you think of him? Did they get a DNA sample from him?"

"That's right. And from Kyle Jackett. Kyle made a fuss. He wouldn't let them swab his saliva. But he lets them prick his finger. They—are—dumb."

I say, "What about the women? Can a woman stab someone like that?"

"Yes. If she's had enough. Susan is a tough broad. She's had to deal with a fisherman husband for thirty years."

"What about Tony's daughter Braunwyn?"

"Braunwyn has capability," he says.

I see *capability* as vague cop vernacular, like *orbit of opportunity* or the maddening term *possibles*, instead of the taboo word *suspects*.

O'Keefe says, "Imagine—Braunwyn's dad had an affair. Christa shames him and the family. Then her husband, Keith, gets into it. That's a double insult, you know? That spins it deeper. Christa wasn't sweet. The more we learn, the more it gets ugly."

More ugly than Braunwyn, who's as hard as an industrial diamond? "What about Porter and Toppy?"

O'Keefe says, "Toppy bought a blow job once a week for a sum of money, whatever. Porter probably doesn't give receipts."

"There's no truth about Porter being Toppy's 'love child' daughter, right? Did Trooper Plath get a sample from Toppy?"

"Not yet. If our samples turn up only a few different markers, then we get her father's DNA. All her ex-lovers say they've had no relations with her for months. DNA will prove if otherwise and then we go for a grand jury investigation to spook them."

I'm a little embarrassed to have to admit to O'Keefe that I don't know what that is—a grand jury. I've heard of "Grand Prix," "grand slam," "grand piano," but—

"A grand jury investigation is an arm of the court to bind a person over to trial. We bring them in to *ask* them about things. We get serious. They get spooked. So they get lawyered up, take the Fifth, and maybe we grant immunity. They confess."

"Oh, so it's like a shortcut? Like in Monopoly, 'Pass Go' and 'Go Straight to Jail'?"

"Without the play money."

He turns in at Mashpee Commons, a pod of boutiques and restaurants that looks half outlet mall, half Disney–concept neighborhood, with sparkling curbs and cheap white trim on every storefront.

Getting out of the car, I spill the contents of my handbag.

I retrieve my hairbrush, my wallet, miscellaneous girlie things, as O'Keefe waits. He says, "Christ. You're going to be high-maintenance."

At a little bistro, we sit down in the bar so he can smoke. When the waitress comes over, he orders a chicken potpie. It amuses me—it tweaks my heart—to see the steely DA order a potpie. He might just miss home cooking; his ex-wife is a judge, overworked, and he might have dined alone even before she left him. "I usually order meat loaf," he says, "but for variety—"

Meat loaf. Potpie. These are comfort foods. Truck-stop cuisine for lonely hearts and workaholics.

He asks me, "You talk to the Worthingtons yet?"

"I've been trying. They slam the phone down. I called her cousin Jan. She says, 'We're not talking. Only the Worthingtons can talk about the Worthingtons,' *said Jan Worthington.*"

"She bit your head off?"

"I'm not writing the 'Worthington Story.' That's their own mythology. But I know that when people don't want to talk, they're hiding something. Like you said, it's sex or money. You know what Emerson said?"

"Who?"

"Ralph Waldo Emerson. Ralph Waldo? He wrote, 'Sunlight is a great disinfectant.' "

O'Keefe looks across the table at me with the patience of a saint. He isn't accustomed to having chow with English majors.

"I guess the Worthingtons aren't reading Emerson," I say.

We're finally eating when he asks me, "So, do you think Tim Arnold croaked her?"

"You're asking me?"

"You've been talking to him."

"He's pretty distressed. He said the police took his shoes."

"The door was kicked in."

"Tim says they still have his shoes. He thinks he'll never see them again." I tell O'Keefe that I wasn't talking to people to try to solve the crime. That's his oeuvre, not mine. But I wonder if O'Keefe is sitting there trying to *work* me. So I turn it around again. "You haven't mentioned this—was there any evidence that Christa was raped?"

"We haven't got all the samples back. There were some stains, a dried smear on her inner thigh. If it comes back as semen on her leg, then it's fresh, or she would have already showered. But she did have some semen inside her."

"It was a sexual assault?"

"We don't know that yet. The semen was old."

"Old?"

"The semen was degraded. Its age could be anywhere between four to eighteen days old. It didn't have tails."

"No tails?" I picture a frozen constellation without its typical whipping propulsion. I remember when Tony Jackett had once complained about having had a bad run on his boat, the *Josephine G.* His site was fished out. He had said, "Fish have *tails.* They go where they want to go."

I say, "That means Christa had been seeing someone, right?"

"That's usually how it works."

O'Keefe tells me about someone named Dr. Henry Lee. A forensic genius. He'd like to have a powwow with Lee, but he doesn't have money in his budget to hire him. He tells me about a murder in Centerville that took seven years to solve. Ernie Marino was murdered in '86. The case was cold until a rat in Boston mentioned he had bought a gun from a man who said that the gun was "dirty" from a murder on Cape Cod. Then things started to click and tumble like a Rube Goldberg machine. The crime scene was at a house that had since been torn down. Dr. Henry Lee built a model of the house from the original plans in order to figure out blood spatters on the stairwell landing. O'Keefe says, "Tried the case in 'ninety-three. Lots of trashy details: drugs, porn, dildos—"

"How's your potpie?" I say.

Since his marriage busted up, I wonder how many meals he eats in restaurants. But instead I ask him where he grew up. He says, "Brighton. Waltham. Milton." He went to Boston College, then to New England Law. He was a cop down here on the Cape while he studied for the bar exam. I ask him, "Is it true that while you were working in the Dennis Police Department, you rescued a woman from a burning building?" For that, he had been awarded a Medal of Merit for Bravery. But he's more concerned that I know that he prosecuted nineteen homicide trials to jury verdict. "I'm nineteen and one."

His bravado is hard-won, but he sounds like a pugilist. You don't hear doctors say, "I'm nineteen and—" They don't admit their failures. But cops, pitchers, even outlaws refer to numerical proof. Notches on bedposts, on guns, and notches on "the bench."

As we eat, people flow up to our table to talk to Mike. I try to gauge if his popularity comes from being a regular at the restaurant, like any divorced man trying to get his three squares, or if these tableside chats are political applesauce.

"So you say you play golf?" I ask.

"I'm a serious golfer."

"How serious?"

"I wager."

"No kidding?"

"For supplemental income. Do you play?"

"As a kid, I walked the course with my father, but mostly I liked to saw through golf balls to get to the rubber bands."

My little asides don't seem to faze him. He says, "Well, tonight we looked at pictures. Next time I'll show you the video."

"There's a videotape?" I imagine the camera panning back and forth across Christa's cluttered place, zooming in tight on her naked body, inching over her head to toe, from her widow's peak to the tiny halfmoons of her toenails, and everything in between. In close-up. Some killers like to imagine the photo shoot.

There's a whole shelf of these forensic flicks at O'Keefe's office. "You won't need your Blockbuster's card," he says.

COLD SNAP

Each year, with winter coming, many Cape Codders escape the bad weather and retreat inland. For health reasons or to avoid Massachusetts' income taxes (we call it "Taxachusetts"), a lot of oldsters maintain primary residences elsewhere. Some return to New York and New Jersey, but most of them run off to the Sun Belt. Florida. These folks migrate with the seasons. Locals call them "snowbirds."

Year-rounders tough it out. In the off-season, the north wind and the east wind collide and reconnoiter, becoming one destructive phenomenon. Gale force. These infamous hissyfits happen several times each winter and can accelerate to a serious contest. A New England nor'easter isn't a velvety mist or spring shower; it's not a sissy drizzle or impersonal downpour. A nor'easter is a lateral assault, a horizontal force, a wall of wind and icy needles that plows into the coast. Not really a hurricane, these gales aren't assigned official names, but the damaging storms earn their titles from local word of mouth, like one called the "Halloween Nor'easter" and another called the "Ballston Break," when a storm surge tore through the barrier dunes on the back shore and flooded the Pamet estuary, burning the freshwater marsh. Another destructive storm, a few years back, is remembered as the "No Name Gale."

Winds churn up the sea, lifting curtains of water off the deep and slamming them, one after the next, across the little hamlets clustered along the arm. Storm doors whip loose from houses and patches of shingling are torn off and hurled aloft. You find bits and pieces of your neighbor's roofing when you trowel your garden the next summer. Driving easterlies shoot glassy spears of rain, soaking weatherworn shingles until one side of your house is drenched dark black. A shake roof can look like a pyramid of waterlogged sponges, until the roof ridge swells and later shrinks, settles again, deformed. Often, when the soaked houses begin to dry out, clouds of steam drift up, and inexperienced passersby alert the firehouse.

To prepare for a hard winter, residents can lock into a discounted price per gallon from Cape Cod Oil if they prepay their estimated costs. After 9/11, experts said the price of oil would shoot higher, and so you'd probably be saving if you paid up front.

After a mild autumn, it wasn't until the first weekend of the new year 2002 that the temperature dipped below freezing. The air started to "smell" like snow, that familiar, almost arid scent of pressed white handkerchiefs. The skies were a pewter smear, a curtain of dirty chain mail that never permits the sun to squeeze through. The mercury was sinking, the barometric pressure wobbled and dipped, making people's ears feel blocked. There would be freezing rain at least, maybe snow, that weekend.

Tim Arnold sat at his desk in his father's house. That weekend he had been house-sitting for a friend in Wellfleet but he came back home to work on a painting. His father's place, a traditional Cape on a wooded lot on Old County Road, had once belonged to an aunt and Tim had spent his childhood summers in Truro. He retreated here when his marriage broke down a few years before. If he wanted to see his two kids, he had to meet his ex at the Bourne Bridge, where she waited at the Tugboat, a landmark dry-docked at the rotary. But he didn't have his kids too often anymore. His ex told him that his daughter had dance lessons every day and was too busy. He felt it was just another excuse for her to avoid the long drive. She didn't have to face him. She didn't like "the reminder," she would say.

At his father's house, a little second-floor bedroom doubled as a studio, a tight garret where Tim spent most of his time writing or painting. The wind was shrieking through the awning window frame. He called down to his father, who sat mortared to his armchair watching the New England Patriots on TV, to tell him to crank up the thermostat.

As Tim worked on a new painting, he had to keep the palm of his hand over one eye. He suffered from double vision, the result of recent surgery for a "cavernous malformation" of blood vessels clustered along his brain stem. To see clearly, he had to keep one eye covered up. His sudden health troubles had been a factor that tipped the checks and balances of his marriage beyond remedy. He separated from his wife soon after his first onslaught of dizzy spells caused by the idiopathic knot of blood vessels. His wife took his two kids and he moved to the Cape, where he would meet Christa. He liked to blame his health problems for the demise of his marriage, for the end of his brief stint at fatherhood, and he was certain it had rushed the ending of his love affair with Christa, too. They'd been together less than six months when his balance trouble worsened and she shooed him out.

Tim looked forward to snow. But Cape Cod didn't always provide. He grew up in Ohio, where winters were white. He moved to Kansas City to take a job as an illustrator and copywriter for Hallmark Cards, and of course it snowed in Missouri, too. Midwestern winters were reliable. Snowplows cruised up and down streets with the same aplomb and regularity as American Harvester combines tacking back and forth over seas of wheat. At Hallmark, he had met his wife. Although the Hallmark job had provided benefits and insurance, the "golden handcuffs," he didn't want to spend his life illustrating greeting cards, and he took his bride and came East. But that seemed like a chapter in a musty book that he had never read through to the ending.

Waiting for the first snow is like hoping for clean laundry after everything in the closet is soiled. Snow is a "mental thing." A blank screen or whitewash that hides ugly landmarks in the psyche. Snow is a curative. Snow is forgiving.

Tim had written and illustrated a children's book called *The Winter Mittens*, a story about the magic of snow. A girl finds a pair of mittens. Each time she tugs the mittens on her hands, snowflakes start to swirl and spiral down. As the snowflakes carpet everything, the neighborhood is transformed. The little girl's friends are delighted. Discovering her magic power to control the weather, she decides to unleash the skies. She wears the secret mittens. " '*Snow*,' *she whispered . . . 'I've seen more snow than this. Harder. Snow harder!*' " Her impulsive commands cause a destructive blizzard. Trees and power lines come down, until, in order to save her town, she must return the mittens to the hiding place where she had found them.

Tim wet his brush and dabbed an exact glob of paint on the Masonite board, then used his brush to feather the color until the tiny inch of surface was reworked. As he continued to paint, he hoped it would snow. A white seaside is an enchanted place, a blinding diorama of frosted beach grass, powdery hillocks, snowcapped dunes, open beaches white as bedsheets. If there was a winter storm, he might go over to Christa's house, just around the corner, and help Ava build a snowman. He pictured all three of them in the alacritous whiteout of a mini-blizzard. He saw them lying down in a row to make snow angels in graduating sizes. He imagined Ava's squeals and giggles, but it was Christa's face he pictured, glowing, rosy with cold and exertion. She was sometimes happy to see him, despite the breakdown of their short-lived affair. She had turned to him after her romance with the hunk fisherman from P-town. She had told Tim that he was the exact antidote she needed to flush a powerful toxin from her system.

Tim was attractive, but from the opposite color chart, blond and fair. Midwestern, or just modest, unlike Tony he didn't swagger or strut around like a satyr. Christa had told her friend and nanny, Ellen Webb, "Tim doesn't know how handsome he is."

He imagined the kiss. He always wanted the kiss. But even when Christa had kissed him, he had often felt her body tense up. She'd straighten her back, nudge his shoulders with the heels of her hands, and gently push him away. Ellen had felt that resistance, too. Whenever she had tried to show affection, Christa would edge away with delicate reserve, as when you lean too close to a butterfly, it lifts away. It doesn't mean to cause insult to you or to the flower it departs from, but it wants to escape to the next bloom, and the next.

At the holidays, she went to New York City to see her fabulous friends and to introduce Ava. She put on her party dress and went to celebrity soirees where she saw Woody Allen and his wife, Soon-Yi, at Ben Brantley's party. But when Tim saw her again in Truro, she was wearing Polartec sweatpants. Christa had hugged him, and for once, she didn't instantly let go. She tucked her head against his lapel and really held on. She seemed to want to climb into his pocket. He wondered what wolf was at her door, or what had precipitated her change of mood and had made her melt against him. In the delayed embrace, he felt a trickle of springwater begin to freshen a ravine of bad feeling between them. But again she resumed her distance from him, and for Christmas they had exchanged "reading material." He bought her Kay Graham's autobiography and she gave him a novel, *The Shipping News*. Christa had said she had read the book and thought he might identify with its hero. He was dismayed to discover that the story was about a beleaguered man in Nowheresville, and he didn't want to recognize himself.

Tim hadn't returned Christa's flashlight that he had borrowed when he visited her the day after New Year's. Because of his blurred vision, his father drove him everywhere. His father had to drop him off and later retrieve him like a preschooler. But that night at Christa's, he insisted that he could walk home through the woods. She had made him take her flashlight.

The Maglite waited on the corner of his desk. It was the unofficial chit he waited to cash in, the perfect excuse he needed to go over to Christa's house again.

He looked down at his new painting, one in a series he was working on with the titles *Singularity I, Singularity II*, etc. Without one eye covered, he saw a confusing duplicate that didn't make sense. He squinted to correct the blurred picture, but squinting made him dizzy. Again, he cupped one eye with his hand and looked at his finished work. The painting was of a central orb with extending vines and tendrils. The image was organic, a natural chaos of branching root systems or like a swirl of knotted blood vessels.

"Ganglia," Christa would say. "You're obsessed with ganglia since your operation."

He had told her, "My paintings are nonobjective realism. They evoke energy, movement, patterns."

Truro has been home base to a lot of artists. On the next hill over is Ben Shahn's house. Edward Hopper had a little place farther down the road. The "Hopper House," a stark and beautiful white cottage above Fisher Beach, is a beloved landmark in Truro. Art enthusiasts and painters hike out there through the sedge and brambles to see it in person, hoping to absorb its mojo.

Contemporary painter Jim Peters built his house just behind the knoll where Hopper's house sits. Peters hung his bayside windows so that they frame a vision of Hopper's house. It looks like a glistering sugar cube on the crest of the bluff. Hopper's famous paintings of Truro, especially the painting of the old red gas pumps on Route 6, are beloved to local residents, but Tim wasn't painting Hopperesque landscapes. There were scores of derivative landscapes for sale in local galleries.

Tim also worked on a new book. He explained that he was reinventing the Diana myth, inverted. "She becomes the protectress who runs away from an overbearing environment." He didn't want to think it might be something spurred by his love affair with Christa, but she seemed to be central in everything he did. Even now, when it was over.

MERCENARIA

That same weekend, shellfish constable Tony Jackett worked at a grant site east of Pamet harbor. He had staked that acre last year and was transferring seed clams from intertidal nursery trays to a pen or "runway" for grow-out to full harvest size. The juvenile quahogs were little white gleams, like baby teeth, as he sifted through the sandy sediment. The genus of the northern hard-shell clam is named *Mercenaria*, because of its deep-blue border that was once used to make Indian money, or wampum. Tony thought if he had a nickel for every one of these little seed clams under his supervision, he'd be doing all right.

Tony worked alone on the flats. He looked for a new location with acceptable substrate for the seed clams to mature. Soft bottom mud was inhospitable, and he towed the haul to an intertidal cul-de-sac where tidewater was always changing in silky sheets at half tide. His waders had Thinsulate linings, but sluicing back and forth in icy ankle-deep water, the cold was starting to creep into him. First his feet got numb, then his hands stiffened. His sinuses began to ache with cold. He hurried to take water samples for fecal coliform bacteria, but in winter it wasn't as necessary. Next, he inspected the trays called "Chinese hats," where a lessee cultured an oyster crop. Once these teensy oysters "set," the little miniatures, called "spat," would attach to any hard surface, even to the backs of crabs.

Aquaculture wasn't his first love, but he tried to adapt to his new position. He said, "My attitude is you don't take a job, you *make* a job. Before someone else tries to make rules for me." There was a lot of science to absorb. He wasn't a bookish type, but a hands-on whiz kid. He had been forced to change careers when his boat sank, and he took it hard going from being captain to being a kind of nanny for bivalves. It took some downsizing in his self-esteem, and his vanity took a hit. Shellfish wardens before him were beloved town characters and Tony knew the lore. John Gaspee, "Lord Protector of the Quahogs," even has a quahog carved on his tombstone. But being shellfish constable didn't have the glamour factor he had enjoyed as a dragger captain. Aquaculture was a no-man's-land somewhere between traditional agriculture and traditional fishing. Real farmers don't understand fish, and fishermen don't like the competition with leaseholders. There had been some violent scuffles between culturists and commercial fishermen, sometimes involving gunfire, boat-burnings, and the destruction of product. These skirmishes were called "quahog wars." Being shellfish *constable* still seemed like an odd fit for Tony. He'd never been on *that* end of law enforcement rituals.

For the last twenty-five years, he'd been a fisherman in the dwindling Provincetown fleet. His new work didn't carry the same clout or have the same romance he had known when he steamed out every day on the *Josephine G.* "Shellfish constable" seemed a ridiculous term, like "sanitation engineer" for garbageman, or like calling a gum-chewing manicurist a "beauty technician." It wasn't glamorous to be out in the cold, in the muck, in the raw elements, taking conference with mollusks. It was a one-sided powwow. But when he had been in the wheelhouse of his boat, a fifty-foot steel-hulled eastern rig, he was on top of the world.

His grandfather came from Portugal. He had harpooned swordfish until he was past seventy. And Tony's father was the renowned captain of the *Plymouth Belle,* a highliner in the Provincetown fleet. As a kid, Tony didn't really want to be a fisherman. The rolling swells and the smell of fish had made him seasick, and he had seen the hard lives his father and grandfather had lived. But Susan got pregnant. He needed the money to get married. In his early days, Tony had tried going out on his father's boat, but they didn't get along. On the *Plymouth Belle*, his father was all business. "You had to *move.* Crank the Hyster. Pick through the fish. Put another basket before him. Throw the junk out the scupper." If Tony made any suggestions, his father would say, "I'll do the thinking, you do the doing."

At that time, his father had found a girlfriend and was ditching his mother. Tony was in the middle. If his father hadn't left his mom, Tony might have stayed on the *Plymouth Belle*. But when Tony saw an opportunity to buy his own boat, he refinanced the house he had bought for his wife and he took possession of the *Josephine G.* He'd fallen head over heels in love again. The first time he was in over his head, it was for Susan. Susan had already been lovingly nicknamed by a consensus of native residents, both men and women, "the undisputed most beautiful girl to ever graduate from Provincetown High School." The next time he fell hard, it was for the *Josephine.* Both were drop-dead gorgeous to him. He'd said, "If I get bored with my routine—marriage, the boat I have—I'd rather get a bigger boat than a different woman. I'd go into a bigger boat and that would revive my challenge." But for the time being the *Josephine* was the perfect-size boat. He told his father, "She's the perfect *little* big boat."

He knew that with bigger boats "you have to know banks." He said, "Money just leads to a lot of problems with money." But if he was late making his payments on the *Josephine,* he knew the money was out there in the ocean. He could steam out and scrape up enough dough. "I bring it in. The bank gets some."

In good times, he hired two mates and went out every day. A small operation, he needed only a small crew. Dragging is a gamble, you have a good stretch, a bad stretch. You might have a big week, so you haul out again. You're always looking for that *big week.* But it doesn't always come around. "You're doing great one day, and so the next day you're charged up. Then, steaming out—your propeller hits a log." Over the years, the fishing got worse, both from government regulations and from decreased catches due to dwindling fish populations. He tried new sites— "Fish have *tails.* They go where they want to go"—but his catch wasn't enough to carry his crew. He rehauled his boat for a stern rig so he could go out alone. The net was coiled in back and he could point into the wind. When it's an eastern rig, you need two guys to pull the net up the side; it's not as efficient and it's sometimes called "ass rigged," but he didn't need a crew to handle a stern-rigged dragger. He liked the autonomy. He was one to one with the sea. It was a time when a lot of boats weren't making it. The middle man takes all the profit. "It's businessmen or it's weather; you can't control either end of it."

In 1984, when he wasn't meeting his mortgage payments, or his boat payments, Tony was lured into a little drug connection. Two strangers, well dressed and all business, showed up at MacMillan Wharf in Provincetown. They asked him if he was interested in captaining a boat from

Colombia to Boston Harbor, where they wanted to off-load forty thousand pounds of marijuana. They promised that his take would be $2 million.

Two million dollars was an absurd promise. It was easy to ignore the temptation. A smaller amount would have been easier to visualize—perhaps $10,000. Now that was a realistic figure, and he might have agreed to it.

He declined the offer. But at night Tony imagined the actual mass and bulk of $2 million. He tried to guesstimate how much actual physical space he would need to hide that sum, would he need to rent a storage bin or could he keep all that money in his tiny place with his wife and six kids? The strangers came back two more times to talk to him. Seaman's Bank had been sending letters refusing to reschedule his payments. They were threatening to foreclose on his house.

He told them he would captain their boat.

But as he waited several weeks for his plane ticket to South America, Tony waffled. They sent his friend, another local fisherman, Skip Albanese, instead. They put Tony in charge of scoping out a drop off at the Neponset River in Quincy, just outside of Boston. The Neponset is a favorite spot for miscellaneous KP duties assigned by local crime kings. Even now, in 2002, police have continued digging along its banks searching for bodies; one in particular is presumed to be mobster Whitey Bulger's girlfriend.

After repairing some engine troubles, Albanese steamed north without difficulty, following the East Coast from Florida to Block Island. But alerted to a pileup of coast guard patrols in Boston Harbor, Skip turned the boat around and brought the load of dope home to P-town. Worried that more DEA agents might be waiting at MacMillan Wharf in Provincetown Harbor, Tony, Skip, and a couple of Colombian crewmates off-loaded forty bales in the dunes at Herring Cove. They decided to sink the boat with the rest of its eight hundred bales still in the hold. Later, when things cooled down, they would dive for the booty and dry the weed out. This was common practice ever since moon cussers had mastered the technique in the eighteenth century. But when they scuttled the vessel outside Wellfleet Harbor, it had an empty fuel tank and the boat wouldn't sink. Its ass popped up.

Local law enforcement, federal agents, and DEA were all over it like ants on a honeypot. To make things worse, in order to disguise the vessel, Skip had painted the name of a local Provincetown dragger, the *Divino Criador*, on its stern. When the boat was discovered, foundered plain as day right off Great Island in Wellfleet, all three towns became hysterical, fearing that its crew had been lost. Women in Provincetown, Truro, and Wellfleet started a phone tree, trying to locate their men.

Tony agreed to testify before a grand jury. He said, "I might as well snitch before I'm indicted." He didn't do any time, but he didn't get his mortgage money. He lost the house and worried that Susan might never forgive him.

He started fishing again. He went out alone for a few years but he never climbed to the highliner status his father had earned. To make ends meet, he was driving an oil truck and collecting garbage, but he kept fishing until the *Josephine* sank. Twice. In '96, she went down in the Pamet, where he took her to ride out the storm surge from Hurricane Edouard. He had put out a dragger door to help his anchors set, but the door ripped his skeg and tore out his rudder post when he tried to haul it up. She went nose down as the tide surged in, flooding his wheelhouse. But he pumped her out and got her back up. By this time, she's a rust bucket. After everything she'd been through, wind and gale, twenty-foot seas, night fogs— like the time she almost got plowed into at midships by a freighter. Or one haul when he snagged a wreck—instead of cutting his gear loose he towed the heavy wreck into port to save his net. He was almost capsized. After so many adventures and near misses, she finally gave up the ghost in Provincetown Harbor, "in her own goddamn mooring."

The weather was mean that first weekend in January and he didn't find anyone raking clams or asking for a shellfish permit. Usually, there'd be a few diehard amateurs looking to buy a license off him wherever they found him, right there in knee-deep water.

Each time he came down to Pamet harbor, Tony worried he might run into her. She lived right up the street at the end of Depot Road. As he worked, he was looking for her. He had a familiar anxiety each time, like when he was a kid and cranked a jack-in-the-box with a scary clown inside it. He never knew when she'd pop up. He had met her at the harbor in 1997 when she was living in the small Worthington cottage, the one they called "Tiny's Hut." The name was tongue-in-cheek or they just wanted to make a distinction between the shoe box and their more substantial houses. Tiny's Hut was right on the harbor, left of the parking lot. He was standing on the finger pier, minding his own business, when he first saw Christa. Tony was a movie buff, and one of his favorite pastimes was trying to match up local beauties with current movie stars. Christa would be tough. She was different from the typical Hollywood sexpot. He tried to go through his mental *pictionary* of movie stars to get the right one, but it wasn't coming.

Christa liked to hang around the harbormaster's shack, talking to Warren Roderick. If Tony came in or out, she'd make room for him in the tight closet. She kept finding some reason to show up when he was around. She complained to him that there were too many boats being launched at town landing. "They make a racket every morning." Or she didn't want the port-o-johnnies set up near her property. Or she didn't like how people rode their Jet Skis right up onto the beach. "Those things leak gasoline." She had her little pet peeves and expected him to do something.

She was beautiful even when she was snippy. Her chestnut hair lofted to her shoulders. Her pale skin was getting too much sun, and when she faced him to gripe or argue about something, he noticed a sprinkle of tawny freckles, like flecks of cinnamon across the bridge of her nose. Suddenly, he recognized her actress twin. She was Julianne Moore's doppelgänger. But then of course there was "the mouth on her." She could talk circles around him.

Christa caught him off guard; he was suffering some sort of midlife thing. He was on the rebound from the *Josephine*. He wasn't himself since his boat sank.

He thought he'd be fishing until he was as old as his granddad. But here he was, only fifty years old, and just about landlocked. He still had a full head of jet black hair. People teased him about it. He'd tell them, "Hey, it's not Grecian Formula, just look at my beard." It was true, only one hour after a shave, his deep whiskers emerged, black as magnetite. Even so, he was having trouble adjusting to his career change. Harbormasters were usually geezers.

He didn't see it coming. She was two or three steps ahead of him. Finally, when he saw she was taking a fancy to him, it was too late to reverse engines or drop an anchor chain. She'd beached him.

It was snowing when he stowed his kayak on the roof of his Jeep, a grizzly temperamental cloud of ice crystals that stung his face. He worried that at any time she might come down to find him and have it out. But she wouldn't take the baby for a walk in the raw weather. She was a worrywart when it came to Ava. Last spring, she had asked him to put the baby on his health insurance plan. She wasn't just letting the cat out of the bag, it was more like she threw the cat out a car window in a bag of Coke bottles.

Christa had told him he had to tell Susan. His wife had to know about Ava before the little girl turned two. Ava was already talking a blue streak; soon she was going to be asking about her daddy. "I'm not keeping secrets for you," Christa told him.

When he had told his daughter Braunwyn about meeting Christa at the harbor, he had said, "She was already hunting. I didn't see it coming. I went for a buggy ride."

Braunwyn told him he had to confess to Susan. Ava was almost two years old when he was finally ready to talk to his wife. On D-day, he drove down 6A toward home. He cruised right past his turnoff. Trying to get his nerve up, he rolled up and down Route 6, from Herring Cove to the Wellfleet Cinemas, and back down Route 6 to Herring Cove again. He'd turn around with the resolve to go home and face Susan, but he was driving up Route 6 again. He made the hesitating loop enough times, he could have been in Boston before he finally inched home to face the fireworks.

There's a beloved legend in Provincetown, memorialized in Susan Baker's illustrated *History of Provincetown*. Every year at the Fourth of July, the town presents its annual fireworks display from MacMillan Wharf. The whole town: summer tourists, year-rounders, shopkeepers, and restaurant personnel stop what they're doing and head to the town beach. Blankets are thrown down, and people sit elbow to elbow, until the whole sandy hem is obscured by "the human condition." Families, honeymooners, knots of gay men and women, party animals, divas, and the town manager, Keith Bergman, and his two blond daughters—everyone comes down to the harbor at sundown to watch the sky.

But one year, the crew hired to oversee the pyrotechnic fandango were out-of-towners. They didn't understand the whimsical weather patterns at Land's End and they didn't notice a wall of fog drifting in from Pilgrim Lake. The show went ahead as planned, just as a wall of mist surged over the town. You couldn't see anything. There'd be intervals of explosive thunder behind a woolly curtain that tinted red or green, but hardly enough to notice.

When Tony told Susan about Christa, he had expected a full blowup, but her reaction was like that foggy Fourth of July. Susan didn't explode or burn up. A curtain of mist came down between them. After her painful sobs, she went to her father's house to cool off. She called Tony "Dumbdick," but it was mostly affectionate. She was acting like a saint or something. She had raised his four kids and two she had adopted with her first husband. She had always had a capacity to love children who weren't her own flesh and blood. And when Tony told her about Ava, Susan told him, "I could raise this one." She tried to stake her claim in her husband's boondoggle. She didn't want to be left out. Some people thought she was crazy, but others who knew Susan were certain of one thing: "The most beautiful girl to ever graduate from Provincetown High School" just loved Tony to death.

If his wife had been playacting the role of jilted-wife-as-heroine, if she was shell-shocked, in denial, or sleepwalking through his nightmare, soon she was going to wake up. Christa wanted money.

THE HOUR BETWEEN
DOG AND WOLF

Tim took a short walk down the driveway to clear his head before heading back to his house-sitting job in Wellfleet. The sky looked like a tarnished platter, its soiled filigree edged the horizon. It started to come down, the first powder. Even with just a little scrim, he left footprints. He explored the woods bordering his father's house, careful to walk with one eye pinched shut; otherwise the trees were a confusing mural of blurred poles. He tried to see if Christa's car was in her driveway. Busty rhododendrons blocked the view. The snow was turning into needle ice. "Oh, these bleak winds, and bitter, northern skies," Brontë wrote of Wuthering Heights, in prescient commiseration with residents of remote and stormy places like Land's End. When Tim came back to the house, his father said, "Where were you?"

"Nowhere."

"Is it doing anything yet?"

"It can't make up its mind." He went to his room and tried to call Christa, but she didn't answer the phone. That didn't necessarily mean she wasn't at the house. Earlier that week, he had asked her if she wanted to go out to dinner on Sunday, but she had put him off. She'd said, "I can't plan that far ahead. I can't be sure what I'll be doing." She often hemmed and hawed, as if hoping for a better invitation to arise, but eventually she'd give in. It wasn't likely Prince Charming was barreling up Route 6 to rescue her from her doldrums. She'd had her fair share of spectacular nobodies. Her closet was filled with glass slippers: wedgies, huaraches, stacked heels, Ferragamo sandals, cheap stilettos, boots, pumps.

When Tim couldn't get her on the phone, he sat down to watch the Patriots game with his father. Then he asked his father to drive him over to Christa's house. He would bring her the flashlight. Maybe, if he caught her at twilight, before she'd started chopping carrots or cooking rice, he'd convince her to drive up Route 6 to Land Ho! despite the freezing rain. Ava was well behaved in restaurants. She wasn't a screamer or a whiner. Some children, he knew from experience, when crammed into portable high chairs, can behave like little hostages.

Tim's father aimed the remote at the TV, clicked it off, and got up from his chair. He grabbed his car keys and saw the flashlight on the kitchen counter. "Don't forget this." They got into the wagon. They drove down County Road to the corner, and turned onto Depot Road. It was a short distance and without his vision trouble Tim would have liked the walk. His father didn't grouse about the limo service, but Tim was never comfortable. He felt like a child or like the feeble seniors who rode in the shuttle van that he used to drive for the Council on Aging. Before his vision had failed, he had ferried oldsters to the A&P or to doctors' appointments at Outer Cape Health. He had liked the job at the COA and he often joked with the old-timers. He'd say, "Some of us need a Council on Middle Aging. We could call it COMA."

When his father turned in at the bungalow, climbed the hill, and rounded the curve, Tim saw Christa's car beside the house. The kitchen light was burning. She'd been home all along, just as he had thought. He left his father in the car with the engine running. If Christa didn't want company, she'd have run outside to meet him before he reached the porch. That was her typical routine, to run interference when people showed up unannounced. When she didn't gallop outside, he was hopeful Christa would want to drive somewhere for dinner and he could tell his father that he didn't need to wait.

As he walked up to the house, he noticed that Christa's view of the withered marshland looked much more sinister in the hour between dog and wolf. He hurried to her bright kitchen. He knocked on the back door and peeped through the window.

He saw Christa lying on the floor.

He thought, Jesus, she must really be tired to lie down on the floor right there. Ava was snuggled beside her mother, nursing. The floor must be cold, but Christa had often stopped whatever she was doing to unbutton her blouse for the baby. Tim tried to find the logic in the scene before him. Christa was cuddling Ava right there on the floor. No big deal. He opened the door and called to Christa, "Hello?" Ava lifted her head. Her face was smeared and dirty, her eyes wide and unblinking, like a rag doll that fell from a moving car and tumbled along the shoulder of a highway.

Ava didn't seem to recognize him or acknowledge any aspect of the scene she was part of. Then her frozen eyes pinched shut. She began to sob. "Mommy fell down," she told him, her little shoulders heaving.

He imagined that Christa might have rushed to get the telephone when he had called her earlier and might have slipped and banged her head. He thought of her diving to answer his phone call as he waited on the other end, getting increasingly irritated. He felt an immediate jab of guilt and a corresponding *resistance* to guilt. Two sensations, guilt and disassociation. He couldn't calibrate the intellectual problem before him with the emotional explosion he felt.

He saw a ribbon of blood. Another congealed streak was smeared where Ava had left little footprints back and forth to the kitchen sink. There was a thickening pool of red scum beneath Christa's head. He edged forward on watery ankles over the vast desert of flooring and bent down to look. A plastic Tippee Cup was beside Christa, smeared with color. Ava might have tried to offer a drink to her mother to revive her. Then he understood that Ava had been nursing and had also sipped juice from the little cup, smudging one with the other. He touched Christa's face. Her cheek was bruised and puffy. Cold as putty.

He tore from room to room looking for the cordless phone. Her house was messy, even more than usual, and he couldn't find the telephone anywhere in the wreck of it. The whole house was like an overturned junk drawer with everything spilled out. He didn't notice the cell phone on the cluttered kitchen table.

He lifted Ava in his arms and walked outside to his father's car. He waited an eternity for his dad to crank the window down. Tim had the presence of mind to spare Ava and he carefully masked what he told his father. He said, "Dad, I think Christa is d-e-a-d."

Tim recited the first consonant, the two vowels, the final consonant, but it was a surreal alphabet, nonsensical in its suspension. Again he said, "I think Christa is d-e-a-d." It was the infamous "spelling scene" that newspapers would describe gleefully in print nationwide.

His father left Tim with Ava and went inside the house to address the facts. He had to see it firsthand. Then he searched for Christa's telephone. He didn't have any better luck.

Following some ingrained notion of crime scene etiquette, they agreed that one of them should stay put while the other went home to call the police. His father sat down in the car with the little girl, the heater going, and Tim started through the woods behind Christa's house. Her property abutted his father's land. When they were lovers, Christa had once introduced him to a friend, saying, "This is Tim. We're abutters," laughing at the innuendo.

It wasn't far, but the hike was difficult. He walked into the dark stand of trees and prickers. He was grateful for darkness. He wanted to flee from illumination, recognition, perception. But estimates and arguments were already warring through him. He was thinking that Christa had been "a moth that circled the flame." He recognized it was the "blaming the victim" syndrome that people fall prey to when they are in shock, a strange, unbidden wellspring of accusation. He had recently asked Christa if she was seeing someone. She had told him, "When would I have the time to do that?" But he felt she was dodging the question. She continued, more mysteriously, "I'm not *involved* with anybody, if that's what you mean." Tim had made the translation: "I might be screwing someone but I'm not 'involved.' "

She liked the intellectual battle around sex. The tension that builds to an unfulfilled aggression. The competition to seduce. Who would initiate sex first? He knew that in their brief relationship she ratcheted up the sex component, but her sex life and her emotional life were always separate. Her warmth was for Ava. She compartmentalized love and sex in separate, climate-controlled archives.

He examined the immediate past and farther back. His thoughts surfaced in non sequiturs, one after another. As he trekked in the half-dark, a Stephen King gloaming or eerie Hitchcock monochrome, his blistering jealousy collided with his remorse and pity. He was paralyzed, a useless bystander. In the horrible one-to-one in Christa's kitchen, a place where he had once belonged, he had been left out. He felt robbed of the privilege. He wasn't even a witness. His participation was after the fact, like a jogger who comes across a body in a city park. This is how he would describe it to police.

When he reached his house, he dialed 911 and told them, "It's Christa Worthington. Please come. I think she fell down." He knew she had not "fallen." She'd been on the floor a good while. Already, there was a rank, unpleasant odor like a stale refrigerator drawer with the sticky residue of meat drippings.

Tim turned around and went back through the woods to the bungalow. He sat down in the car with his father and waited. Sirens advanced, a disharmonious tangle of sneering bleats and tremolos. He held Ava close, unwilling to look at her face stenciled with watermarks of grime, milk, and dried blood. She had tried to nurse Christa despite the stab wound. She told Tim, "Mommy got into my paints."

Christa's cousin Jan Worthington, a onetime TV writer who worked as an Outer Cape EMT, had heard the call on her radio. "Inert body on Depot Road." Jan's initial thought was that it must be her own mother, Lucinda. Because she lived across the street from Christa, Jan was the first one to arrive. She charged into the house without an EMT's typical remove or professional restraint. She saw her cousin on the floor of the hallway, her legs scissored. In seconds, Jan fell apart. She was of little use. In fact, state police have said she was "messing things up." Then the EMT trucks tagged up, one after another. The vans. The cruisers. A whole conference. Tim said, "They collected like a little social club at the end of the driveway." They tromped all over the crime scene. It was the first Truro murder in thirty years. For law enforcement lifers, no murders for such a long stretch wasn't always a blessing but a dry spell. Like a frat house gang, they had all come to officiate, to roll out yellow tape, to snoop and rubberneck. They struggled to maintain deadpan faces, but their raw excitement sometimes emerged in nervous tics, twinkles, and half-smiles. They discharged some of their pent-up jubilation by marching in place, crossing their arms, and slapping their parka sleeves against the cold.

An officer spoke to Tim's father and then he approached Tim. Tim explained how he had found Christa. The officer listened with an affectless expression, tipping his chin up and down at every switchback in the narrative. The officer said, "You better stick around."

Night was falling. It was dark. One of the emergency technicians came

out of the house. He announced, "She's gone." He might have been talking to the other officers, but he looked directly at Tim.

Jan was in pieces. Tim knew that Jan and Christa hadn't been very close;
there was no love lost between them. They had a skittering rivalry that
spiked hotter or cooled down, in cycles, but it never fully waned or disappeared. Jan still owed money to Christa. But Christa was a Worthington.

A Worthington was dead.

Killed on Worthington property. On the hallowed Worthington strip.

A string of distraught Worthingtons started to arrive. John Worthington, Christa's uncle who lived down the lane, came to collect Ava, who
still looked dumbstruck and frozen. Tim was resistant to letting her go.
Then, an EMT took charge of the little girl until a Department of Social
Services psychologist arrived to assess her condition.

In the next two days, she'd be passed around between different baby-
sitters, neighbors, and do-gooders. The police visited with her briefly.
Encouraging statements from children is a sensitive and tricky procedure. But, for now, they all went over to John and Cindy Worthington's
place. All but Tim.

A police officer asked Tim to sit down in a cruiser. The officer drove
Tim to Truro police headquarters at the Truro Public Safety Facility. The
officer was driving at a speed that seemed preposterous. They were crawl-
ing. Tim could see that the police officer behind the wheel was charged
up, he might be thinking that he had the "primary suspect," and he sa-
vored the little journey. Tim was ferried to the station with covetous awe
and caution, as if the cruiser was transporting the Shroud of Turin or the
Hope diamond.

At the station house they waited at the big front window until the dispatcher behind the glass buzzed them through an interior door. Inside
the locked-down hallways, the new station house had wall-to-wall carpeting that gave the place a quiet-as-a-library effect, or it was like an
empty airport lounge. Tim felt a mixed sensation of "traveler's rest" and
icy incarceration.

In a tight office, Tim was questioned by police officers. The officers de-
ferred to one another, but seized a moment to showboat whenever they
could.

Again Tim told them the narrative he had already recited more than once at the Little House. "I arrived at her kitchen door and looked in the window."

"Do you do that a lot? Look in her window?"

"Excuse me?" Tim said.

"You go over there. Look in her window. The harbormaster says she didn't wear a lot of clothes. She liked to go around in the buff, that's okay, that's just bohemian, right? It's okay to look. Or did you just want to see who might be with her?"

"No. I had the flashlight."

"When was the last time you had relations?"

"Months."

"Was she dating anyone new?"

"I don't know. Theoretically, maybe," Tim said.

"What's that? You say 'theoretically' she was involved?"

"I don't put anything beyond the realm of possibility. She had jetti-soned her therapist. She wasn't taking meds. It was the holidays."

"Where would you look?" an officer said.

Tim said, "I think you should take a hard look at Tony Jackett. The whole town knows about his relationships. Based on what Christa told me last Friday, it makes me suspicious."

"What did she tell you?"

Tim said, "They had talked about money. She wanted money from him."

"You say 'look at Jackett.' Jackett says 'talk to Arnold.' "

The table of uniforms seemed to enjoy watching the little shuttlecock of accusation. It was going to be an interesting game.

"So you went over there for what reason?"

"The flashlight. I told you. The day after New Year's I went over to play with Ava. I had borrowed the flashlight to walk home."

"Did she say she wanted this flashlight returned?"

"Not directly," Tim said.

"But you thought it important to return it to her?"

"Yes."

"Why tonight? I mean it's not a video or an overdue library book, right?"

Questions kept circling back to the flashlight. They didn't seem to recognize that it was just a neighborly courtesy to return a borrowed item.

"So you say you sometimes went over to check on her? Maybe see if she had a visitor?" an officer said.

Another uniform added the color. "You look in the window. Maybe you see what you're missing—"

Tim scraped his chair back and stood up.

Their questions had started to accrue in a poisonous, point-blank assumption of guilt. They didn't believe he had any neutral or benign reason to visit Christa Worthington.

"She was my friend," Tim said.

"How do you use that word? Friend? What is your definition of that?"

Tim felt the air pressure sucked out of the room.

They told him he must wait for the state police. He learned that it was the Massachusetts state police who handled murder investigations; local police were just flunkies. Even Truro Police Chief John Thomas—whose nickname is "Popcorn" because friends joke his IQ is the same as his belt size—even he wasn't the kingpin.

When the state police arrived, a trooper asked Tim to remove his shoes. They had found a footprint on Christa's door.

"A footprint on the door?" Tim said.

"For starters," an officer said.

They told him that the door frame had been splintered and the dead bolt ripped off. Tim admitted that he hadn't noticed any damage to the door.

The staties looked back and forth at one another, unable to hide their disbelief. They said the door had been kicked hard.

As he unlaced his shoes, Tim thought of the kind of anger it would take to rip the dead bolt loose and break the door in. He said, "It must have been a big rage." He had sometimes lost his cool with Christa. She could often be hypercritical, instructive without invitation, dismissive and incendiary at once. She cornered him. He thought she was self-destructive when she tried to push him too far, like a child testing her limits. She didn't stop until he'd retaliate with a rebuttal or a fresh harangue of his own. But he could never match her lucid critiques, her exquisite diction of disapproval. She wanted the back and forth. She'd turn up the dial, crank the thermostat, rev the tachometer. Once he had thrown a dish at her.

When Tim returned to his house later that night, his father was sitting in front of the TV as per. He cradled the clicker but didn't stab it.

Tim told him, "They kept my shoes."

His father looked at him and said, "Did you do it, Tim?"

Tim stopped in his tracks. He felt stupid standing in his stocking feet. Like a child in footie pajamas. "Dad, give me a break—"

His father said, "I just want to know. I just want to hear it from you, did you do it?"

TRURO TREASURES

At the launch of every tourist season, and as an extension of good will and commerce after Labor Day, Outer Cape villages host annual events and festivals, with themes specific to each. These unabashed campaigns lure day-trippers with fat wallets, and help boost the morale of year-rounders before the long winter lull. At the start of the season, the Chatham Merchants Association invites visitors to its Spring Fling, featuring a pet show and a Crazy Hat Parade and competition. Brewster promotes Brewster in Bloom, when banks of jonquils and gaudy tulips carpet the berms along 6A for miles through town. In Eastham, it's Windmill Weekend, with an art fair on the town green beneath the antique windmill. Originally built in Plymouth in the seventeenth century, the windmill was dismantled and sailed across the bay when a group of Pilgrims, with unexpected pangs of nostalgia, decided to return to Cape Cod, where they had started from. In May, Wellfleet makes a big to-do about the seasonal mating rituals of horseshoe crabs, the little monsters of the tide pools, beloved by naturalists but poached by fishermen for their tubs of bait. The Horseshoe Crab Festival inflames the controversy. And the first weekend after Columbus Day, it's Wellfleet Oysterfest, where you can vote for the best fried oysters (crisp light batter with sweet and plump, almost raw, middles), watch oyster-shucking contests, or compete in the Shuck-n-Run 5k race.

In Provincetown, at the traditional Blessing of the Fleet, a priest stands on MacMillan Wharf or on the deck of a trawler, wielding his aspergillum to douse the prows of fishing vessels and pleasure boats with holy water. Captains come alongside one by one, in a procession, each vying for sea room closest to the holy father. But after the sober ritual, it's a wild party in the harbor, with beer, babes, balloons, and horns blasting. The Blessing of the Fleet is followed by the annual Portuguese Festival in the heart of town. Restaurants enter a "soup-off," where people can sample the best Portuguese recipes for kale soup and squid stew. Another favorite ethnic treat on offer is the notorious "flipper," a paddle-size confection of fried dough dusted with sugar. You can watch the flippers churn and tumble in a huge fryer vat behind a plate-glass window at the Portuguese bakery, across from Town Hall. These events celebrate Provincetown's maritime and ethnic connections—without a Lisbon, there wouldn't be a Provincetown the way we know it. But deeper into the summer, it's wholly different with Carnival, pronounced "Carnie-vahl," an over-the-top gay-pride extravaganza. Its famous annual parade down Commercial Street, from the East End to the West End, is a full-color dictionary of divas, queens, and shirtless, steroid stallions who queue up with shop owners, town selectmen, the new police chief, the fire department, high school athletes, and the mayor, Keith Bergman, who dresses in the loudest sport jacket this side of the canal.

Since 1988, a major event in Provincetown is the annual Swim for Life, a competition with a festival atmosphere, where sponsored swimmers earn donations for AIDS services in Provincetown. Swimmers paddle and splash across the harbor en masse, from Long Point to the Boatslip.

Then, in October, at the launch of the off-season for the diehard tourist trade, the town hosts the internationally renowned transvestite festival, Fantasia Fair. Hundreds of Marilyn, Madonna, Princess Di, and Diana Ross divas strut up and down Front Street abreast of their frumpy sisters, those gals who prefer to dress like American housewives in Edith Bunker shirtwaist dresses and housecoats accessorized with clumsy handbags and Shirley Booth orthopedic oxfords.

Also gaining a reputation, the Provincetown International Film Festival invites both indie and major studio directors to attend a week of informal chats and screenings. Gus Van Sant, local resident John Waters, and actor Kevin Bacon sit down to have a chin wag before a big turnout of movie buffs that fills Town Hall. This year's festival had an unfortunate incident when during the screening of a movie, the theater went dark. The projectionist was found slumped in his tight cubicle unconscious and was carried away on a stretcher. It was rumored that he had OD'd, but in fact he was someone who suffered epilepsy and the flickering light of the projector might have set off a grand mal.

I had family roots in East Sandwich, a historic village up-Cape, at the opposite end of the peninsula. Although I spent most of my childhood in Wilmington, Delaware, "The Chemical Capital of the World," summers I went to Cape Cod, where my mother had lived with her uncle, Dodge MacKnight, a landscape painter, whose paintings have their own room at the Isabella Stewart Gardner Museum in Boston. In Wilmington, DuPont produced Teflon, Stainmaster resins, and toxic pigments. Dow and Monsanto made napalm. Fumes from their smokestacks blistered the paint on parked cars in our neighborhood, but in July I was picking wild blueberries on the Cape, filling the hem of my white T-shirt. The indelible stain of that wilderness seeped into my bones.

When I came to live in Provincetown in 1980, my family had disappeared from Cape Cod. I had come for a writing fellowship at the Fine Arts Work Center, my six-year-old daughter in tow. The Work Center supports ten writers and ten visual artists for the winter season, and I arrived with only two trunks, my Smith Corona typewriter (its backspace key missing), and within a week we had a new kitten. In Provincetown, toms parade from the West End to the East End and litters are dropped in odd places: restaurant pantries, wheelhouses on draggers, and in unexpected file drawers and crannies in Town Hall.

My daughter was starting first grade the following day. I set my alarm clock in order to arise in time, but as I cranked the knob, the clock fell apart. This instant, when the little clock disintegrated at my touch, was a turning point for me. Time warps on the Outer Cape, when "length of stay" is transformed to "way of life." And having a sticky "backspace" key on my typewriter seemed to be meaningful: from here I should only go forward.

Like Christa, I had come back to Cape Cod to work on my writing. But Christa didn't have the support of a built-in community. She might have had family nearby—a mixed blessing—but she didn't have the focused society and fraternity one finds in an institution with a highly charged "vision statement." I was a single mom, but I brought my kid almost everywhere, to poetry readings and communal dinners. The long, hard winter at the Fine Arts Work Center can be spartan and austere as a gulag, but that autumn, before the first freeze, Fantasia Fair was going full tilt.

I met a young man standing before the vanity mirror in the women's room of a local bar called the Back Room. Dressed in a skintight evening gown with a plunging neckline, she primped before her transformed reflection. She was shading her cleavage with a pot of powdered rouge to enhance the illusion of a real bustline and to give it a little more oomph. "It's all about depth perception," she said.

Without warning, she took her sable brush, smeared it with color, and dabbed my breastbone. "See? Not that you need extra help," she said. Of all the women I've met in "powder" rooms, she was the most guileless and cheerful. But straight tourists, who are caught off guard to find themselves in town during Fantasia Fair, are often heard whispering the same old chestnut: "Toto, I don't think we're in Kansas anymore."

Unlike Provincetown, Truro is a lot more like a small town in Kansas. It's a sleepy hamlet controlled by the weather. Kansas has its twisters and dust bowls, and Truro has gales, nor'easters, and "perfect storms" crashing into the shoreline of the narrow peninsula. The sea surrounds. But the people here or in America's heartland have a similar foundation in family, in work, and in familiar goals of unhindered capitalism, whether the town's first economic foothold was in salt cod and barrels of whale oil, or in wheat fields and grain elevators.

Truro is what people imagine when they think "small town." In the eighteenth and nineteenth centuries, the town's growth fluctuated with the success of its fishing fleet, but its population had declined and leveled off by the early 1900s. Incorporated in 1709, a mystery emerged regarding the original name given to the town. On the records of the General Court of 1709 is a passage left unexplained even to this day: "The part of the Cape lying between Eastham, and known as the Indian Pamet, shall be a separate town by the name of 'Dangerfield.' "

Thoreau wrote, "This is a very appropriate name, for I read on a monument in a graveyard near Pamet River, the following inscription:

SACRED
TO THE MEMORY OF
57 CITIZENS OF TRURO
WHO WERE LOST IN SEVEN
VESSELS, WHICH
FOUNDERED AT SEA
IN THE MEMORABLE GALE OF
OCT. 3RD, 1841."

The reference to "Dangerfield" in the record of the General Court is the solitary documentation of any such place on Cape Cod. Christa might not have known that she was coming home to "Dangerfield" when she left New York. In later town and church records, beginning with a petition written by Captain Thomas Paine of Pamet, the town is incorporated by the name of "Truro," making it the seventh township on the Cape. The town was organized under the specific provision "that the inhabitants of the said town do procure and settle a learned orthodox minister to dispense the word of God to them, within the space of three years next after the passing of this act or sooner."

Truro, like many New England towns and cities, is in fact named for an English burg. "Truro" in Cornwall County, England, dates back to the mid-twelfth century. Truro was a center for tin and quite prosperous. In fact, Reginald, the Earl of Truro, had lived in a grand manse known as Truro Castle. In the nineteenth century, the population of Truro in Cornwall was over eleven thousand. But in 2002, Truro, Cape Cod, has a year-round population of only eighteen hundred.

"It's Nowheresville," Truro resident and Pulitzer Prize–winning poet Alan Dugan likes to say.

Painter Susan Baker calls it "a nexus of Spectacular Nobodies." Dugan and Baker love it this way.

Yet others complain that it's remote. Backward. Off the map. Most surprising for such a wilderness setting is the fact that although Truro has no manufacturing plants or industry, Truro has the worst air pollution in Massachusetts. A scientist at the federal Environmental Protection Agency calls Truro "the tailpipe of the nation" because it takes a direct hit from the prevailing westerly winds that spew smog and ozone from sources far inland. Sulfur dioxide, nitrogen oxide, and fine particulate matter created by industries and power plants in the Midwest, augmented by pollution from the heavily populated Northeast Corridor, from D.C. to New York, are funneled over the Outer Cape. Charles Kleekamp of Cape Clean Air said that the EPA issues warnings when ozone levels reach one hundred, but the monitoring station in Truro records ground-level ozone at two hundred. People can drop dead.

And yet in all of Truro there is only one traffic light, and it's a blinker. There is no mail delivery, no sewer system, no fire hydrants or trash pickup. People dig their own wells, septic systems, and must haul their refuse in the backseats of their cars to the Truro dump. There are no shopping centers or fast food chains. One grocery store remains open in winter, an old mom-and-pop establishment called Dutra's Market, with very slim pickings: sour milk; green fuzzed lemons; brown bananas; a few loaves of bread.

Civic matters are chewed over and voted on by a show of hands at Town Hall meetings. In a recent public debate, residents argued before the Cape Cod Commission, a tree-hugging panel investigating an outsider threat from a "huge corporation." Privileged summer folk who call themselves "nonresident taxpayers" feared that the "rural character" of Truro was threatened should the Stop & Shop corporation build a new supermarket. Working-class year-rounders (people who clean the summer folks' homes, mow their lawns, wait tables, baby-sit their grandchildren) want the convenience. The meeting was held at Nauset High School because Truro Central School was too small for the testy crowd. Working year-rounders took the bleacher seats and rich geezers sat in the orchestra pit. It was living proof of our town's cross-demographics, both the "Appalachia by the Sea" poor folk and the well-heeled retirees from Sun City. Individuals from both sides got up to stand before a microphone on a long boom, which had an upsetting effect on the shy, inexperienced chambermaids and fishermen who weren't used to public speaking. The other side, most of whom owned musty diplomas and who might have been debate team captains at their prep schools, had no problems filling their allotted time. Two days after the confrontation, I received a thank-you note from a Stop & Shop exec, Ray L., praising me for supporting the project. He said, "If I could use a boxing analogy, I think they had us on the ropes in the early rounds—but we closed with a flurry at the end. . . ."

These class struggles exist everywhere, yet Truro, a typical small town in most ways, is not as simple as most legendary American settings—for instance, River City in *The Music Man*. Based on Mason City, Iowa, River City is an archetypal American hamlet wherein a disingenuous grifter falls for "Marion the librarian" and reforms himself to win her hand. But Truro neighbors are not the Marions, not the Cleavers, not the Donna Reeds, and, even with Christa's murder, they're not the "Clutters" of *In Cold Blood*.

Truro, aka "Dangerfield," has beginnings that are a little more charged and edgy.

Still steeped in its brutal Yankee history, Truro is a pin dot famous for its outcasts. Washashores keep coming, but the original story still packs a wallop: an overcrowded square-rigger full of men and brides, fleeing oppression and bondage in England, set out for the New World. When the *Mayflower* makes landing on the Outer Cape, the Pilgrims are greeted by a wind-torn wilderness with savages, and topsoil *less than an inch thick*. Some of these new arrivals will starve or freeze to death that first winter.

In 1609, Henry Hudson claimed to have sighted Cape Cod, where he anchored at its north end. He sent his men ashore to collect wild grapes. Hudson's log said that they returned with a bounty of fruit, and also a live mermaid. There are still wild grapes in the Province Lands, but of late no mermaids have been sighted. Some believe it was a harp seal that aroused romantic interest by Hudson's crew. After months at sea, sailors wear rose-colored glasses.

Hudson named the spit of land "New Holland," and it is printed that way on antique Dutch maps, but Captain Hudson left these shores and sailed southward to the river that bears his name.

There is still some argument about who was first to set foot on Cape Cod, Sir Francis Drake in 1586 or Captain Bart Gosnold in 1602. But there is no dispute that on November 11, 1620, the *Mayflower* rounded Race Point and set anchor in the safe waters of "the Bay of Cape Cod," or what today is known as Provincetown Harbor. After sixty-three grueling days at sea, their journey was almost over. On the same day that they set anchor in the harbor, even before heading ashore, the men sat down to write the Mayflower Compact.

The text expressed their oath to "covenant and combine ourselves together into a civil body politic, for our better ordering and preservation. . . ."

Although quite brief and economically written, this simple document is the foundation of all the democratic institutions in America; its salt-stained papyrus is the sturdy plinth on which the Republic was built.

Regardless of their sterling intentions and vow of independence, the weary party faced a certain risk of perishing en masse that first winter. Yet, on Wednesday, November 15, sixteen men left the *Mayflower* for their first expedition into Truro. As the men went exploring, the Pilgrim women prepared for a washing day, and they went ashore with their tubs.

Miles Standish led his men from Long Point to East Harbor in Truro. A further hike brought them to a roiling spring where they took their first drink of fresh water in the New World. Today, the clear brooklet, just east of Head of the Meadow Beach, still trickles and purls. It's called Pilgrim Springs, a well-hidden, almost secret attraction, managed by the National Seashore.

Leaving the spring, the Pilgrims saw Native Americans, a few Pamet Indians who roamed nearby, accompanied by pet dogs. The Englishmen chased them, but the Indians knew the terrain and fled. The English were not used to marching in hillocks of sand and soon grew weary.

After trailing the savages, Standish and his men discovered a kettle and baskets of seed corn, the famous booty they would steal from their native hosts and bring home to the *Mayflower*. Before taking the grain, they discussed how they would one day return the kettle and settle payment with the Indians. The corn would keep them from famishing, and what would be the proper remittance?

On the Pilgrims' first expedition into Truro, they discovered the Pamet Inlet, a peaceful waterway that flowed with the tide into a broad valley and marshland. On their next circuit, they sailed their "shallop" up the river. As they navigated the estuary, they sailed past the sloping hill where today Depot Road meanders upland to the Worthington bungalow and the scene of a murder.

In 1992, I returned to live in Truro after several homesick years in the Bible Belt at a small college with a "work program," where students ran the physical plant. More than once, when I turned on the faucet in the women's room, I found my feet soaking wet. A student had forgotten to reattach a trap elbow or had neglected to tighten a locknut. In Black Mountain, North Carolina, I looked out my windows at Mount Mitchell, the highest peak on the Eastern Range, and a bowl of surrounding mountains, called "the Seven Sisters." The vista made me claustrophobic. I was landlocked. I had to get back to sea level, to Truro, the "tailpipe of the nation," or not.

In '92, I settled into a small house on the "back side," east of Route 6, across from Corn Hill. I was getting the Dixie residue off just in time for the town's first stab at "quaint bait" for day-trippers, a gala christened Truro Treasures Weekend.

Truro Treasures festivities start each year with a Friday-night spaghetti dinner. The launch is attended by year-rounders who are happy to sit beside one another again after the grueling summer season. With business winding down, neighbors can again be sociable, seeing one another as brethren and not as the competition. Outsiders leave town. A seasonal gourmet food emporium, Jams, chains its doors after Labor Day, when summer folk disappear. The out-of-town shop owners graze their profits and take off. Residents are glad to see them go. They never give anything back to the local community. My daughter had worked at Jams one summer under the icy manager. After breaking five glass coffee carafes against their chic granite sink, she was fired. She was much happier doing changeovers at the Horizon Motel on Shore Road. Jams can't get local help and has to hire Irish girls, who come to the States every summer to work for nothing. But the "nothing" in the States is more than the nothing in Ireland.

In its first years, the annual spaghetti dinner was held at Goody Hallet's Tavern. Goody Hallett was an incorrigible teenager who in 1715 was found lying in a barn with a dead baby in her arms. Historian Jeremiah Digges

(Josef Berger) writes in the beloved WPA guide, *Cape Cod Pilot:* "Goody was at once whisked into the village, seized up to Deacon Doane's fine new whipping-post and given a lashing preliminary to the real punishment that awaited the outcome of her trial for murder." In fact, she was arrested for having had a child out of wedlock, whether dead or alive, and was imprisoned. The devil visited her at the Eastham Gaol. "Can ye write, Goody?" he asked her, and he offered her his quill so she could make her mark on a contract. "As Goody took the quill, she observed that its tip glistened scarlet." The demon aided her escape and for years she rambled the Outer Cape doing misdeeds, believed to be "betaken" by the Witch of Billingsgate. She earned her real fame bedding "moon cussers" and pirates; she caused tempests and hurricanes, sinking ships and looting their fortunes.

In 1999, Goody Hallett's Tavern was razed for the new Seamen's Bank building, and the spaghetti feast shifted to the tight little cafeteria tables beneath fluorescent lighting at Truro Central School. Today, Goody Hallett would be welcomed at the spaghetti dinner; her famous escapades are an over-the-top romantic legend, but residents have a different feeling about Christa Worthington and her out-of-wedlock baby. If Christa sat down in the cafeteria, she'd wear a "scarlet letter" on her spaghetti bib.

On alternate years, Truro Treasures sponsors a parade through town. The oldsters and dowagers who organize the event say it's too tiring to create the spectacle *every* year. Saturday morning, it begins with a line of classic cars. In one car, a seat is reserved for Truro's oldest resident, a recipient of the *"Boston Post* cane," a mace handed down year by year to the person whose bones have remained aboveground the longest. Then it's a beauty pageant for local businesses. Men drive their fresh-waxed vehicles: fire trucks; Cape Cod Oil tankers; or it's Quahog Electric and Royal Flush Plumbing (with crisp white playing cards stenciled on its driver's side door, and long tubes of white PVC pipe tucked piggyback across the roof). There are pickups from Joseph's Dump Runs and Brian Davis's well-drilling rig, like a giant corkscrew. A "monster truck" from Ducky Noons's sand and gravel pit rolls past with shoulder-high tires. Fishing boats are hauled on trailers, wives, widows, and children on deck throwing candy and prizes to their friends on the sidelines. Billy Souza's lobster boat, the *Raider III*, gets a round of applause. A wine vat on wheels from

Truro Vineyards sloshes past and following that an E. Z. Doze It flatbed truck carries children from Miss Hutchings' computer class. The kids hold fishing poles, jigging for floppy disks (already hooked on their lines). A banner says "Fishing for Knowledge." And Nick Brown, good-natured as always, is dressed in yellow oilskins, as he pushes a dolly carrying a giant papier-mâché steamer clam. When he pinches a rubber bulb, the clam sprays a stream of water at the crowd. Closing up the rear, a float with a cardboard lighthouse commemorates the successful relocation of Highland Light, the first lighthouse built on Cape Cod. Erected upon the clay pounds in North Truro in 1796, it was recently moved back from the eroding cliff. The work needed to be completed before the next big storm could chew further into the bluffs, leaving no room for the equipment needed to come in to save it.

With fanfare and national press attention, the Army Corps of Engineers jacked up the lighthouse with hydraulic lifts and built a plywood pallet beneath the structure. They rolled the beloved landmark in tiny increments, just a few inches an hour, to make sure its antique bricks and mortar didn't topple. It took a full week to relocate.

In the afternoon, there's an art fair on Sonny Roderick Field at the grade school, where "crafters" sell tea cozies, needlework pillows, scrimshaw rings, and "clam clocks" made from seashells. Kids can dunk the principal in a vat of water.

Neighbors loiter around the concession tent, eating bowls of chowder or Portuguese sausage. Then, with a mix of charged machismo and technical grace, the Truro Fire Department and EMTs demonstrate their newly acquired Jaws of Life equipment, sawing through the roof of a clunker donated for the spectacle, a gift from Ducky Noons' junk heap. For eggheads who boast that "the pen is mightier than the clam rake," there's a used-book sale at the library, and in the evening a poetry reading or a slide show.

But the social highlight every year comes at sundown, when residents meet at the Truro Transfer Station for the annual Dump Dance. Young couples think the incongruous setting romantic, finding private niches between the towers of trash to kiss and hold hands. Families have tailgate parties, parking their cars beside organized mounds of junk: glass and plastic recycling bins; the metal pile; the appliance heap; the wood mountain where contractors dump mitered scraps, stubs of two-by-fours, mismeasured planking, and whatever mistakes accrue at work sites, refuse from the lucrative build-out that's increased for the last few years. The local rock-a-billy group, the Jug Band, has been performing at the Dump Dance since its inaugural bash ten years ago. You can't imagine someone saying, "How do you get to the Transfer Station?" . . . "Practice, practice, practice," but it's an upbeat gig.

No alcohol allowed. Not since the year a tight Dump Dance partygoer drove his car into a police officer directing traffic. It's forbidden to have booze, but there's plenty to go around. The golden therapist is poured discreetly from coffee urns and lemonade jugs regardless of Chief Popcorn's eagle eye.

The year winding down, Thanksgivings on Cape Cod have a little more clout than elsewhere in the nation. After all, we have the local cranberry crop. You can even pick your own berries in secret dune bogs where the cranberry mat grows thick, along with the poison ivy. But most of our pride comes from the heady recognition that the Pilgrims landed *here*. They drank their first sip of potable water in Truro, before heading out across the bay to Plymouth. The South Shore might have "Plymouth Rock," but we have the Pilgrim Monument, and that's a whole lot more granite. In December, Provincetown presents Holly Folly to entice holiday shoppers and partygoers. The town strings guy wires mounted with colored lights from the top of the monument tower, the lines stretched taut from its gargoyles to its base, in a perfect cone. When lighted, the monument is a colossal Christmas tree visible for miles around. It can be seen from the wheelhouses of freighters steaming offshore in the Boston shipping lanes and by pilots on their approach to Logan Airport in Boston.

After Christmas, the Outer Cape settles in for the blear of winter. Daylight fades fast and the sun sets before 4:00 P.M. Only in Nova Scotia does night fall faster than in Truro. Thoreau noted the unique sensation of standing on the edge of the jutting peninsula and wrote, "A man may stand there and put all of America behind him."

January through March is downtime for year-rounders who work in the tourist industry. Cottages are boarded up; water lines are flushed; fish stores hose their cases one last time; restaurants disconnect refrigerators; motels store toilet paper and paper bath mats in their dormant ice freezers and display "Sorry" on their signposts. But nobody is sorry. They're closed. They don't have to worry about opening up for four months.

My work follows the academic calendar. I was teaching in Boston, driving up a couple of times a week. In the winter slowdown, the traffic on Route 6 slacks off. Empty businesses post signs that say "See you in April." The off-season standstill is contagious. It's the ebb and flow of a tourist town that earns its keep in summer. In winter, workers find respite, time for hobbies, self-improvement, and personal growth. A friend of mine took a welding class at Cape Cod Tech.

Long before tourism, fishermen learned to accept the winter lull, when the weather turned and they couldn't steam out. They spent these months mending nets and building new lobster pots. They still do handiwork like this, and some captains even put on their wives' dusters and aprons to help around the house. Others go into the Wellfleet library for yoga lessons.

I had broken my ankle in December. I couldn't drive my own car because of its clutch, but I could get into Boston driving a friend's automatic. Mostly, I was homebound.

On January 7, I was listening to the local weather report on WQRC, when I heard the newsbreak.

WQRC begins each news segment with ships' bells clanging. Then it's a recording of breaking waves, a crack of surf, and a grinding curtain of sand and pebbles. The tide pitches and pulls back as the announcer recites the station's call letters. Each day he salutes different Cape Cod pin dots on the map: "WQRC, from Spectacle Pond to Newcomb Hollow" or "from Springhill Beach to 'Tween Channels"; "from Scorton Creek to Jeremiah's Gutter." It's a hats-off to beloved Cape Cod town landings, waterways, and fishing holes. Landmarks and seamarks.

The native flag-waving reminds listeners that we are a world apart from Boston. Forget the commute, the congested Southeast Expressway, the HOV lanes, and the tangle of highway construction at the "Big Dig." The local radio patter admonishes anyone who wishes to be elsewhere. Cape Codders believe they can stomach events, whether it's 9/11 or NAS-DAQ nosediving, as long as we have ships' bells and breakers to buffer the hard news. But it's different when there's trouble east of the canal, when the news flash comes from deep within our own bounds.

"Sunday, a Truro woman was found murdered in her home on Depot Road."

I adjusted the Velcro closure on my clunky boot cast, and the plastic teeth made a ripping sound, so I wasn't sure I had heard right. At the same time, my sixteen-year-old son had plugged in his amp cord, making a clatter of audio sparks and feedback snarls, a sound like throwing the switch on a penitentiary armchair. He rolled into a bone-pulverizing, disruptive, but full of pathos riff, crunching chords up and down the neck of his electric guitar. He specializes in punk subgenres called "crust" and "thrash" and "grind core." I turned the volume up on my radio until the newscaster was screaming. "On the weekend, Truro resident Christa Worthington was found murdered, her little girl clinging to her side. Police estimate Worthington had been dead for up to thirty-six hours, during which time the child was left unattended. Former boyfriend Tim Arnold discovered the victim when he went to the residence to return a flashlight—"

Depot Road is a couple of minutes by car, and as the crow flies it's less than a mile from my house. I didn't know Christa Worthington. Her name was new to me, although the radio announcer said that she was a writer, had family here, and she had returned to Cape Cod to "live a quiet life." Like me, and many other Truro folk, a reclusive life is the ideal. But I was surprised to hear, "Truro shellfish constable Tony Jackett, father of six, has acknowledged that he is the father of Worthington's out-of-wedlock baby. Worthington was raising the child alone."

Although I already knew Jackett, and I would soon meet Tim Arnold, I felt an immediate affinity and identification with the victim. She was a single mother.

This detail was the first little synapse that sparked. The *single mother thing*. A nerve that shivers and connects, in perpetuity.

I think of July weather when mothers and their kids crowd the opposite shore of the Pamet Inlet. The red and yellow beach umbrellas like a row of giant, irradiated zinnias. And a few nylon awnings that look like half a pup tent. One of these wind-torn, raggedy tilts would be missing from the Pamet shore next summer.

NEWSBREAKS

Staff reporter Emily Dooley broke the Worthington story in the *Cape Cod Times*. She had been at the Provincetown desk for a little more than a year, and had had her hands full the summer before with the Churchill saga. She filed at least fifty stories about the stricken right whale. She fielded the national press and TV teams who wanted both the scientific and the hokey details about the endangered animal. Churchill's dilemma seemed to strike a nerve and it spawned PC rants, wildlife columns, and vacation spot features. Dooley tipped her head back, looked at the ceiling, and said, "Oh, please, I never want to hear about another whale."

Whales come back to these waters each season, but there hadn't been a murder in Truro for three decades, not since Tony "ChopChop" Costa killed two girls from Rhode Island and hacked them up. He tumbled them deboned and gutted into a shallow grave in the Truro woods. It was the same clearing where he planted marijuana seedlings. He called it his "garden." The infamous site is less than a mile from Christa's charming bungalow.

Emily Dooley is an attractive woman in her mid-twenties, with dark hair, pale skin, and big, liquid eyes like a movie starlet. She looks a little like Natalie Wood in one of her youthful roles, maybe the jaded teen in *This Property Is Condemned*. But Emily is no-nonsense, all Lois Lane when she sits at her keyboard banging out a story by deadline—anything from mercury poison in the water system to a feature on taffy pullers getting back into practice for the summer season. Or, more recently, she was on the phone with a source in Plymouth, England, where they are building a new replica of the square-rigger *Mayflower*: *Mayflower III*.

A reporter has to have a healthy mind-set to work in Provincetown.

Dooley has mastered the perfect calibration of generous tolerance and a wry distaste for her setting. On occasion, Dooley might shed her professional reticence to deliver a zinger about the nutty place where she has found herself, but usually she's down to business. She came to the *Cape Cod Times* from Littleton, Colorado, where she had covered the Columbine massacre for the *Littleton Independent* and *Highlands Ranch Herald*. For a young reporter, the Columbine incident was a brutal and demanding assignment where she was baptized by fire. Hired by the *Cape Cod Times* to head the bureau desk in Provincetown, she soon found that her beat wasn't a typical small town assignment but something else entirely. P-town has an idiosyncratic populace of urbane sophisticates and hedonist decadents, of underground lifestyles out in the open, of long-established countercultures elbow to elbow with diehard Yankee puritanism. In a hothouse of sexual diversity, where town landmarks earn names like the "meatrack" and the "dick dock," there are still the steadfast virtues of seaside living: last-chance fishermen at work, landscape painters, weekend sailors, naturalists and spiritualists. Everyone packed in like sardines, sometimes happy as clams, sometimes at each other's throats.

She covers town meetings or reports on the high school's junior prom and its annual grand march of "dates," where teens dress in their formal wear and parade through town. To her horror, the prom's chosen theme song is the same treacle her high school had showcased at her prom ten years ago: "Wonderful Tonight." The Provincetown school system is shrinking; each graduating class is smaller, with few hetero couples in town raising children. These last P-town prom kids are like dinosaurs on parade.

In the summer of 2001, Dooley wrote several stories about *Naked Boys Singing,* a nude musical at the town's beloved drag bar, the Crown and Anchor. The performers sang to the audience in their birthday suits, with full frontal exuberance as they soloed and harmonized with glee club enthusiasm. When selectmen voted to close the show, there was an uproar. The summer of 2001 was mostly Churchill and *Naked Boys Singing.* There are always stories about coyote troubles: should they be pampered or shot on sight? And stories about the annual war against personal watercraft. Jet Skis in the harbor, should they be banned?

Dooley had been getting restless at her P-town desk and had started to think about sending her résumé to other dailies. Working in a gay town is hard on a single girl. She missed being in a larger city with its more woman-friendly demographics. She says, "Once I'd like to see a man in a suit!" She is more likely to see a buff young gent walking up the street bare-assed, dressed only in a thong and buckskin chaps, a boa constrictor coiled around his shoulders as his only accessory. Beefcake, bruisers, Nancy-boys on parade. Winter and summer. For a while she had to commute to Connecticut to date a man she had met off Cape.

She was writing a follow-up story about the untimely deaths of two lesbian pilots from town, whose single-engine plane had crashed during a snowstorm over Iceland. She was recapping the bios of the local heroines, ho-hum, when the Worthington murder fell in her lap.

Not since she had covered the Columbine shootings had she sorted through such a wellspring of murder lore.

The story had legs.

She entered the maelstrom, a vortex of cross-referenced details and information that was gaining momentum, escalating by the hour like a supercell thunderstorm.

Dooley's newsbreak begins, "The violence that shattered three decades of relative serenity in this bucolic Outer Cape town was enough to disturb even the most veteran homicide detectives." She lassos the story in her first sentence, evoking its charged dichotomy—the small town ethos disrupted by the sudden appearance of law enforcement's glamour cop: the homicide detective.

"Tim Arnold, a former boyfriend whose father lives near Depot Road, found the body Sunday afternoon. According to Arnold, he had watched the New England Patriots game at his father's house on Old County Road." The New England Patriots. Football. Supporting the home team. This is the familiar detail readers can identify with; most New Englanders were watching the game, and Dooley sets the stage for what comes next. "After the game, Arnold went to return a flashlight he had borrowed from Worthington earlier that week.

" 'I could see something bad had happened. There was blood under her head,' Arnold said."

Within days of Dooley's story, the talk around town was skeptical. "A flashlight? What a crock!" a woman said at the Truro post office, where WBZTV had set up a camera tripod. A reporter held a microphone under a woman's chin as the tape rolled. Holding a white fan of neatly addressed envelopes, she told the reporter, "We never locked our doors before this. Now, I don't know. I think it's that boyfriend." Then, she turned and walked into the little post office. The Truro PO is the social nexus of the town, where people stop to gab and compare notes; it's just like the old Feed & Grain of the nineteenth century. People meet at the PO or at the dump to exchange information, hearsay, and rumors about the Worthington murder. Until now, the rumors were familiar recountings of the latest news about Churchill, the endangered whale, Lady Di, or John Jr.'s plane crash in the waters off Martha's Vineyard. One old favorite: sightings of the Truro mountain lion surfaces now and again. The rumor of a Truro mountain lion emerged most recently when someone found large paw prints in the sand, but these turned out to be the tracks of novelist Denis Johnson's Great Dane.

Other than the strictly local folklore, there had always been a cushion, a distance, between Truro residents and the national tabloid stories that cropped up. But now Truro was ground zero. All details and references were site-specific, and familiar to one and all. *People knew the people involved.*

A Fox News van rolled into the PO's gravel parking lot and a cameraman jumped down. He sidestepped WBZ's tripod and with a shoulder cam he followed on the heels of people as they came and went with their mail. He blocked access to the blue metal drop boxes, forcing people into a face-to-face.

He asked a resident her opinion about the *New York Post*'s pulpy headline, SLAIN FASHIONISTA'S PALS JOIN CUSTODY FIGHT FOR DAUGHTER, that had seized the tabloid-packed story about Tony Jackett's traumatic battle with Amyra Chase and her husband, Clifford, the couple Christa had designated as guardians for Ava in her recent will. It was a neck-to-neck race for custody of Ava. Whether it was talk of Ava, Toppy and Beth

Porter, a report of a "mystery van" leaving Christa's place on the Saturday before she was found murdered, or the rumor that she was stabbed with a flagpole broken off a relative's nearby home, residents said that they didn't know if it was better to learn it was an outsider or one of their own who had killed Christa.

Chief John "Popcorn" Thomas was quoted in the paper: "Lock your doors. Although most murder victims knew their assailants, it's a good idea to be vigilant. But her life didn't begin when she moved to town."

News of a murder is shocking, but when Tony Jackett's open secret circulated, few people seemed surprised. Jackett had a long-standing reputation as a high-profile playboy on the town pier. He was handsome and guileless and quite successful with women. One resident, sixty-five-year-old plumber Robert Meads, spoke with unbridled admiration about Tony's effect on women. Meads told the *Boston Globe*, "Tony would stand on a corner. I think it would take maybe five minutes and there would be a waiting line. He's charismatic. I'd like to go through life again being like Tony." This time, however, Tony might have got in over his head.

I had met Tony Jackett years ago, when he invited me onto the *Josephine G*. I was fact-checking my information about draggers for a novel I was writing. I walked out to MacMillan Wharf looking for anyone, captain or crew, who might be willing to verify my facts and to explain to me how the Loran navigation system worked. I wanted the definitive how-to about a fishing boat's rusty rakes and cables, the placement of its scuppers, were they kept open or plugged? What are the brand names of its screeching winches? How many grommets on that netting? How many feet of chain? Tony was generous with his time and walked me around deck. I couldn't help but notice his mystique. He was muscular and tan. His thick black hair glistered as the late sun bounced and fractured through his curls. I had done a lot of reading beforehand, and I went through a litany of equipment, asking him if I had my list right. He said, "Hey, Miss Dictionary, you don't need my help. What are you doing here?"

This was a time when he was steaming out alone, without any crew. He had only a plastic bag of shucked scallops to show for a whole day out. After tying up, he got on his bike that he had left chained to a piling, and he pedaled into town to sell his catch directly to the kitchen of a restaurant, maybe to the Lobster Pot or to Napi's. If he was in the mood, he'd go home to Susan, but more likely he'd pedal to the Surf Club for a round or two.

Back then, I was writing a novel that had a fishing disaster as the core anxiety. I studied an incident that had happened in 1976, when the *Patricia Marie*, a dragger out of Provincetown, was lost in a "queer sea," steaming back from Chatham. She was overloaded with a mountain of scallops. The catch was left on deck unshucked and not stowed in the hole when she hit "freakers," those rogue waves that can capsize an unstable boat. She went down in one blip on the radar. All mates were lost. That tragedy had a commonsense explanation. From the transcripts of a coast guard hearing, it was suggested that the accident resulted from a deadly combination: greed and bad luck.

What I have before me now is more prickly and unsettling. Unlike the time I walked out to MacMillan Wharf to find Tony Jackett on the deck of the *Josephine G.* and he was nice enough to invite me to come aboard, Christa isn't anywhere. She can't give me a guided tour. I can't ask the direct questions I had asked Tony: "Is that your VHF? Is that a Hyster winch?"

I didn't know Christa Worthington and I have to work backward to find her without the help of a mentor. Her family isn't speaking. Her ex-lovers are more cooperative, but their agendas are charged, mercurial, and sometimes contradictory.

Writing fiction, I have obligations to my characters. I make demands on them, but they are my compatriots, my friends, even the wicked ones. They are in front of me, but Christa is behind me. She shadows me, an apparition who ducks behind a tree and teases my peripheral vision. Every day is haunted like this.

Writing about a murder victim, I'm all mops and brooms. Worthington, once a total stranger, has become the center of my world. Christa Worthington lived a kind of double life, and that's all too familiar to me. The more I learn about her, the more I understand she isn't the sum of her parts, or any one thing.

I think I can approach her from that same fractured place in me. Christa and I shared a landscape, not just the Truro wilderness, but as woman, mother, even as mistress. Our strongest connection might be writer to writer.

Emily Dooley tells me she is working on a feature story about people's "fear of clowns." The Clyde Beatty Cole Brothers Circus is in town. Every year, the fifth-rate operation comes to Provincetown to set up its tent in a sand parking lot behind the water tower. A clown named "Mr. Jiggs" told Dooley, "We regard ourselves as red-nosed philosophers." But a ten-year-old explained her fear of clowns to Dooley: "They have big, scary-happy faces." Dooley admits that she, herself, is uncomfortable with clowns.

"Clowns?" I say. "Clowns are nothing compared to the ghost in front of me." "Scary-happy" is one thing. I'm facing "scary-sad," "scary-desperate."

CAPE FEAR

Within a week of the murder, several individuals in "the orbit of opportunity" were introduced in the press. These subjects would say "introduced" isn't accurate, they were "dragged" through the tabloids. The story flickered briefly, then blazed. Readers immediately recognized the Miss Marple atmospherics that emerged day to day. The national newspaper *USA Today* ran a story that listed block biographies of Christa, Tony, Tim, Porter, and Toppy, "a cast of characters worthy of a game of Clue."

EX-HOOKER EYED IN TRURO KILLING. The headline in the *Boston Herald* was the newest dollop of sleaze to be ladled upon a story that grew more and more unflattering to Truro. The prism had revolved a quarter-turn to reveal unsettling news about Christa's father, Christopher "Toppy" Worthington. Worthington, a former civil prosecutor for the state attorney general's office, had surfaced as an indefatigable ladies' man. At seventy-two, he had befriended a twenty-something ex-prostitute and heroin addict named Beth Porter. The daughter of a Boston cop, Porter had had a ten-year battle with heroin. She hadn't kicked it. A neighbor said, "She's totally engrossed in the whole drug world and living for the next fix. She manages to find one person after another to support her habit." Toppy financed Porter's rent at a Quincy boardinghouse, the Ritz Manor, and he had recently renewed its lease. A week after Christa's murder, Porter was arrested on drug charges with her boyfriend, Ed Hall. Police found her sitting on a stoop with a needle in her hand. "She's a two-bag-a-day heroin addict," a courthouse official said.

Suddenly, the Truro tragedy was linked to the heroin dens of Roxbury.

In the "orbit of opportunity" Porter had the most volatile profile. She'd been arrested nine times for possession of heroin, for larceny by check, and for noncompliance with drug testing. Her boyfriend, Ed Hall, had already served two sentences in the Suffolk County House of Correction. After his recent arrest, police questioned him about the Truro murder twice in his cell at the Nashua Street jail.

Porter had earlier been a key witness in the high-profile murder trial of convicted wife-killer Dr. Dirk Greineder. When Porter had worked for a Quincy-based escort service, she had made business appointments with the Wellesley physician at local hotels, where he had treated her to champagne and chocolate-covered strawberries.

When the *Boston Globe* published photographs of Porter, the pictures showed Beth in a courtroom, wearing handcuffs. The shots of a woman in restraints encouraged people to believe that the police had nicked someone. "She's the murderer. Toppy Worthington is her hapless pigeon." But as readers studied Porter's photograph, some thought Porter looked like Christa's half-sister. The two women have the same oval face, impish smirk, and loose auburn hair.

When Christopher Worthington rented a small apartment at the Ritz Manor in Quincy, he had told the building manager that he had left his wife and was "looking for a place to live." But when Beth Porter moved in, Toppy told the new building manager, Rocco Vasile, that Beth was his "stepdaughter."

Christa's closest friends saw a resemblance between Christa and her father's shack job. Kim Gibson said, "The resemblance is unbelievable. I've got it all figured out. Beth was adopted by this Boston cop Arthur Porter—so, years later, she decides to look up her wealthy father. She's Toppy's daughter from an affair he had thirty years ago."

DNA testing would prove that this wasn't true. O'Keefe said, "Oh, please. Worthington just got himself a girlfriend, that's all." Amateur psychologists say that he fell for Porter because she resembled his daughter. For Toppy, Porter's coloring, physique, her smirk was the familiar ideal.

Kim Gibson's theory, that Porter was Toppy's "love child," spread online. *CrimeNews2000* gabsters developed the story: Toppy had searched for the daughter he had once abandoned to social services years ago, and now he was making it up to her. Or Beth herself had tracked him down, like the girl in the British movie *Secrets & Lies*. Either way, Christa would have had to share her inheritance; she would have had to go "halfsies" with Porter.

Toppy, a partner in the Dedham law firm of Parasco, Worthington and Chase, before retiring in 1993, had become a bit of an embarrassment to his colleagues. His old associates tried to shrug off the assumptions people were making about him. They didn't believe he could have kept a second daughter a secret. But when law partner Francis Chase learned about Worthington's love nest in Quincy, he said to the *Globe*, "It's a big mystery to everyone. It's a total mystery." Another colleague, David Hopwood, said that Worthington had been a mentor to him. Chris Worthington having a mistress in Quincy "doesn't sound like him at all."

After the murder, Christa's New York friend Steve Radlauer notified police that Christa had had suspicions about Toppy's girlfriend. He said that when Christa had visited him in the city right before her death, she had aired her concerns about her father's offbeat relationship. He said that Christa had told him, "He's giving Beth all my money." Christa was also concerned because Porter was HIV positive and was facing hefty medical expenses.

Police assured Radlauer that several others had contacted them about Porter's murky background.

O'Keefe said that the scenario wasn't extraordinary. Mr. Worthington had found a little chippie and had put a roof over her head. No big deal. The Ritz Manor apartment was a dive. A last-chance bachelor pad. The Ritz Manor had a long history of drug troubles and had been the site of some overdose deaths, and Christopher Worthington, a former state assistant attorney general and upper-middle-class home owner, wasn't a typical tenant at the seedy apartment complex. But he seemed to welcome his new perch, in digs that straddled the line between modesty and decay. Visiting Porter at that "borderline" building, he shirked Worthington expectations and rejected the patrician code.

As if giving the whole world the "bird," Toppy made sure that both their names, "Worthington/Porter," were displayed on the felt board directory in the lobby of the rooming house. For more than two years, Christa had battled with her father about Beth Porter. She never told him directly that she disapproved. She didn't want moral judgments to cloud their straightforward discussions about money.

But it was sizzling tabloid news to read that when Gloria was dying and Christa was with child, Toppy was having a Vegas-style honeymoon. Tim

Arnold said that Christa was both wounded and embarrassed when her father had confessed to her, "I'm in love."

"He was spending quite a bit of money each month on the young woman," Tim Arnold said. "We all thought he was being used by Porter. But he'd had previous affairs with women even before Porter. He might have loved his daughter, but they were so distant. It was almost a moot argument—did he love Christa or not?"

Christa's aunt Patricia Worthington Bartlett told the *Boston Globe* that she knew that Christa had been concerned about Toppy's "inappropriate girlfriends." As Gloria Worthington was bedridden, close to death, Bartlett said, "He was never home enough. He was going off with some girlfriend."

WOMAN TIED TO TRURO CASE UNDER ARREST. When it emerged that Porter had been arrested with her real boyfriend, Ed Hall, a Dorchester man with a string of drug convictions, Toppy's infatuation seemed even more pathetic. He didn't even have Porter to himself. The *Boston Globe* reported that "Porter was driven by two plainclothes State Troopers to Quincy District Court to face a probation surrender hearing and potentially six months in prison." Ed Hall was charged with heroin possession, jailed, and later released on $500 bail.

But the very next day, January 16, Porter appeared in a Dorchester courtroom. She was wanted in both Quincy and Dorchester courts on warrants for earlier probation violations. Porter believes that they trailed her to entrap her when they found her shooting up with Ed Hall. Since Christa's murder, Beth's right to privacy was being messed around with.

She was on her way to do three months at Nashua Street jail for her probation violations. But before she got her orange overalls, she was seen with Toppy again. Toppy was spotted escorting Beth to the hospital. Her pneumonia symptoms had come back.

Later that afternoon, when she returned to Ritz Manor, she was told she was being evicted for her new heroin arrest. The building manager said that they didn't want the place slipping back to what it had been in the old days. Back then, the lobby was littered with sleek little polystyrene syringes, the needles crunching underfoot, like walking on dragonflies.

Reporters covering the Worthington story like to compare notes about their abbreviated conversations with Toppy Worthington. There's an unofficial competition to see who will win the record. Four words. Six words. How many words will Chris dribble out before the receiver slams down. Lightning exchanges with Toppy can be quite comic. From the get-go, Worthington wouldn't talk. Ellen Barry of the *Boston Globe* writes of repetitive stalemates. "A man answering the telephone in Worthington's Weymouth home said he would not comment on any relationship to Porter" or "A man who answered the phone at Christopher Worthington's house declined to comment."

"Reached at his Weymouth home, Christopher Worthington declined to be interviewed. 'No thanks. Sorry. Over,' he said, before hanging up."

I have had no better luck. Chris has responded to my telephone greetings with: "O-kay. No. Gotta go." And "J-oop, here we go. Nope." "Not. Thanks a lot." "Stop here. Leave me out."

His rapid-fire, monosyllabic retorts seem almost infantile, both defensive and childish in their clipped defiance. Yet sometimes his haikulike simplicity and his awkward half-rhymes seem all too poignant, quizzical, and sad.

Christopher Worthington has emerged in the press as an unstable character, and his unwillingness to be interviewed has cemented opinions about him—he's a "cranky Yankee." His transparent relationship with Porter seems to upset people for its bold, "in your face" evolution. To some, he's just the clichéd "dirty old man" with a trust fund to squander. But others are more sympathetic; he's alienated, a naïve prep school boy who never grew up, like a creaky Tom Cruise in *Risky Business*, who scuttles his Princeton application process to fall into cahoots with a working girl.

Christa's friends have different responses to her dad. "He's socially awkward. He never bought into the patrician mystique. He wanted no part of it," said her friend the novelist Eli Gottlieb. Another friend said, "Christa had always told me he was always drinking, but even when he wasn't he was still just so awkward."

But Christa's friend and Ava's onetime nanny, Ellen Webb, said, "I like

Toppy. He stuck by Christa's mother in an unhappy marriage. But when Gloria died, he was done. He was ready to go. I think Toppy was tired of being a Worthington."

In an incongruous addendum to this seedy mural, the *New York Times* Sunday Styles section ran a beguiling full-color photograph of Christa seated on a luxurious velvet divan. The headline said, A MURDER IN CAPE COD JOLTS THE FASHION WORLD. The fashion world was usually un-ruffled by anything but insider gossip, glamour glitches, celebrity rivalries, and faux pas. Nothing very serious. Until Versace was gunned down.

Alex Kuczynski wrote about Christa, "Her story sounds like a paperback mystery: vulnerable beauty and privileged fashion writer comes home to remote New England town from her world travels, has affair with ruggedly handsome fisherman, has a child and is murdered, the case under investigation."

New York magazine sent a pretty young reporter to Cape Cod who chronicled events the first week after the murder. Vanessa Grigoriadis is a diminutive sprite, with big eyes and a childlike tilt of her chin, but she has an adult-size appetite for slasher information. She nosed her way into taboo and "off limits" settings. She barked up every tree, like a Jack Russell terrier on methamphetamine milk bones, to get the story. She visited Jackett and his wife in their kitchen, and she crashed the private funeral service for Christa the following weekend in Hingham. She braided the seedy and poignant strands of the story, cinching a sensational ligature for the stylish weekly. Weeklies are in the incinerator in five days, but the *New York* magazine cover story resonated for much longer in the Truro community. Some people she interviewed—Tim Arnold, for instance—had seemed to want to hang themselves. She was a fireball who talked a mile a minute, and she absorbed the story like a Bounty paper towel.

The TV news program *Dateline* asked the *New York* magazine reporter to analyze the Worthington segment on their newsmagazine. Like a juvie Margaret Mead, Grigoriadis, who hadn't set foot in our little town until a few weeks before, was suddenly an expert. A tsunami of TV newsmagazines followed suit: *48 Hours, Dateline,* and *20/20* activated their phone trees, contacting "suspects," friends of the suspects, neighbors of the victim, community bystanders and busybodies, anyone who wanted to add their two cents. One TV reporter interviewed a local schoolteacher. The teacher was originally from New York and had married a Provincetown fisherman. The reporter thought that the local couple's story might shed some light on Jackett's and Worthington's class diversities and explain their incongruous union. The teacher didn't know Worthington, but she was familiar with the Jacketts. Tony's daughter Braunwyn had a child enrolled at Truro Central School.

When *48 Hours* broadcast a segment called "Secrets of the Heart," Tony told reporter Susan Spencer what Christa had once said about him. He said, "I was a slave to my ego, and an addict to my senses." And ever since the murder, he's been staked to the anthill of the national media. Tony has become what Janet Malcolm had called convicted murderer Jeffrey MacDonald—a "prisoner of publicity."

But *48 Hours* producers received their comeuppance the following day when *New York Post* reporter Don Kaplin wrote, "A salty expression for 'serious trouble' accidentally slipped unbleeped on a news report on Wednesday night's *48 Hours* about the murder of former fashion writer Christa Worthington.

" 'When I heard she was dead, I knew I was in deep s——t,' Worthington's ex-boyfriend, Tony Jackett, said on the CBS show."

"We intended to bleep it, but it got past us," said *48 Hours*' award-winning executive producer, Susan Zirinsky. "We immediately corrected it for the broadcast that aired on the West Coast."

Tony's "salty" mouth was nothing new to local residents, and what might have been a grave or comic irregularity for network prime-time TV was hardly noticed. What people in Truro found most unsettling, especially Tim Arnold, was that the news program showed little Ava playing on the Jacketts' living room carpet. She was singing "We're a happy fam-i-ly" in a sweet, angelic singsong. In the vortex of an emerging custody battle between Tony and Christa's friend Amyra Chase, Ava's appointed guardian, the TV segment portrayed Jackett as a doting father. Prompted by Braunwyn, who asked, "Who loves you?" Ava said, "Daddy!" her eyes wide with wonder and just a trace of suspicion. Tony Jackett was almost a stranger to her.

The public grew more obsessed with two central mysteries: who was Christa's killer and what would happen to the baby?

And then there was the money.

Tony Jackett, if he won custody, could be charged with the authority to oversee his daughter's trust, worth over a million dollars in both Truro real estate and Wall Street assets. State police detective Bob Knott, who had been doing much of the "forensic accounting" for the case, said, "She had a lot of money. A lot more than was reported in the newspaper." But a probate lawyer said that even if Tony won custody, he'd have to jump through hoops of red tape and file monthly requisition slips before he'd see a dime of it.

In the national media, there hadn't been a tabloid story this hot since Gary Condit's mysterious connection to missing intern Chandra Levy the summer before. Soon after Condit's troubles, the Towers fell. Anthrax lofted through mail rooms and hallways of our most sacred institutions. The media's response to Christa's misfortune, in early January, seemed to signal the first signs of our nation's "cultural recovery" from 9/11. The media blitz over Christa embraced the good old American appetite for celebrity mishaps and tragedies, everything from JFK Jr.'s nosedive in waters off Martha's Vineyard to murder suspect Robert Blake's *Baretta* flashback. The media attention awarded Christa had a sheepish alacrity or "sigh of relief" aspect. Christa's pretty face was easy on the eyes after looking at photographs of ground zero, and reading the daily obits of 9/11 victims in the *New York Times*.

Curly-top Ava captured hearts. Not since little "Baby Jessica" fell into a well in Texas had parents felt so much knee-jerk worry for a child. But the media blitz in Texas took its toll on one hero who had rescued Jessica. When all the attention finally evaporated and the do-gooder was altogether forgotten, he committed suicide.

The Worthington family was not cooperating.

"We're not talking. Only the Worthingtons can talk about the Worthingtons," *said Jan Worthington*, in a shrill telephone call.

Jan was distressed as the media persisted to dig. But in fact she had made a deal with Hollywood producers to write her own TV movie script about the crime. She signed up with an outfit that had produced *The*

Jayne Mansfield Story and *A Tale of Two Bunnies,* a TV flick about Hugh Hefner's empire.

When the *Boston Herald* ran a story with the heading CAPE FEAR, about Truro's growing unrest and obsession with the murder, some people remembered that movie buff Tony Jackett had kept a *Cape Fear* movie poster tacked in the wheelhouse of his dragger. Day by day, as no arrests were made and nothing crystallized, anecdotes and rumors provided the only succor for townspeople. Every day, a new confabulated rumor emerged. "Christa was stabbed with a flagpole from Tim's house." "A black van was seen careening down her driveway Saturday afternoon, 'like a bat out of hell.' " "Beth Porter is Toppy's love child." "Tony's daughter Braunwyn had charged into Christa's bungalow last spring, raging about the shift in her father's financial obligations." Or "Braunwyn's estranged husband, Keith Amato, and Tony's handsome son Luc, the one with the fiery eyes, must have bedded Christa. Both men had been seen using Christa's outdoor shower."

In fact, the summer before the murder, after Tony confessed his secret to all his kin, Braunwyn, Luc, and Keith Amato had sometimes stopped at Christa's house to use her outdoor shower after swimming at Corn Hill Beach. To some, it was proof of Christa's genuine hospitality to her new extended family, since Keith Amato was especially susceptible to the "Pamet Crud," an allergic reaction to noxious properties in harbor muck, if he didn't shower immediately after clamming. But others believed it was a form of harassment by Jackett's clan.

One local woman said that she thought Susan Jackett, the jilted wife, "had a valid complaint, and more reason than anyone to lose it, to crack."

Truro wanted to be assured that the state police were doing something. People felt some relief to learn that Christa's closest contacts in town, both her ex-lovers, Jackett's children, and even her father, Toppy, were given polygraph tests. Tim Arnold was the first to get hooked up. Barnstable County Sheriff James Cummings told Emily Dooley, "A polygraph is an investigative tool. It helps eliminate someone as a suspect, or it might persuade a guilty person to confess. The first people you start with are those closest to the victim." Other professionals debate the usefulness of the test, claiming that a machine can't measure someone's truthfulness. If a person curls his toes or tenses his bladder sphincter, it doesn't mean he is lying. Nervousness, grief, and fatigue interfere. There's simply no clear-cut proof with a polygraph.

When police had asked Christa's circle to take the test, it might have been a public relations tactic as much as an "investigative tool." The Truro community wanted to hear about the test results, hoping that the polygraphs might lead to a conclusive "Liar, liar, pants on fire" accusation and arrest. People were pleased to learn that Ed Hall and Porter had been tested. However, according to police sources, when Porter was hooked up to the polygraph equipment, the results were inconclusive. The *Cape Cod Times* reported, "Police surmised that Porter might have been edgy and in need of heroin at the time of the test." They want to administer a new test.

The never-ending newsbreaks sometimes didn't add up. Often a blurred detail or tidbit of character assassination drew fire from readers. Wellfleet resident Eric Martinson wrote to the *Cape Cod Times* scolding the paper for a tickler headline: RAPES IN ORLEANS AND TRURO CALLED UNRELATED TO WORTHINGTON CASE. Martinson wrote, "You could just as well have titled the piece 'Orange juice found not to contain uranium' or 'No links yet between Bin Laden, Worthington.' "

CHIEF POPCORN

I went to see Chief "Popcorn" at the new Truro Public Safety Facility on Route 6. I asked someone how he had earned the nickname, and was told that Chief Thomas had a short temper. Another cop told me that the nickname came from his boss's snack food habit: "Just look at his waistline."

The Truro Public Safety Facility has a name too big for the building, a plain structure with a blank façade of sterile gray clapboard and three garage doors for EMS vehicles and pumpers. With its bays closed, it looks like a supersized "double-wide." It sits just south of Ducky Noons' "pit," a landmark junkyard of scrap metal, gravel, and abandoned cars.

Just behind the station is a cellular tower, hoisted skyward soon after the headquarters were christened. It has become the tallest structure in town, overshadowing other landmarks, like the beloved Cape Cod Light, a cone of antique white brick, the turreted Jenny Lind tower where the singer once performed, and the "golf ball" radar dome, for transatlantic air traffic control. The dome's matte-white sphere looks like a puffball mushroom. Even the yellow crane at Ducky's pit, once the tallest contraption in Truro, isn't a match for the cell tower. The tower is the town's one concession to modern demands, and it was a long time in coming.

My meeting with Chief Thomas is at two o'clock. At this time of the afternoon, the station is quiet except for a man who has come to ask for a burning permit. The dispatcher sits behind a tall Plexiglas window and shouts instructions. I wonder why the expensive new facility doesn't have a simple speaker system like you would find at a drive-up window at Wendy's.

I have to raise my voice slightly to tell her I have an appointment with the chief. "Second door on the left," she says, as she buzzes me inside the inner sanctum. Its wall-to-wall indoor-outdoor carpeting gives the place the hushed soundproofing of a physician's office, unlike the creaky, bare floorboards at Town Hall.

Thomas rises from his desk to shake my hand and flops down into his chair again. A compact man, with a round face and steady eyes, he watches me carefully with mild apprehension. Yet something about him reminds me of an impish kid, a middle-school student who, when left alone, sits behind the principal's desk, opening drawers, twisting paper clips, lifting the telephone receiver, and mocking the authority figure.

He tells me, "We don't have a suspect. We don't have a motive. This isn't typical."

"What makes it different?"

"Usually, they are co-residents. The suspect and the victim. There was no one living in the house with Christa. No one had an opportunity to be there."

Opportunity to be there seems like police rhetoric. I ask him to explain. He tells me that her body was found at 4:30 on Sunday, but the murder could have happened twenty-four to thirty-six hours before that.

"So no one you have questioned had 'the opportunity to be there,' is that what you're saying?"

"So far. The evidence takes a while to gather. Like this, say you tell me that on Sunday you went to Dutra's Market and you bought a half gallon of milk and a loaf of bread. Then someone says they saw you there and saw that you had also purchased a dozen eggs. You didn't say you bought *eggs* in our first conversation, so we have to go back to the beginning."

"You go all the way back to the beginning with each new controverted tidbit? Is that necessary?"

"We've talked to fifty, maybe seventy-five, people, some more than once. Investigation is like a circle. You start from the center and move out farther."

"Can you tell me, did they find a weapon? I've heard a couple crazy things."

"The flagpole?"

"Yes."

"There's been a lot of errors in reporting. That flagpole detail came from one of the Worthingtons. It's not correct. Something about someone using a flagpole in a domestic matter. It doesn't factor in."

"Was the door damaged?"

"Yes. The dead bolt was smashed. The door has been removed by CSS."

"CSS?"

"Crime Scene Services."

I imagine a group named this. It sounds like a carpet-cleaning operation rather than a law enforcement unit.

But I picture Christa's Yankee door removed from its hinges and carried off to a lab. The doors on Cape Cod cottages are idiosyncratic to each house. These are usually paneled "Christian doors," with divided lights; their fir planking warps and settles from year to year, according to each season's weather: hard freezes and sea fogs, northeasterly winds that pry into every crevice, rain that slams in horizontal sheets. There is something evocative about a door, especially here on Cape Cod. And "doors" is common vernacular for the rakes used on draggers. I think of Christa walking in and out of that door, having left her New York life for a new life here with Ava. Both Tony and Tim had entered and departed from this missing door. The door as the gate to Eden. The door as entry to the "narrow house," the door as coffin lid.

I want to ask Chief Thomas how he got the nickname "Popcorn," and verify my facts, but instead I ask him if he thinks I can ever see Christa's papers and journals taken from the house. I tell him, "She was enrolled in a class at Castle Hill. She was writing a narrative about her mother's death while she was expecting Ava. I'd like to see it—"

"These papers will be held until there's an arrest and trial. Then maybe they might be available. Or you can see investigative reports, arrest reports attached to an application for complaint—these eventually go on public record. But there's no arrest. Yet."

Driving home I think of Dutra's Market. Milk. Bread. Eggs.

If it's really so simple, why don't they figure it out?

SINGLE MOTHERS BY CHOICE

In 1997, Christa wrote a piece for the *New York Times* about African fertility dolls. "They offer a talisman and a tonic for the aging baby boomer struggling to conceive in the age of multiple births and sci-fi technology." At the time, Christa had been attending meetings of a non-profit support group called Single Mothers by Choice, or SMC. She herself was struggling to make a decision to have a baby without a husband. She wrote in a "First Person" column for *Harper's Bazaar*, "There is, at the moment, no father for a child of mine, no husband for me, and what if there never is?"

Christa recognized that childlessness was "the lament of her generation," and she went to meetings with other wannabe mommies. Some members had already become pregnant with medical help, and others, like Christa, were still thinking it over. Christa wrote that SMC calls this sort of woman "a 'Thinker,' someone who is still in the Rodin pose, who has not yet gone prone, into 'trying,' through insemination by an anonymous donor."

Women at these meetings were usually college-educated and earned more than the national average for males their own age. Like Christa, many had successful professional lives and had postponed thoughts about children and family. Christa wrote in the magazine article that she had let half her life go by and had put off the urge to have a child until "one day when I was absolutely safe and sound." That day had come, and gone.

Christa progressed from a "Thinker" to "Stuck Thinker" to a "Tryer," and she began the process of finding a donor. In bed at night, she read herself to sleep scanning "long forms," the detailed medical and genetic histories of sperm donors. She also listened to tape recordings of donors' voices, as they recited their "distinguishing characteristics." She fell head over heels in love with the sound of one man's voice. "I thought I heard a voice I could listen to for a lifetime," she wrote.

But when she tried to order donor samples from the "voice" she admired, she found out that her choice was "sold out."

In her article about fertility dolls, Christa wrote, "Most appealing, they can be activated by faith alone." But since the man with "the voice" was sold out, blind faith wasn't going to help.

An editor at *Harper's Bazaar* who worked on that article, Eve Mac-Sweeney, remembers Christa as being "a sad case," her unhappiness sometimes visible in her big, woeful eyes, whether her mood came from her being childless or from her battle with other, secret demons. She said that Christa at that time had looked "especially hangdog" in the hubbub of that glamour mag's stylish offices, as if she was searching for a solution, a different perch in life, but still hadn't found her footing.

Although statistics prove that almost 40 percent of mothers in America are single mothers, not everyone has sympathy for those who are single parents *by choice*.

When Christa agreed to appear as a guest on the Leeza Gibbons talk show to discuss the ideology and expectations of Single Mothers by Choice, some of her friends didn't think it was a good idea. But Christa had been a student in the seventies, the heyday of women's lib, and she had attended many of Vassar's tutorials in feminist action. From the get-go, influenced by her grandmother Tiny's spunky style, Christa had learned to speak her mind. So Christa walked out onto the apron of the stage at the tabloid gabfest having a sincere interest in supporting single women who wanted children. What was all the hissing about?

Friends have said that Christa was not only surprised but also wounded by the audience's response. They jeered and disapproved of her SMC premise and theories. The audience was typical of the current TV sleaze-fests: young, low-income or unemployed, uneducated, tattooed, fat or pregnant. They looked at Christa, her fair skin, sorrel hair, tiny physique; they listened to her biographical information and chic CV and immediately pounced. Here was a privileged, Ivy League graduate turned fashion writer turned ball-buster ice queen. Here was the upper crust complaining she didn't have the fruit filling. Why didn't she just get knocked up and shut up about it. They let her have it.

And like the Leeza Gibbons audience, many Truro residents couldn't digest Christa's independent lifestyle without a little heartburn. "Who did she think she was? First, she wants a glamorous career and then, uh oh, before it's too late, she decides she wants a baby?"

"She steals another woman's husband."

"Like a stud service—"

But local Provincetown folks seemed to side with Jackett. The *Provincetown Banner* printed letters of support for the beleaguered shellfish constable.

> To the editor:
>   Please have compassion in your hearts for this little girl and the Jackett family. Any choice of lifestyle is none of our business. We live in a small town under a large magnifying glass. All of us.
>
> —Barbara Perry
> Provincetown

A lifelong resident of Provincetown, Barbara Perry's husband owned the Foc'sle, the town's most notorious and beloved tavern on Commercial Street, patronized by fishermen and artists alike. She told me that most local Portuguese families showed tolerance after the Worthington murder. "The murder connected our two towns, and two of their most important families. The Portuguese here are warm and open-hearted. We accept our neighbors' troubles because we have the same troubles, too."

In the close-knit Land's End population, there sometimes seems to be less than "six degrees of separation." Barbara said, "My mother told me not to talk badly about other people. My mother liked to say, 'It's easy to run somebody else's life with *your* mouth.'"

It was easy for people to see Christa as a Vassar-educated femme fatale who used her wits to hoodwink "Dumbdick" Jackett. Jackett himself had called Christa a "huntress." He was the unwitting sperm donor, sexy voice and all. Jackett said that when he met Christa for afternoon trysts, he didn't use protection because Christa had claimed to be infertile. A doctor had pronounced her ability to conceive "highly improbable." Friends remember how distraught Christa had been when she had learned she might be barren despite all of her research about artificial insemination and all of her good intentions.

Billy Kimball, a TV producer who at one time was Christa's neighbor on the North Fork of Long Island, had hired Christa to operate a "real time" on-line chat room for AOL New Line Productions. A forerunner of on-line fashion gossip columns like the popular site *Chic Happens* (www.hintmag.com), Christa provided cyber fashion advice in her column called *What2Wear?* Web browsers would ask Christa questions: "Can I wear white to someone else's wedding?" "Are open-toed sandals okay with socks after September?" "I don't wear panties under my tight jeans to avoid panty lines, but can I wear a mini-pad?" The live site didn't do well on Friday nights. Kimball changed it to a static format where people e-mailed questions for Christa and she would post her answers. *What2Wear?* had a flurry of hits after that.

Kimball and Christa remained friends after their business connection concluded. He was in California, Kimball said, when he received a phone call from Christa. She had just visited her gynecologist and was traumatized by some very bad news. The doctor had told her she couldn't have a baby. Kimball said, "She hadn't called me for ten months. I thought it was odd she would call right out of the blue, but I guess I felt good that she wanted to confide in me. She was devastated by the doctor's bald statement. Then I realized she was having a hysterical reaction and was probably going through her address book, telling everyone."

Kimball said that he was familiar with Christa's dramatic monologues. She chronicled her current problems. She talked through little bumps and valleys. "I was used to her being a little bit unhappy, a little unlucky. There was always a bittersweet story attached to a lot of the circumstances in her life. But that was part of her charm. There's a manner in which that sort of thing, I'll call it 'world weariness,' is associated with sophistication, and that might be the persona she decided on. She wasn't a gloomy gus all day. But she had a melancholy coupled with a sense of humor about what she perceived as a certain amount of misfortune in her life. But this time, when she told me the news from the doctor, she didn't joke about it."

Jackett told me, "Yeah, she said she couldn't get pregnant, but I should have suspected something. I'd stand up and button my fly, but she wouldn't get out of bed. She'd lie there with her knees up, her hips tilted, you know, so the sperm wouldn't spill out. I don't know what a doctor had told her, but she promised me we would 'use each other' with no strings attached. She said, that's how it's done in Europe."

The community's reactions to Christa's single parenthood, and to her adulterous relationship to local legend Tony Jackett, were often vindictive. People within Truro and from far afield discussed their ideas on Web sites and chat rooms. *Cape Cod Times* forums and the busy site *CrimeNews2000* had new postings every day. People expressed hot feelings and anxieties. It was mostly a lot of armchair quarterbacking of the events unfolding on the Outer Cape. Site members submitted their speculations about Tim Arnold, Tony and the Jackett women, and of course Toppy and Beth Porter added hot sauce to the delicious table spread. Site members scrounged up details and would wring the pixels out of them. In these postings, Christa came under attack as often as the "suspects" or those persons in "the orbit of opportunity," the poor slobs detectives called "the possibles."

The sticking point was Christa's Single Mother by Choice profile. She was known to have many suitors, Ivy League pals, writers, magicians, and once she had dated a Vanderbilt scion. Why did she pick on a local fisherman? Someone wrote on *CrimeNews2000*: "A person seeking single motherhood who miraculously conceives with a married man and then willingly arranges with this fling sperm donor to keep his paternity secret, THEN she changes the rules, shows no acknowledgment that she's been calling the shots all along."

And "There have been a number of puff pieces on Christa and even those entries have trouble supporting the 'career woman turned selfless loving mother' picture."

But because of Ava's lineage as the great-granddaughter of beloved Tiny and John Worthington, some loyal townies relented and felt more inclined to pity her slain mother. She was a Worthington. The Worthingtons were one crumbly pillar of Truro's history. The town was split; some felt loyalty, others felt their tolerance wearing thin. Yet within a week of the murder, the public's curiosity and needling wrath soon shifted from Christa to a different Worthington, Christa's father and his real-life hooker pal.

Christa had previous knowledge of her father's relationship with Porter. "She's sponging off him," Christa told friends. Being an only child, Christa would inherit her father's estate, money she needed to raise Ava. She saw her trust quickly dissolving teaspoon by teaspoon. Even before Christa's concern about Porter, her father had often threatened to leave all his money to his prep school, the Kent School, although as a student at Kent he had had mixed feelings about the place. This, along with his later threat to sell the house in Truro where Christa was living, might have been an ugly power game he played with his daughter. But some friends have said that Toppy Worthington had conflicted feelings about living a privileged life. He wanted to shed the "Worthington baggage," their expectations for wealth, success, social status. He wanted Christa to shake them, too, and get them off her back.

But when Christa saw him slumming with Porter, she had told friends that she was looking into having Toppy declared legally incompetent. She wanted full control of his finances. When she learned that Beth Porter was HIV positive, Christa worried that her father would deplete his trust paying for Porter's medical bills. Unlike some HIV "nonprogressor" athletes, who even train for the Boston Marathon, Porter looked sickly, with chronic respiratory symptoms. Christa's friends, searching for a motive for Christa's murder, discussed the theory that Porter had gotten wind of Christa's interference. A friend said that Christa was trying to get Porter's "oil well unhooked," and the addict and her boyfriend, Ed Hall, would have done anything to stop her.

Christa's quest to clarify her blurry financial picture was, of course, motivated by her concern for Ava. But some friends felt it was a kind of premature ambulance-chasing. She had become obsessed with getting what was rightfully hers. The Worthingtons were land-poor, and they often bristled about who rightfully owned this or that house within the several properties bequeathed to them by their elders. Christa had recently hired a private detective to find out information about some money owed to her by an aunt in Florida, Alice Truitt. After the recent sale of a property that had belonged to both her aunt and Christa's mother, Gloria, her mother's profits were supposed to come to Christa and she hadn't yet seen a dime of it.

Within a few days of the murder, Christa's door was missing from her house. The door and samples from the crime scene were shipped to the state crime lab in Sudbury. DNA testing had not yet begun, but Christa's complex financial entanglements, coupled with hers and her father's carnal secrets, had entwined in a double helix around the town of Truro.

WALKING AT MIDNIGHT

The Truro police log lists the usual small town mishaps and misdemeanors: DUIs; marijuana busts; domestic disturbances (a woman chased her husband with a piping hot Sunbeam steam iron); deadbeat dad complaints; nuisance dogs; hoax shark attacks; a flurry of tip jars lifted from the counters of local ice cream parlors or souvenir shops. Recently, a heartbroken teen who had lost his sweetheart went on a rampage. Buck-naked, he drove a sit-down lawn mower across his neighbors' lawns, through flower beds and picket fences. And the *Cape Codder* printed letters of support for the victim of "Mrs. Perry's Rosebush Heist," after a thief had swiped the eighty-year-old's pampered flowerpot from her front stoop.

Before the Worthington case, the most publicized criminal incident in the last few years involved a veteran Truro police sergeant, David Costa, who is second-in-command of the Truro Police Department. Like other police officers who in their free time conduct other business, doing everything from underwater welding to pumping gas at the Route 6 Gulf station, Costa moonlighted as a lobsterman. But in 1999, Costa was arrested on his fishing boat for illegally harvesting "eggers," or egg-bearing lobsters, a crime called "lobster scrubbing."

Only unscrupulous lobster fishermen pull their traps and neglect to release egg-bearing females. Instead, they scrub the lobsters' bodies to remove the eggs, globs of micro-tiny tapioca pearls with black specks, before taking their catch to market. It's illegal to sell egg-bearing lobsters. Harvesting eggers pulls the rug out from under strict lobster conservation measures.

Fishermen identify egg-bearing females by sight because of "extra fur on their swimmerets." The law requires that these lobsters be released if

103

trapped during this stage in their reproductive cycle. In three more weeks, the females would be legal. Selling scrubbed lobsters was considered to be impatient, reprehensible greed.

Costa, captain of the *Nana-Molly*, was arrested east of Race Point after numerous tips brought surveillance by the Massachusetts Environmental Police. The *Nana-Molly*, a thirty-five-foot lobster boat, is a beloved landmark in Truro, where it's wintered in dry dock outside Costa's fish market on Route 6. Beloved landmark or not, its owner, Costa, was charged with seven criminal offenses, including failure to obey commands when officers tried to board his vessel; Costa didn't comply with "safe boarding and inspection instructions." Costa had pretended not to hear commands as he dumped scrubbed eggers over the side and hosed his boards and gunnels to get rid of evidence. Telltale clumps of lobster eggs were everywhere on deck. Later, at Costa's trial, the evidence included a white scrub brush with lobster eggs embedded in its bristles. A *Provincetown Banner* editorial said, "The violence, such as it was, was rendered with a scrub brush, not a gun or a club."

After Costa's arrest, the *Nana-Molly* was impounded, and later returned to him with a bill for its storage and transportation, but Costa was forced to relinquish his fishing permit and was not allowed to lobster in the state again. The *Nana-Molly* was again dry-docked in the parking lot of Costa's Route 6 fish market, but this time it displayed a FOR SALE sign on its prow.

News of a local police officer charged and tried for scrubbing lobsters angered the town. A *Cape Codder* editorial said, "This has been going on for decades. The guys in Chatham will tell you that Provincetown is a scrubber port, meaning that they all do it down there. . . . Throwing an egger back is like finding a $20 bill in the water and throwing it back, and times are tough enough for all fishermen without throwing back money." But in another editorial it was asked, "How is breaking laws on the water any different from breaking laws on the land?" Truro residents believed that the victims here were not the lobsters but the other lobstermen who had enough integrity to release their unlawful catch. Truro's last link to olde time Cape Cod is its fishing fleet. Costa had sullied their reputation. In his renowned history of Truro, *Landmarks and Seamarks*, published in 1883, Shebnah Rich describes Truro's fishermen as being "leaders of the fleet. . . . Truro has had a remarkable succession of leading or lucky skippers. I know of no time during hooking days when some of her skippers were not acknowledged kings." Rich describes the difficulty fishermen had to face in order to earn such recognition, "Going to the Grand Bank meant leaving in April for a three to five months' trip, with no communication until the return . . . to be shut up in fog, exposed to ice bergs . . . and cut off from the world as if alone on the planet. Doctor Johnson said, 'Going to sea was going to prison, with a chance of being drowned besides.' " Costa's trial, at Barnstable County courthouse, caused ripples for more than a year. People waited to see what Chief Popcorn would do. The Truro Police Employees Federation issued a letter stating a unanimous objection to Costa remaining on duty. He shouldn't be with the force as he faced charges. The town selectmen joined the fracas when Chief Popcorn had first suspended Costa for only two weeks, and had bumped him from second-in-command for a mere thirty days more.

Finally, after his conviction and the denial of his appeal, Costa wrote an apology to the town in which he said, "I pledge to work with the members of the Police Department and the citizens of the town to restore any lost respect for the Department and to regain any lost confidence in my ability to perform my police duties." Yet the selectmen had already voted to strip David Costa of his second-in-command position, this time for six months. Costa lost his lobster permit "for life." No one sympathized when Costa told the court why he had scrubbed lobsters on deck of the *Nana-Molly*. "The temptation was too great. I couldn't help myself."

This was the same excuse Jackett had used to explain his stopovers at Christa's bungalow.

Costa's fish market still operates across Route 6 from my house. Informed residents might rather choose to shop at Sonny Roderick's Pamet Seafood, but tourists who don't know the story of the *Nana-Molly* walk into Costa's place to buy fish, oblivious of the controversy.

The misdemeanor crime of scrubbing lobsters is not exactly heart-stopping. It's nothing compared to a murder.

The Outer Cape towns of Wellfleet, Truro, and Provincetown are still quite rural and bucolic, safe as the teacup ride at Disneyland (people just never lock doors or windows), but they have had occasional grisly incidents. These uncommon events stand out like a tarantula on an angel cake. For instance, in 1998, a woman's body was found in the trunk of a Lincoln Continental in Truro. The car was stuck in the sand ruts on a National Seashore road at High Head. The woman had been strangled. Her boyfriend was found slumped outside the car, dead of a gunshot wound to the head, the gruesome "bookend" to an apparent murder/suicide.

The couple had lived in Danbury, Connecticut. The woman, thirty-four-year-old Rita Cebik, had been asphyxiated in the condominium where she resided with her boyfriend-turned-killer, sixty-year-old Donald Gabriel. Gabriel had placed the body in his Continental to make the five-hour journey to Cape Cod. He tooled up Route 6, his lover concealed in the trunk with the spare tire and a bright blue gallon of window washer fluid. He drove east, all the way out to the tip, only to be thwarted by deep sand. Cape and Islands District Attorney Philip Rollins speculated that the dead man was driving into the Province Lands to dispose of the body, but when the car got stuck in the dunes, he committed suicide right where his tires were spinning in deep sand, sunk all the way up to the wheel wells. Rollins said, "I don't know this for certain, but the theory is, getting stuck in the sand was the last straw for this man."

The "last straw" is often piled on to people's backs out here at Land's End. Something about the Outer Cape attracts desperate people. Suicides have happened at sunset in the parking lot at Herring Cove. In Porsches or beat-up pickups, in Chevies and Jeeps, different lost souls pull into the long line of empty parking spaces, facing the surf. The grid looks due west across the Cape Cod bay. As the sun sets, one can see the white cliffs at Plymouth and the ghostly coastline of the South Shore silhouetted against the cadmium sky. The hubbub of the everyday world seems a million miles away. The Herring Cove parking lot is as far out as you can get from the mainland of Massachusetts. They can't get any farther away from their problems unless they can walk on water. This is "the spot."

And in the summer of 1996, a red Mercury Villager minivan was found abandoned in the beach parking lot at Cahoon Hollow on the backshore in Wellfleet. The driver, a thirty-seven-year-old wife and mother of three from Hingham, could not be found. On the previous day, a beachcomber had come across a woman lying facedown in the sand. When the beachcomber tried to talk to the woman, the woman replied "in a strange, high-pitched voice," but her speech was garbled because she never lifted her face out of the sand. The hiker went home to call the Wellfleet police, saying she had seen a "distraught woman" on the beach. Police went to find her, but she was gone. The police later issued a report, identifying a woman, Patricia Minniassian, as a "missing and endangered person."

The young mother had been depressed, and her husband had found notes she had written to him and to their kids. Her husband said the "cards indicated she needed her own space and couldn't live with herself the way she was feeling." Yet he insisted that the messages weren't suicide notes. Weeks turned into months, and after many search efforts, nothing proved hopeful. The wilderness in Wellfleet is rugged terrain. The underbrush is so dense and impenetrable even dogs can't nose through the most difficult thickets. That autumn, when the leaves fell, helicopters buzzed over ponds and kettleholes unreachable on foot. Police posted signs in the woods that said:

HUNTERS TAKE NOTE

A woman has been reported missing in this area, perhaps somewhere between Newcomb Hollow Beach and White Crest Beach. Should you come across anything unusual, such as: abandoned clothing, or personal belongings, please notify the Wellfleet Police Department as soon as possible.

For decades, there has been a familiar billboard at the foot of the Sagamore Bridge. As drivers cross the canal and come onto the Cape, they are greeted by the sign: DESPERATE? CALL THE SAMARITANS. It's not the typical upbeat slogan, WELCOME TO CAPE COD. The sign remains there even after the recent installation of a suicide fence. Across the steel-tied arch, the Army Corps of Engineers have added tight metal tines that depressives can't wriggle between. Since the suicide fence was installed, the Herring Cove parking lot might be a little more busy.

Suicide at the seashore has an exaggerated flourish. There's something poignant or just plain melodramatic about persons who travel far distances to the remote edges to end it. And murder, when it happens in rural settings, when wrongdoings emerge in wide open spaces, can seem twice as gothic and unnerving.

Nowadays, with cable TV and digital cameras, people no longer depend on AP stills but can watch real-time on-line updates, and live-action homicides, everything from the Waco fire to a one-to-one holdup in a liquor mart on your own corner. We watch bird's-eye chopper chase scenarios, and live-cam "suicide by police" final episodes. But real connoisseurs still prize old Weegee visions. Working for Acme Newspictures and later for *PM Daily*, Weegee, aka Arthur Felig, got the reputation for getting to a murder almost faster than its victim. His signature flash-bulb shots are high-contrast, silvery-skinned death cameos. In Weegee's monochrome murder shots, there is black blood on curbstones. Black blood on lavatory tiles. The *New York Post* called him "O. Henry with a Camera." Today, it's full-color car-jacks. Drive-bys. Yellow police tape luffing between street signs. Bodies chalked in neon on concrete sidewalks. Pictures without narrative.

It's impossible to draw a chalk outline on a sand dune.

The seaside has veils of mist, clanging mast poles, mournful foghorns, a cottage doorway beshrewed with climbing roses. The Truro sand flats are like the empty snow plains of Fargo, North Dakota, as in the Coen brothers' movie. Murder in a rural town, in the sticks, has a certain secrecy, a sylvan screen, a mystery frame as dreamy as it is jarring.

Christa Worthington's murder happened thirty-three years after the last local murder victim was discovered in a rural neck of Truro. At the time, Christa would have been twelve or thirteen years old, spending her summer weekends in the Worthington beehive on Depot Road. The Worthington retreat is less than a mile from a small clearing in the Truro backwoods, near the Old Truro Cemetery, where Tony "ChopChop" Costa had pampered a small plot of marijuana plants. Antone Costa, who was not related to lobster scrubber David Costa, had called the rural site his "garden." A Provincetown handyman and married father of three, Tony Costa committed at least four murders in the Truro woods. In 1968 and 1969, Tony Costa brought two local teen girls and two women from Providence to his "garden," where he killed them and performed necromantic rituals and sex acts before dismembering the bodies.

Provincetown Police Chief James Meads said, "Each girl had been cut into as many parts as there were joints." Costa buried his victims in shallow graves. One was found alone, and the other three victims were piled in a heap on top of one another, everything jumbled together. There were teeth marks on the body parts, and the hearts of the victims had been removed. The hearts were never found.

One of these girls was Barbara Perry's niece, Susan.

Cape Cod News reporter Leo Damore published a book in 1981 about Costa's murder spree entitled *In His Garden*. Many local residents were alarmed that Damore seemed sympathetic to Costa. He describes Costa's doomed life, his addiction to amphetamine drugs, and his forced marriage to a fourteen-year-old girl, Avis, when she became pregnant. Because of a substance-induced void, he tumbled from woman to woman, many of whom disappeared after their involvement with him. At least six other missing girls are assumed to be his victims. Damore's book chronicles Provincetown's drug culture in the sixties, and the town was unhappy with his portrayal of their pristine fishing village. Damore said, "It's a place where people come to let their hair down and the town looks the other way. So I'm a little astonished to learn that Provincetown is adopting a moral posture."

In 1970, Costa was tried only for the murders of the two young Providence women, a grammar school teacher and a college student, whose weekend trip to P-town concluded weeks later with their remains being sent to a crime lab in Pocasset. Costa was convicted and sentenced to life in prison. At his sentencing, when he was asked if he had a statement to make, Costa said, "Keep digging."

In 1974, Costa was found dead in his cell in Walpole State Prison. He had hanged himself.

Costa was dead only two months before the next murder was discovered in the sand dunes of the Province Lands.

In July that same year, a twelve-year-old girl, walking her beagle east of Race Point, came across a woman's naked body, facedown in the sand. The girl noticed the victim's pink-painted toenails and her dungarees neatly folded under her head. But the woman's skull was caved in, and her neck almost completely severed. The woman had been placed on her stomach with her hands in the sand, in the bizarre posture of someone doing push-ups. The girl ran with her beagle a full mile to her parents' house and the police were informed. When Provincetown Police Chief James Meads arrived on the scene, he, too, was shocked to see the victim's body propped up as if to mimic someone performing calisthenics, her arms buried to their wrists in the sand. He soon discovered that the woman's hands had been crudely cut off. "The fingerprints went with the hands, which have not been found."

Cape Cod's most haunting unsolved murder mystery, known as "The Body in the Dunes," is a long-lived saga of a "cop who won't quit." The discovery of the unidentified woman's body kick-started a two-decades-long investigation, headed by Chief Meads, who eventually retired with the case still unsolved. But not because he hadn't been trying. The case was stymied from the start due to decomposition of the body in the summer sun, and because its hands were missing. Meads said, "Without an identification of the victim, the search for the murderer can't begin." Meads spent his career exploring every new breakthrough in forensic science; he had the woman's skull reconstructed and from that he asked a sidewalk portrait artist to draw a probable likeness. She had no fingerprints, but the woman had several gold crowns. Meads researched dental records from Cape Cod to Canada, after help from a psychic who claimed the unidentified woman was a nurse from Ottawa. He tracked a dentist from Canada who had rented a motel room the week of the murder, believing the woman might have been his girlfriend because she had had so much expensive dental work. He contacted mob officials in Providence, following a lead that didn't pan out. The mob denied any involvement. Although DNA testing wasn't yet available, he had the body disinterred to take blood samples.

The case seemed to be nearing a possible conclusion when Meads investigated a chronology of events surrounding a girl named Rory Kessinger. Kessinger, a teen runaway turned bank robber, had escaped from the Plymouth County House of Correction at age twenty-five and went missing in 1974. The body in the dunes, between five-foot-six and five-foot-eight, matched Kessinger's height and weight, and the two women had similar features. "The hair and the face are right on," Meads said. So, in March 2000, the current Provincetown police chief, James Anthony, had the remains of "the body in the dunes" exhumed a second time from a gravesite in St. Peter's Cemetery in Provincetown for modern DNA testing. The stone at the site was put to one side, it said:

UNIDENTIFIED FEMALE BODY

FOUND RACE POINT DUNES

JULY 26, 1974

Police had finally located Kessinger's eighty-year-old mother in Colorado. She had not seen her daughter since she left home at fifteen. But results of DNA testing proved Kessinger had no connection to the woman in the dunes. Chief Meads had retired from the Provincetown force with *his* unsolved murder still in his craw.

"The Body in the Dunes" mystery was linked to another ongoing murder investigation with a Cape Cod connection. Hadden Clark, a crossdressing and cannibalistic serial killer, had summered in Wellfleet at his grandfather's house, and as a young adult had lived in Wellfleet and Provincetown. In 1992, he was arrested for the murder of a young Maryland woman, Laura Houghteling. At that time, Houghteling's body had not yet been found, but Clark's fingerprints were identified on a bloody pillowcase. Luminol, a chemical commonly used to identify hidden blood evidence, was sprayed on the victim's mattress and the Posturepedic lit up the room. Clark had also been seen leaving the woman's house dressed in his victim's clothes. Clark owned a collection of women's wigs. Maryland police discovered a map in Clark's truck depicting a Wellfleet cemetery where some of his family members were buried. Clark had drawn a crude *X* on the map and police believed Clark might have buried his victim in Wellfleet. Wellfleet Police Chief Richard Rosenthal was asked to check the highlighted area on Clark's map to see if there were any irregularities.

When Rosenthal investigated the site, he discovered that soil was disrupted near the grave of Clark's grandfather, Silas Clark. A "cadaver-recovery" dog was brought in the next day. The dog began scratching at the disturbed earth, a signal that it had found something. Rosenthal, state police officers, and detectives from Maryland started working, passing shovels back and forth between them. They didn't find anything.

HUMAN BONE FOUND IN P-TOWN, a headline in the *Cape Cod Times*, surprised readers but was another irksome twist for the police investigation. In May 1993, a femur bone was turned into Provincetown police. A resident had found the bone in the dunes months before but its novelty had worn off; he didn't want it anymore. Police believed that the bone might be a link between Hadden Clark and the murder of "the unidentified woman in the dunes." Hadden Clark was scheduled to go on trial that month for the murder of Laura Houghteling, the Maryland woman whose body had not yet been found. Because Clark was on Cape Cod in 1974, and was also very recently seen by witnesses "carrying what may have been a body," it is suspected that he might have buried both victims in the Province Lands. But forensic examination had revealed that the femur bone was from a male victim.

In jail, Clark confessed other murders to his long-haired cellmate he called "Jesus." Clark told Jesus about the murder of a six-year-old girl, Michelle Dorr, whom he had murdered in 1986 and had buried beneath a box spring in a ravine in Silver Spring, Maryland. He later brought the Maryland police to the site. He told Jesus he had killed girls from Vermont, Pennsylvania, and a young girl who was missing from Wayland, Massachusetts, Sarah Pryor. Clark said he buried her in Wellfleet along with a bucket of jewelry he had collected from his different victims.

In one of his late-night confessions, Clark told Jesus that he had killed "The Woman in the Dunes."

In Wellfleet, Chief Rosenthal found the bucket of jewelry where Clark had said he had buried it. Some of the items were quite expensive, but others were children's trinkets and cheap beaded bracelets. After finding the jewelry, they searched the Wellfleet woods but never found a body.

In January 2000, Maryland police escorted Clark to Wellfleet when he had agreed to help detectives locate the graves of his victims. Before he would cooperate, he insisted on dressing in women's clothing, and police purchased a bra, nylons, and panties at Kmart in Hyannis, which he wore under his outer clothes. Winter storms made their efforts difficult, and no remains were found.

Yet Chief Rosenthal thinks there's at least one of Hadden Clark's victims in the cedar glens and high bush blueberries where summer folk take their nature walks.

In the *New Yorker* article "A Hole in the Ground," Alec Wilkinson, who had once worked on the Wellfleet police force, tells of his conversations with Clark. He asked Clark to describe what had happened in the dunes in 1974. Wilkinson quotes Clark's explanation, but one will never know if it's a candid recollection of a serial killer or morbific musings of a raconteur just riffing: "I came across a beautiful girl; I lured her into the dunes . . . and then I cut off her hands and stuffed her arms into the sand like she was doing push-ups. Then I took her hands and put them in her purse, like a beach bag. I cut off a couple of her fingers and used them for fishing bait. . . ."

It was never discerned who Clark's "beautiful girl" might have been, or if the beauty in the dunes had, in fact, belonged to another killer.

Currently, O'Keefe has been working on a case where another victim, Kelly Ford, was found buried in the sand at Scusset Beach in Sandwich, a historic Upper Cape town at the west end of the peninsula. Two boys playing Frisbee discovered the victim. The victim's head had been severed from her body and has not yet been recovered. For identification, the victim's mother gave the police a photo of a tattoo Kelly had had on her back, a Chinese symbol for "summer love." O'Keefe said they had interest in a suspect who was presently incarcerated in another case, Eugene McCollum. McCollum is in jail awaiting trial for a different but similar murder off Cape. McCollum is charged with killing a woman after a "sex for money" deal went awry in his room at the Greater Lynn YMCA. Forensic technicians are studying Ford's headless body against evidence from McCollum's prior victim, examining "tool marks" on the cervical vertebrae where their heads had been sawed off, to see if there is a match.

When Christa Worthington was killed, it wasn't Hadden Clark, Tony Costa, or the "unidentified female body found in the dunes" that first came to mind. When the news broke about Christa, residents remembered Linda Silva, whose murder is still unsolved.

In 1996, Linda Silva was killed in Provincetown right in the center of town, one block from Town Hall and the police station. She was shot in the head as she inserted her car key in the driver's side door. Her car was parked in the side lot of a busy convenience store on the corner of Bradford and Alden streets, directly beneath the Provincetown Monument.

Silva's murder scene was more like the archetypical Weegee milieu: nighttime, rain-slicked pavement, crowds. Silva was shot once behind her left ear, at close range. Her killing looked like a professional hit. She lay supine on the slick asphalt of the parking lot in a steady rain for three hours as police waited for the medical examiner to show up. He had a long drive up Suicide Alley.

Unlike the "unidentified body in the dunes," Linda was a local girl, and everyone knew her. She worked for the Department of Social Services as a child abuse and neglect investigator. Police wanted to find out if Linda had angered any of her clients after she had taken action in cases and, because of her recommendations, a parent's rights were restricted by court order. She had a huge family network in Truro, where her parents, sister, brothers, and nieces and nephews lived. Even the Rescue Squad knew her; she had been one of their bright young secretaries, years before.

Linda's one striking connection to the crime lore of Cape Cod is Avis Johnson, her good friend since childhood. Avis Johnson is killer Tony Costa's widow, the pregnant fourteen-year-old he had married at the start of his murder career. Linda had visited Tony Costa's marijuana garden several times with Avis and Tony before the world turned upside down for the couple. After Linda's murder, Avis said, "Linda loved a challenge. She might have lived on the edge but she was not afraid of it. . . . Her killer could be anybody. Do you think a killer walks around acting like a killer?"

If anyone knew the answer to that question, Avis certainly would know.

Linda Silva's unsolved murder threatened to change the way people feel about the Outer Cape town. Provincetown has always been perceived to be a haven from universal threats common to most larger American cities. Soon after Silva's murder, town selectman Irene Rabinowitz said to a reporter, "This is an intrusion from the real world. That's what it feels like. People are familiar with every street corner. We feel comfortable walking at midnight. This is an intrusion into our feelings of peaceful-ness." Despite its carnal edge and fringe population demographic, even town officials had bought into the idealized vision of Provincetown as a sanctuary from everyday modern problems and worse-case evil perils.

With Worthington's death, rumors began to circulate that Linda Silva's unknown killer had struck again in Truro. Both Provincetown and Truro seemed all too willing to see a connection between Linda and Christa, perhaps hoping to share the yoke and to dilute the painful aftermath of two distinct tragedies. Yet similarities did exist. Reports of similar vehicles fleeing the murder scenes triggered speculation that the murderer was the same person in both instances. The *Cape Cod Times* reported that after Linda's murder "the police put out radio broadcast bulletins on a dark-haired man in a yellow sweatshirt driving a full-size dark-colored pickup truck." Jackett has black hair and drives a dark blue SUV. His son-in-law Keith Amato drives a black pickup, and the armchair sleuths are quick to point this out. After the Worthington murder, Truro resident Girard Smith told police that he'd witnessed "a black truck speeding from the Worthington driveway on January 5, the day before Worthington's body was found." Again, the driver had dark hair. State police visited Smith and showed him photographs of trucks and SUVs. Smith said that one or two of the photos resembled the truck he had seen. Linda and Christa were the same age when they were killed. The women had similar builds and color-ing, loose shoulder-length hair. Neither woman had ever married. In fact, Silva and Worthington seemed to share the same history with men.

There were a lot of them.

Avis Johnson said that her friend Linda "was spontaneous and she un-derstood from the time she was young that marriage doesn't always mix with being spontaneous." Linda's sister-in-law Caryn Silva said, "Men loved Linda. She was attractive, sexy, sultry. She always had a lot of suit-ors." In other words, she was "a little promiscuous," and so, too, people believed, was Christa.

Jackett had stated several times that Christa told him, "We'll use each other for sex."

In some people's view, the two single women, who had refused to be doormats in marriage, had encouraged their similar fate. It was the *Looking for Mr. Goodbar* moralism that circulates through small towns in coffee-klatch table talk, at bar rail tête-à-têtes, and at filling station chin-wags. Yet sympathy emerged for Linda Silva, whose working-class back-ground was a solid plinth or caisson and not the pedestal that Worthington kin seemed to stand or teeter on. Linda had many friends. One old boyfriend of Linda's was a beloved EMT and firefighter in P-town, Doug Trumbo, who was dying of Lou Gehrig's disease when Linda was murdered. In only six weeks, he'd have his funeral ceremony at the Shankpainter Fire Station with wrenching bagpipes whining as the Outer Cape force, in full dress, stood in two rows to form an aisle for the widow as she entered the firehouse. Before his death, Trumbo told Linda Silva's father, "I'm the one with ALS. I didn't think Linda would get there before me, but I guess I'll be seeing her soon. I'll give her your love."

It wasn't long before discussions erupted about Tim Arnold's connec-tion to both murder victims. Without a speck of evidence, Arnold was accused by armchair sleuths on the Web site *CrimeNews2000* and in chat rooms at *Cape Cod Times* forums. Every day, wannabe Kojaks theo-rized, preached, and plumbed the possible links between the Silva and Worthington murders. Electronic rubberneckers with IDs like "not-awashashore," "TheOutsider," "Sunrise," and "Caper" submitted their two cents in daily gabfests on-line. Tim Arnold complained when an elec-tronic rumor blossomed that Tim had once dated Linda Silva. The inven-tion asserted that he was a serial killer who targeted independent women, women who "enjoyed" sex and who shirked domestic responsibilities and traditional roles. But Tim Arnold had never met Linda Silva.

One member of *CrimeNews2000* disagreed that the murders were linked. "Are they connected? No. There's no comparison between them. Christa was from a different group of people, an 'upper crusty' type and Linda was more of a 'salt of the earth' type."

Crime buffs found it easy to categorize each victim. But it was true that Linda Silva came from a blue-collar background. Her father was a fisher-man. More than two hundred local people attended her funeral service. Rescue personnel wore their uniforms with black tape over their badges. The day was noted for a gesture friends had made on their way to Sacred Heart Cemetery. When leaving the church service, they formed a long line of at least one hundred cars and, instead of taking a direct path on Route 6, they snaked slowly through North Truro, following Linda's favorite back roads. Truro police had to shut down intersections for the procession to pass through.

Even with such community sympathy and attention, Linda's face, photographed by the state police forensic photographer, has one frozen dimension. But Christa's death mask is different somehow. It's a complex transposition—one of Weegee's brutal snapshots coupled with John Singer Sargent's ethereal portrait of society mistress Elizabeth Winthrop Chanler. And because Christa had Ava, add to her picture a scarlet letter.

THE SEA SURF MOTEL

Linda Silva's unsolved murder splintered her family. Within a year of the murder, Linda's sister and brother-in-law, Nancy and John Burch, started to express their snowballing opinions about the crime. Their suspicions caused a very public disconnect from the rest of the their family. For the past six years, the couple have been actively involved in their own investigation. They say that Trooper John Kotfila, of the Massachusetts State Police, has been both a mentor and a stumbling block for the couple. When they give him information and "leads," they aren't certain he follows through on all of them.

Trooper Kotfila told me, "Boy, are we sorry we ever gave the Burches our eight-hundred number."

After Linda's murder, people didn't suspect Linda's last boyfriend, but everyone knew about a local man who had been arrested and jailed twice for "violation of a protective order" after repeatedly harassing his ex-wife. His ex-wife was the bartender at the Governor Bradford, and Linda Silva had been seen sitting with her on the evening that she was murdered.

Both women drove red coupes and had parked their cars in the same lot where Linda was gunned down.

The Burches never moved past this initial cobbled-together narrative about mistaken identity. Because of the Burches' suspicions about the local man's involvement, and their dogged and obsessive amateur sleuthing, the rest of the Silva family has little patience left. In an interview in the *Cape Cod Times*, Nancy Burch told Emily Dooley, "My family and I don't speak anymore. I have been pretty much shunned." Dooley wrote, "The loss of Linda drove a wedge between Burch, her three brothers, and parents."

I visited the Burches at the Sea Surf Motel on Shore Road in Truro, where they manage the place in the summer and live year-round. In winter, Shore Road is two miles of boarded-up motels and cottages. It's a cozy ghost town, without the summer bustle, and winter people like it this way. On the overcast day I visited, the bay was like a huge zinc penny. Worth nothing in the off-season. The little house and office at the Sea Surf is a redwood A-frame uncharacteristic of Cape Cod, but several motels along this beachfront strip look 1950s retro, and could be as easily found on Route 66.

After two thousand man hours were spent on the case the first year, the Burches sensed a growing apathy by law enforcement personnel. They believed the police were letting the case go cold. In constant communication with Trooper Kotfila, Nancy says that after a while, whenever she called the barracks, whoever answered the telephone said with sarcastic glee, "Oh, Nancy, it's *you.*"

When I first talked to John Burch, he said he was dismayed by all the attention the Worthington murder was getting, when after six years their sister's murder was still unsolved. They saw the dichotomy between Linda's "nobody" status and Worthington's more glamorous workup in the press. If Linda's case had been forgotten, they hoped Worthington's murder would rekindle interest in it. The Burches' fifteen minutes of fame had been flickering out, and Christa's case had a bellows effect.

At the motel, I walked past a koi pond in the front garden, the large fish visible beneath a scrim of ice. When I entered the house, I was face-to-face with a fifty-gallon aquarium. I liked seeing the fish. I always feel comfortable with hobbyists; not only does it show a little initiative and diligence to clean fish tanks, change air filters, and keep up a successful routine, but I'm impressed when people plunge body and soul into something until it's almost a fanaticism. Then I looked closer at the tank. A blue crayfish crept along the bottom gravel, between darting fish. Its pincers had been snipped. The maimed creature was an unnerving sight. What kind of people dismember little creatures like this?

Nancy Burch is compact and blonde, and doesn't resemble her sister Linda. Her husband, John, is muscled, broad-shouldered, but softspoken. The couple seem very close, unified by their common obsession with Linda's murder.

Sitting in their bayside living room, John and Nancy described their distrust of the said same local resident. Nancy said she saw his car parked in the turnabout on Route 6 behind their house. "What was he doing there, I'd like to know," Nancy said.

John said that he had once found a burning cigarette left on a can of acetone in their garage. "If I hadn't found it in time, this place would have gone up."

Nancy continued, "Our tires have been ice-picked."

When I had asked Kotfila about this mystery man, he had told me, "It's true, he's a wingnut, but right now, the investigation is moving back to the DSS angle."

The couple leaned back into their cushions and began to relax. Their accusations seemed to steady them. They sighed and breathed deeply, as if enjoying the sweet orchid perfume of obsession.

I told them about O'Keefe's theory, and I asked, if they were to put Linda's murder in one category, did they think her trouble was "sex" or "money"?

"Money," Nancy said. "A couple weeks before she was murdered, Linda asked my parents for ten thousand dollars."

John walked away and came back, holding a gun that he had purchased from a local man. He handed it to me.

"Shit. This weighs a ton," I said, unable to find the appropriate nuance of appreciation for the chilly item. I put it on the coffee table.

John picked it up. "This is a *serious* gun," he said. "Smith and Wesson. This is not a sport gun, it's for defense. Or offense. I called the cops and asked them if they wanted to test the gun. They said if they did that, they would have to redirect the search."

I asked them both what they thought about the Worthington case.

"I hope that family doesn't have to go through this for as long as we have," Nancy said.

Harboring suspicions or assigning blame can be an exhausting workaday obligation.

John grinned and said, "Now Tony's another story. Tony's an institution. Tony always came off his boat already all dolled up. He looked *pretty*. He'd come off the boat ready to go into town. He likes girls. He had no worries, maybe just worried about his hair."

Everyone knows Tony. His demons are so familiar. Even Trooper

Kotfila had told me, "Tony, oh boy, his only trouble is he thinks with 'his little head.' "

John Burch said, "Before the secret leaked, I had heard he had a kid in Truro. No surprise there."

I asked Nancy, "Linda's murder has been so destructive to your family, how are you going to work that out?"

"We don't talk to anyone. I never see my mother. She knocked on the door. I didn't answer."

The next week, I visited Linda's parents, Doris and Alfred Silva, Sr., in a little house on a private road east of Ducky's gravel pit. Doris was nicely dressed, as if she had expected to meet Connie Chung. Alfred Sr. was more casual, but very attractive with a thick head of hair like silver floss. In all my years here, I don't think I've yet to see a bald pate on any boat in the Provincetown fleet, today or yesterday. Alfred Sr. had been captain of the *Tom & Joan*. He said he had known John Worthington in the old days when he delivered fish to the cold storage plant in North Truro, back in the forties. He said he had really liked Pop Worthington. At seventy-six years old, Alfred Sr. had sold his boat to his son Michael. But he still went lobstering on a smaller boat. "I've got a plastic boat," he said, acknowledging its inferiority to the *Tom & Joan*, the big wood-hulled dragger he'd captained most of his life. "Lobstering is summer work. All winter I'm fixing gear and traps. But I'm getting my knees replaced this summer. Scalloping is hard on your knees. But I'll go tuna fishing. You can sit down when you go for tuna." He couldn't stop smiling when he talked about fish. He told me about hurricanes and when his boat rolled over in a storm. He remembered the *Snoopy* out of New Bedford, a dragger that exploded when it caught a German torpedo in its rakes. His wife, Doris, let him gab, but she was a little more cautious with me, at first.

Then Doris said, "Nancy and Linda weren't close, they had problems, and Nancy wasn't so nice. Sisters. I think she's doing all this detective work out of guilt about Linda."

"She said Linda asked you for ten thousand dollars?" I said.

"What? That's news to us," Doris said.

Alfred Sr. said the "cops have missed something." They have never found a weapon. He said he wants the police to ask the Boy Scouts to comb the hill behind the parking lot where Linda was gunned down. Alfred Sr. said, "If it was me, I wouldn't have shot her in the parking lot, I would have waited on that hill to shoot from there. Then I would have thrown the gun into the brush on that hill."

It was alarming to hear a father speculate and troubleshoot about his daughter's murder, offering pointers in hindsight for her killer. In self-protection, he had removed himself from the real crime, transforming it into a narrative, an entertainment. He talked the way people might talk after seeing a detective movie, rehashing plot elements, reconstructing clues and adding their two cents.

Meeting Linda Silva's family might not be representative of the Worthingtons' assimilation of events surrounding Christa. Linda Silva was a notch above "blue collar," but she was in the trenches of the worka-day world, and her job in social services often tugged her down into underclass squalor. Christa's family might be grieving for her, but their remarks always sounded imperious. Linda Silva's family's disintegration seemed more poignant. It's difficult to watch hardworking, meat and potatoes, salt of the earth characters turn against one another. Patricians seem to be born with silver thorns in their sides, and begin their bickering in vitro.

I said, "Nancy says someone put a lighted cigarette on a can of acetone at their house."

"Acetone? A cigarette? Now that would be bad—" Alfred Sr. said, showing some excitement for the details. He was about to describe how that story might unfold, but Doris interrupted.

She said, "They aren't speaking to us. They haven't spoken to us at all. They haven't been in my home for years. Not since Linda was murdered."

TEN THOUSAND TONY JACKETTS

Tim Arnold came to my house to talk. His father chauffeured him to my kitchen door just as he had dropped Tim off at Christa's door that gloomy night in January. His father backed out of the drive, resigned to his role as Tim's footman or Jeeves during the recent mess. I told him that I would drive him home when we were finished. For the next few months, I often went to retrieve him from his cottage on Old County Road. Tim warned me that since 9/11, his father had placed an American flag decal on the mailbox, and that's where I should make my turn. I often brought him back to my house, or we sat at the Truro Library. We rolled up Route 6 to Chatham for lunch and on the return trip home we stopped at Mid-Cape Center in Wellfleet so Tim could buy Masonite boards and art supplies. My appointments with Tim provided him with a little change of scene or a chance to run errands.

And he seemed to like our subversive jaunts—he wasn't supposed to be talking. He had also been warned: "We're not talking. Only a Worthington can talk about a Worthington," *said Jan Worthington.*

After his father dropped him on my doorstep, I asked him about his malady. "Is it improving?"

"It might be getting better. It's incremental. I have to retrain neural pathways. I have a magnesium plate, so I have headaches. I still have to close one eye to see clearly," he said. "I'm getting kind of used to it. I've done some painting. Early on, the police told Amyra Chase that I was ruled out because of my condition, I couldn't have physically done it. It's funny that they didn't say I couldn't have morally done it. But Amyra waited to hear from the police that I wasn't thought to be a primary suspect before she would let me visit Ava. Now I can go up once a week with Christa's aunt, Diana."

But a state police investigator had told me it was "interesting" that Tim was so obsessed with Ava when he rarely saw his own two kids. And O'Keefe had talked about Tim's affection for the baby. It was transparent to him that before Christa was killed, the baby was Tim's excuse to visit his ex-girlfriend. Warren Roderick had said Christa had the habit of walking around the house naked. Unannounced prowlers outside her windows could see whatever they wanted to see. Tim's extended commitment to Ava might be in mourning for her mom, or in loyalty to the little girl, or just plain loneliness in that winter wasteland. But Ava and Tim have a connection no one else has. It was Tim who had found Ava clinging to Christa on the kitchen floor.

We sat at a big glass table. We could see one another through the surface as we shifted in our chairs and crossed our legs to get comfortable. Sitting at a glass table can sometimes be awkward. It's the same feeling I had when as a child I sat scantily clad in a wading pool with my friends, daring one another to tell secrets. I poured him some coffee. He leaned forward, squinting. He tried to make respectful eye contact, but as he pinched one eye shut, it was hard for me to look at him without feeling a little dizzy myself. He peered at me intently, affecting an expression of sincerity and genuine intentions, but maybe he was trying to gauge *my* sincerity, or perhaps he was trying to see just one of me.

To see clearly, he needed to cover up one side of the warring retina screens. With his hand over one eye, he could relax the other eye and look at me directly. It was a peculiar sensation to speak to someone holding one hand to his face. Vanessa Grigoriadis had told me that she thought it was "creepy" talking to him.

Tim has nice features and sandy hair, almost Nordic coloring quite fitting for someone who had painted white-on-white snow scenes for his book *The Winter Mittens.* He was affable, soft-spoken, refined. But there was something slightly discomfiting about his physical condition. Like mythic heroes, the disabled Achilles or even the Cyclops—a charged, masculine, and beguiling character whose disadvantage can arouse both pity and suspicion—Tim evoked that same unsettling confusion.

And Tim himself complained to me that his condition had greatly changed his appearance. Because of his poor vision, he didn't walk naturally, and he had gained a little weight. When he was ambushed by a

48 Hours news crew, the broadcast footage had been a shock to him. He said that he didn't recognize himself. His face was furrowed when he squinted at the camera as he lumbered in a dizzy line along the sidewalk in front of the Wellfleet Library. He joked about the video clip and said that the figure exposed on the TV screen had looked "like Sasquatch." He said, "If it wasn't for my AVM, Christa and I would have lasted longer."

There is often a suggestive metaphoric resonance in a person's distinctive ailment, like in the case of one local resident here, a notorious loudmouth who developed throat cancer and who had to have his larynx removed. I wondered what might be the "character is fate" correlative for Arnold's double vision.

"When did you meet Christa?" I said.

"Let's skip that."

"Okay, you were born in Ohio, right?"

"In Chardon. The sugar maple capital of Ohio."

"In your bio note in one of your books, it says you grew up in Worthington, Ohio. I thought that was a strange coincidence."

"Christa got a laugh from that."

"When did you come to the Cape?"

"Six years ago. Right after I first had this vision problem. It was the final blow to my marriage."

He had attended Columbus College of Art and Design, but he said he had met his wife working as an illustrator at Hallmark Cards in Kansas City, Missouri. This was the first in an accretion of bland and saccharine details that emerged to underscore the mild presence before me. Born in "the sugar maple capital," having worked at the famous corporate monopoly of smarmy greeting cards that's been nicknamed the "General Motors of Emotion," I wondered how he had ended up in O'Keefe's "orbit of opportunity." While at Hallmark, he was saving money for graduate school. He said his wife was a fellow malcontent. Of the many "talented people" who worked at Hallmark, Tim and his fiancée weren't "Hallmarkers," not like the drones who stayed on for the security of insurance packages, benefits, and the like. He and his wife moved East. In New York City, he went to graduate school at NYU, taking courses in education. He was interested in children's literature. He started student teaching at Manhattan Country School, and was later hired full-time.

"Our first child was born in 'eighty-eight. Kathryn. It was when I published *The Winter Mittens*. I remember coming home from the hospital. They were inflating balloons for the Macy's parade."

This was another dollop of Americana that helps to dilute his "killer suspect" profile.

"Our second kid, Andy, got infant botulism. That was the first blow to our marriage."

Tim seemed to have cataloged all the wallops he had endured in his marriage, from the first blow to the final knockout punch or TKO he had first mentioned, when his marriage was strained by his AVM symptoms. I wondered if his relationship with Christa had the same distinct demarcations. How many times had Christa "clocked" him.

He said that the baby recovered, but he and his wife were growing apart. "Money pressures. Other things." When they moved to Princeton, she was getting more freelance work than he was. He was staying home with the kids.

"How are you finding your way through all this, since Christa's death?"

"I can't answer that one either. Too soon," he said.

I asked him what a miserable bachelor does down here, stuck in Nowheresville?

"I ran a lot. I ran around the loop. Old County to Depot, to Mill Pond Road. I can't bear to do that now, on Mill Pond Road you see her house."

I imagined him running down the country lanes holding one hand over his eye. His resistance to wearing an eye patch, which he could have bought over the counter at CVS, seemed like stubborn vanity or an unwillingness to accept that his condition might be permanent. He said, "The A&P are all out of eye patches."

I learned that Christa had been an amateur runner, too. She had competed in the Truro Treasures 2001 Pamet River Run, a 5k race that winds along Depot Road to South Pamet Road, and finishes at Ballston Beach. On the *Cool Running* home page, there's a list of race contestants and their finish times.

On the list, I read, "Christa Worthington (R.I.P.). Time: 23:26, Pace: 7:32.5."

Tim met Christa in the fall of '99. Tim said that a woman he had briefly dated, Ellen Webb, had acted as matchmaker. Ellen Webb was working for Christa in an all-around nanny-homekeeper position. Christa had been overwhelmed being a single mom, which isn't a single job but a thousand tasks in one. When Ellen took the job, Christa waited for her to show up before she could hop in the shower. And even then, it was only with Ellen's urgings that Christa finally put the baby down. Her postpartum depression, although mild, was causing her to have obsessive panic reactions about Ava's safety. Christa had read about a new mother who threw her infant out a high-rise window. Christa talked about wanting to nail every window sash shut, in case she fell into a psychotic trance and tossed her baby outside. Ellen coming to the house each day was a calming influence. Christa really looked forward to hearing Ellen's car winding up the gravel drive.

In the Wellfleet Library one afternoon, Tim saw Ellen Webb. Ellen said to him, "Tim, have you met Christa? She lives right behind you on Depot Road."

They joked about how it was good to have a neighbor nearby in the wintertime—it's nice to see another house with some lights on across the moors. Ellen told Tim he should call Christa. "Why be alone?" she said. The next day she told Christa about Tim. Christa said, "Who would want to date me with the baby and all?" But Ellen saw she was pleased and looked forward to hearing from her neighbor.

After Christa met Tim, she told Ellen, "He doesn't know how handsome he is."

And Tim gave Ellen a box of chocolates to thank her for telling him about Christa.

On their first date, Christa and Tim took an afternoon walk with Ava. Christa wasn't dressed very "Mommy Chic" but looked more like Ma Kettle, in a rumpled jacket, her hair blowing into her face. Tim said, "She appeared very plain to me at first. But it was clear she was very bright."

Christa talked freely about how she had become pregnant in an affair with a married man. She told Tim, "When things got too hot for Tony, he broke it off." But about Tony, she said she could only blame herself.

A savvy woman won't air her dirty laundry to a prospect. She can't assign blame to her last lover without risking the impression that she's a bitch, a princess. She wasn't going to spend her first moments with Tim deconstructing the Tony problem. She was admitting her role in order to leap over it. Tim commiserated and told her that everyone knew about this guy except his wife. He could see she was very hurt by Tony. "She was plagued by ambivalent feelings about him."

They spent the next few afternoons together. When the weather allowed, they walked in the Wellfleet pond district, or when it was too raw, they rented movies. The Wellfleet Library has a very good movie collection. When at last he started to spend the night, he was careful not to complain when she asked him to go upstairs when it was time to turn in. Christa was nursing Ava and she slept with the baby in the same bed on the first floor. He didn't argue. "Sleep was so important, and neither one of us were getting enough. But I told her more than once that most couples would have had a year or two to fall back on when the child comes. There was a lot of pressure on us to become an instant family."

But he was falling for her. He would have slept hanging by his ankles, upside down, if she had asked him to. She was witty and liked to laugh. Once she told him, "I just had my bush trimmed by two lesbians with a chain saw." It took him aback for an instant, until he realized she was talking about the landscapers who had come to the house that day.

Tim said, "She'd introduce us as 'abutters.' She'd say, 'We abut one another—all the time.' " He believed that she had inherited her wit from Toppy; Toppy could be searing.

He gave her a copy of *The Winter Mittens*, and showed her some of his new paintings. She praised him in careful words, in which he noted a slightly instructive tone, but he didn't let it bother him.

Tim asked her if she would go back to Tony if he wanted her again. "She told me, 'You're worth ten thousand Tony Jacketts.' "

Ten thousand Tony Jacketts don't exactly fit on the head of a pin.

But Tim said, "That's one of the nicer things a woman ever said to me."

At our second meeting, we started where we had left off. I said, "So on your first date, you walked down Depot Road?"

"She looked a mess. Her hair was disheveled."

"Single moms don't have time to brush their hair."

Tim said, "She didn't immediately knock me out."

"What did you talk about?"

"The first thing we discussed was how she had come to have this child. She was very up front. Her first boyfriend had been from a fishing family like Jackett. Christa had this egalitarian streak. A lot of the women in the family dated fishermen. The Worthington family has a rulelessness, no boundaries. That's what Christa had for an example. Christa's habit of attaching herself to the dispossessed comes from her father. Toppy, too, went toward chaos with Porter. When Toppy sold the big house in Hingham and moved into a dump in Weymouth, it was a political statement. He wanted to lose the Worthingtons."

"But then you became intimate with Christa?"

"Heading in a direction I'm not ready to talk about." He smiled apologetically, put his hands in his lap and squinted at me. I began to understand that when he didn't hold his hand up to cover one eye, the conversation would shut down.

Tim said, "Amyra's position was that Christa shouldn't have gotten involved with Tony. They had many conversations about it. Christa was lonely. She was depressed. 'It was part of the disease,' she would laugh."

"The disease? You mean part of being human?"

"Yes."

I told Tim, "Most men don't want to get near a single mom, but that didn't stop you?"

Tim said that Christa was a great mother. Christa was immersed in Ava. She was a natural. That's what had impressed him.

"You sound too good to be true."

"Not really. Sometimes we would butt heads. She was critical."

"What did she criticize you for?" I said.

"Humming. I'm walking down the street with Ava, humming something, and she'd say, 'Stop humming. You'll make her a hummer, too.' She seemed to think her criticism was well deserved, it was researched."

The more he began to reveal about his relationship with Christa, their union seemed strained from the get-go. I asked him if they ever had fun.

"I wouldn't describe it as having *fun*. If we went into Provincetown for an art opening, we might see Tony standing in the doorway of the gallery. We'd have to walk past him. He's known to hang around the art scene like that. I'd have Ava in the baby backpack, he'd see us, and take off. I was there for the baby. He wasn't."

I pictured Tim wearing the baby backpack, like so many yuppie pops who march up and down Commercial Street every summer. Sometimes men wear the baby in front, as if to copycat the heavy pull on their back muscles that their pregnant wives had complained about. For Tim to walk around with another man's papoose was all too noble or, some might think, too beaten. To see Jackett dolled up, standing in the doorway of a premium art bin as Tim is "carrying the load" of his daughter, was understandably vile to him.

"Did you fall in love with Christa?"

"Yeah, yeah."

"Was it reciprocated?"

He got up and took his coffee cup to the kitchen sink. He emptied the dregs. He came back. I refilled his cup.

He said, "It was reciprocated."

"What made you fall in love with her?"

"Let's skip that."

He stared through the glass table. He had noticed a hairline crack that began at the beveled edge and disappeared the way a ripple on a lake dissolves.

He said, "She had this 'modern irony.' She couldn't make a distinction between emotion and sentimentality. It made her kind of unapproachable. Once, when I said I loved her, she said, 'God, I want to push you off the sofa.' "

"She had trouble being affectionate?"

"Affectionate? That's not a good word," he said.

Fun isn't the word. *Affection* doesn't fit. *Let's skip that.* He couldn't find the right diction to define their relationship.

I said, "Ellen Webb told me that Christa 'couldn't hug right—she'd push away.' "

Tim said, "Right, she'd control it. If I kissed her, she'd say, okay, that's enough—she'd never let the embrace be over when it was naturally over."

What might be "natural" to one might be abhorrent to another.

Christa's resistance to connect was immediate and organic, but to Tim it seemed calculated: a little invitation, a little dismissal—to keep things where she wanted. A man in Christa's playwriting class had described the same characteristic. Jim Dalglish said that "Christa would look at you directly but give nothing emotionally until she had pinned down the exact response from you she wanted. You would try to say something to make her smile and she might grant you the merest little smile, a quiet smile, but that quiet had so much power. It was overstatement that seemed very demure, regal. But it was such a narrow passage between you and her."

Tim said, "Christa had this thing, this idea that other people were stupid. 'I can't believe everyone around me is so stupid,' she'd say. Meanwhile everyone is there helping her clean her attic."

Tim said that fierce criticism was what he had been used to with his own parents and he might have overreacted to Christa's complaints about him. "She didn't consciously want a battle, but subconsciously this was what she was used to in her own family. If there wasn't enough high tension, high drama, she'd make it."

"Was this part of her carnal life, too?"

"Yeah, I think so. I didn't go that way. That kind of sex."

"Did she want rough sex?"

"No, she didn't *request* that. She liked the intellectual battle around sex. The aggression. The competition to seduce. Who would initiate sex first. Her sex life and her emotional life were separate. They never merged. If she kissed in sex, it was sexual rather than loving. That's what she was used to. In her relationships, she ratcheted up the sex component."

"But, then, she never put the baby down. When she did, she'd say I didn't touch her the 'right way,' and I'm not allowed to say 'this' or 'that.' "

"That sounds like when an animal is injured in a trap. It snaps its jaws at you if you come too close."

"Yes. She was in pain. A woman whose mother died, has a new baby, and was jilted by another man."

"That's kind of a big yoke for you to step into."

"It was. Recently, I've been staying in bed."

"What keeps you in bed."

"Who did it. I want to know."

He said that he thought they should look hard at Jackett.

I told Tim that Tony says the same about him. Tony just assumes that everyone is a sports fan when he says, "That Patriots game—it wasn't over when Tim says he and his father left the house to give back the flashlight. No one leaves the house with the clock still going. The Pats were hot. Heading for the Super Bowl. That's the first clue that they were lying."

Tim said, "It's no coincidence that Christa had told her friends that she was going to ask Tony for child support, and the next day she turns up dead. She told me about her plans to talk to Tony about support. The money she had invested from her portion of her mother's estate wasn't doing as well, because of the market, you know, after nine-eleven. It wasn't as good as she hoped. But there was also this moral question that it just wasn't right for him not to contribute. The idea that she was keeping Tony's secret really started to bother her. She had a father like that—"

"Do you find yourself examining all the data? It sounds like you're defending a dissertation."

"I just want to know who did it."

When I asked him if he was certain Jackett was guilty, Tim said that there were many different little stories that could "fit." Tony's daughter Braunwyn had chastised Christa for bringing it out in the open. He said that Braunwyn had claimed that her family had been here since the *Mayflower*. "That's not true, I'm the one with the Bradford in my genealogy," Tim said. "But that's what everyone is looking at—this fistfight between the Jacketts and the Worthingtons."

Christa's old friend Jay Mulvaney had called it so "town and gown."

Tony had told Braunwyn about Christa and Ava before he told Susan. Susan was the last to know. She's the golden doormat. "But I don't see how Braunwyn could have kicked the door in," Tim said.

"In your day, how often do you think of these things?"

"It used to be like a tape loop. I do still get these intruding visions, but not as regularly. I want them to find the killer."

I drove Tim home. His driveway on Old County Road is just east of a street sign that says WORTHINGTON WAY. DEAD END.

"The press keeps taking pictures of that street sign," Tim said. "They showed it on TV in the *Dateline* segment—"

"Tacky," I said.

"Sick," he said.

He invited me into the house to see his new paintings. We walked up the Yankee staircase to the second floor. The almost vertical stairway had no banister, and in its place was a knotted rope like an old boat painter. But the rope had an unsettling suggestion of a gallows pulley. As I followed him up the steep risers, I was careful not to twist my ankle again. It was a little awkward for me to enter the bedroom and studio of my low-key friend, who was, in fact, still in the circle under police scrutiny.

His room was tight with a rumpled antique bed and a drawing desk against one window. He showed me his new paintings spread across the coverlet of his bed. *Singularity I, Singularity II,* colorful Masonite boards with finely worked surfaces. The images were oddly similar, central orbs with radiating appendages, tendrils, and bursts of color. Animal or vegetable.

He gave me a copy of his children's book, *The Winter Mittens.* The illustrations were eerie, almost too mournful for a children's book; the faces of the kids had big, haunted eyes like those unsettling Walter Keane paintings that were popular in the sixties.

When I left him there, I drove up to Christa's house. The yellow police tape had been removed from her driveway, and Ava's plastic toys were gone. Her "Cozy Coupe" had been packed up and sent to Amyra Chase's home, but not before a state trooper had knelt before the little toy car to brush it for fingerprints. Forensic examination of romper-room items is an unforgettable vision. I walked up to the kitchen window and looked in. I saw familiar cookstore gizmos and white stoneware bowls identical to my own; the occasional Fiestaware oddity, unmatched, and a candle burned down to a stub in a pool of hard wax, just like the miniature paraffin topiary I, too, have ignored in a saucer on a bookshelf at home. Of course, Christa's kitchen had been dusted and rubbed down in a crime scene spring cleaning as good or better than Heloise. Her kitchen was never this tidy, nor is my own. But where Christa's back door had once been, there's a blinding sheet of plywood.

In midwinter, Pamet harbor looks changed. Indifferent. The sea has lost its anthropomorphic applications. A little dory overturned on the boat ramp looks stranded, hopeless. The landscape vernacular is different now. The water too quiet, too smooth, a glass table where the guest of honor never showed up.

99.9

T he *New York Post*'s headline SLAY-TOT TUG OF LOVE angered friends and family, but its decisive tabloid diction had put just the right English on the accelerating custody battle for Ava. It was a battle cry. On Monday, January 7, one day after Christa's body was discovered, Cohasset residents Amyra Chase and her husband had filed an emergency motion to take custody of Ava. They took the baby home the next day. On January 10, Tony Jackett filed a motion in Barnstable County Probate Court seeking custody of his daughter. He requested of Judge Robert Scandurra that he vacate a "temporary custody" awarded to Amyra Chase. The judge ruled that Amyra Chase should keep Ava for the time being. In November, Christa Worthington had named her longtime friend Amyra as guardian for her daughter in a codicil to her will. Her first choice had been her British friend Barbara Holloway. Barbara was a highly charged professional woman, a woman with similar signposts as Christa's. But most important to Christa, England was half a world away, across the Atlantic and far enough from Susan Jackett. Christa didn't want Susan to raise her daughter.

But as Ava got a little older, Christa realized that Barbara Holloway might not be the right person to raise her. Barbara was a "high altitude" career woman working in the international entertainment business, organizing showy events and film festivals. What would Barbara do with a little girl? Amyra Chase, with four kids of her own, was in charge of a joyous monkey house where Ava would be welcomed.

Anyone who looked at the curly-haired toddler could see she was Tony's little girl, but his name was not listed on Ava's birth certificate. A DNA test to verify Jackett's paternity was ordered to be completed before a hearing scheduled for February 7.

Tony told me, "If I'm good enough to make the baby, I'm good enough to take the baby."

I recognized Jackett's typical "foot in his mouth" guilelessness that some people think is a put-on, but in fact is the real McCoy. Tony isn't trained for the podium. His public-speaking finesse was honed on deck, working elbow to elbow with the saltiest mouths, and he polished his modest vocabulary at the bar rails at his favorite haunts in Provincetown: the Surf Club; the Foc'sle; the Old Colony; and the Governor Bradford.

On February 7, I traveled up Cape to Barnstable Village to see if I could elbow my way into the custody hearing for Tony Jackett and Amyra Chase. O'Keefe had told me it would be up to Judge Scandurra, but he believed I might be lucky. When I got into Barnstable Village, I had time to kill, so I stopped at the Cancer Ransack Shop on 6A across from the courthouse. My mother had volunteered at the Ransack shop years ago. Proceeds from thrift shop items are donated to medical research. My mother had liked to stand over one particular glass display case where dowagers came to donate keepsakes from yesteryear, paste jewelry and stickpins, mementos of first and second marriages. I like to enter rag and bone shops where people have left little stories in their castoffs. Unmatched forks nested in a basket; butter knives from hotel dining rooms; miscellaneous coffee cups; a tower of bone china plates with the classic "wheat sheaves" pattern almost worn away; one willow-ware pitcher with a chipped lip; a melon-baller; a cheese grater; oddball gizmos from the domestic lives of nobodies. The morning of the hearing, I browsed around in my mother's old domain and I found a child's weighted cup like the one Ava had left beside her mother. And on the same shelf, a row of empty jelly jars with white tin lids, the threads rusted tight. These jars were identical to the one I had found smashed on the sidewalk in front of the DA's office. I thought it strange to see these items side by side, the Tippee Cup, the jelly jar, as if my mother herself had arranged the charged items to make my jaw drop.

I meet *Cape Cod Times* reporter Emily Dooley at the Barnstable County Courthouse at Deeds and Probate. We wait in line at the security kiosk as cameramen unload their equipment, extra lenses, microphones, film canisters, battery packs, anything that can fit into the scanner. The shoulder cams are given a cursory once-over with a rod, and one by one, different crews from Boston news stations and a few journeymen network pros push through the bottleneck. Reporters stand in clusters around the downstairs lobby and start to crowd the hallway upstairs.

WBZ wins the pool, and the WBZ cameraman is allowed to set up a tripod in the courtroom. I sit down on the blond maple benches and watch the room fill with reporters and curiosity-seekers. The WBZ technicians test their sound equipment. The cameraman curses as he takes out a handkerchief to dust off his camera. He tells his buddy, "This eff-ing sand. I had to do a Truro beach shoot. I hate shooting on Cape Cod."

A court deputy stands up front and says, "Everyone but attorneys are asked to leave the courtroom."

We all trudge out to the hallway. Through its glass door, we can watch Jackett's attorney and the opposing counselor in a heated discussion. I see O'Keefe in the courtroom and our eyes meet. He's got his deadpan mug down to a science. Trapped in the hall with the press, Amyra Chase and her husband stand quietly, their shoulders squared, as the oglers surround. Amyra is a pretty brunette. Because of her heart-shaped face and her shoulder-length hair in a sixties-style flip, she looks like the familiar sitcom mom—beloved and nonthreatening—the all-American housewife.

Her husband, Clifford, is at her side, nudging her out of harm's way when a reporter plows too close. He runs a successful liquor store franchise, and Amyra and Clifford own a nice home in Cohasset with enough room for Ava. But Clifford's face sometimes locks up and worry drifts over his features. He seems to have had the wind knocked out of him to find himself at the heart of the sudden custody war. Reporters force their cards on the couple and try to nab a statement or to encourage any quotable complaint. At one point, Amyra sits down on a bench against one wall and begins to weep, her dainty hands fanned over her face. Reporters nudge their camera crews so they won't miss the opportunity to shoot her little breakdown. A swarm of shoulder cams and large boxy cameras swing in that direction. The photographers rise on their tiptoes, dipping and swerving around one another to get their shot.

The first time I spoke with Amyra she told me how she felt about

Christa's codicil to her will. Amyra said, "It's such an honor. I can't tell you how much of an honor it is." She was almost tongue-tied with emotion, with awe. Her unspeakable shock at Christa's death was tempered, overwhelmed, by her allegiance to her friend and her immediate acceptance of the role she had been thrown into. Under the spotlight, she doesn't flinch. Her momentary fit of tears isn't self-pity. Amyra is simply in the very first stages of a long grieving process for her friend Christa.

The more I learn about Amyra, the more down-to-earth and good-hearted she seems. A lifelong friend of Christa's from her old Crow Point neighborhood in Hingham, Amyra had been Christa's dearest confidante. Amyra's immediate devotion to Ava reminds me of Miss Temple, the stoic and kindly schoolmistress in *Jane Eyre*, who takes Jane under her wing after Jane is brutalized by the wicked Miss Scatcherd and the icy Mrs. Reed.

Tony hasn't appeared, but his daughter Braunwyn and son Luc parade into the huddle, stopping to talk with writer Peter Manso. Manso, a local author who had penned biographies of Norman Mailer and Marlon Brando, had recently captured for all posterity a snapshot of our native heartthrob Tony Jackett in his new book *Ptown: Art, Sex, and Money on the Outer Cape*.

I'm amused to see Manso's slacks have hanger marks, sharp horizontal creases across his knees. This fashion faux pas is a geezer thing, similar to when older women apply makeup without their reading glasses and it smears in uneven dollops. Next to crumpled Manso, Braunwyn is a startling vision. She's slight but graceful, with looping ass-length bleached tresses. She looks like a hybrid of a slutty Tuesday Weld and a Court TV Rapunzel. I don't know if she and her mother are natural blondes, but it would take more than one bottle of "Preference—Because I'm Worth It" to lighten that mane. Luc is dark-haired and handsome, with his father's sharp features. Luc's chiseled profile resembles Tony's, but at fifty-two Tony's eyes have little pouches. Luc's complexion is smooth and cold as marble; he's like a gorgeous life-size statue that just broke off an Alexandrian monument. I watch newswomen try to hide their knee-jerk responses to Luc. I see one gal's little Adam's apple shiver, as she bites her bottom lip, smudging her lipstick. He's an eyeful. Women try to shift their gaze, but they come right back to Luc as if hypnotized, like marks in a card trick.

Emily Dooley has seen Luc before. She doesn't react to the simmering soap opera. She's too seasoned or maybe just too familiar with these Jackett kids. Luc and Braunwyn look strained. Braunwyn's marriage is crumbling, and her husband, Keith, doesn't stand beside her now, but sits by himself. Just one more chip off the old block in "the orbit of opportunity." In a few weeks, Braunwyn and Luc plan to flee Cape Cod and move to Colorado. Luc wants to accompany his girlfriend, India, and her new baby to India's hometown, and Braunwyn hopes to tag along, at least for a breather from the jangling events with her dad and her husband.

Watching these tense knots of the two opposing clans, Emily's little grimace signals me. We smile in amusement as we wait to hear if we'll be allowed to attend the hearing. We both know that Manso's new book has fouled things up for Tony Jackett. Manso laments the loss of P-town's old charms, the exodus of artists, the decline of its fishing fleet, and the disappearance of beloved Portuguese old-timers, all due to the gentrification in town by wealthy gay landowners, gay businessmen, and lesbian shopkeepers. In his tirades against Provincetown's "theme park" of gay yuppies, or "guppies," Manso describes Tony as a high school heartthrob turned fisherman turned "drug smuggler." Manso's portrait of Tony is one of a guileless and bumbling maverick, suggesting to the reader that despite Tony's nefarious escapades, he might be the last high-profile hetero man in town. The *Cape Cod Times* described the book: "Readers will be treated to the inside scoop on the life of Tony Jackett, father of the love child of murdered Truro fashion writer Christa Worthington. Manso describes Jackett's brief career as a wannabe drug smuggler, back in the days when marijuana bales washed up on Outer Cape beaches." As Keystone Kops as Tony's escapade had been, Manso's fresh recounting of Tony's run-in with the DEA was sure to be a coffin nail as big as a railroad spike in his custody bid for Ava.

Tony finally arrives just as the deputy squeezes out of the courtroom door to stand in our ranks. He announces that everyone, press and busybodies, will be allowed to be present at the hearing. He tells us that we may "file in, sit down, but families get the first rows."

Emily and I choose a bench right behind Jackett's entourage, almost as many as a baseball team. It's the whole family. Tony's son-in-law, Keith Amato, looks a little distracted, uncomfortable to have his own secret life exposed on deck with Tony's public operation. He knows that his wife is preparing to leave him, and as Tony's drama unfolds, Amato sits there stewing and brainstorming about Braunwyn. The brunette men and blond women are a vivid tableau of hard-bitten survival techniques and sexual frisson. Every one of them is under scrutiny. It's a burden, even to the most narcissistic Jackett, Tony, to feel everyone eyeballing his family in a courtroom setting.

Tony is dressed in a brushed imitation suede jacket with leisure suit tailoring. He must have purchased the item two decades ago when disco clothes started to appear in bargain bins. But Tony is trying. Other times, when he gets dressed up, he wears a white shirt with a pleated bib and ruffles, like Errol Flynn. I think twice about saying hello to Tony because Amyra and Clifford have just entered. As in wedding protocol, they sit down directly in the opposite aisle, or it's like a Hatfield and McCoy showdown.

The court deputy says, "All cells off."

Everyone reaches into their pockets or rummages in their handbags to accommodate.

Barnstable County family and probate judge Robert Scandurra sits down at the bench. I'm surprised to see that he is bearded and looks like a graduate student. But he has a sharp, attentive expression. He understands the gravity of the case and that it's not a typical custody squabble, but a "story unfolding." There's an unsolved murder at the core of it and it's not a run-of-the-mill plea for "every other weekend" visitation rights.

Tony's lawyer is his cousin, Chris Snow. Snow has thick hair combed back in a classic John Gotti coif that accentuates his high forehead and deep-set eyes. He has the similar hetero bulk and Mediterranean traits as Tony. He's Tony Jackett in a Men's Warehouse suit.

In contrast to the John Gotti lookalike, Amyra and Clifford's lawyer, Paul Mayer, has an instant resemblance to "Mr. Rogers." It's his mildness and thin voice. His comments emerge in tentative phrases, and he stumbles over multisyllabic words due to his escalating nervousness. One feels it may get so bad he will stop talking altogether. I wonder about Amyra Chase's choice of counsel. His bumbling is especially pronounced juxtaposed against Attorney Snow's colorful locution. Snow has vocal force from the get-go, but most of his comments reek of blanket moralism and paternity "rights" and accusations of kidnapping, when Chase's lawyer speaks only about Ava's well-being.

Proof of Jackett's paternity is officially submitted to the court. DNA tests have proved 99.9 percent likelihood of paternity. Snow tells the court that if Jackett is Ava's biological parent, his claim of custody would take legal precedence over any designation of a guardian that Worthington might have made prior to her death. "Otherwise, you could will away your children like chattel, or a grandfather clock," Snow said.

The row of Jacketts bob their heads in agreement, making little geese noises.

"This is a court-ordered abduction," Snow said. The room is silent, impressed by Snow's accusation.

Snow continues, "Tony is a law officer, in a law enforcement team as shellfish constable. If there was any reason for him to be named a culprit, they wouldn't allow him to be a law officer.

"In the meantime, the whole community is suspect. We're no closer today to finding the murderer. This could go on forever. Tony, the father of Ava, shouldn't remain under a cloud of unfounded suspicion."

Scandurra asks Cape and Islands First Assistant District Attorney Michael O'Keefe to address the question of culpability. He asks O'Keefe if Jackett or any of his children are suspects.

Snow says, "Objection. This is not appropriate."

But O'Keefe rises and walks to the left of the bench. He says, "Jackett stands in a position similar to a number of others where he cannot be ruled out."

With O'Keefe's statement, it doesn't appear that Tony has much chance of bringing the baby home today. But the arguments are just beginning to simmer.

I watch Emily Dooley scribble her notes. I can never transcribe a conversation as fast as my thoughts explode. She whispers, "It's the pen. You have to have a good pen. I can only use a Gel-rite."

Attorney Mayer is saying, "There was never any intention that Jackett would be the primary caretaker. Christa was well traveled, a famous writer. Christa did not intend to stay in Truro.

"From May 1999, when Ava was born, until February 2001, Jackett had zero contact with Ava. When Christa was walking at Pamet harbor with a friend, Francie Randolph, Jackett fled when he saw her pushing the stroller. Jackett openly abandoned the child. At two and a half years old, she doesn't know her father.

"The fact that he's a shellfish warden doesn't make him innocent."

Despite his thin voice, Amyra and Clifford's attorney was hitting the right notes.

Snow again stood up to express his disbelief in Amyra's integrity. He said that on the night of the murder, Tony took possession of Ava with approval of the town police, the state police, and the Worthington family. Then the police picked up the baby to "take her to the hospital" but she went to Francie Randolph's, and then to Amyra. He said, "There was no warning of the surreptitious behavior of the Chases. Within twenty-four hours, Jackett sought recourse of the court decree. Meanwhile, the child is without her father.

"Susan is the hero here. Susan has nurtured the relationship between the four of them."

Attorney Mayer said, "It was EMT Malloy who took care of Ava for the three hours after Christa was found. Tony and Susan did not interact with Ava. There was no viability of a relationship between Ava and Susan. Susan was heard to say, 'You can't believe anything that child says, she fibs.' "

Snow stands up. He says, "That's hearsay. The burden rests on the Chases to prove Jackett is unfit."

Mayer requests a trial for fitness with witnesses. He says, "Parents have rights but the state has the right to intervene. We are asking for our day in court."

Judge Scandurra says, "This is a tough case. Tony Jackett has biological rights, but here are two facts:

"One. It is uncontroverted that Jackett didn't step forward legally to be adjudicated until after Worthington's death.

"Two. The district attorney has stated that Jackett cannot be ruled out.

It is in her best interest, at this time, for Ava to be with Amyra Chase. This is what Christa Worthington wanted. I am giving due respect to those wishes. Visits with Jackett must be arranged by counsel, and issues of support should be addressed. There will be a pretrial conference."

Scandurra is keeping in place a temporary custody order given to Chase immediately after Christa was murdered. Within the structure of a Barnstable County program called "Children and Parents," Scandurra says he will appoint attorney Peter Hickey as counsel to the toddler. Hickey will be directly involved with any decisions made in Ava's behalf.

The hearing is over. The judge slams the gavel once in the silly tradition of closure that everyone expects. It would be pleasing, I guess, at the end of every argument between husbands and wives, between lovers, between parents and children, if we could wallop the dinner table with a wooden hammer. Amyra and Clifford rise from their chairs, teary-eyed. Amyra grins weakly, showing some respect for her opponent or maybe simple exhaustion. Walking out of the courtroom, I hear Tony say to his kids, "That's that." He seems resolved to find some relief, like a gust of air, as the first door slams in his face.

I introduce myself to Amyra, but I don't try to chat. I don't want to invade her hard-won halo of immediate triumph, it's a shaky penumbra.

Leaving Emily behind, I walk downstairs to find Keith Amato. He's sitting by himself, with that same distracted countenance. He isn't feeling good. His wife is dumping him and the cops aren't leaving him alone. They have come to "talk" about saliva samples. I introduce myself and tell him I want to see him sometime. He looks at me, smiling, but with distrust, as if I were telling a leopard I wanted his spots.

THE DELFONICS

Unlike the writer from *New York* magazine, I didn't crash Christa's memorial service in Hingham. But her old friend and Vassar classmate Jay Mulvaney, the author of *Diana & Jackie: Maidens, Mothers, Myths* and *Jackie: The Clothes of Camelot*, had attended the event. He told me that he was amused to see that her aunts and cousins were decked out in "Talbot's WASP" attire. Tim Arnold was there, huddled in a corner, but of course Tony wasn't going to show up. Mulvaney said, "Her father, Toppy, didn't seem to be very upset at the funeral. When I walked over to him, he said, 'There's the big guy, I remember you. Sorry there's not a bar here. Yes, I'm sorry there's not a bar.' "

Mulvaney had asked him how he was feeling, and Toppy answered, "I just want to go home and put my feet up on the hassock." The funeral home was an old Victorian with two parlors. Toppy stayed to himself in one room, and in the other room was Christa's coffin. Mulvaney was surprised to recognize that the casket was the same one he had ordered for his parents, the "Britannia," walnut with a matte finish and white rayon lining. Twenty-eight hundred dollars. Christa's former employer, Fairchild Publications, had sent a huge basket of flowers, a four-hundred-dollar arrangement, whites and pale greens, with eucalyptus. It was beautiful. There was only one other nice arrangement, but the rest were "fabulously tacky." Carnations stuck in Styrofoam. Toppy kept to himself with a couple of Yale prof types. "That WASP stiff upper lip," Mulvaney said. "He didn't go near Ava once. Amyra was very nice; she kept telling Ava, 'Here's someone else who loved mommy.' "

Ava looked enchanting in a blue-green velvet dress and yellow barrettes in her copper hair. "Beautiful," Mulvaney said. "She has Tony's coloring."

Many of Christa's high school friends attended the memorial, including her first boyfriend, John Wotjacinski. Christa had often said he was the "love of her life." Her good friend Gail Motlin said, "We all went out to a bar afterward, all the Hingham High friends. John was really upset. He whispered in my ear how much he missed Christa, after all these years. The music was loud or I was drunk, I couldn't hear his whole confession. But he was bad off."

I might have missed the memorial for Christa in Hingham, but I did attend a local vigil for Christa at the "UU" in Provincetown. The Unitarian Universalist Meeting House is a beautiful white church in the center of town, set back from boisterous Commercial Street by a wide lawn, its pure white spire a focal point second only to the Gothic green copper steeple of Town Hall. For as long as I can remember, one of the town's reliable entertainments appears each week on a signboard in front of the UU. The sign announces the quirky titles of each Sunday's Sermon: "Give It a Rest," "The Finger of God Points at You," "Him and Hymn," "Now, Then, or Never Again."

Two weeks after the murder, some of Christa's local friends had organized a program entitled "An Hour of Peace for Christa Worthington." I read the announcement in the *Banner*, P-town's local weekly.

Still on crutches then, I had parked on MacMillan Wharf and windmilled down Commercial Street in the bitter cold. The sanctuary at the UU is on the second floor, and I had to climb the stairs crabwise on my hands and seat, pulling my crutches after me. I didn't feel it was a respectful way to arrive at the somber occasion, but once on my crutches again, I entered the prayer hall and was greeted by the mousy women hosting the event. I didn't recognize anyone. Tim Arnold said he missed the memorial at the UU because that's when he was getting a lie detector test.

The UU has stunning trompe l'oeil wall paintings of ivied Corinthian columns. As I worked my way down the aisle to find a seat in the forward pews, flickering candlelight at the altar exaggerated a sense of faux reality in that pseudo-ethereal setting, half church, half courtroom. Someone played the piano in a leisurely style, not somber, not jubilant; in fact, without any particular emphasis at all. It should have been one or the other, sorrowful or celebratory, and not merely so boring, I thought. I didn't recognize a soul. Mourners stared at me with a sort of imperious patience, like schoolmarms one and all. None of these local residents were in my immediate circle, but a woman gave me a program and pointed to a basket of lavender sprigs. She encouraged me to take some of the dried flowers in remembrance of Christa. I declined, since I needed both hands to grip my crutch handles.

The service began with a woman named Irene Paine standing at the raised pulpit. She commanded mourners to curb and scuttle their bad reactions to Christa's murder. "If we've been concentrating on the negative elements of her passing, we must now do the work of changing our focus to ease her spirit's journey. From this time forward, picture Christa bathed in white light, emanating peace and acceptance."

This was a little too fruit-and-nut and New Age-y for me, and I began to wonder about what kind of friends Christa had cultivated. The *New York Times* article had described someone who had been sophisticated, wry, and urbane, and I was surprised by her friends' tepid testimonials. One after another stood up to deliver the most bland and boring rhetoric. It was like being force-fed lukewarm Cream of Wheat. The candlelit sanctuary reeked of sweet, white bread. "Feel the air on your face, smell the scents of the seasons, appreciate the beauty, and know that Christa loved it." I found out that some of this group practiced yoga and "reiki," a massage therapy that transfers "healing energy," and most everyone was vegan. "Let us not allow negativity to starve our souls." They were gardeners and furniture-makers, an art gallery director, a collector of Eastern art, a mandolin player, but the UU turnout was only a tiny pie wedge of Christa's broader circle; most of her friends lived in Europe and New York City.

These guided meditations were punctuated by a mandatory five minutes of silence between each new installment. We were asked to spend these minutes concentrating our "energies" in order to urge Christa's soul to its resting place without further delay.

The pianist David Wright played Bach, Brahms, and "La-La Means I Love You" by the Delfonics. A song, some of her closer friends have told me, that would have made Christa cringe. After the final "guided meditation," we were asked to sit quietly for the remainder of the hour, a good thirty-five minutes by my watch.

As the others, about thirty in all, dipped their heads to tough it out, I got up from the second pew. I teetered for a moment, losing my balance, trying to center my crutches under the armpits of my bulky jacket. I was making a racket, and I felt a little conspicuous in the face of so much mandatory quiet and meditation, my face coloring.

Again, I went crabwise down the stairs. As I stood up in the dark anterior foyer, I saw a figure swerve away and tiptoe quickly into the dim hall before me. She had her back to me, but refracted light from the street illuminated her silhouette for an instant. I saw her reddish hair bloom over her shoulders. Then she was gone. She was an apparition, a spook, or probably a homeless woman taking shelter in the church doorway. Yet her movement was inaudible, silent, like a ghost. She disappeared before the heavy door, but I didn't see or hear her shove it open.

I hobbled outside and looked for her. There was no one, just a line of cars parked on Commercial Street before the church. I counted more than one "Free Tibet" bumper sticker. Although the UU ceremony was heartfelt, I didn't believe Christa was really one of that group. I imagined the spirited zingers she might have whispered under her breath if she was forced to sit through that goofy hour with me. No, she wasn't one of them, but a lost soul they had adopted.

And her childhood friend Gail Motlin said that when she had left the stuffy Hingham memorial, her first thought was to run home and call Christa. She wanted to tell her about all the people she had seen: Christa's high school pals, her New York friends, a few of whom had formed a little glam squad of fashionistas. Christa would have had a little giggle or snort about this one or that one.

Gail said, "Then I remembered, Christa was gone."

THE DEBBIE SMITH ACT

O'Keefe telephones me one night. "What's your feeling about Law?" he says.

"Law? You mean the legal system? Tax law, criminal law?"

"Not that."

I don't know what he's talking about. It could be anything. "Law of the jungle?" "Law of gravity?"

"The Catholic Church. Cardinal Law," he says.

"You mean cardinal *sin*?"

He laughs. One abbreviated deep note, gone before he can seem to enjoy it. "I'm talking about the archbishop in Boston. Cardinal Law? At last, law enforcement has the green light to go after these creeps."

I had read about the recent scandal in the Roman Catholic Church in the *New York Times*: PEDOPHILE ISSUE SHAKES THE AUTHORITY OF BOSTON CARDINAL. The names involved seemed synchronous to the charges against them. Not only Cardinal Law, but a priest was suspended from duty at a parish in Wellesley for sexual misconduct and his name was Father Power. "Father Power" was the perfect moniker for a child molester.

Calling me after hours to discuss newsbreaks, O'Keefe has caught me off guard, but I try to keep up with him. "So you think Law should go to jail for rubber-stamping pedophiles?"

"That'll never happen," O'Keefe says, "but we've got people speaking out. These boys are grown men now, and they're mad."

O'Keefe was a Catholic kid himself. I wonder if it's personal.

He says, "Meet me in Orleans."

"Where?"

"You tell me."

"How about Land Ho!, the Fog Cutter, the Homeport?" I say. Almost every bar and restaurant on Cape Cod has a nautical tag. The Boatslip. The Foc'sle. The Reef Café. There are not too many Western steak houses east of the canal.

O'Keefe says, "The Binacle. Six o'clock Tuesday."

The Binacle isn't my favorite spot, but it's dark as hell in there, and maybe that's the way he wants it.

O'Keefe is sitting at the bar with a Diet Coke. He takes my elbow and steers me to a corner table in the dark. The Binacle, even on a Tuesday, is filling up. Our little table wobbles, and a waitress comes over with a deck of cards. O'Keefe waits for her to bend down to shove the pack under the uneven pedestal, but she tells him, "I'm not reaching through your legs, you do it." She gives him the pack of cards.

For a moment, I think he must choose this table every time. He's indulging me with another chinwag about the murder in my own backyard. O'Keefe's "backyard" is everywhere on the Cape and Islands. Like Weegee, he's at every murder "almost before the victim," but I'm a novice. I had read about murders in forensic paperbacks like *Dead Men Do Tell Tales*, and *A Fly for the Prosecution,* about entomological evidence, when I researched a novel I was writing. But my expertise is at the layman level of Court TV, the O. J. Simpson trial, and the John Walsh syndicated extravaganza, *America's Most Wanted*.

I told him I wanted to learn what happened to Christa, and understand the conflicts that preceded the final instant that she didn't survive. Why did it happen? No one can understand the arc of the victim's life until her killer is ID'd.

"*How* tells us *who*, *who* tells us *why*," O'Keefe says.

He didn't care about "why." "Who" was his meal ticket.

O'Keefe shows up at the endpoint, at the crime scene, and works backward. "I've stood over every dead body on Cape Cod for eighteen years," he says.

"So, what is it like to show up at every murder for a score of years? How does it affect your life?"

"It's a job. Like any other," he says.

"Not exactly."

He says, "Look, say you have a plumber. He doesn't think about plumbing twenty-four hours a day. Late at night, he doesn't dream of augers, washer bonnets, and locknuts."

He paused. Giving me time to imagine what cops might dream about.

"Most criminals are stupid. Most crimes are a target of opportunity. They leave mistakes everywhere."

"So you don't think this was premeditated?"

"That's the sixty-four-thousand-dollar question. The door was kicked in, but maybe this was done afterward to mimic a burglary. We see a footprint on the breast or vagina and gauge the 'anger factor.' "

"A footprint on the vagina? How is that possible?"

"I'm being a gentleman. I'm not using slang, okay?"

"Oops. Well, gee, thanks."

"We can tell if it's a female perpetrator or a male, shoe size, force, the position of the body. We look at where and when people left prints. Several people have a perfect legal right to have left evidence. Jackett. Arnold. They'd been in the place. But *when* it was left, and *where* it was left, can be informative. Statements of trace evidence can be controverted." He tries to explain the difference between "specific and articuable facts," "evidence short of probable cause," and "proof beyond reasonable doubt."

I'm scratching down what he says as fast as he speaks, but when I look up, he's grinning.

He says, "Did I lose you? Are you following this?"

"Shit. Do you have to make fun? Haven't you read *Men Are from Mars, Women Are from Venus*? You're supposed to give me some encouragement."

"No, I didn't read it. No wonder I didn't do so well."

"Excuse me?"

"My wife. I guess I should have read a book."

His wife is a judge, but even with her background in law, I wonder what it was like for her when her hubby's routine is finding "footprints on vaginas," but I don't want more explanation. I say, "What was your day like?"

"I had a two-hour meeting with *three* troopers, and then a three-hour meeting with *two* troopers."

"And the Truro police?"

"We don't worry about them. We need to have a 'uniformity of resources' and state troopers handle the murders for local police. People read the papers, then they call up Chief Popcorn with their big ideas and comments, and make felonious press. That wastes our time following up. A chain reaction of felonious information confounds our time and resources. It makes us chase stupid things."

"She was stabbed with a flagpole? That one?"

"There's a list of this crap."

A man sitting at the bar asks O'Keefe to remove his overcoat from an empty chair beside him. O'Keefe obliges and tells me, "So if a woman comes along and wants to sit down next to him she can." He asks me, "You want a drink?"

"No, thanks, I don't drink anymore. A Diet Coke for me, too."

"If you wanted to have a drink, what would it be?"

"I didn't say I don't *want* a drink. I said I don't drink." I wonder if he's curious about my downfall, my weaknesses; does he want to know what kind of carrot to dangle before me?

"What did you drink in olden times?"

I tell him, "Some kind of single malt. Glenfiddich, I guess."

"No kidding?"

"I wasn't an amateur, if that's what you mean."

"You mean you weren't a cheap date. What about Christa? What was she?"

"Her friends say she didn't drink much. Because of her father's problem—"

"But she wasn't an amateur either. The more we look at her, the uglier she gets," O'Keefe says. I don't know if he's referring to her money problems, to her disassociative family on Depot Road, or to her long history with a virtual barnyard of boyfriends, leading up to her high-octane adultery with Jackett.

O'Keefe says, "She was an equal opportunity employer. She'd fuck the husbands of her female friends. The butcher or the banker. Her family

says, 'Oh, no, she wasn't promiscuous, she really liked Mr. So-and-so.'
Married or not."

O'Keefe sometimes reacted to Christa's adulteries with a visible Jerry
Falwell–Rush Limbaugh tic, that sexist, patriarchal, Republican thing.
Women fit into two specific categories. Saint or tramp. But I understand
the complex prism that blinds a woman as her lover sits on the edge of
the bed to lace his wingtips and reknot his tie before going back to the office or home to his wife. They complain about their wives being unwilling
to go that extra mile into the heart of the desert of sex: their wives don't
swallow; they don't roll over; they don't sit on top or they *always* sit on
top. You're their goddess of chic sex, mean sex, taboo sex, but you start to
wonder who's the doormat, the jilted wife or the mistress left behind to
sort out her evenings alone. It's the wives who get their backs rubbed, cars
waxed, checkbooks balanced, pictures hung, drains unclogged, spiders
squashed.

O'Keefe explains that the DNA results are coming back at a snail's pace
from the lab in Sudbury; it was taking months for results to dribble back.
Christa's friends are impatient. Some of her pals in New York want to
raise money to hire their own DNA technician. O'Keefe says he won't give
samples over to just anybody in a lab coat, although he is still waiting for
samples to be completed at the state lab. O'Keefe tells me, "It's a serious
situation. The Massachusetts Crime Lab services eleven district attorneys' offices. Ten years ago, A-B-O blood group analysis was all we had to
match blood left behind by a perpetrator. This changed with the advent
of DNA. DNA is the 'fingerprint' of the twenty-first century. But most
states are way ahead of us, although Massachusetts has the greatest teaching hospitals and scientific brain trusts. The best universities. But we're
the worst in time of delivery of this forensic tool to police. We have just
four chemists doing DNA for the whole state. Boston has eight chemists,
just for the city. You know about Debbie Smith?"

"Debbie Smith?"

He tells me that Debbie Smith is a rape victim who is crusading in
Washington to clear up the backlog in DNA testing. Across the country

there are more than eighteen thousand rape kits containing physical evidence waiting in cold storage like a backlog of Girl Scout cookies. And in the FBI data bank, over half a million samples from convicts haven't been processed for use in cross-identification. The House of Representatives has a bill on the table, House Resolution 2874, called "The Debbie Smith Act." The bill earmarks $200 million for funding to state labs, for training of hospital staff to conduct sexual assault examinations, and for DNA testing and inclusion in the CODIS, or "Combined DNA Index System" of the FBI's DNA analyses of samples from crime scenes.

So far, DNA samples from Christa's body don't match anyone in "the orbit of opportunity" and CODIS would be of use to O'Keefe if all systems were up and running.

O'Keefe says, "Christa's killer was probably the creep who fucked her that weekend. We don't know from our DNA who that is. The other scenario might be that whoever left his DNA was just her houseguest one night. He visited. They did it. He left. Someone else comes in and kills her, a stalker. Tim Arnold might have seen her with someone and—"

"In a jealous rage—"

"Maybe. But just because Arnold is obsessed doesn't make him the killer—"

"Or someone could have followed her home," he says. "We have her on a videotape at the supermarket in Orleans. This happens. Someone follows a victim home from the store. Remember when they used to have conveyor belts that sent your groceries outside to the sidewalk with your address clipped onto the box and delivery boys would bring it over? These address slips got snatched by sex offenders."

"This DNA from Christa—didn't you say it was old?"

"Turns out that the DNA on her breasts and nipples matches the semen inside her. So unless she didn't shower every day, it's fresh that weekend."

"DNA on her breasts?" I imagine "who" shooting his mystery load all over Christa. O'Keefe notices my thoughtful expression.

He says, "Not what you're thinking. It was saliva on her breasts, I'm saying."

"Oh, right." Ava was found nursing, clinging to her mother, even though Christa couldn't move a muscle and couldn't hug her. If Ava was nursing, of course the baby's saliva would have mingled and combined with the killer's.

"What's the matter?" O'Keefe says. "Did I lose you again?"

It must be on my face, the "single mother thing." I can't describe it to him.

PART TWO

FILENE'S BASEMENT

She stood in a tight aisle between long racks of marked-down clothes in Filene's Basement, a discount store in downtown Boston as big and blinding as a hockey rink. The racks were shoulder-high, but for Christa, who was not yet five foot two, they were just about eye-level. She liked being pinned inside the snug tunnel of clothes. She felt like a nymph lost in a cornfield, a sprite hiding in a secret garden. Her friend Kim Gibson was on the other side of the crowded rack. Kim's mom was across the street getting her hair done and the girls had two hours to browse. They were choosing halter tops. At thirteen, they were finally starting to fill out a cup size. It was a slow process, like watching a tin of popovers rise behind an oven window.

Kim held open a shopping bag as Christa crammed a halter top in. Then Christa held the bag as Kim tugged a prize off a hanger and shoved it out of sight. In the overstuffed rows they made their transactions, screened by heavy poles of merchandise, ruffles, pleats, and shoulder pads. If someone walked by, Christa would step back and nonchalantly drag some hangers left and right as if still searching for the perfect item. Nope, can't find it. Walk.

They got nicked on the way out the door.

Kim's dad was deputy sheriff for Suffolk County Superior Court and Mr. Worthington was a district attorney. The two friends should have been red-faced and contrite. Other girls, whose dads were bankers or teachers, weren't under such a spotlight. When the security office called their homes, the girls begged their moms not to tell their fathers. They made a pact. If their mothers buttoned up, the girls promised never to do it again. But after a breather, Christa and Kim were nicked again in ninth grade. On this junket, they were caught lifting costume jewelry from Ann Taylor's in Social Plaza. Kim said, "We had no fear."

I told O'Keefe about Christa's shoplifting sprees. I thought these details made Christa seem like an all-American girl. Teenage girls go through a little bout of kleptonarcissism; it corresponds to a phase when they begin to primp before mirrors, jutting their hips, turning back and forth to study their new curves. They want to get decked out, curl their eyelashes, accessorize, but can't afford bangles on their meager allowances. O'Keefe wasn't so tolerant.

I said, "Oh, come on, you never lifted anything when you were a kid?"

"Never."

"Are you serious?"

"I never stole anything." He wasn't smiling. I wondered if he was truly a moralistic fuddy-duddy, or if he was whitewashing. Maybe he was careful not to admit to his juvie wrongdoings because he was up for election.

"You never swiped anything? Not even a candy bar?"

"I did worse things," he said, as if shoplifting was a wasteful use of one's allotted sum of forgivable sins.

I guess he had his Irish background, and a Catholic childhood to shrug off. Christa was from a WASP patrician tutelage, which sometimes shirks God. It's not just trailer-trash teens who get picked up for pinching things. Privileged mall rats and working-class kids have this one common denominator: after-school hoisting, an extracurricular that flowers in adolescence on both sides of the tracks. Like teenage Christa, Linda Silva didn't resist an occasional item that glistened at her fingertips.

Christa was born in Brookline, Massachusetts, on December 23, 1955, but growing up in Hingham, a waterfront community on the South Shore just fifteen miles outside the city of Boston, seemed like the ideal American backdrop for a promising coed. In the 1930s, Hingham was still rural, with twenty working farms. Eleanor Roosevelt once said, "Main Street in Hingham is the prettiest street in America." But at the start of World War II, the town was changed forever when the navy spent $25 million to build a shipyard at Hingham Harbor. Experts from Bethlehem Steel Works helped build a steel mill at the shipyard, and sixteen concrete bays, so that ships could be mass-produced. The shipyard built ships for the English navy before the United States entered the war, launching ninety destroyer escorts, or DEs, in one year. After Pearl Harbor, when America had entered the war, there weren't enough men to work at the yard. School-age boys went to work and local women were trained as welders. Some Hingham women talk about the scars on their breasts from soldering slag that smoldered through their work jackets.

Hingham Shipyard also built the infamous flat-bottom ship, the LST, or landing ship tank, that swarmed the coast of France on D-day and helped turn the tide in that war. After the Allied victory, the shipyard stopped production. The plant closing caused a vacuum in the small town, but the shipyard had launched 227 boats in that brief window of time.

In the next decades, Hingham became a popular bedroom community for Boston professionals. Christa's mother, Gloria, worked in the city as a portrait artist and at a photography studio where she did color tinting of photographs as Toppy continued as assistant attorney general in Boston. Still peeved that his parents, John and Tiny, had sent him off to boarding school in Connecticut, he wanted Christa to go to public school in Hingham. But some have said that he just didn't want to spend the cash for private school.

Their first place on Sycamore Lane, in Bradley Woods, was in a good neighborhood. By most everyone's standards they were well housed and lived in a prime location. But Gloria always hoped they might do better, and when Christa was in ninth grade, her parents bought a grand harbor-view house in Crow Point with a big wraparound porch and a dock where Toppy could moor his sailboat. The house looked across the harbor to the Boston skyline—the Prudential Tower, the Hancock Building—but from their windows one could also see the sewage treatment island and the constant traffic in and out of Logan Airport.

Kim Gibson said, "I was Christa's *first* friend when she lived on Sycamore, across the street from me. My mother used to baby-sit both of us, because Christa's mom worked all day in Boston. Back then, she was putting Toppy through law school and I guess they were saving for the Crow Point place. They weren't ever home."

Christa took piano lessons, ballet classes, and she went to tap lessons with her friend Kim. Kim said that Christa was very gifted and excelled. "I was the klutz," Kim said. "I was a Christa wannabe, but she wanted to be like us because I had two older sisters and she was an only child. She was like the fourth sister and was always at our house. When she went to Truro, her cousins, who were all sisters, made her feel like a misfit." So, summers Kim went to Truro on weekends with Christa. She remembers that the cousins weren't always nice, and that she and Christa went off by themselves. The girls liked to sneak up to the nudie beach on the Pamet River and watch the naked men. "Most of them were really old, sixty and seventy. We'd see their little 'marble bags' bouncing up and down when they played volleyball."

Her summer friend, a boy named Ethan Cohen, sometimes tagged along. Christa thought he was very smart but a little too full of himself. At his brother's bar mitzvah, Ethan jumped to his feet and took center stage when his brother had fainted. He began reciting where his brother had left off and was trying to steal the show. So, if Christa saw that Ethan was in a "me mood," she ditched him.

When she had no friends with her, Christa loved to explore the tidal flats. She caught baby green crabs and Jonah crabs. She let them walk over the palm of her hand like pet spiders. One year, Christa did have a pet spider. A big garden spider had built a broad web across the T-bar clothesline behind the house. Christa had never seen such a beautiful spider. It had a bright yellow starburst across its back. Orb weavers sometimes devour their own webs every morning, just to rebuild them at nightfall. But this one maintained the same web in the exact location, mending any holes. Christa went to the big web twenty times a day to admire the spider. Its stillness. Its perfect indifference to her was what seemed so attractive. She wiggled the pole to make the web bounce, but the spider ignored her. Christa decided to catch moths, flies, crickets, mosquito hawks, and she carefully tossed these offerings into the gauzy wheel. Sometimes her gifts escaped, but more often her pet spider charged to the squirming bread-and-butter gift, wrapping it up in a foamy hanky for a later snack.

Her mother told her, "I've seen everything now." Gloria hovered around Christa, always feeling a little lost in Truro, her husband's stomping ground. The Worthingtons didn't accept Gloria. "She was a really short, I guess you'd say 'petite,' Italian woman who wasn't classy enough for Toppy," Kim Gibson said. "Toppy had gone to college, Gloria had never been given the chance. Christa's mom told me, 'My in-laws ignore me.'"

Christa's friend Steve Radlauer said, "The Worthingtons thought Gloria was intruding on their patrician world. She was bohemian, a painter, and socially awkward, too." Gloria tried to fit in, to "look WASP." Although Toppy was growing more resistant to family pressure to keep up the patrician mystique, Gloria tried to adapt. A friend said, "She was trying too hard—that's like shooting yourself in the foot." In the fifties, Gloria had had a rhinoplasty when few women were getting "nose jobs." Years later, when she was dying from cancer, the doctors had difficulty inserting oxygen tubing due to scar tissue and adhesions in her nasal passages.

When Christa was a girl, Gloria bleached Christa's hair. She wanted her daughter to look 100 percent Anglo, and she was careful to watch for Christa's roots growing in darker than the rest of her head. When she needed a touch-up, Gloria would take out a bottle of peroxide and a toothbrush and scrub Christa's scalp where her hair was parted. Gloria had many issues about her ethnic identity. Her family name was changed from Santosossa to Sanders. She was "Gloria Sanders Worthington." But even with her sanitized alias, she was always a little too bohemian for Toppy. As a girl, she had lived in a working-class neighborhood west of the Route 128 beltway. She moved into Cambridge, where she started painting. "She was an excellent portrait painter," said John Cornachio, at the Scituate Art Association where Gloria had showed her work. "We had a portrait group that met every Monday morning. We'd get volunteers to model. It was more about having a place and finding a model to sit. She worked in pastels. She was very good with textures. She talked a lot about her husband. Her husband was a character. When she talked about him I used to say, 'You should be on television with the stories you tell. You could call the show *The Bickersons*.'" Gloria complained to the art group that Toppy was always riding his bicycle, at the drop of a hat he would disappear for hours. He told Gloria that he rode to 'the library,' but she didn't always believe him. His ten-speed was never in the bike stand.

Cornachio said, "I met him when Gloria was ill. I brought flowers over to her home, a gift from the Art Association. He didn't have much to say.

I met him again at her memorial service. He didn't seem to be a man in mourning. My wife noticed it, too."

Toppy's blank indifference might have been construed as the common impenetrable Yankee countenance, but in fact his affair with Porter was in high gear and his mind was elsewhere. His separation from Gloria had been a long-earned, even a lifelong process.

In the last year of Gloria's illness, Toppy took a job as some sort of courier, at least that's what he had told his wife. He drove off every day. He had met Porter in a shoe store. Gloria was surprised to find boxes of new footwear crowding the floor of his closet. Gloria had told Christa, "Why does he need so many new shoes? Where's he going to wear all these different pairs of shoes?"

When she had married Toppy, Gloria was already pregnant. A friend said, "She was no spring chicken when she had had Christa, and after the baby, she spent so much effort trying to maintain her youthful looks." Christa's friend Ellen Webb said, "Because she was a 'mistake,' Christa always felt responsible for forcing her parents together. She knew they were too different. But Christa's mother was a toughie—a lot of strong energy. She was such a *little* woman. Christa once showed me one of her mom's tiny blouses. Like doll clothes. We were in awe of it. But Gloria was a little powerhouse with big soulful eyes."

Toppy was unsociable, almost invisible, and because Gloria drove her VW bug with her miniature poodles, Louie and Happy, yipping on the dashboard, and she was known to take in feral cats and kittens, people in Crow Point thought Gloria too eccentric. At the Mahoney Studio, where she attended a portrait workshop, her fellow classmates thought she was both "a sweet person" and "a little peculiar." One member of the portrait workshop, Kay Shaw, said, "We'd bring a sack lunch. Gloria would unwrap a parsley sandwich. Just parsley and two slices of bread, without any butter or mayo. She was trying to keep svelte."

Gloria tried to find her niche in a patrician world where Jackie Kennedy's slight build was suddenly considered the sublime standard for the feminine physique. Jackie had usurped the Marilyn Monroe body ideal. Women wanted to look like Jackie. Adding to this impossible burden, Gloria went prematurely gray and had to dye her hair black. Kim

Gibson said, "She dressed in black. It made her feel skinny, but she looked like she was always in mourning." She spent a good deal of energy "keeping herself up," as she pampered Christa and encouraged her daughter's hypochondria.

Gloria kept Christa home from school if she had the slightest sniffle. She went to work in Boston and left Christa at home alone to lie about, watch TV, and play the piano. When Christa started to have her period, she'd miss school every month. Kim Gibson's family tried to take Christa under their wing. On Sundays, Christa started going to the Episcopal church with Kim. Toppy and Gloria didn't attend. Gloria's own mother died when she was young, and her father took a new wife who was a Jehovah's Witness. Her stepmother's religion was a turnoff to Gloria, and she avoided the church after that.

Christa's friends speak of her difficult childhood with her parents. Her girlhood friend and lifelong confidante Gail Motlin is a pharmacist and widowed mother with two young children. She has balanced insights and an understanding of Christa's childhood. She knew that Christa's mother had worked, and Christa's parents were removed from the fabric of the neighborhood, when other parenting couples were more visible. Gail said, "Her mother is where to start if you want to understand how Christa got messed up. Her mother was a wreck. Both her parents were difficult, but her mother was the victim." Kim agreed that Christa's parents were both "very eccentric people. They stayed together for Christa but lived very separate lives." Kim said that Toppy used to drink, and she was nervous to go over to do homework with Christa because Christa's father would yell from the other room when he wanted a refill, "Gloria! Get me another one—now!"

Christa said she always feared coming home and finding her father's car parked diagonally across the lawn. That meant he was three sheets to the wind. She tiptoed into the house so she wouldn't disturb his "unwinding" process. If he didn't have Gloria nearby, he'd interrogate Christa for whatever minor infractions he might notice from where he was sitting. "Why is that window open?" "Who left the light burning?" "The bottle opener isn't where I left it. It doesn't have legs, does it?"

Christa's mother tried to stay out of his way.

Her parents rarely socialized with other couples. Even in an era known for suburban harmony, when neighborhoods had barbecues, organized picnics, bridge clubs, and block parties, Christa's folks were invisible.

Kim's mother, Laura, asked Gloria to come along on a train trip to Vancouver and the Canadian Rockies. Gloria accepted the invitation. Kim's mom said Gloria was fun to be with, she had a very dry wit. This rubbed off on Christa. But Kim's mom was bewildered to see that for the weeklong train trip, Gloria had brought only one pair of panties, and every night she washed them in the little sink and put them on the radiator to dry. It was some remnant of frugality from her ethnic background. She didn't buy panties by the dozens. Hearing this, I thought of O'Keefe's photo of Christa's double bed sprinkled with rows of Victoria's Secret underthings.

Toppy's drinking had a lasting effect on Christa. Not a drinker herself, when she moved back to the Cape, Christa went to Al-Anon meetings for children of alcoholics. There she saw Helen Miranda Wilson, the daughter of Edmund Wilson, who had also been a drinker. Because of her father's affliction, Helen Miranda Wilson developed an exaggerated aversion to spirits. She says she's "allergic" to wine. She won't even eat grapes. At dinner parties, she grills the hostess, "Are there any grapes in this dish?" Helen doesn't want to see a grape anywhere in the place. Tim Arnold said, "These two had similar personality traits, but even Christa wasn't as extreme." No one is as Wagnerian as Helen Miranda Wilson.

When Toppy stopped drinking, he soon fell victim to another compulsion: he started cycling.

He quickly became addicted to trekking long distances on his ten-speed. He never got off his bike, it was like a portable hamster wheel. He never stopped pedaling. He didn't just take casual bike rides, he disappeared on his bicycle for long outings. He rode out to the coastal peninsula of Hull, and he circled its arm repeatedly to avoid going home. He took overnight trips throughout New England.

Belinda Oliver, who met Christa at the University of East Anglia during Christa's junior year abroad from Vassar, remembers the tension she had felt when she visited Christa in the States. "Being in Hingham gave me an insight into Christa's family background. Christa's mother put on a gala meal for us—slaving over lobster and the rest of the spread for hours. Meanwhile, her father regaled us with his cycling exploits, demonstrating his cycling glasses complete with rearview mirror, and laboriously showing us all of his cycling picture albums."

Toppy wore his cycling glasses and showed Belinda and his daughter how he would make defensive maneuvers on his bicycle if he found himself in unpredictable traffic. When the dinner was on the table, Belinda sat down with Christa and Toppy, but Christa's mother didn't join them. Belinda said she had the feeling Gloria was "crouching in the hallway," or maybe she'd just gone to bed. "Christa was mortified. She laughed it off, but it must have been very painful."

Belinda said that Christa's parents had always embarrassed her. She didn't think they were normal. But, in Truro, Belinda met Christa's grandparents, Pop and Tiny. "They were a great couple. Tiny was imposing and outspoken. Pop was quiet, but firm, a little deaf. Tiny told us about her fishnet business and demonstrated the versatility of her products. It was kind of like Toppy showing us his cycling glasses. But Christa loved her grandparents without reservation. She was relaxed and happy in their company. But it wasn't that simple."

Belinda described how Christa felt within the rest of the Worthington family. "Christa's branch was the poor relation. Not so much in money terms but in standing." Other friends have said that Christa had talked about a chasm between her parents and her paternal grandparents. And Christa had always felt ignored, even snubbed by some of her cousins. As an only child, Christa desperately wanted to fit in. Christa felt "in" the family but not "of" it, an anxiety she would again suffer from working in the fashion industry.

Belinda said, "Her mother often presented herself as having a distant, arty air." Whether it was hostile or merely a self-protective mechanism, Gloria kept her distance when she was surrounded by Toppy's unwelcoming clan. Gloria developed her own circle of "art friends," and showed her paintings at the Scituate Art Association, where she found acceptance.

Another friend explained, "The deal with her dad was that he is just an awkward guy. He never really seemed to find his place, never did that well professionally, never fulfilled his promise. He was part of that WASPy generation that was supposed to inherit wealth and go along comfortably. Then Christa hit that cusp and had to work harder than she was brought up to believe she had to."

Christa had learned how to throw up a wall around herself just like her mother had done. Tim Arnold said, "Gloria was difficult, a perfectionist, hypercritical." And, like Gloria, Tim said, Christa was always finding fault, making judgments, pushing people away by making pronouncements and relentless intellectual observations. Her strict appraisals and caveats, her voluminous critiques, emerged in her writing, but she made the same harsh criticisms as she watched Tim stir soup, sort mail, or chop carrots. Tim said, "She would be critical because it made her feel better. It was a family-learned thing. Christa's anxiety was turned up so high that she found everything around her wrong. She was bossy. She would criticize the little things she could control, to fight her anxiety about things she couldn't control."

Her father's behavior was something she couldn't curtail. Toppy's secret life extended beyond his cycling exploits. He sought relationships with women even before Porter. Once, when Christa was in high school, her mother showed her a snapshot of a blonde and buxom ketty that she had found in Toppy's wallet. Together they stared at the dog-eared snapshot. In Christa's eyes, her mother had suddenly plummeted down a level, into an arena where she stood side by side with her daughter, in a house of betrayals.

When Christa saw the snapshot, the safe haven of childhood dissolved like Kleenex in a glass of water. Toppy's indiscretions were just one facet of her family's disintegration.

Gloria turned to painting to remove herself, both from the Worthington mythology and from her husband's wrongdoings. Gloria worked on her paintings obsessively to create exactly what she wanted to see. Her landscapes were almost surreal because of the intensity of the colors she used. Her portraits also seemed charged by something more than the subject who sat for her, and in her work one sensed Gloria's desperate secrets, her brutal isolation and buried feelings. But her mother's industrious example gave Christa a discerning eye and she learned to hone her critical skills from her mother's intense impatience with anything that fell below her impenetrable, private standard. More than the piano lessons, ballet classes, or all of the extras her parents provided, it was Christa's inquisitiveness, her razory viewpoint, sometimes defensive, but always highly alert, that made Christa turn to writing. Just like painting, writing begins on the reverse screen of the retina. Like Gloria, Christa was rarely happy with what fell in front of her. She wasn't ever seeing what she wanted to see—not until she was face-to-face with Ava.

One of Christa's college boyfriends, David Brophy, had once met Gloria in Poughkeepsie. He said, "Christa's mother was really peculiar. There was a picnic at Vassar on Parents' Day. We said only two words to one another, but Gloria was unforgettable. She was trying too hard. She was trying to be beautiful and young. Trying to compete with Christa."

VASSAR GIRLS DO GREAT THINGS

In high school, Christa was voted most popular. Her friend Gail Motlin said that Christa was a central member of the Crow Point gang, kids who were a little wilder, more adventurous. They were called "the cool kids" but, in fact, some of them were disenfranchised loners, and were soon to be future "Friends of Bill." Amyra Chase saw Christa drifting into trouble and she became someone Christa could entrust with feverish secrets and distressing details of her adolescent exploits. Amyra wasn't afraid to criticize Christa's bad choices or mistakes, and Christa depended on Amyra's honesty, even if she didn't always take her friend's advice. Amyra would later tell Christa that she disapproved of Christa's meanderings with married men, especially when Christa had started seeing Tony Jackett. These arrangements can only backfire. Amyra had married and was raising kids, and she warned Christa about the complex repercussions that Christa's role as "the other woman" might create for her and for the unsuspecting family members of her paramour. Christa didn't always listen, but Amyra's straightforwardness was a reliable solace to Christa; Amyra never backed down.

The Hingham High School yearbook listed Christa as the girl with "the prettiest smile." She was a cheerleader. She wrote for the high school literary magazine, *Pegasus*. Christa played piano, sometimes classical pieces, but she also could bang out top-forty tunes. A friend said, "Everybody looked up to her. She was a natural beauty. She was smart. She loved to dance. She had everything going for her. But, later, her taste in men! She went for guys who were handsome and buff, but they were losers. It didn't take me long to figure it out. She didn't have a good role model in her parents."

Christa had her first sexual encounter on a class trip abroad to Spain, a

privilege awarded to students in the accelerated program at Hingham
Junior High School. One sultry evening in Madrid she went out with a
couple of her friends unchaperoned. They were immediately shadowed
and hounded by a group of young men. She disappeared for an hour with
a handsome twenty-something boy who bragged that he was a count and
a race car driver. She was impressed by his story and listened to his tall
tales as he nibbled her neck. She allowed him to lead her away from the
group. In a thicket of fig trees, he kissed her. He explored her body with
his fingertips in a deft, focused, almost technical examination that for
some reason reminded her of the piano tuner who often came to her
house in Hingham. He bent over the piano to adjust complex levers, wip-
pens and dampers, testing the action of each key. With the faux count, she
felt her body begin to resonate at his touch, her nerves begin to vibrate
like piano wire. She didn't protest. Then, he tugged her hand and gloved
it upon his penis. She was alarmed at its transformation, surprised by its
girth and heat. Being completely green, it was her first introduction to the
physiology of sex. Before then, she had thought that a penis was a floppy
thing, like a monkey sock. Not like this. It was rigid, difficult to interpret
and to manipulate. It was like her father's bicycle pump! She jumped to
her feet and ran back to her classmates. She told her friends about the "re-
pulsion" she felt for the opposite sex, but her fury came from her own impatience. She had hated to be so uninformed, and to be left still feeling
curious. Curiosity made her feel anxious and incomplete. The "count"
who raced cars had made her feel stupid and this was the worst offense.

But later that year, Christa met a boy in her seventh-grade class in
Hingham who would give her her first tutorials. Friends say that this boy
was "the love of her life Number 1." John Wotjacinski was an attractive kid
with long shoulder-length hair, and a wiry physique. He was barely 95
pounds at the time and topped out at only 120 in high school. He was
one of five brothers in a local family, whose father ran a successful fish-
processing business in Hingham. John's father had known Pop Worthington from the Cold Storage plant in Truro. John's mother was ill and he, his
brothers, and one sister were raised by their grandmother. He told me, "My
grandmother loved Christa."

John said, "Christa was a standout. She had thick, rich, gold hair and was about as cute a package as you could want. Bright, serious, she was challenging intellectually, but I guess I had this great physical attraction to her."

John had met Christa when she was still living in Bradley Woods, but when her family moved to Crow Point, he lived directly up the hill from her house. He said, "Crow Point had so many places we could get away to. We would hang down at the sea wall and escape from our parents." He said that Christa was "standoffish with her father. Their relationship was very distant, chill. It grew out of his treatment of Gloria. Toppy was so demanding and abusive. It was chronic. It was de rigueur for him to be waited on hand and foot. I remember how he had a way of enunciating his commands, always at his convenience and leisure. I don't doubt that she pulled his shorts on in the morning. Gloria was just a slave.

"You can't call it dysfunctional because it *functioned* for such a long time."

John and Christa were very close in junior high school. In ninth grade, John transferred to a local private school, Thayer Academy, where writers Malcolm Cowley and John Cheever had once attended, although Cheever had been expelled. Even though he didn't see Christa in school, John and Christa remained "a couple." Summers he went to the Pamet with Christa and stayed in Pop Worthington's barn or at the Little House. He said that being in Truro with Christa are some of his fondest recollections. "I guess these memories are idealized. There's nothing like being an adolescent in love." He said that it was "one glorious summer between eighth and ninth grade" when he and Christa consummated their relationship. "She was a sweet and complicated person. I loved her deeply," he said.

He continued, "I spent a lot of time at her house. She played the piano as her mother painted or colored in pastels. I loved being in that house, looking out at the water, as Christa played Mozart. I think that's why I love classical music and listen to it in my office."

In her senior year, Christa became pregnant. Her health teacher had recently explained to the class, "A girl is just a flowerpot." Boys were told to think of this "flowerpot" any time they got carried away. Christa figured that they didn't give the boys at Thayer Academy the same practical lesson.

John said, "It was a painful decision for us. But we were unanimous." Christa had an abortion just before her high school graduation. They continued to see one another when Christa was at Vassar and he was enrolled at BU. He went to Poughkeepsie on weekends, but he saw that their bond was fraying. Friends say that for years to come, whenever one of Christa's many love affairs went bust, she had always pined for John. In her postmortems, she would tell her old friends that she wished they had ended up together.

But John eventually married a very stunning blonde named Toni. Learning this, Christa had felt a simmering rivalry. Friends say that "a real blonde" was demoralizing to Christa. Kim Gibson said, "It's funny there was a 'Tony' or a 'Toni' at both ends of Christa's life." And, like Jackett, John is from a fishing family. But John's is a white-collar position. He owns a seafood-processing plant, Atlantic Sea Cove, where he imports and distributes swordfish, tuna, sea bass, grouper, and snapper, in volume. He jets on business trips, and bikes through the Andes. His company imports from all over the world, China, South America, Indonesia. When I asked him if he was hated by local fishermen, he said, "Their hate is focused on the regulators. Besides, my other company, AB Seafood, processes domestic ground fish. We have a seat on the auction floor in Gloucester."

Christa would go on to date patricians, wealthy do-nothings, two-timing scions. And she would have her fair share of bohemian wastrels, art cons, a magician, none of whom were the genuine article. But John's Purex blue to white-collar background, connected to fishing, an all-American supply and demand industry, was the example Christa felt a strong sentimental attraction to. Her grandfather Pop Worthington had been the archetype. He was the catalyst for Christa's romantic fascination with the solid, entrepreneurial fisherman. As John settled down to raise a family with Toni and to run his import and distribution business in Hingham, Christa told friends she envied John and Toni's situation. It was so much like what Pop and Tiny Worthington had had.

John has a photograph. He's sitting on his motorcycle in front of Christa's house on Downer Avenue. He says, "It's my BSA 650 'Lightning.' I loved that bike. In the picture, I have my leather jacket on, and my arm's around Christa. Gloria was very fearful. She hated me to take Christa on the bike. In fact, I wrecked that one."

Christa's friends say that John Wotjacinski was "an overall great guy." But in the next years, in her dating career, Christa seemed most comfortable with less sterling prospects. She'd attach herself to the dispossessed and choose men who had a little glitch, so if the relationship didn't survive, she wouldn't have to blame herself. She was attracted to ground-up people. Tim Arnold said, "Toppy, too, went toward chaos with Porter. It was almost a political statement. They wanted to lose the Worthingtons."

In 1973, Christa enrolled at Vassar College in Poughkeepsie, New York. Writer Mary McCarthy, author of the notable books *The Group* and *Memories of a Catholic Girlhood,* had attended Vassar in the thirties. In her essay "The Vassar Woman," she describes the college as "less intellectual than Radcliffe and Bryn Mawr, less social and 'weekendish' than Smith, less athletic than Wellesley and less bohemian than Bennington." So, what is Vassar all about? McCarthy writes, "Vassar can stand for whatever is felt to be wrong with the modern female: Humanism, atheism, Communism, short skirts, cigarettes, psychiatry." McCarthy could have been describing Christa when she says that a girl "will have chosen Vassar in all probability with the idea of transcending her background." McCarthy describes the effect Vassar teachers hope to evoke in a young Vassar woman. Vassar teachers seek to "shake her up," "emancipate" her, make her "think for herself." This dynamic conception of education is "Vassar's Hallmark."

Christa's models were Tiny and Gloria. Both women had tried with varying degrees of success to etch out a niche for herself or to find her own mountaintop in a world of men. Gloria had difficulty "fitting in" to the patriarchal WASP landscape where Toppy had pastured her, and where he himself lived distractedly. But Tiny had always been her own buggy driver; she held the double reins of being female, being both matriarch and businesswoman. To Christa, her grandmother's independence seemed all-in-one.

A good thing about Vassar, one could leave Poughkeepsie and get to New York City by train before she had digested her lunch. McCarthy writes, "New York, plays, concerts, night clubs, Fifth Avenue bus rides— all this seemed to foretell four years of Renaissance lavishness, in an academy that was a Forest of Arden and a Fifth Avenue department store combined." But when Christa first arrived on campus and she walked through Vassar's famous Taylor Gate, with its tall iron tines that could look like a giant upended mousetrap or a catapult for Amazon warfare, depending on a girl's frame of mind, Christa was overwhelmed. She spent her first days at college hiding in her dorm.

Christa was savvy in her negotiations with Admissions counselors, and she snagged a single room as a freshman. She complained about her intense menstrual cramps. She told them that she had to sit in the bathtub during the first day of her period to relieve her pain. But in a single, she could make a cocoon for herself, with room for only one. Gail Motlin said, "In her first year she fell into despair. She had been the queen of her high school, but her first year at college she was depressed and couldn't get out of bed." But her classmates remember how Christa always aced her final exams. She would procrastinate until the last minute, then she'd borrow someone's extra Dexedrine or if she couldn't find someone with a prescription, she'd buy NO DOZ, and like a long-haul trucker, she'd stay up all night to study. Christa never turned in a paper on time, but when she finally had it finished, she'd walk up to her professor with a smile that could melt Shackleton pack ice. Gail Motlin said, "If she couldn't turn in her freshman assignments, how would she ever meet deadlines when she later became a writer?" New York friend Steve Radlauer did say that when Christa was writing fashion journalism, "She was always deadline-crazed."

An English major at Vassar, Christa studied with Colson Johnson, who remembers that Christa received a very good grade in his senior seminar, but he can't remember much about her. She took a course in surrealism taught by visiting professor Michael Benedict. Barbara Page taught classes in modernism and was the Woolf scholar at Vassar. Christa's senior essay was on Virginia Woolf, but Page says she, too, can't remember having Christa in her classes. Christa's classmate Carole Maso said, "Christa and I were in a lot of classes together. I can see why Barbara can't remember her. Christa was very quiet, unassuming, studious, very serious. I guess you might say she was shy, or protective. She always seemed to be protecting something. Maybe it was her decorum, a little mix of shyness and patrician decorum. It was kind of a relief, really, when other girls are so bent on confessing every little problem. With Christa, there was a sense of polite disapproval, not unkind, but certainly judgmental, dissatisfied. It was just part of who she was."

Nancy Willard taught creative writing at Vassar, and Maso said, "There was a handful of us who wanted to be great writers, and Christa was in that group." Maso went on to publish several novels. Years later, when Maso saw Christa in Provincetown, she said that she thought "Christa looked so together, so fashiony. She had a glamorous job in Paris, I was envious. But Christa told me that she had all this regret and sadness about not being a real writer. She wanted to write a book. She knew she hadn't done any of the hard work, and fashion writing wasn't satisfying."

Maso said, "I recognized her as a sensitive, talented person who couldn't get to the thing that might save her."

When Christa was at Vassar, men were a fraction of the student body, only four hundred men in a class of twenty-three hundred. Christa had no trouble winning attention from a handful of gorgeous boys on campus, but after usually very brief entanglements, she shrugged them off.

When Christa arrived at Vassar, the senior class president dressed in drag and called himself "Jack St. James." Christa's classmate Jay Mulvaney said, "Jack St. James had Shirley Temple hair and looked luscious and funny with a bare midriff. He was sprinkled with glitter." It was the latter days of "glam rock" when Bowie and Iggy Pop wore androgynous costumes. Several male Vassar students performed cross-gender gags.

Jay Mulvaney, the author of *Diana & Jackie: Maidens, Mothers, Myths,* a book that Dominick Dunne praised for revealing the "extraordinary parallels between their front-page famous lives," and that *Publishers Weekly* called "irresistibly readable," also published two other books on the Kennedys. Jay was in a tight group of about eight drama students at Vassar and Christa tagged along. He said, "She was a receptive audience. She was very low-key, quiet, but there was something off-kilter about her sensibility which was good. Her sense of humor was sharp; she was spritely, even fey. She would *get* it."

Mulvaney said that Christa never wanted center stage. She let her drama student friends be the stars and didn't compete with them. He was from Watertown, Massachusetts, and they sometimes shared a ride in and out of the Boston area. He said, "I was a scholarship student and I felt really separate from all the rich kids. I felt that great divide, but not with Christa. There was something really accepting about her. I don't want to say 'earth mother' because that's the wrong visual."

David Brophy felt the same acceptance. He said, "At Vassar I was rubbing shoulders with millionaires. There were climbers at Vassar. I hung out with these wealthy scions but I never got the impression from Christa that she felt she was a blue blood."

For Christa, Vassar College was both a nurturing cloister and a feverish "fuck den." Typical of most college campuses in the seventies, Vassar students experimented with alcohol, drugs, and sex. Christa didn't often indulge in booze or dope. She borrowed "uppers" when she crammed, but she wasn't a pothead, and she wasn't an acid casualty. A good friend tells a story about Christa's naïveté or innocence with controlled substances. He said, "I used to live with my better half in a rambling farmhouse in the Catskills. We had blowout weekends and Christa was a regular. She was a terrible driver and she'd always get lost. One time, a friend brought some mushrooms and we all took some. Christa hadn't arrived yet. She was lost again. We had wanted to wait for her so we wouldn't be tripping and out of sync with her, but she was late. So we took a lethal dose and were pretty far gone, when lo and behold, here comes Christa's Honda Civic. She comes in. We didn't want her to know we had indulged, and we tried to pretend we were straight. It was awkward. She was too perceptive and we finally had to say, 'Christa, we took these mushrooms!' "

He said that Christa asked him to give her some. He said that it wasn't that she wanted to get high, but she didn't want to rain on their parade. "She didn't want to dampen our psychedelic blitz so she took a tiny dose to keep us company. The little bit she sampled couldn't have done anything, but she immediately *pretended* to be high. She said the funniest things. She looked at the windows, which had curtains way too short, and she said, 'I don't feel like my *hem* reaches all the way down to my *sill*.' " Her remark seemed like the perfect assessment of her friends, who were teetering thralls to the mushroom.

Like Jay Mulvaney's belief that Christa was a "receptive audience," a sprite who helped the party flow along, her voluntary mushroom trip was an offering of "self" more than it was a desire to experiment with drugs.

Another Vassar classmate, Jody Cohen, said that Christa might not have been a big drinker or drug user, but she said, "Christa was cool. Christa always looked together. She didn't wear expensive clothes, but she always looked different. She wore tall boots, and those bohemian high-necked sweaters. And Christa knew how to talk to men."

Christa had her share of college romances. David Brophy said, "I was one of very few men at Vassar. It wasn't as bad as being a transfer student at Smith, but I was in only the third graduating class at Vassar—the odds were pretty good. I love women. I loved Vassar."

Brophy said that he and Christa were classmates in an English-lit seminar together. "Christa was a goddess. Bright, articulate, sweet but not a pushover. She had a childlike look about her, endearing, in that she had these big eyes. I read a magazine article about young animals and baby humans. They have these helpless, big eyes and high foreheads, *so their parents don't eat them.*

"I'm not going to paint her as a sad sack. There certainly were more lighthearted people. But there was that wistfulness, that unrequited thing, even then. She always had a serious sobriety. With her Anglophilism, we hit it off. We dated for a while. It was not for very long; what should I say—we were friends afterward."

Mulvaney said that Christa's breakup with Brophy "hit her hard."

Brophy said, "It just didn't work out, but we managed to remain friends. I went to a party at her Gramercy Park place after college. The last time I saw her was ten years ago in my apartment. I made dinner for her. Christa was an editor at one of those glossy lipstick ad magazines—I don't know which one, she brought me a copy, *Elle*, maybe, one of the big glamour-puss magazines. Which is not to demean it. I had her come to dinner to pick her brain, I guess. We were chatting about life, careers; mine was in a shambles. She gave me good advice. She put me in touch with Ben Brantley, who was at *Vanity Fair*. That was very nice of her. It was before Brantley had started writing for the *New York Times*. He was not a theater critic then, but he was very kind to talk to me, and I'm sure it was drudgery to give me tips, but he was very gracious. Christa was kind to help me with what I thought was my next career move.

"I told her she seemed to be doing well, but I sensed something about her. A little sadness. There was something going on behind her eyes. She was a little wistful, a little unrequited. She expressed her frustration: 'Well, I should have at least two books written by now, if I was going to be a real writer.' She was a little self-deprecating about her fashion career. Later, she called me and asked me to go to some glam function that she wanted me to squire her to, but I declined. I couldn't make it, honestly I couldn't. I hope she didn't think I was blowing her off.

· "When she was killed, I read somewhere that she sought out abusive men who were shitheads. I could say, yeah, that's me. We had a fling. And it ended. But she was a cutie, why wouldn't I jump her bones?"

David Brophy wasn't alone when he said, "I've met more lighthearted people." At Vassar, Hugh Cosman dated Christa, and he said, "She was extremely sweet, but a profoundly sad person. She was very much damaged goods. I guess it was her family baggage. She was a melancholiac—no, I shouldn't say that. But she was melancholy. That's a beautiful word, isn't it? Melancholy? It didn't work out, but she never reproached me for not wanting to be her boyfriend. But it was like this—remember Nelson Algren's famous three rules?

" 'Never play cards with someone named Doc; never eat at a restaurant called Mom's; and never sleep with anyone whose problems are bigger than your own.' "

In 1975, Christa went to Norwich, England, to spend her junior year abroad at the University of East Anglia. UEA was established in the early sixties as one of England's new "campus universities" based on the American model. Its architect, who had designed the Royal National Theater on the South Bank, was famous for what critics called "concrete brutalism." The buildings were naked concrete; both offices and classrooms were built of unpainted "breeze block." The central structure was a zigzag wall of offices and classrooms, almost a quarter-mile in length. Student housing was called the Ziggurat, after the ancient Assyrians' temple, a terraced pyramid. But wind and rain came straight off the North Sea and the cement-block buildings were dreary. Rooms on the ground level of the dormitory abutted a river meadow and were often invaded by flocks of geese. Geese waddled through the halls and turned up in unexpected places, in closets and in lavatories, a welcome comic distraction from day to day.

Other diversions were few. The drinking age was eighteen, and students spent a good amount of time in the Student Union tavern or marching down a straight line of pubs that dotted the road from campus all the way into town. Christa preferred to wander through the Castle Market in Norwich, a congestion of distinctive antiques and junk shops that sold everything from handmade table linens, soap, sweets, raw wool, rare teas, hammered-tin jewelry, retro gizmos, and curiosities.

Christa felt an immediate connection to the medieval town of Norwich. She admired its famous twelfth-century Norman cathedral, and was in awe of its grave statistics during the years of the Black Death, in the fourteenth century. But, most of all, she was impressed because she had learned that Norwich had been a great center for Puritan revolution. Rebels had smashed the stained-glass windows of all the churches before they migrated to Lincoln, then to Holland, and hence to Provincetown and Plymouth. The UEA campus was on the Yare River, which emptied at the town of Yarmouth—the familiar name of a mid-Cape community. And, in fact, many villages in Norfolk County and throughout England had inspired the names of beloved Cape Cod towns. Only fifteen miles from campus was the original Hingham, the hamlet that Christa's hometown had chosen to ink in when it was incorporated. Hingham, England, is famous for being the birthplace of Abe Lincoln's grandparents. Dirt-poor farmers, they emigrated to America to produce a favorite son.

Soon after her arrival, Christa had asked a classmate to drive her through Hingham's sister town. Of course, she would often visit London, which was a little over a hundred miles from the UEA campus, but Truro was in Cornwall County, at the opposite end of England, and that would be a five-hour drive.

At UEA, Christa met writers Malcolm Bradbury and Angus Wilson, who had launched the UK's first creative-writing program at East Anglia, when other renowned academic institutions in Britain still thought creative writing a frivolity. Novelists Ian McEwan and Kazuo Ishiguro were the program's first offspring, both of whom were on campus during

Christa's year abroad. McEwan's first book, *First Love, Last Rites*, had just come out and was a sensation. His success proved Bradbury's statement, "You can't teach someone to be a writer, but if you have talent, a program can knock off six or seven years of struggle." It was an exciting environment for an American student. Helen McNeil, a professor in the School of English and American Studies at UEA, said that Christa's workload would have required rigorous essay writing. "Unlike Oxford or Cambridge, UEA had a concentrated emphasis in writing. At least two thirty-thousand-word essays were expected in each eight-week term. The really top essay had a kind of sparkle, a verbal elan, a *sprezzatura* or gaiety that comes from tremendous intellectual confidence." She said that British students "were still gender-divided in the classroom. The young men monopolized conversation in seminar while the women held their fire; but the women would write very long, elaborate essays." Christa's writing was honed and tested during her year abroad at East Anglia University. Christa began to exhibit that kind of confidence McNeil describes. From early in her academic career, Christa's writing showed the lucidity and finesse she would display in her fashion journalism in the years to come.

At UEA, Christa met two British coeds, Barbara Holloway and Belinda Oliver, who became lifelong friends. Barbara Holloway had been the *original* name penned on a codicil to Christa's will when Christa had first drawn up official plans for Ava's guardianship. Her revision, naming Amyra Chase as Ava's caretaker, was a later development.

Belinda remembered meeting Christa at Norwich. She said, "Christa was with a merry crew of Americans—mostly men. She was brown as a berry and freckled, with a wayward mane of nut-brown hair, and a brown duffel coat to match. She wowed the men and entranced us all. Although she sometimes seemed confused and tormented, she was more often luminous. I never saw her luminous again, except maybe when she was back on the Cape."

At UEA, Christa was very much part of the group, yet somehow always apart. Her friends say that Christa didn't want to be consumed by group dynamics and often disappeared without warning. Belinda said, "Dependency issues seemed very big. She wanted to be completely independent. Her whole life, she never even shared an apartment. She'd let someone squat for a while, but she never wanted another person's name on a lease."

Christa dated a few different classmates when she studied abroad. She met a young man who was born in America but had been raised in Wales. He had just returned to UEA from a year in the States at Brandeis University. Christa called him her "Welshman." Her friends from UEA see a similarity in Christa's Welshman and Tony Jackett, her "harbormaster." Their wild hair. Their coloring. Their physicality. "The Welshman" was a gifted actor and quite a dancer. Barbara Holloway said that they all loved to dance and had grown up on soul music. "Christa and I really bonded dancing to Motown. She was poetry in motion. I was also very impressed by her wardrobe of leotards and wraparound skirts, years before anyone else in Europe had found warm-up clothes fashionable enough to wear to parties.

"She'd come to my room. She taught me how to do the hustle to George McCrae as I counseled her on the Welshman's emotional insecurities. With men, Christa took no prisoners when it came to standards. She expected an awful lot and it was hard for men to live up to her expectations. She always had a drama going on."

Christa met another student at UEA who was to become a lifelong friend and confidant. He spoke on condition of anonymity and said, "Christa and I met at UEA. We dated for five seconds. No big deal. Everyone, at that time, was in flux."

Himself a journalist, her friend said, "The ultimate intellectual straitjacket that consistently made it difficult for Christa was that she got that Vassar indoctrination and although she turned it into a literary persona, she never quite attained in her journalism that intellectual dimension."

But during her year in England, Christa was pleased when Angus Wilson invited her to his annual party. She was singled out from many other students who vied for the honor. Wilson had seen a sparkle on the pages she had written in class, or perhaps he had thought her charming and a delightful party attraction, but Christa was excited by the invitation. She wandered through Wilson's bohemian antique house, where he lived with his partner. The house had interesting artwork and bric-a-brac, but was impossible to heat and every room had its own weird, oddball electric radiator, each with a distinct anthropomorphic persona.

McNeil said, "Visiting Angus would have been, for Christa, like visiting Woolf's eccentric hangout in Sussex, where the walls were painted red." Christa aspired to be accepted in a literary circle of serious writers, and when she attended Wilson's soiree, she drank it up like ambrosia. But these highly charged literary events were few and far between, and would soon take a backseat to the fashionista flings where she'd be a regular on the guest lists for the next two decades.

Christa took a walk into town, happy to leave her oppressive breeze block confines at the university for the rich Georgian architecture of Norwich, which is one of the last intact medieval cities in England. Students liked to meet at a pub called the Ten Bells. Christa liked the name of the place, but she walked past the landmark. The Norfolk landscape is flat, and for centuries it had been a farming empire. The fields and pastures were symmetrical squares separated by lines of oak trees. She had been told that her very own Truro's moors and highlands looked similar to the topography of Cornwall, but she still hadn't found someone to take her there. The motorway hadn't been opened yet, and the drive would be rigorous.

In the overcast, the English landscape was dreary. It had the flat tonality of a basic tube of paint, the standard Payne's Grey, a staple you can find on every artist's palette. As she trekked, she lost track of destination points. Some people might say she looked "lost," but how can you be lost when you purposefully embark on a getaway journey? Her whole life sometimes seemed like a getaway plan that she constantly revised and remapped, just to start out again.

She thought adulthood should be like walking across a river on stepping-stones that sink away behind you—you can't turn back. She could never flee from her mother's feverish expectations, from her father's conflicted paralysis and distance. Even here, across the Atlantic, she tried to shove off, but she'd get a scary sensation as if she were standing on the end of a pier as its pilings collapsed. She had read somewhere, "A pier is a disappointed bridge."

She was reading what Vassar students had dubbed as the "tortured female writers," like Woolf and Jean Rhys. The Brontës didn't hold a candle to the modernists. Professor Bradbury was deeply committed to modernism and taught it forward and backward. Christa liked to find a window seat in a shop or carrel somewhere to sit by herself. She had a bound notebook, a sketchbook, really, with coarse-textured cream-colored pages. She liked to smooth the palm of her hand over the paper and feel its tiny fibers, like a thousand little spiders' legs embedded in its grain. She was keeping a journal. She was trying to write poems. One of her instructors said, "Poetry is the highest literary art." She thought she might as well begin at the top, on the high bluffs of Parnassus, although Christa was finding it a steep climb. She struggled to find the right image for the Payne's Grey sky, but after scribbling in her journal for an hour, she slapped the covers shut. She pronounced poetry a Sisyphean pastime, so to hell with it!

But Belinda said, "She came to the university bar one night to give me a poem she had written for me. I can only remember the first line: 'We both like corners, you and I.'"

"I was an impressionable little freshman from New Jersey," Avery Chenoweth said. "I got to Vassar and Christa was part of this very cool crowd of seniors. I suppose, looking back, they were fairly pretentious, but at the time I didn't quite see that. You know, they were very cosmopolitan, smoking their cigarettes up at an angle, talking about artists and all that sort of thing, anything that the impressionable are impressed by. She went around with seniors who were sort of cynical, who wrote for the college newspaper."

Avery said that Christa was very "vivacious" and "sparkling," but she saved her quiet, sweet smile for him. He said that seniors could be patronizing to freshmen, but she wasn't like that. She was more down-to-earth.

He had a serious crush on her, but he "kept getting smoked out of the scene" by older men who had already graduated and who came back to campus with gifts for her, sometimes trying to persuade her to take whatever drugs they had brought along. He described his competition as "kind of sleazy, kind of wealthy racy types. They wore black tasseled loafers with *no socks* and beat-up dinner jackets. Or a tuxedo jacket, jeans, and *no socks*." He said that they would show up bombed out of their minds or stoned.

"I'd be after Christa ineffectually all night. And one of these guys would arrive in a Jaguar and show up at her door very late. He'd find me and say, 'Well, kid, see you around. Bye.' "

The next day, Avery would have lunch with Christa. He wrote a column for the school paper, the *Vassar Chronicle*, under the pseudonym "Susan Avery." Susan Avery was a persona, a freshwoman radical who was disgusted with the indulgent disco crowd, and she'd write about being picked up by West Point cadets, giving pointers about snaring one. Everyone in Christa's crowd was always trying to figure out if Chenoweth was the femme fatale in the newspaper. He became their enfant terrible, their favorite pet.

"Christa looked different. Way ahead of us. Tall leather boots, very, very adult when the rest of us freshmen were schlepping around like we were still in high school.

"Her hair was very long. Kind of girlish. She did have a weight problem. You know about 'the freshman ten'? At Vassar you can put on thirty pounds. Vassar has endowments to make cafeteria food haute cuisine, and the cooks are all from the Culinary Institute. The women were giving me grief for growing an inner tube, myself. I noticed a certain degree of malicious joy other girls had when Christa had the weight problem."

Chenoweth said that the culture of the seventies, especially at Vassar, was not interested in working out. It wasn't sophisticated or suave to exercise. No one had jogging bras. Yet Christa had a great deal of high energy. He said, "I'm attracted to high energy. She could be languid and droll, but she had real genuine energy. I showed up at Vassar and was sort of like Woody Allen. If someone showed up at my door with champagne, I would say, 'I have to study.' Christa seemed to have confidence. But it was a pose, I think." He described going to her room one night. He said that she was naked under the sheets, but he just stood there. "I was a gentleman, but it wasn't going to advance my gene pool, was it? And then there was a knock on the door. This creepy guy in a navy blazer stumbled drunk into the room, filling the room with this feeling of wealthy sleaziness, and he said, 'Yeah, man, I remember you, kid, I guess you're going now, right.' And I looked at Christa. She wouldn't meet my eyes.

"It's a terrible thing when you see women you care for go out with assholes. Sure, they're more exciting. They do more daring things. I knew girls whose mothers liked me but the girls were bored stiff. I think she went out with these sleazeballs because they were disposable. She could keep them at a distance. No one gets too close to people who are bombed."

Yet Vassar in the seventies was a hotbed of feminist idealism. Her UEA boyfriend said, "At Vassar, Christa was indoctrinated into the whole 'female as victim,' women's rights thing. Vassar turned it into an actual ideology. That, coupled with being a single child of older parents who were distant and unhelpful in guiding her, Christa had to discover things herself, by knocking around and finding out."

Parents are supposed to spare children from basic "learn by experience" traumas. Few parents allow their kids to touch a hot stove, and will teach them how to avoid injury without firsthand knowledge.

Vassar seemed to have extreme expectations for its students, both for their academic success and for their ongoing, lifelong accomplishments, even fame. Vassar girls are supposed to do great things. Mulvaney said that Vassar encouraged a myth-making mode in its female students. The myth was that women could, with a Vassar education, "have it all." Career and family. It was an expectation that previous generations never considered realistic. Career girls were childless. Even Mary Tyler Moore, a pop culture icon of women's lib in the seventies, didn't dandle a baby on her knee in that long-running TV series. But, in fact, the actress's own son fell into despair and ended his life with a pistol during a dramatic telephone call, illustrating that a career woman like the actress might not be successful in both worlds. The fast lane and the mommy track can't be paired up without the derailment of one, if not both.

And two decades later, at Christa's twentieth Vassar reunion in 1997, alumnae women were split down the middle. Two distinct groups attended the reunion party: women who had chosen high-altitude careers, many of them quite successful, and those who had opted to have kids. These offspring were already teenagers. Christa realized how much had passed her by. Some of these Vassar women were well adjusted, but others bristled at being face-to-face with decisions they had once made and had tried to ignore were permanent. These women eyed one another with longing and self-hate, regretful about the lifestyles they had chosen and envious of career opportunities or the family lives they had dismissed.

Mary McCarthy, who had been a student at Vassar decades before Christa, described this tortured Vassar woman: "The Vassar alumna is two persons—the housewife or matron, and the yearner and regretter. The Vassar graduate who has failed to make a name for herself . . . is more inclined to blame herself than blame society . . . and to feel she has let the college down for not becoming famous or 'interesting.' " If a Vassar girl isn't famous, if she hasn't been elected to office, hasn't published a novel, hasn't been a noted spokesperson or figurehead in a political movement, if she hasn't rocked the boat and made a big splash in a big pond sort of way by the time she attends her twentieth reunion—well, she better have a happy family to fall back on.

Jay Mulvaney said, "It was a big desperation time for Christa. Her close friend Carol Ostrow had had four kids. Carol had earned an MA from Yale but couldn't pursue a career for a while because of her children. She's working now, running Flea Theater in Manhattan with Jim Simpson, Sigourney Weaver's husband. She'd caught the brass ring. But others, at least half a dozen of our friends, were frantic. They were over forty and wanted children."

At the time of the reunion, a classmate and old rival of Christa's was trying to get pregnant and was taking hormone injections, a combination of Lupron and Pergonal. When they had been students together, her classmate and not Christa had been chosen the "heir apparent" by the Vassar English Department, and she was expected to be a successful writer. Instead, like Christa, she had gone into magazine writing. Neither Christa nor her rival had become serious literary sensations, and neither had yet had babies. When they met again at the reunion, they recognized their stasis or limbo, where they connected, and they disappeared into the women's lounge, where Christa helped her friend inject her hormone shots. It seemed just like Christa to be helping someone get what she herself so desperately wanted. Seeing the divide between women with careers and women with kids suddenly crystallized for her the severed world within herself. Her obsession to have her own baby, once on a back burner, was suddenly on full flame.

Jay Mulvaney said, "I had another childless friend who took a trip to Turkey and got pregnant with the Turkish tour guide just because she wanted a child." Christa's Vassar classmate Carole Maso became pregnant in her forties, from a chance meeting with a stranger she met on an airplane, and she had a baby girl a year before Christa had Ava. Maso said, "I wish Christa and I had connected. She once wrote me a letter after she had read my novel *Ava*. When I found out she had named her baby 'Ava,' it was so odd. It haunts me, because I was nearby in Providence, but we never got together with our babies. There are so many odd stations of time with Christa."

Jay Mulvaney said, "Me, I don't have children. But I had recently produced a PBS TV show for kids. The show got Emmys but it was a kind of 'Barney' nightmare. But I saw what was happening to Christa. Right about this time, Christa's mom got sick. Christa told me, 'I have no husband, no child, but I have to be a parent to my parent, I have to mother my mother. I feel gypped.' "

THE PETRIFIED WOMAN

The Susan Baker Memorial Museum is a landmark in North Truro. Twenty years ago, Susan Baker purchased a rambling bungalow with a gallery out front that used to be called Eldred's Rock Shop, where different mineral specimens, semiprecious stones, rara avises, and geodes were sold. The rocks are gone, and in their place is a startling output of landscape paintings, handmade books and graphic novels, painted furniture and sculpture. She's near the North Truro PO and across the street from Hayden Herrera, the renowned biographer of Frida Kahlo. The "museum" is perched at the top of the hill on a sharp curve above Dutra's Market and the one blinking traffic light in town. A guardrail had to be erected on the neighboring home's front lawn, a busy zendo, after someone drove a car into their meditation room. But there isn't a New Jersey barrier before the big windows of Susan's museum. She's accessible to everyone.

Since Susan Baker moved into the Rock Shop, it's become a hitching post for local folk who drop in unannounced to sit before their offbeat but highly acute counselor. Both subversive wastrels and Upper Crustacean summer folk have fallen in love with the artist and they drop in to get the newest Marconigram and to treat themselves to a hearsay pick-me-up. Beloved for her humorous political art, she has gained a reputation for her graphic novels, especially her *History of Provincetown*, which the *New York Times* described as "an irreverent compilation of notably absurd happenings, past and present." Local resident Norman Mailer said that the book "captures the spirit of the town for men and women who have lived here fifty years and for people who just came yesterday and fell in love." But Susan Baker is also noted for her landscapes of France and Italy, half a world away. Her specialty is paintings of cathedrals, obscure duomos, temples, and famous baroque churches in cities where the native tongue is a Romance language. The animate force of these paintings makes empty churches seem inhabited. Her recent book, *Following Proust*, is a collection of paintings portraying the dreamy and poignant, sometimes claustrophobic locations described in *Remembrance of Things Past*. In a foreword to Susan's book, Richard Howard writes, "She has made a sequence of sacramental objects. . . . She is not illustrating Proust, she has allowed Proust to make her art illustrious."

Baker's husband, the poet Keith Althaus, author of *Rival Heavens*, says, "Yes, when people come to Cape Cod they aren't looking for seaside landscapes and mementos of lighthouses, they're searching for paintings of Italian and French cathedrals." Alongside Baker's work, her studio is charged floor to ceiling with canvases by a local resident, the late painter Mary Hackett. Everything from Hackett's famous portrait of Nikita Khrushchev to paintings of bridges, public buildings, kitchen sinks, and cluttered bedrooms, Baker's gallery might be more accurately called the "Mary Hackett Memorial Museum" rather than its tongue-in-cheek shingle.

Baker has her thumb on the pulse of Truro's seething "community imagination." Susan Baker is head comptroller in charge of the town's pileup of implausible but electrifying gossip. Her roomy but cluttered kitchen is the nexus of bar-stool tall tales and breakfast-nook examinations of events in town, a wellspring of mythology that eddies and purls after every public spectacle or eviscerated secret. After the murder in Truro, people sought audience with Baker to spill their worries and speculations. She is neither a fire-starter nor a sprinkler system. She's a listener. And a medium. She's the final word in its boldest exaggeration.

A friend came to Baker after hearing about the murder in Truro. The woman was too scared to go home to her small cottage in the woods. She had to stay overnight with a friend for the first weeks after Worthington was found. Baker began to call her friend "the Petrified Woman." For the next several weeks, the Petrified Woman would sit with Susan and discuss the newest tidbit, rumor, or armchair evaluation of the case. "Braunwyn has left Keith. She went to Colorado with Luc and his girlfriend, India." "Someone thought they saw Tony with a new girl, parked in the lovers' lane at the cemetery."

The litany halts so they can discuss if "cemetery lovers' lanes" are distinct to Provincetown, or are they in fact the most common makeout glens all across America. Then, it's back to business at hand. "Beth Porter violated her parole and went to jail. Toppy comes to visit her every day." "Braunwyn is back. She got knocked up." "And, guess what, India dumped Luc and went back to her old boyfriend." These rumors were mostly true, but the most amusing invention was, "The knife used in Christa's murder was stolen from the Kennedy Compound."

People ask Susan, "What did the Petrified Woman find out today?"

Recently, I walked into Susan's parlor. I saw she had replaced her ratty couch with a new one. Susan gets most of her furniture this way, hand-me-down items from friends; white elephants from yard sale washouts; sometimes nonequitable trades for her paintings. Her decor is half subway tent town, half Yankee *Sanford and Son*. Her paintings are dramatic, fresh—everything else in the place has "lived" a tortuous previous life, long before she gets her hands on it. Someone gave her a new refrigerator, but the old one still sits on the back stoop. They should take its door off.

Like the best parlors in Montmartre Susan Baker's place is an integration of real art and Salvation Army artifacts. But I was a little surprised when Susan told me where she got her new sofa. Susan's old friend, Diana Worthington, had just delivered the divan.

It was Christa's.

A charming overstuffed settee, its floral fabric has a supersized fleur-de-lis pattern, what UEA English professor Helen McNeil has since told me isn't actually a fleur-de-lis design at all, but a popular British fabric pattern called "Pomegranate." The settee is overstuffed with down cushions but delicately crafted. Christa bought the sofa in London, and it had been a central piece in her Fabergé egg apartment in Gramercy Park.

I sat down on Christa's sofa.

I sank in.

The pillows were plush and billowy, but for me they were like quicksand. As the roomful of people chattered, I kept sinking deeper into the cushions. Of course, I was thinking, here is where Christa nursed her baby, or spooned with suitors, or penned her one-act play in a notebook, or nibbled an apple as she read a novel, maybe her third journey through *Mrs. Dalloway*, her favorite book by her number-one "tortured female writer."

Diana also delivered to Susan Christa's ergonomic desk chair, where Christa might have one day sat down to begin work on her first novel. Diana then brought over a little maple table. Diana must have known that Christa admired Susan Baker and wouldn't have minded the transfer of these items.

Tim Arnold said that Diana might be planning to buy the Little House if she could sell a parcel of land first.

The same week that Diana gave Susan the sofa and desk chair, the local used-book dealer, Tim Barry, called me to say that he had just bought Christa Worthington's entire library from Diana Worthington for $600. He'd been up at her bungalow packing twenty-five boxes with books from Christa's lifelong collection, including her marginalia, receipts, bookmarks of all kinds, plane tickets, birthday cards, photos of old boyfriends. He said, "Are you interested?"

I had already seen some of Christa's books stacked in high towers when I peered into the windows of her cottage as I prowled around the foundation. I wasn't supposed to be there, it's private property. But one afternoon, again I rolled up the gravel drive that curves like a nautilus through the wooded hill until it reaches the top of the bluff. I parked my car beside the T-bar clothesline, its wooden pegs clipped in brisk, even lines, like birthday candles. An empty clothesline, without socks or towels, doesn't usually seem so mournful as this one.

This is the same clothesline where Christa had pampered her pet spider and clipped Ava's bonnets to dry.

I walked around the house and looked inside the windows. I tried to read the book titles in her study, but the light was dimming. There were mystery novels. Literary fiction. But much more prominent were her baby books. Books on nutrition and child-rearing. Pop psychology paperbacks and game manuals, everything she might need to raise a daughter. In the corner of one room, there it was.

The gleaming mirror in its unhappiness. Empty without its mistress.

I wondered if Diana would try to sell it.

The bookseller, Tim Barry, described Christa's collection of books. He said there's an overdue volume from the New York Public Library, and a book called *The Will Handbook,* probably bought when Christa was making arrangements for Ava. There are volumes of fashion texts, such as a book called *Choosing Pearls,* and there's a paperback called *Workbook for Single Girls.* He wants me to buy it all.

Trying to tempt me, he said that in her stacks, Christa had a history book about ancient Greco-Roman traditions. Christa had underlined an interesting passage about swapped partners, borrowed wives and daughters traded without ridicule or retribution. Written in the margin, Christa had penned "Adultery is no sin." He told me that a buyer in Hollywood is interested in Christa's library, but he will sell it to me, did I want it? "Three thousand dollars for the lot."

"Try Hollywood," I said.

"Why don't you sleep on it," he said.

"I don't think so. But you might have something in your shop that I want—do you have the CliffsNotes for *The Scarlet Letter*?"

In her book, *Crossed Over: A Murder, A Memoir,* Beverly Lowry was lucky to meet her subject, Karla Faye Tucker. Karla was living on death row in Texas, but the writer spent many hours face-to-face with her subject. Lowry describes how they would end their conversations with a "hug," even when they were separated by a partition. "We press our palms against the Plexiglas until our fingers turn white, then pull back and cross our arms over our chests and, holding tight to our own shoulders, rock back and forth, hugging ourselves as a substitute for one another."

I have never been face-to-face with Christa. If I hugged myself, in order to hug her, she'd never know the difference. And in my dreams about Christa, we had not yet spoken. But last night she was standing before me. She smiled, her face beautiful, almost childlike, transposed with Ava's face for an instant, but completely guileless. Her sorrel hair fell across her face, and she walked her fingertips over her temple to comb it out of her eyes. She was very worried about something, she said. She crisscrossed her arms over her fawn cardigan, not in a defiant posture, not in a "Karla Faye hug," but as if she had felt a chill. She told me, "Someone took my sofa. Can you believe it? Do you know who would do this? Could you help me get it back?"

THE DNA GALLERY

O'Keefe's gala election campaign launch is a happening. The parking lot outside the Sons of Italy Lodge is full, and I roll into an adjoining field where lines of cars are packed in tight across the stubble; it looks like an auto mart at a county fair. I want to get a bumper sticker and I walk into the busy hive of Barnstable County GOP bigwigs and wannabes, a Republican shindig where I normally wouldn't belong. But I'm thinking that maybe, for once, I won't be a yellow dog Democrat. I might vote for O'Keefe.

I'm funneled up to a banquet table, nudged before a pretty centerpiece, a crystal punch bowl layered with Easter pastels, colored flower petals and leaves. It isn't a decorative centerpiece, after all, but a cut-glass piggy bank filling up with personal checks, and even some hundred-dollar bills. I take a bumper sticker. A button. I write a check for fifty dollars and let it float into the bowl. The Kennedy machine is funding O'Keefe's opponent and Mike will need every measly donation.

O'Keefe is on the other side of the hall, dipping from table to table, working the crowd. He had told me it's like having two full-time jobs being DA and running for office; he's the lion tamer *and* the no-nonsense GOP workaholic who pushes the broom behind the elephant. Despite his campaign grind, he's working his regular hours—night-and-day turf prowls from crime scenes to the courthouse, to a meeting for crime lab accreditation in Sudbury, then it's a golf tournament fund-raiser, a benefit walk. It's legit head-banging, hand-pumping, and careful rationings of his deep baritone in telephone interviews, radio spots, and dinner dance speeches. He's also showing up at Kiwanis Club lunches, bake sales, Cape Cod Hospital soirees, tea dances here or there, at high school assemblies where he warns students about the illegal manufacture and sale of false IDs, and there's the side of beef banquet at the Ancient & Honorable Artillery Company. He's chumming with gubernatorial candidate Mitt Romney, who's running against the blond Democrat Shannon O'Brien. In July, he's already been written-in to march in four different Independence Day parades, on the most sweltering day of the year, in 90 percent humidity.

He sees me and weaves his way in my direction. He says, "I need a smoke. Follow me." We walk across the ballroom and go out the fire door. I feel everyone's eyes zooming in as we cross the wide parquet and disappear. I know he's conscious of the pivoting heads and I feel a little used. He once told me that his opponent is never seen with a woman, and he's not going to let that happen to him. But I give him the benefit of the doubt as we stand on the stoop and he hunts for his lighter. After all, he's having a nicotine fit. Meanwhile, I'm peeling a tab of Nicorette. "It's a huge turnout," I say. "Congratulations."

He reaches out and rubs his thumb across my mouth. "You've got red stuff on your front teeth," he says. "I hate that."

Red stuff.

I scrub the lipstick off my top shelf with my fingertip. "Is it gone?"

He can't find his light. No matches. Nothing. Without a smoke, his nerves are jangled. Or maybe it's the launch. He's come a long way to stand on the lonely gangplank of political life, when in the beginning, as a rookie on the Dennis police force, he had felt safe and snug in a cherry top. He's all law enforcement, and politics is a nuisance to him. Having to square off with his Democratic opponent who flunked the bar exam ten times in a row in ten years, when O'Keefe and everyone in his office had passed the first time, is beneath him. O'Keefe has been working at the DA's office for twenty years. His opponent has had little experience as a prosecutor and spent more time behind the wheel of a limo, as a driver for Ted Kennedy. After that, he had actually taken time out from practicing law to be a real estate agent. That was before the Kennedy machine puppeted him back into competition. I couldn't imagine Callahan on the job. I couldn't see him standing over the body of Cheryl Tavares last month, a woman who had been strangled and left in the trunk of a car parked in a lonely commuter lot in Bourne. But O'Keefe was there, as per.

We walk back into the din. I find a table with an older couple, and sit down to watch the notables climb up to the podium, one by one. Sheriff

Cummings. DA Rollins, who is gleeful to be winding down. He's ready to hand the baton like a hot potato. Republican state representatives and local officials walk to the lectern to read O'Keefe's praises. They love Mike. They tell us that O'Keefe was "Massachusetts Prosecutor of the Year" in 1994. He personally prosecuted 250 jury trials and 19 homicide trials to jury verdict. He established the first Elder Abuse Unit, and also established a Juvenile Diversion Unit. He's a member of the Federal-State Anti-Terrorism Task Force. He's Tough on Crime. His golf handicap is impressive. He was awarded a Medal of Merit for Bravery when he rescued a woman from a burning building.

I picture O'Keefe saving the woman from her tinderbox house. But he was too late to rescue Christa. She was a flash fire behind closed doors. A flicker reflected in the eyes of her killer, burning out.

A message on my machine says, "Been swamped. Don't worry. We'll rendezvous."

O'Keefe's use of the French idiom seems tragicomic. We have our little get-togethers for one official reason. He's the brain bank of Barnstable County law enforcement, and I'm the little egghead pest, trying to sponge it up. I climb into the fishbowl with O'Keefe, a guppy circling the king fish. Our meetings are supposed to be cut-and-dried table chats about the Worthington ordeal. Sometimes it seems more layered than this. A nervous, edgy, simpatico connection has emerged between us. His divorced status seems to be on his shoulders, when most men feel it's a weight removed. He never tells me what went wrong, but it's brewing across his features. He hasn't shrugged it off.

I meet O'Keefe in Barnstable one morning. He brings me into DA Rollins' corner office. It's a nice room in the old Victorian, shaded on both sides by old elms, and twice the size of O'Keefe's cubicle. We sit down before Rollins, who is cheerful and tan, already enjoying his retirement lifestyle. He opens correspondence with deft slices of his letter opener and waves the blade around as he talks, like a TV chef gesturing with a paring knife. He stacks separate piles, sorting important memos from the expendable junk mail. He says that he looks forward to stepping down and handing the reins to Mike. He teases O'Keefe, tells him that soon Mike can sit here, in the corner office, behind the towers of paper.

O'Keefe tells me that last night he was in Boston at the Park Plaza Hotel, a guest at the Ancient & Honorable Artillery Company wingding.

"The ancient what?"

"Ancient & Honorable Artillery Company," Rollins says, grinning. He explains that it's an ultra-private club of blue bloods with ancestors of historic military importance. Or so they claim. Some dress up for the event in authentic brocaded jackets.

O'Keefe is juggling his campaign duties with his more important routine as a prosecutor. He scolds me for not attending a trial last week in Nantucket where he tried a murder case and won. *Commonwealth v. Peter Chongarlides.* "It was a piece of surgery," he says.

I tell him, "I followed it in the *Cape Cod Times.* I guess I should have come over."

"Should-of, would-of, could-of."

He explains how he had grilled a *Boston Globe* reporter who had written a story about the death of Pamela Bouchard, a young woman on the skids in Nantucket. He said about the reporter, "She didn't know if she was working for the *Herald*, the *Globe*, or the DA's office by the time I was through with her."

He describes his opposition, a public defender, as a "bow tie lawyer." He says that the defendant, a local Nantucket man, had only been "off the rock" three times. It took three whole days to get a jury who weren't blood kin or neighbors. Nantucket natives have more than ten toes.

He questioned the *Globe* reporter about her notes for her story. She had interviewed principals in a drug deal that brought about the death of Miss Bouchard from an overdose. Her body was found floating in the harbor, where she had been unceremoniously dumped by the defendant. He shows me a transcript of the reporter's testimony before O'Keefe's cross-examination. There's a comic instant like a Bud Abbott "Who's on First?" confusion when O'Keefe tries to get her to clarify her note-taking:

Q. (By Mr. O'Keefe) What does that say? I'm just having trouble reading your—

A. "He stopped by my house"—this part right here?

Q. Yes.

A. "to sell his"—and then I wrote down "house."

Q. To sell his *house*?

A. Yeah.

Q. What does that mean?

A. What that means is that I was probably paying more attention to what he was saying than to what I was writing down. But obviously he did not say "house."

Q. Okay.

A. He meant drugs.

Q. He meant to say drugs?

A. Yeah. I mean, that was the whole—

Q. Let me ask you, ma'am, could he have said "horse"?

A. No.

Q. Do you know that horse is slang for heroin?

A. I guess.

Q. Have you ever heard that?

A. I think I have, yes.

Q. Okay.

A. But I wrote "house."

He seems a little disappointed that I didn't make the effort to get on the ferry. "Why didn't you invite me?"

"It's not exactly a fun date, I guess that's why," he said.

But taking the ferry to Nantucket to watch a murder trial is a morbid little sojourn I might have enjoyed. Most times the ferry is crowded with tourists or wealthy Bostonians who have second homes, and I try to avoid it. O'Keefe's irritation with me for missing his "piece of surgery" seems a little personal. But he says he wants to get breakfast.

We sit down in a back corner of the little breakfast spa on Main Street. He shows me the current issue of *People* magazine. There's a photograph of Christa.

She's the new poster girl in the campaign for the bipartisan "Debbie

Smith Act." The article states that "even high-profile crimes aren't exempt. In Massachusetts, investigators collected dozens of samples of DNA and other forensic evidence from the Cape Cod home of fashion writer Christa Worthington, whose bloodied body was found in her kitchen on January 6. . . . To date, all the results are still not in, and the crime remains unsolved."

O'Keefe orders a linguiça omelet and a Diet Coke. That's a lot of garlic to start out the day.

I have coffee.

"This Debbie Smith problem? In a ball of wax, that's what's holding you up, right?" I say.

"This might take three or four years to solve. Within the samples we have gotten back so far, no DNA jumps out at us. The semen DNA is from a lover who might be the perp. If her fingernail DNA matches, then he's our guy."

"Fingernails not back?"

"Nope. In the meantime, the state police go back through everything. They will assemble the case again as if they had never done it before."

"They start all over again, from square one?" I think of what Popcorn said. "Eggs. Milk. Bread."

O'Keefe tells me that her phone and bank records are still being investigated. That's a lot of paper. Forensic accounting is done by troopers working the case. They look for repetitions and patterns in telephone numbers dialed from the house.

"We want to find her sexual partners," he says.

"That's a haystack."

He says, "This was someone she knew. That house isn't easy to find."

"It's tucked away. But you must have something?"

"She was struck in the head several times, probably with the phone that's missing."

"He took it with him because his prints were on it?"

"I guess he didn't take it to call us or to call his mom." His eyes almost twinkle, but, even better, he likes to make fun of me without any expression on his mug.

He tells me that Jan Worthington has been trying to organize putting

up a reward for information. When Toppy heard about this, he argued
with O'Keefe. "Toppy was against it. He didn't agree with his niece. He
didn't want the publicity. I told him that the DA's office doesn't give a
fuck about his privacy issues or his concern about his girlfriend.
Beth Porter is doing a little stint at the Nashua Street jail for a parole violation."

"I know. She's supposed to call me collect."

"His girlfriend's a mess. So what? We don't care. So then he gets real
and changes his mind. He said go ahead with the reward."

A reward can sometimes help encourage someone to cough up what
they know, but if his office is going to help Jan Worthington set it up, it
has to be according to their rules. So far there's no movement on it. The
reward is a Worthington "concept."

He puts us in the car and starts driving west up 6A. "You smell nice," he
says. "Too bad."

"Too bad for who?"

"You. Me. Us." He doesn't tell me where we're going. I'm used to it now.
He's always in motion. Driving his car, I see his shoulders relax. He says,
"I was going to take you to the beach."

"So where are we going instead?"

"To my house. I want to show you my political science."

"I've heard it called a lot of things, but I've never heard it called 'political science.' "

"No. Political signs. We had them in a storage bin, but we were paying
rent. Now they're in my garage."

His neighborhood is plush. Big homes with rolling lawns and rhododendrons big as pink blimps. He pulls into his driveway. His property is
manicured by landscape professionals. It doesn't have a woman's touch.
The bushes are sheared with a military exactness, flat on top, as if his lawn
boys used a spirit level.

We walk into the garage. As he had explained, there are hundreds of
campaign signs for Sheriff Cummings and DA Rollins stacked against
three walls. "We can use the posts and frames again," O'Keefe explains.
"We pinch pennies this way."

In a clearing on the concrete floor, I notice a little runway of green indoor-outdoor carpet, and beside the swatch rests a heavy golf bag. A full-length closet mirror hangs on the wall. It's a Kmart item, nothing like Christa's treasure.

He says he practices his drives out here. He walks over and chooses a club. He stands on the little square of green carpet. He swings. A smooth and forceful motion. The empty air churns and I feel its wave of nothing wash over my face and lift my hair a little.

"Very nice," I say.

He swings again.

"That's good," I tell him. I think of him out here all alone at the end of the day, swinging the club with the same controlled, refined fury.

He says, "Come here. You try it."

"I don't think so."

"Come on, take a swing," he says, holding a driver by its whipping, offering its grip end to me.

I look at the wood. The mirror. The man.

"No, thanks." I understand the physiology of the amateur golf swing—it *begs* for instruction. If I try to take a swing, he'll spoon against me and put his arms around mine, grip over grip. I don't want the test or the temptation. I wonder how many girls he brings out here to stand on the green sliver so he can teach them how to swing a golf club.

"No?" he says. "You sure?" He tugs a terry head cover on the club and jams it back in the bag.

We walk into the big house. A pool glimmers in the back. "We swim raw here," he says. "It's private."

I ignore his relentless surf casting in my direction. I look at the pool. Its surface shivers for an instant, stills, and shivers again. I circle the kitchen island and prowl into the next room. There's a weight bench and barbells, abandoned in a lonely huddle like a scene from a prep school movie, maybe *A Separate Peace* or *Dead Poets Society*, when an empty weight bench suggests the teenage id. The big house feels empty. It pitches and yaws with that feeling of being suddenly vacated, like finding a sailboat adrift. Its galley pillaged, its lady figurehead removed from its prow.

He tells me to sit down in the living room. The sofa is tousled with scrunched pillows and a throw rug kicked to the foot of it. It's lived in. He tells me that since his wife left him, he doesn't like to sleep in the big bed upstairs. Now that's a candid confession or it's a pitch. Some women are suckers for violin music.

"I saw her in the mall," he says. "We had a cup of coffee."

"You saw your wife in the mall?"

"The mall is neutral, right?"

I sit down in the DA's "bed" and pretend not to notice its musk, its disarray. I tell him I saw Tony Jackett in Provincetown. He's back on the street, getting his legs back after so much publicity.

"Where'd you see him?" O'Keefe asks.

"I was at an opening at the DNA."

"Excuse me?"

"An art opening."

He still looks confused, and I recognize the crazy confusion. The "DNA" Gallery is a popular Provincetown art bin, a loft upstairs at the Provincetown Tennis Club on Bradford Street. The gallery is run by Nick Lawrence, a straw-hat-wearing "Margaritaville" maverick, son of famous editor Seymour Lawrence. I realize that the gallery has the coincidental name of O'Keefe's pet peeve, "DNA."

"DNA. It stands for 'Definitive New Art.' It's a silly acronym and not what you're thinking," I tell O'Keefe. But he must be picturing paintings of double helixes, or computer printouts of the grids and columns of DNA markers that forensic technicians study to find Christa's killer.

I say, "Tony is back in the loop. He goes into a lot of art galleries. He used to like to window-shop for bohemian goddesses. Now he takes Susan."

O'Keefe has a big-screen TV across the room. Stacks of videos are arranged in lopsided pyramids and unstable towers beside the VCR. We can watch the Christa video that O'Keefe has dangled like a carrot, right here, side by side on his lonely sofa bed, a spartan pallet that tweaks your heart. I ask him when he'll show me the tape.

"They've got to make a copy for me. The original is in Sudbury."

"At Blockbuster's they have the foresight to make multiple copies. They have racks. There's a wall of De Niro and a wall of Mel Gibson."

"We're on a budget," he says.

"Yeah, yeah, those Democrats won't budge." I don't tell him that Christa's tabloid photos and three-by-five crime scene glossies are always plastered in front of me, floor to ceiling, like shrink-wrapped porn at Noirtown Video, shelves of Christa on the wall of the psyche. I wonder what the killer is renting.

"LOW-PROFILE LOVELIES COME OUT OF HIDING"

Joan Didion wrote about her arrival in New York, "It's easy to see the beginnings of things, and harder to see the ends . . . enter a revolving door at twenty and come out a good deal older, on a different street."

Christa moved to Manhattan in the early summer of 1977. She had graduated with honors from Vassar, earning a bachelor's degree in English. Of course she had written her senior essay on Virginia Woolf when other students chose Plath or Sexton. And that year Tillie Olsen had finally been recognized as a popular new feminist martyr. But Christa defended her choice, saying that she believed Woolf had been "more stylish than ghoulish" when the writer had walked into a river with stones in her pockets and had not merely swallowed pills, like cowardly American housewives.

In the city, she hooked up with Jay Mulvaney and they crashed at an apartment on Seventy-first Street and Broadway. Soon, another apartment opened up when some actors went away for the summer. They rented the place for only $200 a month. The unit was deep inside the building and always dark. But Jay and Christa spent most of their time elsewhere, looking for jobs and partying. Jay said, "There was a big party right after graduation at the Beekman Towers. A penthouse restaurant. Everyone dressed very Fred Astaire and Ginger Rogers. And those days it was Studio 54 five nights a week. You stand there, your nose pressed up to the velvet rope of Studio 54. The first time Christa was allowed into the place, she was wearing this big denim skirt and an off-the-shoulder hippie blouse. I was in those awful red duck 'Nantucket' pants and a green-and-white-striped Brooks Brothers shirt. Steve Rubell picked us out of the line. He just *looked* at us and we got in. It was like getting into Oz or something. For Christa, it was a very 'Stella Dallas' type of life." Stella Dallas was King Vidor's 1937 film heroine, the ultimate caricature of a liberated woman. Sprung from matrimony, but with enough money to live freely, she could wear trashy clothes and sleep around. But in the movie, of course, Stella would have her comeuppance later on and she'd reform her wild life for a conservative maternity role.

Mulvaney said that he and Christa had worked out a plan. They wouldn't bring any of their conquests back to the apartment. "A guy finding another guy there would freak them both out." Because of this contract, they didn't have a very romantic or promiscuous summer.

Mulvaney said, "My best memory of that summer was when we read *The Importance of Being Earnest* out loud in the apartment late at night. She would let me play Lady Bracknell. She did it to accommodate me, but she had a lovely voice. A real Daisy Buchanan voice, à la Mia Farrow. Christa's voice had a lilt to it, a precision—always a slight hesitation. She used words specifically, to make a point or make a wry aside. She could present herself as this really big ditz; she would twirl the ends of her hair, her eyes looking up from under big eyelashes, but she was focused on what you were doing."

Christa looked for writing work and she was thinking about starting a novel. Instead, she took a job as a paralegal at Sullivan and Cromwell. At her interview, she was told that "a legal assistant cannot actually give legal advice." But under the supervision of an attorney, Christa's "work product" would be "merged" with the attorney's daily output. She was told she'd be asked to interview clients, conduct legal research, draft documents, correspondence, and pleadings. She might have to locate and interview witnesses and attend executions of wills, real estate closings, depositions, and trials with the attorney. But, in fact, Christa spent most of her time bent over the Xerox machine, spilling toner on her shoes. She spent many painstaking hours looking up docket numbers, running out for sandwiches, or stacking paper cones at the watercooler. The flimsy tower had the habit of tilting left or right and spilling across the floor.

Jay Mulvaney said that he and Christa had had a falling out. When he was working for a theater company, driving a minivan, he had promised to help her move into a new apartment. "I bagged on her and didn't show up. She was stuck, standing there, with her boxes on the sidewalk. But we reconnected later in Paris. She didn't hold a grudge."

In the spring of 1979, Christa took her first job in the fashion industry, as assistant to beauty editor Mallen DeSantis at *Cosmopolitan* magazine. DeSantis said, "It was a beginner's job, more like a secretary. Christa fielded phone calls and protected me from pests; she saw PR people who came to show products and samples of beauty products, everything for teeth, hair, cosmetics, exercise equipment."

DeSantis remembers Christa as being extremely quiet compared to some of the other jittery or bubbly newbies. "She was reserved, very poised. She was obsessive about her writing, she couldn't dash it off. She took it too seriously, but she wasn't impressed by the fashion world. She thought it was a joke. She had a polish, a refinement, that wasn't just a surface appearance." DeSantis said that she had once run into Christa at the theater. She was with a young man. The next day Christa told DeSantis about her date. She told DeSantis that she had already dismissed him because he had told Christa "You're a class act." DeSantis said, "Christa's response to his remark had many layers. First, she had thought the remark was such a cliché. Second, she knew it was true, but it was so unclassy for him to say it!"

At *Cosmo*, Christa worked on a monthly column called "What's New and What It Does for You." Her friend Belinda Oliver said, "Basically, it was rewriting press releases on beauty tips, but she agonized over it. It seemed to take her all month and she usually finished it in the wee hours of the deadline day. She was living in the Village over Trudi Heller's dance studio. The thumping music drove her mad, especially when she labored to meet her deadlines." In one of her "What's New and What It Does for You" columns, Christa advised women to use a homemade hair-setting mixture made of egg white to create body and luster for overworked and color-treated hair. The technique had not been well researched. Women wrote letters complaining about their personal hair disasters after following the magazine's explicit directions. The mixture was "organic" and healthful and it did in fact add body to limp hair.

It dried into a stiff meringue that hardened into a helmet.

DeSantis said that Christa herself had "an enormous amount of hair. She had enough hair for ten women." Helen Gurley Brown had once grabbed Christa and said, "Look at that head of hair. It's gorgeous."

But DeSantis said that Christa was often ill with painful female troubles. She had often found Christa doubled up with cramps, lying on the women's room floor. "She said the doctor had told her she had endometriosis. Even then, she worried that she wouldn't be able to have a baby," DeSantis said. Having had her first abortion, she fretted she'd been scarred.

Around this time, Christa had found a different apartment where she could camp out until she got her feet planted. She lived on the corner of Ninth Street and Sixth Avenue, sharing the space with a woman named Susie Doe. Her friends have a funny feeling when they remember this minor detail. It seems to have a tragic resonance now. Susie Doe. John Doe. Jane Doe.

Their building was across the street from Balducci's, and Christa liked to window-shop, making sure she'd already eaten something so she wouldn't be tempted.

Her cousin Jan Worthington was living in the city, working as a camera operator, shooting baseball games for TV. Jan introduced Christa to Steven Radlauer, or Radz, a writer whose books include *Step by Step: Keyboarding on the Personal Computer* and *How to Choose, Change, Advance Your Career.* More recently, his book *The Historic Shops and Restaurants of New York,* a guidebook with accompanying stories about American immigrants, offers a much welcomed look back after the events of 9/11.

As two young writers, Christa and Radlauer started dating. When I first talked to Radlauer he told me that Christa had had a lot of friends who were writers. He said with a snippy, proprietary tone, or perhaps it was nostalgia, "There's a pile of us. Media persons; TV writers; movie people. We're a *wall of writers* around Christa."

He complained that the media were painting a false picture of Christa. He said, "Christa would really be laughing if she heard how everyone is calling her glamorous. She dressed more often like a bag lady. She bought clothes at the flea market."

But others say that wearing tatters is, in fact, a "conscious glamour statement." Christa knew how to evoke the exact nuances and style inventions of "shabby chic."

Radz said, "Friends talked about her even when she was in the room, they were adamant that she write a novel—she just exuded story." I thought, "Poor little match girl." "Little girl lost." Even "The Lady or the Tiger."

Radz says he still owns a copy of the 1980 *Cosmo* issue in which Christa was enlisted to be one of the "plain Jane" subjects for a *Cosmo* makeover, with the typical before and after photographs. The article is titled "Low-Profile Lovelies Come Out of Hiding." Christa's "before" photo shows her unpainted face, her hair pulled back, her mouth a flat line, almost a frown. She is plain, plain, plain. DeSantis said, "We purposefully made the 'before' shot look really bad." But in her "after" shot, Christa is glowing. Her hair tumbles in lovely auburn waves across her shoulder; her eyes are enlarged by Elizabeth Arden shades, and her eyebrows are penciled; her mouth is dewy. Her pale, ivory neckline is revealed in a low-cut gown. Her friend Kim Gibson said, "Christa had fun with it. She was really thrilled that they had made her look as if she had some cleavage. You know, she was pretty flat." Christa always felt a little short-changed. Tatyana Mishel, a writer who had worked with Christa at *Elle* magazine, said that her strongest recollection of Christa is when Christa had once complimented her. Tatyana had worn a sundress to work with an open neckline. Christa told Tatyana, "What a lovely dress. You have such a nice décolletage." Tatyana said that Christa's compliment was so unexpected, so oddly heartfelt, almost mournful, it stuck with her. Tatyana said that sometimes, when she gets dressed in a revealing item, she thinks of Christa's oddball comment: "You have such a nice décolletage."

Radz said that Christa "wasn't blissfully happy" at *Cosmo* but was happy to have a job. "She was so 'starting-out-y' that it was kind of a lark to have a job at all."

Working at *Cosmo*, Christa met an editor, Jane Lane, who asked Christa to apply for a position at *Women's Wear Daily*. Christa was tempted by the prospect of moving into a more substantial position as accessories editor at *WWD*, and she spent hours preparing for her interview. DeSantis said, "She asked me about how she should wear her hair. She decided to pin it up in a chignon to look very serious. She was stunning."

But when Christa left *Cosmo* to begin working at *Women's Wear Daily*, she was launched into a much more harrowing environment, a realm of chic savages and tribal threats that formed a dizzy, elliptical orbit from Manhattan to Paris. It was an instantly thrilling but pernicious setting.

When she walked through the doors at *WWD*, she entered the nasty, gothic underworld of chic. It was the most glittering, exaggerated nothingness. What *Women's Wear Daily* publisher John Fairchild himself called "the empty pit."

Trying to gain her footing in the high-powered and spiky world of icy fashionistas and wage-war garmentos, she felt like the familiar character in the *Little Prince* illustration, a figure who stands alone on a tiny globe in the middle of space. She felt too small and too self-conscious to stand by herself on this new "glamour planet." But soon she was brisking from desk to desk at their offices, a huge open floor where only the writers and "creators" could mingle. Advertising execs weren't allowed access to the golden beehive where John Fairchild reigned.

Women's Wear Daily had emerged in nymph form from a Fairchild Publications enterprise that began as a clothing trade paper in Chicago at the end of the nineteenth century. Today, *WWD* is a powerful, edgy, both beloved and reviled fashion bible of worldwide importance to the fashion industry. Its influence dictates standards for designers, Seventh Avenue manufacturers, and retailers, but it also cuts across demographics and cultural boundaries in a never-ending trickle-down effect. If it's in print in *WWD*, it becomes both word-of-mouth and "page image" across the world. For instance, when John Fairchild coined the term "hot pants," within months Sears, Roebuck and Montgomery Ward marketed their versions of the fashion hiccup that to this day is most often seen adorning "business girls," streetwalkers like Jodie Foster in *Taxi Driver*.

The "Best Dressed Lists," the "In and Out Lists," the "Fashion Victims Lists" eventually influence every woman's wardrobe choices. Even farmers' wives who have never once seen a copy of *WWD* will purchase new sewing patterns that reflect the current ready-to-wear trends. When a farm girl sits down at her Singer sewing machine in the flatlands of Kansas, the final product will have the echo and the architecture, although watered down, of Paris couture originals. Thanks to John Fairchild and his empire—writers like Christa—each season's particular silhouette is decoded for the world.

Time magazine once called *WWD* "that gossip-y, bitch-y newspaper of manners, friends, and scandal." Christa joined the staff and found herself instantly immersed in a consciousness exactly opposite to what she'd practiced as a fledgling feminist and budding intellectual at Vassar. Couture isn't directly mentioned in the archival stacks of original poetry manuscripts by T. S. Eliot or in F. Scott Fitzgerald novels, nor in Woolf's bitter tomes, but it's there in every idiosyncratic description of the feminine mystique. Fashion is the undulating conduit between death and beauty. Christa understood this connection. There was one meaning in each meaningless trend, the same message, a constant in every new design signature: beauty fights death.

Christa met John Fairchild, the man *Time* magazine had described as "the owl with a crew cut," and she immediately liked him. He would become both mentor and monster in the years to come, but she was already learning the ropes from him. Fairchild had attended Kent, the same Episcopalian prep school where her father had been educated, and this was an ice breaker in one of their first conversations, although Christa was a little alarmed by the coincidence.

As accessories editor, Christa found herself entombed in tilting stacks of samples sent to her desk by designers, manufacturers, and reigning department stores. Gloves. Purses. Bracelets. Watches. Scarves. Boots and bangles. Gold. Silver. Silks.

Radz visited her often at her offices. He said, "She's sitting there in this hideous environment, completely overworked, deadline-crazed. She's at this desk piled high with junk, except the junk was very expensive stuff, like S. T. Dupont pen sets and Chanel handbags. It was like she was in a junk shop and she couldn't find her typewriter. She was not impressed by any of it. She wanted to do journalism. I never had the impression that fashion writing was what she was setting out to do. But suddenly there she is with her own byline. And she's only twenty-three!"

Having her own byline was heady. Her friends from East Anglia University, Belinda and Barbara, argue about whether Christa had been swept up by the glamour and wealth of her new environment. Barbara said, "She was immune to glamour." But Belinda disagreed. She said, "You could see it in her eyes, like the cat who ate the canary. She was really impressed by all the trappings. The free gifts, the flashy people, the sexy designers. If she had a choice between an evening with friends and a fashion event, fashion won out every time. It was exciting, but difficult for her, too, because although she mixed with these people, she was never one of them."

Writing an accessories column, Christa had to closely examine items of jewelry, clothing, sportswear, or lingerie. She fingered samples of cashmere and velvets; she slipped jewelry on her hands; she sniffed the sweet and supple leather of a new pump, or a snakeskin belt. It was an entirely sensual exercise. She became intimately schooled in "texture," "color," "scent."

Her keenness was both a gift and a curse. She noticed absurd details jumbled into the beautiful tables of pricey junk. Once, she found a tag on a garment with a color identification in six languages. She was hypnotized by the little totem that said: "Bleu. Blue. Blau. Blauw. Azul. Blu."

She tacked the sticker to her desk.

She learned to discern between luxury and lavishness, between beauty and opulence. What made some accessories alluring and others overdone and repulsive. There was a difference between the truly exquisite and the mundane plumped up, masquerading as abundance.

Fingering. Wording. Rewording. She often felt as if she were trapped before an arcade game where you must operate a little crane to try to pick up a necklace or a stuffed animal, but you never can get a grip on it.

Christa was intellectually curious; she studied her subject, when other writers were satisfied to write a quick gloss. Christa researched background information, sometimes seeking technical explanations often ignored in fashion writing. Describing Oscar de la Renta's new jewelry collection for Flavia, she wrote of the designer's necklaces and rings: "There's more to de la Renta's rainbow effects than he lets on. The stones, including aquamarine, peridot, amethyst and citrine, had to be cut in reverse—buffeted on top and faceted on the bottom—in order to achieve such smooth color transitions." Then, of course, the obligatory: "The de la Renta collection will make its debut at Bloomingdale's, New York, on September 22, with prices ranging from $200 to $3,000."

She was often placed in a position of having to stir up some excitement about banal products, gaudy baubles, and every kind of fashion ejecta, for instance, a new Lacoste tennis racket bag: "Durable bags, in Cordura, para rip nylon and vinyl, that appeal to the sportsman's senses. A trapezoid shape, the design coup of tennis pro René Lacoste, makes them look perpetually on the move."

With a literary ear for sensual diction and a no-nonsense economy of line, Christa could find the seductive detail of a new product that would buffer the shocking price list. Christa had quickly learned she was working for a trade paper, and its whole raison d'être was to "sell, sell, sell."

But she also started to enjoy her forays into five-star hotels and restaurants to cover Seventh Avenue soirees and events. She needed an escort to go with her to a luncheon at the Waldorf-Astoria, a bash organized by the Fragrance Council. Women are expected to have acceptable escorts. Fairchild called this sort of man, the very stylish rent-boy, a "walker." A "walker" will ferry nouvelle matrons and "social cyclones" to important events whenever their husbands don't wish to attend. These "walkers" are just as fabulous and celebrated in style pages as the socialites they squire around.

But Christa telephoned her old Vassar boyfriend Hugh Cosman, and he agreed to go with her to the Waldorf luncheon. Ted Kennedy was the speaker, of all people, and Cosman said, "Kennedy was in his cocaine and boozing stage. He looked like a deer caught in headlights. He had to keep referring to his notebook, and when people asked questions, he'd make the most tangential statements. Christa and I couldn't stop laughing. I could see she really enjoyed going to these rubber chicken dinners."

Her relationship with Radz was steady, but slowing down. Once, when Gloria visited Christa in New York, Radz invited them to his mother's apartment for dinner. Radz said, "Christa's mom sidled up to my mom, and said, 'So when are they tying the knot?' "

But their friendship was more enduring than their bedroom trysts. He said Christa had once confided to him that she had a definite idea of what she wanted in a man. Radz said, "At one point, when we were winding down, Christa told me, 'I'm looking for a WASP with a sail bag.' It's a funny oxymoron. She wants the chunk of royalty, but at the same time she wants him to be beneath her."

Christa's vision of the perfect man reminds me of a friend who once told me that her ideal man would be "a poet with a tool belt."

Radz said that Christa was sometimes very self-aware. She was probably really looking for that kind of ideal. The well-heeled patrician with a yacht, but she also wanted the man who built the yacht.

In 1981, when Christa was having trouble finding new digs, her father plunked down $40,000 for an apartment at 32 Gramercy Park South. It was a seventh-floor studio and tiny, but she immediately decorated it with her own flourishes and touches, tapestries and throws, velvet pillows, oddball flea market finds. Soon mounds of reading matter and Gutenberg litter piled up until it looked like a rag and bone shop with Christa as proprietor. She also had many photographs of her grandparents John and Tiny, and of her summer days on the Pamet. But she was putting some roots down in New York, the greatest city in the world. Didion wrote, "To be young in New York, six months can become eight years with the deceptive ease of a film dissolve." The Gramercy Park apartment would be Christa's foothold in New York for the next fifteen years. She would sublet the studio each year she was abroad. She held on to it even when the building was condemned and had to be evacuated after a Con Ed explosion resulted in an asbestos scare. The little place had great impact on her life; it signaled her official separation from her family in New England. She was a New Yorker now; the "WASP with a sail bag" could wait. It was both the promise and the lie she told herself.

At WWD, she was immediately recognized as a "comer," but she was in a career track that she didn't yet feel completely committed to. With Radz and her friends, she was always ready to make fun of herself, as if she understood her perch was tenuous, her writing career in the fashion world ridiculous. Bob Morris, a New York Times columnist for the Sunday Styles section, said, "There's a deep disappointment for most of us who ended up as fashion journalists and who are actually, in some ways, being valorized for it. Like, 'Oh, wow, a contract with Travel and Leisure!' "

Morris says that he finally found a more rewarding perch writing for the *Times.* His columns are slightly edgy, sometimes poignant, but always have a gleefully comic voice about New York life. In a recent column, Morris describes a new trend in Manhattan restaurants:

> This summer they are dancing on tables. . . . Maybe it's a tarantella to shake off the spider-bite-like toxins of the times. "You know you've had a good night when you've broken a pair of heels dancing on a table," said a 23-year-old publicist, and "We don't dance on the tables," a young girl said, as the club filled with skinny young people, "we only dance on the banquettes."

Although there have been a few noted writers such as Joan Didion and Daphne Merkin who began their careers writing for fashion magazines, Morris said he understands how Christa might have felt conflicted writing fashion journalism. "Most of us came into the game as sensitive creatures who thought, 'I'll write a play.' We think we'll be an author or a poet, but fashion writing ends up seducing you. Not everyone can have jobs at glossy magazines, but on the other hand it's so meaningless. When you write for magazines you really have to fool yourself. I sometimes have that personal sadness, but I don't write about silverware. I write about the anxieties of the privileged and being single, a bachelor, a gay uncle. I'm closer to expressing myself in my work."

Christa wasn't "expressing herself" in a novel, or writing a play, but John Fairchild recognized she had something wonderful to say. In 1983, Christa sublet her Gramercy Park apartment and went to Paris to work as fashion editor at *WWD* and the fashion monthly *W* at their infamous offices on Rue Cambon.

THE NURSERY OF FASHION

Her first weeks in the "City of Lights," Christa wore her Nikes and trekked all over town, like a walking sponge. She browsed sidewalk book racks at Vanves and prowled the most splendid and deluxe flea market in the world, at Clignancourt, where she accrued comforting nesting materials for her tiny apartment. She wandered the Luxembourg Gardens and took a touristy jaunt through the sewers. At a patisserie on her corner she discovered a little pick-me-up that she would buy every day— a tiny apricot tart, its golden fruit mounded in a flaky cup, frescoed with a rosewater glaze. The more routine sights, like the Arc de Triomphe, the Eiffel Tower, were so ingrained in her psyche, they looked all too familiar, like landmarks from a recurring dream. She discovered a place where she liked to eat lunch. It was a busy café within the Eiffel Tower.

She joked that it was the only place in Paris where you could relax, sit down, and eat lunch, without having to *look* at the Eiffel Tower.

John Fairchild called Paris "the nursery of fashion," and Fairchild endorsed young talent and gave writers opportunities they couldn't get anywhere else. He threw them into the front rows at runways in Milan and Paris, sent them to parties and events, and taught them how to "see." Fairchild said, "Good fashion is simple. Bad fashion is when a woman exaggerates." Then again, he said, "Simplicity can be boring." "If your toes don't tingle, the show is a flop." "Throw Away chic worn by the right woman can outstyle the best of fashion." "It's sometimes fashionable to be unfashionable."

Fairchild's endless truisms and caveats were a primer for Christa and other young writers. Many of today's bright lights in fashion publishing came from that school. Fairchild gave cub reporters permission to lionize or eviscerate the most intimidating people on earth. Christa once said, "I passed judgment on social titans, political and business tycoons, even as they served me lunch in their country houses. Fairchild handed me a diploma in professional confidence. He gave me eyes to see the grand comedy of personality behind the signatures of style." *WWD* in Paris was a graduate school for fashion journalism. Christa was enrolled and John Fairchild was her don.

Although *Women's Wear Daily* is only a trade paper with a readership of just sixty thousand, it's the most important publication in the fashion business, which is very closed, insular, and coded. Christa did very well to decode that world for an audience; its most important followers were New York society. She was not only very good at decoding, she also knew how to poke fun at "the new thing" even as she celebrated it. When writing for *W*, writers had bylines. But in the daily paper, *WWD*, there were never bylines—writers sacrificed their identity for the common goal: get the glam news out! Find the truism. "Clothes for the workplace." "The Natural Look." "Women wear the pants!" Whether she put her name on what she wrote or threw her handcrafted essays into the roiling melting pot, she was writing to please Fairchild.

Friends recognize that there is a correlation between the way Christa felt about her career life and her family. In each case, she had always felt in it but not of it.

Fairchild encouraged, he even prompted, Christa's cheeky examinations of the very chic (translate that as very rich). Christa soon understood the many layers of the golden onion that included: "The Old Guard" or "Café Society," original old money, politicos and celebs, and those whom Fairchild called the "Wobbly WASPs." And in the early eighties there emerged a whole new glamour demographic called "Nouvelle Society," a label Fairchild extended to "people infused with a combination of money and power that gives them rights and privileges almost beyond comprehension." All of these wealthy factions kneel down before "The High Court of Fashion," the designers in Paris and Milan. Christa's acuity in "decoding" these worlds came from both her Vassar education and her own edgy sensibility, which was half receptive romantic, half blistering skeptic. A professor at Vassar once introduced her to an instructive tidbit of philosophy written by Antonio Gramsci: wisdom is "the pessimism of intellect and the optimism of will."

John Fairchild loved to watch Christa mix it up.

In a 1986 "Letter from Paris" column, Christa reported on high-society Christmas parties and political unrest in the City of Lights. Of course, as required, she begins her piece with a report that Christina Onassis threw a party at Maxim's for fifty guests, and that Philippe de Rothschild had written a book of poetry! But she continues, "The holidays are always a signal to hightail it out of town. This year, the de Ravenels are taking an exotic voyage, traveling with a gang down the Nile. But however far away they get, Parisians will return to the high suspense that has gripped their city of late: the great question mark posed by the March elections in which Mitterrand, with only five years of his obligatory seven-year term served, will lose parliamentary support. 'Paris is numb,' says Isabelle d'Ornano. She will be far from political concerns, entertaining 40 of her children's friends in the Loire Valley over the new year, but she observes, 'There is a sense of expectation and no one knows what to think.' And, Madame Pompidou at long last accepted an invitation from the Chinese to tour the republic in style. With Kim d'Estainville, she roamed the countryside in chauffeur-driven cars—their seats still warm from the Kissingers. . . ."

Christa suggests the brazen incongruities of her privileged subjects' lavish trips and the tense political scene in Paris.

Novelist Thomas Moran, author of *Man in the Closet*, was a writer at Fairchild Publications who had worked at *M* magazine. He said that he had also been nurtured by John Fairchild. Fairchild expected great things from them, and he wanted them to walk on the razor's edge. Moran said about Fairchild, "He was attracted to bright, authentic young people and he really gave them a push."

Yet her friends understood how difficult it was for Christa's transformation from Yankee schoolgirl to instant "glam Francophile." Jay Mulvaney said, "There was a big dichotomy at the Paris offices. As fantastic as it looked on the outside, it was completely horrendous on the inside. *W* was a very political place, and Christa felt very uncomfortable. It was a boys' club. She would say that her supervising editor at *WWD*, Patrick McCarthy, and John Fairchild were pigs to women. It was 'unbelievably loathsome' was a phrase she repeated to me. Another word she used was 'odious.' The whole scene at the time was the emergence of these high-society figures, but they were all ex-hookers, literally, who married well, and who were lionized. Hookers and whores. It should be called *Women's Whore Daily*. These people were the queens of eighties society. The second trophy wives of *W* men. Women, who through very astute marriages to very wealthy financiers, corralled New York society in the eighties and nineties, and Christa had to write about them. How fabulous they were. How stylish they were. It was just a big group masturbatory thing—society based on money rather than real style. Christa hated it and had this sort of resigned laugh.

"But she did it because it afforded her this really idyllic life in Paris. She had this great little apartment near the Eiffel Tower. I went to Paris twice a year in a theater company. In the mid-eighties I saw her a half dozen times. We always went to the flea market. She collected a lot of fabric. She had fabric all over the place—very boudoirlike."

Christopher Petkranas, a writer at *WWD* in Paris at the same time as Christa, said, "It wasn't an idyllic life at all! Her apartment—people imagine it was eight or nine rooms—but it was a tiny box. She lived a very reduced life."

But as tiny as her apartment might have been, her ascendance in the fashion society of Paris and Western Europe was charging ahead. Christa started to appear in distinguished company. In Paris, the couture capital, and in Milan, when Christa attended shows, she was seated in the front row at every runway, beside Mr. Fairchild himself. She was sent to ateliers for previews and to get the skinny prior to the season launch of both haute couture and ready-to-wear collections, spring and fall. She had private tête-à-têtes with every designer worth putting ink to paper about, and from these exclusive interviews, she was first to pounce on a trend or to find the one explosive silhouette that would turn couture on its ear.

Christa had her lips to the vibrating railroad track of fashion. She became adept at feeling the slightest tickle that would erupt into the new sensation. For *W*, she wrote various columns from Paris: "Paris Now," "Letter from Paris." A column in 1984 called "First Look at Paris" is a typical example of Christa's investigative scouring and finesse. She wrote:

> A nonchalant mood is emerging with flirty but simple dresses, warm color—especially peachy-pink—jackets made with the ease of sweaters

and at Yves Saint Laurent, new couture pantsuits that are more feminine than sportive. Saint Laurent is also packing this collection with
color—including blues, greens, and a vivid hot pink he calls "buvard,"
the color of French blotting paper. Meanwhile at the house of Chanel,
Karl Lagerfeld imbues Mademoiselle's classics with a new "easiness" for
spring. Lagerfeld is elongating the Chanel suit in supple wool crepes.
The jacket is cut to the hip—"It all stops here," he says, his hands
shoved deep in his pockets to demonstrate. The black mousseline
featherweight gown will be featured for evening, along with extra-
delicate embroideries which Lagerfeld calls "Chinese porcelain."

And elsewhere, Emanuel Ungaro is pursuing his quest for "liquid"
fashion with fluid clothes steeped in haute glamour. The collection
will include cashmere dresses and suits worn with oversized jackets in
Easter-egg colors: powdery fuchsia, aqua, and canary yellow. "I wanted
something sumptuous and sexy," says Ungaro, unconcerned by the
possibility of warm spring temperatures. His evening wear will include, as usual, a fount of Proustian lace, but this time he is concocting
simple pastel silk cocktail dresses with draped backs, or trompe l'oeil
skirts that flare out from under a seven-eighths blouson jacket.

Celebrity spotlights the couture at Christian Dior, where Princess
Stephanie of Monaco, now a full-time staff member, works diligently at
a drawing table decorated with a stuffed Pink Panther doll.

Christa's "First Look at Paris" column is wordsmithing magic, the
work of a fashion alchemist. Her text combines poetic figure with diction
specific to the trade, descriptive detail that sounds almost too technical or
scientific. Christa identifies fabrics with a clinical, almost a chemist's ac-
curacy: cashmere, black mousseline, organza, crepe de chine, as if these
textiles were elements found in a periodic table in a haute couture labo-
ratory. She praises designers, but she also slaps wrists and suggests that
these geniuses must be careful about how the elements are incorporated.
Ungaro should not be "unconcerned by the possibility of warm spring
temperatures."

Of first importance in fashion is "shape and proportion." She describes
the flounces, poufs, columns, the "bubble chemise," and "slimly tailored
sleeves," with the fussiness of an architect who is careful to blueprint ex-

act roof pitches, ridge beams, first-floor elevations, cathedraled entry-
ways, and flying buttresses. As expected, she folds in a sleek freshet of
tabloid info: Princess Stephanie with her little stuffed pussycat.

And Christa knows the color chart, the complex palette of chic. In couture, there are luxury fabrics and sculpted designs, but *color* is the
medium. Easter-egg. Peachy-pink. French blotting paper, "buvard." Bleu.
Blau. Blauw.

Sometimes Fairchild would dictate what he wanted said, but Christa
did most of the writing "from Paris" during her tenure and she covered
the primary collections. Other fashion writers have said that they could
read a story and instantly recognize Christa's particular sizzle and intro-
spective flourishes. Kate Betts was a reporter at *W* after Christa left Paris.
Betts said, "Christa had the *W* voice down, very particular and sort of
evocative fashion writing, and I remember one of the ways they taught
people to write like that was by showing them Christa's work. She was the
example."

John Fairchild said, "Fashion is a subart and is not intellectual. . . .
Fashion appeals to the senses and comes from gut feeling. . . . True fashion comes straight out of the jungle."

Christa understood that jungle. The "beauty and the beast" motif
seemed at the core of couture romance and all things sensual and lovely.
In her own life, she felt its force. At least for the time being, the wolf at the
door was appeased by "good copy."

A fashion writer has to have an "eye" to be able to pick out the important silhouette. Christa went to a preview, perhaps Christian Lacroix or
Gianni Versace, and she'd see the sudden surprise, something repeated in
a designer's collection that was inherently "new" and yet held authentic
traits. New designs must be novel, but should suggest couture conquests
of yesteryear, sustaining the "grande logique" and have historical rele-
vance. It had to be a "beginning," but it had to be grounded in every
excellent decision made previously. It's a feeling. It's a live spark. Some
designers still cut on live models—and this energy and finesse is palpable
in the final creation.

Christa would view a collection and decide what design would go on
the front page of *WWD*, and it might say "Paris Says Short," or "Paris Says
Velvet." Says "Leather." Says "Bold." Says "Bare."

Not only did she report on collections and designers' triumphs, flops, their tiffs and spats, Christa was charged with reporting on the lifestyles of the wealthy. "The Old Guard," who were both the crumbly European aristocracy and the "Wobbly WASPs," and the "Nouvelles," who were far more wealthy, by the billions.

Bob Morris said, "It was helpful for her to have that name, 'Worthington,' and for her to look WASPy and to have gone to Vassar. For every one of her, there are ten young writers with Italian last names that don't get into the game. That world is dazzled by all things English and WASPy. That's why we've got Tina Brown, Anna Wintour. It's amazing Remnick got *The New Yorker*. But 'Worthington . . .' People associate that name with grandeur."

Christa attended Nouvelle society soirees, weddings, and wingdings. Sometimes she introduced herself, "I'm Christa Worthington, with *Women's Wear Daily*," so they would know what-was-what. The Nouvelles seemed more than delighted to see her, and she could tug out her notebook and mingle freely during cocktails, jotting down *who* was wearing *what*, and just how gorgeous it all was. But at some events, especially with sensitive Nouvelles or very reserved aristocracy, she had to disappear into the ladies' room to write notes on a tiny tablet she kept hidden in her itsy-bitsy clutch. Fairchild said, "It's difficult for a reporter to be both guest and truthful chronicler."

At one glamorous dinner party, Christa discovered that there were a hundred dining room chairs entwined with roses. Hundreds, maybe thousands, of long-stemmed yellow buds were carefully bound by ribbons to the chair legs and high backs. Christa noticed that every rose had been meticulously dethorned. She imagined the florist's apprentices who must have spent hours snipping the deadly prickers, careful not to bruise the budding blooms. Her vision of these enslaved workers was like a scene from the terrifying fairy tale "Rumpelstiltskin." And the room had a sweet, intoxicating fragrance that was almost throttling. For some inexplicable reason, she suffered an obsessive-compulsive disorder episode, and for the duration of the evening, as she chin-wagged and giggled with guests, she examined the chairs, trying to find one thorn that might have been overlooked.

Often Christa was sent to these affairs in borrowed couture, but, even so, she wasn't seated at the table. She was supposed to be invisible. She was sent to cover a magnificent two-day party on the Île Saint-Louis thrown by Baroness Hélène de Rothschild to announce the engagement of her son to a Belgian princess. Christa told her friend Alice Furlaud, a Paris correspondent for National Public Radio and a close neighbor in Truro: "The arrangement was, I could come inside just to get the atmospherics down; I could see all the buffet tables perfectly laid out, all the flower arrangements, all pink and white to match her dress—and the interiors of the mansion. There was a whole bookcase made of lapis lazuli. You can't even get enough lapis lazuli to make a ring anymore."

Christa was permitted to come "inside" but she couldn't attend the actual party. She was treated like Cinderella and kept out of sight. The next day she was permitted to come back to visit the baroness in order to get an accurate guest list for her story. It was three o'clock in the afternoon and the baroness had not yet dragged herself out of bed. Christa was invited upstairs to her opulent bedroom, its windows looking onto the Seine. The baroness propped herself up in her ocean liner of a bed, with its lace-embroidered pillows, its tapestry-draped canopy. She gave Christa the names of her party guests with the precision of a jeweler sorting diamonds and gems with a flat-edge knife, as she nibbled champagne truffles.

Any time someone turned on a radio, all over Paris, Christa heard a thin, whiny but guileless voice singing "Girls Just Want to Have Fun." The American pop single was a hit, even in Paris. Still a bit under the influence of Vassar fem politics, Christa felt somewhere in between Cindi Lauper's anthem and Helen Reddy's "I Am Woman."

Christa sent tear sheets of some of her stories to her mother and father in Hingham, or her mother ran to the newsstand to buy a new issue. Her father didn't think *WWD* was on the same level as *Le Monde,* and Christa felt he didn't approve of all the applause given to such a frivolous subject. Haute couture, and prêt-à-porter, or ready-to-wear, with all the fanfare and hoopla repeated four times a year, was a cycle he didn't appreciate. Toppy knew that Christa could write. He didn't understand why she didn't write something important. He warned Christa that writing about fashion was like being "fried in a cheap oil."

But Gloria was thrilled with Christa's career, and she brought copies of Christa's magazine articles to her Monday portrait workshop at Mahoney Studios to show her friends from the Scituate Art Association. She stood between paint pots and easels to read excerpts out loud. Betty Burke and Kay Shaw, members of Gloria's art circle, said that Gloria was very proud of her daughter. Kay Shaw said, "Gloria was always unhappy about something, she complained about her husband. But she'd bring these big glossy magazines to us, and she'd point to Christa's name at the bottom of a story about Giorgio Armani or Nancy Reagan. She'd be beaming."

Gloria visited Christa in Paris, and Christa showed her the sights, no longer needing to follow tourist brochures or maps herself. Christa gave her mother a whirlwind tour of the old standbys—Montmartre, Notre Dame, the Pompidou Center, four hours at the Louvre one day, and another four hours at the Picasso Museum. She took her mother to lunch at her favorite restaurant inside the Eiffel Tower and told Gloria the inside joke. It was the only place in Paris where you *don't have to look* at the Eiffel Tower. Gloria thought Christa's sarcasm seemed a little too jaded, too Parisian. They went to shop at Les Galeries Lafayette, "the Bloomingdale's of Paris," where Gloria bought one pair of silk knee socks. But Gloria told Christa, "Look at you. Why are you dressed like a rag doll? You're a fashion writer. We're in Paris!"

Christa was wearing a skirt she had purchased at the flea market at Clignancourt. It was ratty. And she wore an old sweatshirt turned inside out; its nubby pile made her look fuzzy as a hamster. She reminded Gloria that she had bought the sweatshirt one Sunday at the Wellfleet flea market at the drive-in on Route 6.

Whether on Cape Cod or in Paris, Christa hunted for comfortable clothes and furnishings. She searched for items that would be little anchors for her wobbly psyche. She was always trying to find the right "soulful accessory" and her shopping trips were intensely serious, almost grave. What was she looking for that she never found?

Writing freelance articles on "decor" for *Elle* and the *New York Times*, Christa was invited to warehouses of antiques and house furnishings accrued by haute furniture designers who collected unique items for "inspiration and transformation." She interviewed designers Garouste and Bonetti, who rejected gilt chairs for their rustic creations: "Sometimes called 'Barbarism,' the label 'neo-primitive' has been applied to their use of rough-hewn materials, such as raffia and dead branches. 'We want to produce furniture in the way a fashion collection is designed—like an idea, a desire.' " On these decor assignments, Christa often found herself plunked before invented "dream rooms." Yet it was in a dark first-floor warehouse of estate sale furnishings, one of the many antiques emporiums in the Village Saint-Paul in the Marais, near the Seine, that Christa first stood before "the mirror." It was a tall, vertical shimmer, like an embodied trance. Its sliver of light evoked the sensation she felt when standing before a body of water. Like the Pamet in a dead calm, or a public fountain when they turn off the feathery cascade and the surface no longer skitters your reflection. The oversized mirror had an immediate tonic effect on her. She felt the facets of her spinal column unlock, the tight muscles in her neck relax. On the other hand, she knew it was a white elephant. It was both these elements—the aura of sublime peace and Christa's insatiable attraction to the idiosyncratic and gregarious totem that made her decide to buy it. The worst problem was getting it delivered to her apartment.

At the *W* offices on Rue Cambon, the street where Henry James had lived when writing *The American*, Christa was living a fantasy life. She had the Rolodex of God. Her address book was a "Who's Who" of A-list celebrities in the arts and fashion. She had the home telephone numbers of designers and movie stars. One friend said, "I remember her telling me about spending the afternoon with Sting and his wife, Trudi Styler, and how fatuous they were, drifting through their afternoon in a self-congratulatory New Age haze."

Her UEA beau said, "At first she had had fun at *WWD*. She was running around in limos and hanging out with Yves Saint Laurent. She had an affair with some aristocrat with his own castle. But it was unreal and she wasn't carving out a niche for herself. *WWD* was a notoriously

twisted place as an organization, but the life that it gave her was a deliri-
ous life, and she understood it was a wild fantasy. It's notoriously difficult
for American women in Europe. You get included, then in the long term
you get excluded. Christa felt alienating elements in the fashion world.
Again, she felt she was in it but not of it. She'd be cut off at some point.
The consolation is that the institution has loyalty to you, but in the end it
didn't for Christa."

Her insider-outsider status was mirrored in her relationships with
men. She had brief, repetitive fiascoes with married men. Parisian infi-
delities generally cause little upset to everyday home life, but for Christa
it was always a little bit of a letdown when her paramours seemed so nonchalant. What's the difference, she asked, between "nonchalant" and "indifferent"? Edmund White wrote about the moral climate in Paris in his
book *The Flaneur*. He said, "It's a city where you can swap your wife if you
want to. . . . Paris is made up of equal parts of social conservatism and
anarchic experimentation, but foreigners never quite know where to
place the moral accent mark. . . . Monica Lewinsky's 'White House knee
pads' made the French hold their sides with continental mirth and superior erotic sophistication."

A friend said that Christa sought unavailable men on purpose, so she
wouldn't have to live up to anyone's expectations. But one college friend
said, "She'd fall into things semireluctantly, but she always hoped someone would come and take that 'halfwayness' out of her."

At *W*, Christa became very close to her formidable colleagues Marion
McEvoy and Ben Brantley. A writer who had worked with McEvoy said,
"Marion was the Queen of Fashion. A diva. Givenchy and Saint Laurent
sat at her feet. She was a real force and carried herself with conscious election. But Christa had some wild times with Marion." He said Christa felt
that she "was very much in Brantley's shadow at *W*. He was more educated, more talented." But she learned a great deal from Brantley and
McEvoy, and she confided in them.

It was at Ben Brantley's holiday party in New York, just weeks before
she was murdered, where Christa had reentered the scene with Ava, who
looked adorable in her party dress. Christa was happy to see her old colleague and friend, and she told Brantley about her desire to leave Truro

and return to Manhattan. She was also considering moving back to Paris. She had told Tim Arnold, "Paris has great schools for Ava. France sinks money in education." If she was thinking about leaving Truro, she still couldn't decide what city, country, or continent was more promising. It was that "halfwayness" again, and she needed a nudge, a shove. But it was too late.

DOCKSIDE CONFIDENTIAL

In February, at the initial custody hearing at Barnstable Probate Court, when Judge Scandurra named Amyra Chase as Ava's temporary guardian instead of the girl's father, her own blood kin, attorney Peter Hickey was appointed counselor for the toddler. "Young as she may be, Ava Worthington has her own attorney," Emily Dooley wrote in the *Cape Cod Times.* Hickey is a member of the Barnstable County program Children and Parents, a group of local attorneys who pledge each year to handle five cases for a measly stipend of $1,250 per case.

"My job is not to be an investigator or make recommendations to the court; my job is to represent the child's viewpoint," Hickey said. But with a nudge from Hickey, the original ninety-day custody order that was set to expire April 8 was extended through June, and another interloper was invited into the huddle. Dr. Kenneth Herman, a psychologist and attorney, was appointed "guardian ad litem" for Ava, someone whose role is to investigate a child's situation with her parents or caretakers and who reports his findings to the court. He started to brisk around the opposing nests, investigating the home settings, family values, lifestyles, and pros and cons of both households. It was a contest between the low-end Jackett milieu and the more affluent Chase homestead. Jackett felt Herman might be biased against a fisherman's modest setup.

But Tony couldn't do anything but bite his tongue and sit on his hands as the guardian ad litem accrued information and compiled a report. The report would be discussed at a pretrial conference on June 10.

The more suits involved in the battle, the worse it looked for Tony. Peter Manso's new book, *Ptown: Art, Sex, and Money on the Outer Cape* was a headline in the front pages of local papers. The book was discussed on local all-talk radio shows, and Manso was interviewed on Boston

TV news programs. The book was the subject of a feature story in the Sunday *New York Times*, entitled "Dockside Confidential: The Talk of P-town." Writer Fred Bernstein wrote, "Mr. Manso's detailed account of Mr. Jackett's part in a botched plan to smuggle 800 bales of marijuana into Provincetown by boat in 1985 seems to have complicated Mr. Jackett's case.

" 'I have concerns about how the book would affect my custody case, and no doubt that's why I'm fearful of going to trial,' Mr. Jackett said."

Tony was also concerned about Manso's portrait of his family. "He makes us sound dysfunctional," Tony said. But in recent months, Tony's family had appeared a little overtaxed. Since the murder, his grown children had to go about their business in town under a cloud of suspicion. They all had had samples taken for DNA testing. The press followed every move the state police made, learning whom they had swabbed, and whom they had pricked. Every day, Tony felt as if his family was vulnerable, exposed, like one time years ago when all his babies were in the car as he tried to change a tire on the highway. As traffic whipped past, the jack wouldn't hold.

Adding to the public swirl, his kids Braunwyn and Luc were in over their heads in jerry-rigged romances gone awry. Braunwyn, estranged from her high-strung husband, Keith Amato, took off with Luc and his girlfriend, India, and went to Colorado. Luc had been loyal to India during her pregnancy, although it wasn't his child she was carrying. Luc had squired her around and had assisted at the birth, but India dumped Luc in Colorado to return to the father of her baby. At the same time, Braunwyn connected with an old boyfriend and after a brief getaway to the Rockies, she returned to Provincetown "in the pudding club." She was pregnant. In her first trimester, she moved back home with Tony and Susan. The ghost of Hester Prynne seems to hover over the Jackett clan.

Keith Amato was acting more erratic, his shorts twisted in a knot by events he couldn't control. He left his job at High Toss Pizza. He looked for work, but was most visible as a regular guest on a local radio talk show, a wannabe sleazefest on WOMR. WOMR is the local nonprofit radio station, called "Outermost Community Radio," in Provincetown; its programming is run by a shabby Rolodex of fringe radio enthusiasts and volunteer DJs. From the late Ernest Cooper, a beloved geezer whose Sunday-morning show *Forward March* had presented two hours of nothing but marching bands to a constantly changing index of disc jockey clones, WOMR programming is always transitioning. It has everything from one diva historian's hour of Broadway show tunes, to another DJ's never-ending Grateful Dead discology on a show called *The Psychedelic Oyster*, to pounding techno dance music, New Age smoothies, and the usual PBS fare of Celtic reels, flings, and fiddle power.

Cape Cod Times reporter Eric Williams hosts a Wednesday-morning talk show where Amato often appears to shoot the breeze. After the Worthington murder, Williams wrote a story about his troubled radio guest for the paper:

"Amato had been questioned by the state police several times. Keith is always included in the 'people-who-have-been-questioned lists' . . . and he's fed up with that. He's a funny guy and a natural on the air. But the show is a no-holds-barred kind of space and he knew if he came back it would mean talking about, well, everything. He answered some rough questions, live, on the air. 'Did you kill Christa Worthington?'

" 'No, no, Eric,' said Keith. 'Of course you know I wouldn't do that.' "

On live radio, they discussed the never-ending Worthington chapter, and Amato shadow-boxed with Braunwyn about their daughter, Etel, threatening a whole new custody battle.

As Tony's kids seemed to mirror the impulsive mistakes and the hard luck aftermaths that Tony himself was enduring, the guardian ad litem report would no doubt chronicle the ongoing ruckus.

Meanwhile, Amyra Chase was caring for Ava. Amyra brought her to weekly counseling sessions at the Child Witness to Violence Project at Boston Medical Center, and she had the more active role in Ava's day-to-day recovery from her trauma.

Added to the Jackett family's boisterous tumult, Tony's digs just couldn't compete with Amyra and Clifford's large home in an upscale neighborhood in Cohasset. In fact, in order to economize, Tony had recently had to move his family out of their small suburban rental house on Sunset

Drive. He and Susan went to live in an apartment on the top floor of his father-in-law's old house on busy Commercial Street in Provincetown. Tony was being downsized. With his kids all grown up, it might seem a commonsense change of locale, but Kyle was still living at home, and Braunwyn had moved back with Etel, as she faced her unplanned pregnancy.

And everyone knew that the Provincetown school system didn't have the same cachet as the schools on the South Shore that Amyra's four kids attended. Tony saw that he wasn't perched on a level playing field on which to win his custody bid. Convincing Dr. Kenneth Herman would be a steep uphill climb.

Tony said that during this time, his cousin Chris Snow was approached by the "other side," who had made an offer to "buy off Tony's parental rights with a lump sum payment." He says, "This wasn't in writing. They'll deny it. But we told them we're not interested."

When you speak with Tony Jackett, you bump up against a strong will. It seems guileless; detractors might say it's witless, but it's frontal. Whether he's on the *Josephine G.*, or in Barnstable District Court, he's determined. As in his realm as shellfish constable, he's resolute, like the bearded mussel that holds on when the surf is pounding. These creatures cling to one another in glistening mats and don't give up.

Tim Arnold regularly visited Ava in Cohasset. He rode up with Christa's aunt, Diana, to see her. Tony is suspicious of Arnold's devotion when Arnold rarely sees his own two kids, who live with their mother less than three hours away near Andover, Massachusetts. The police have said that Arnold's interest in the baby was one way he could visit his exgirlfriend after she had dumped him.

Tim and Diana saw Ava whenever they pleased, but Tony had to adhere to a strict visitation schedule. Tony said he was really "frosted" to hear that Arnold was free to visit Ava whenever he wanted, getting a lift to Cohasset from this or that Worthington crone, usually Diana. Tony saw his daughter only once a week for a few hours, and most of that time was spent on Route 6. He and Susan drove up and down the Cape each Wednesday, in summer traffic, to meet Amyra at the Sagamore Bridge. Amyra drove the shorter leg from Cohasset. Driving back and forth took up most of Tony's allotted time with Ava.

I'm familiar with the "bridge switch." Years ago I met my daughter's father at the Sagamore Bridge every other weekend. And before that period, when I was a graduate student in Iowa City, I drove seventy miles, both ways, on Interstate 80, through numbing rural farmland to connect with Mr. Mistake at a Stuckey's Truck Stop. A Stuckey's is a little patch of American purgatory: Formica tables, watery coffee, gaudy pinwheel lollipops in a jar at the cash register. It seemed like Stuckey's was the spot in that part of the Midwest where estranged couples united to disperse their charges and to reclaim them. Connect, disconnect, depart with their yo-yo strapped into the backseat. If it's your turn to have a getaway weekend, you drive off alone. It's the same meeting ground at the Sagamore Bridge. Even Tim Arnold sometimes meets his ex-wife at the tourist landmark known as the Tugboat, a regulation-sized vessel dry-docked at the Bourne Bridge, the sister span of the Sagamore. These midpoint exchanges happen all over the country. Some ex-wives insist that the father drive all the way if he wants to see his kids—that's his problem. Tim says his ex-wife isn't making the trek much anymore. With his vision trouble, he can't do it either.

But for Tony, after raising six kids, "joint custody" was a new experience. He gets to the bridge and parks in the Dunkin' Donuts parking lot at the rotary to wait for Ava. In the moments before he greets his daughter, he has never felt more sandwiched between two lives. The canal that separates the Cape from the mainland intensifies the sensation of being "in between." His first life seems to have culminated here, with all his wrongdoings come to roost like the black crows collecting on the Texaco sign, while his second-chance life is still foggy, without promises crystallizing. Then Ava arrives. She climbs into his Jeep and he straps her into the new car seat he purchased just for her. She's beautiful. Her tousled curls look like a rufous dahlia. But sometimes Ava isn't too pleased to be locked into another vehicle for the second leg of her long journey to Provincetown, only to be turned around in a few hours. She drums her heels and whines for an instant. On these outings, she's like a kind of perishable cargo—Boston lettuce that wilts fast; she's ferried back and forth for more time than she's entertained or is allowed to play. At her tender age, she can't see the reasoning. In their pinched visit together, she and her father seem like victims of a bureaucratic boondoggle. But every

Wednesday, Tony is there to meet her. On the return trip, after dropping Ava at the rotary, he and Susan might do a little shopping in Hyannis. They browse at the Job Lot or at the Christmas Tree Shop looking for bargains. A little deal on some domestic gizmo takes the edge off after giving his baby back.

Tony is parked at the Truro post office. He calls me to come over and I sit down in his Jeep. He looks tan, honey-toned, healthy. He's dressed in jeans and a leather vest. Wearing a leather vest in summer says "Fashion Victim" by *W* standards. But Tony is groomed as if he knows his local fans expect him to live up to his signature Don Juan profile. I see an old European tradition familiar to me from my own first-generation family members. Men took extra care in their appearance, and somehow seemed to look stylish every workday, like peacocks, even when wearing an oilskin butcher's apron or their tradesmen Dickey overalls.

Today he wants talk therapy. I had come to pick up my mail, and I hold a pile of it in my lap as he tells me about Ava. His Wednesday routine is tough, getting harder to live up to. Sometimes he imagines not bringing Ava back to the bridge. Not handing her over to Amyra. He says, "On the *48 Hours* segment, everyone says Ava was prompted to say she loved 'her daddy.' That's not true. We didn't force her to say that. But you know, the last time we went to the bridge to get the baby, when Susan referred to me as 'Daddy,' Ava shook her head. She frowned at me, like she didn't believe it. I worry that they're telling her not to think of me as her father.

"I keep figuring, after we went to all the effort with Christa, getting our families together, why did Christa make a new will naming Amyra Chase and her husband? I think it was because Christa was surprised to see Susan roll with the punches. She thought Susan would dump me when she found out about Ava. Then she finds out Susan is *sweet*. Christa didn't know how to relate to sweet people. She liked to have battles. Her aunt Lucinda and her uncle John told me they had never met a more difficult person than Christa."

Susan Jackett told me that Christa had trouble believing that Susan could be so forgiving of both her husband and of Christa. Susan's willingness to incorporate Ava into her life, and to even invite Christa into her family circle, was mind-boggling to Christa, when her own family life was measured in chilling distances. It was more natural for Christa to feel rivalry in family settings. Susan said, "I forgave Christa. I felt so sorry for her regarding all the anger she had, because I got over that real quick. She was just sort of pitiful. But I don't know why she had to pick on my husband."

People walking in and out of the PO see me sitting in the front seat beside Tony. Some residents are still eyeing Tony as if he might be a killer, but others are smirking, as if thinking, "Whose pants is he trying to pry into now?" or "There's Tony, thinking with his 'little head.' " Tony's in a fishbowl. "It's like being a fly on the wall of a coffee shop, when I hear everyone talking about me," he said. Yet many of the oldsters, fishermen, leaseholders who see him regularly on the flats, the Town Hall geezers and dump haulers, stop by his window to say hello.

Even dressed in his finery like a Siamese fighting fish, he's just good old Tony, one of their own.

His visibility crested with Peter Manso's narrative about Tony's smuggling days. With that, and the addition of a guardian ad litem investigation, Tony tells me he's beginning to have some doubts about winning the custody battle. He says, "Peter befriended me and then he betrayed me. Because of that book I may have lost my bid. For me to say the book won't have an effect on the court's decision would be naïve. I was naïve with Christa, I didn't see what she was scheming. Thinking back on it now, I see why she didn't want to get out of bed afterward and clean herself up like a woman going about her business. Instead, she'd lie on her back, tilt her hips. Once she put her legs in the air. I thought she was doing yoga. She was trying to get pregnant. Even the Worthingtons knew she was trying to get pregnant. Jan had been hoping to have a baby, too. They were in a race."

Writer Jessica Treadway said that she had met Jan Worthington when she visited *Boston Globe* critic Gail Caldwell, who had rented a Worthington house one summer. When Jan stopped by to see Gail, she and Jessica shared their notes about wanting to have babies, although they were both single. Jan said she planned to attend an adoption fair, but finding a local guy was a more direct route.

Tony said, "Jan's boyfriends weren't so dumb as me. Well, I can't be so naïve now. I'm offended by Manso's chapter headings, 'Tony the Drug Smuggler.' And, worse, he makes us out to be a dysfunctional family. He says my son had only one pair of trousers for school. In the end, he doesn't suggest I matured at all."

I ask him, "Tony, your kids are grown up. Are you sure you're ready for another three-year-old?"

He says, "Susan told me that if I didn't try to get Ava, she wouldn't want to be with me. She'd walk."

Susan seemed to have inexhaustible maternal gifts. More than thirty years ago, she had adopted two Sioux Indian babies with her first husband before having four children with Tony. When she was willing to take on his love child, people thought it wasn't selfless but self-destructive. To many, she seemed like a victim or a beaten-down female. Susan said, "If they think I'm a victim, it's because people confuse kindness with weakness."

Susan still believed in her husband. She still often called him "Dumbdick," but on *48 Hours*, in front of a billion viewers, she had said, "Tony is a good man."

Tony smiles when I mention it. Not like a cat who ate the canary, but like a dog who was just sprung from the doghouse. He tells me, "We were one argument away from splitting up, but this whole thing has brought us together."

In May, Tony and Susan had a birthday party for Ava in Provincetown. That same week, Amyra held a gala event in Cohasset, inviting Christa's friends from Depot Road with their children, and taking care to be inclusive of her own kids, Ava's prospective siblings. Even Toppy arrived. Having two birthday parties seemed just the beginning of an excess of both riches and obligations for Ava to manage in the years to come.

But the first week of June, before the pretrial conference, rumors circulated that Tony was being forced to concede his custody battle. On June 7, five months to the day after Amyra Chase had filed for emergency custody, newspapers reported that the guardian ad litem, Dr. Kenneth Herman, had submitted his thirty-three-page report to Judge Scandurra.

The report favored Ms. Chase. Herman concluded that for Ava "to lose a parent, live with a new family for five months, and then have to move again would be counterproductive to the child's adjustment after the loss of her mother." Ava would be better off in Cohasset, with Amyra. But Tony asked me, "What's better? With me, Ava will grow up in this town known as 'Tony Jackett's kid,' but with [Amyra and Clifford], she'll be known as 'the daughter of that murder victim.' "

Tony and Amyra were expected to appear in Barnstable Probate and Family Court on June 10, but the date was postponed to June 20. Tony sat down with his cousin and attorney, Chris Snow, to discuss the struggle ahead if they went to trial. The money. The humiliation. The caustic examinations of his family life. His criminal record. His dalliances, both his famous detours and his nondescript meanderings. These were nothing to sneeze at. Tony started to see how the fallout might be worse than the triumph, if and when he should win his case. A fisherman knows when to steam out and when to turn around if the weather shifts and the sky turns to slate.

"It appears this case may settle," Ava's court-appointed attorney, Peter Hickey, told the *Cape Cod Times* on June 11, two weeks before the postponed hearing. The trial was never put on the docket, and the pretrial conference became a last-minute, mostly benign powwow between both parties.

Jackett had reached a moment where a turnaround didn't seem like a defeat. He thought of *Jo*, how she sank in the Pamet and he brought her up. When she sank again, she was salvage. She sits in a shipyard now, in more than a few pieces. He wasn't going to let that happen to Ava.

So he agreed to a settlement where Ava would live with Amyra and Clifford. "It is expected that Jackett will have ongoing contact," Hickey said. Chris Snow said that Tony would provide child support but the dollar amount wasn't disclosed.

Tony told the *Cape Codder*, "If we went on to a lengthy court battle, it would have been nasty, and other people would have been dragged into it." He told the *Provincetown Banner*, "It's probably the best decision to make at this point in time, because the baby has bonded with them. She'll always know I'm her father and I'm going to have a relationship with her."

After the decision at the courthouse, Amyra was quite liberal with her pencil line smile. She told the press, "What happened today was the best possible arrangement for Ava." But as Susan Jackett stepped up to hug Amyra, saying, "I think we're all going to be good friends and very close," Amyra's face became suddenly pinched and fragile, like overheated glass.

Response in town was split. Some local folks who had followed the tortuous custody case were relieved that Ava wouldn't be forced to return to the gothic setting where her mother was murdered. Watching Ava grow up in their midst, right on Front Street, would be a constant reminder. Unsolved crimes should be swept away; they're a stain on our bucolic Eden and can't be good for tourism. But many residents believed that Tony and Susan were betrayed by the system; they were martyrs. People recognized the flavor of class privilege in the outcome. The patrician has more rights than the hard-scrabble fisherman. Christa's pretty face in news photos, "like a Sargent painting," was an example of what critic Roger Fry had condemned Sargent for in the first place. Sargent's work was "art applied to social requirement and social ambition." Whistler had said it was "a cold and soulless eclecticism." Added to the haughty picture is what Tony had been saying, "I was outgunned and outresourced."

If the baby had not been a Worthington, if she had been Linda Silva's kid, she'd be coming back to P-town where she belonged.

EAST OF EASTHAM

The unofficial but uncontested "Town Historian of Truro," a woman named Betty Groom, lives in an antique house on Truro Center Road. A quarter-mile from the PO on a busy jog between Town Hall and Depot Road. She has lived in the landmark property her whole life. It's where she was born, where she raised her six kids, and the house where her father died and was waked. From its parlor windows and sloping lawn, she has watched the town evolve. She monitors its growth and transformations; she notes when it's willing to change and, more often, when it sinks its heels in.

With her heart-shaped face and wavy white hair, Betty looks like a "Cape Cod Mrs. Claus." But she's no Milquetoast pushover; she has an unsentimental vision of Truro life. She's no saint herself, she says, and at seventy years old she might be a granny but she's also a bad-ass realist. She knows the town's folks, both its natives and its washashores, its saints and meanies, its fathers and its prodigal sons, and, of course, she's seen some Jezebels and a love child now and again.

Betty's house sits on a winding oyster shell drive, bordered by mature plantings, fifty-year-old yuccas and lilacs, and an old boat on blocks in one corner. (Authentic Cape Cod homes have to have a boat on blocks, or an overturned dinghy, or a dory cloaked in trumpet vine or honey-suckle.) Betty's visitors are sometimes greeted by a large, unruffled pea-cock, or in this case a pea hen. A pair of peacocks had been abandoned by a summer resident years before, but Betty hasn't seen the male peacock for a while. Most likely it became an iridescent dinner for the coyotes. But the female is in residence beneath her back porch. Betty calls it "Pia," an acronym for "pain-in-the-ass."

Betty's father, Tom Gray, knew John and Tiny Worthington, and Betty remembers Tiny's fishnet operation. She said the Worthingtons' cold storage plant and fishnet industries bolstered the town's economy. But her father wasn't a fisherman, he was a carpenter and he had worked for some of Truro's most famous residents. Edward Hopper, John Dos Passos, and Edmund Wilson had hired her father. He did cabinetwork, remodeled antique houses, repaired roofs, and helped summer residents care for their properties. Betty went with her father every spring to "open up" the Hopper cottage. Betty said that Hopper would send her father a note. "Tommy, we're coming down! Open the house by such and such a date."

Her father would prime the pump and remove the "beastly sized" boards" from its big north window.

Betty spent a lot of time at the Hopper house as her father worked. "Hopper was a tall and stately man with very little to say. My father was the same way. They'd sit on the stoop together and hardly say a word. Just grunts and groans. But when my father left, he'd have a list of what Hopper wanted him to do. We'd ask my father, 'Pop, how did you find that out? Hopper didn't open his mouth.'

"But Josephine Hopper was a chatterbox. Hopper would leave her at the post office, go home for an hour, come back, and she wouldn't know he had left. She'd be talking a blue streak. If she ever took the car, she was always driving into a ditch. She couldn't see over the windshield. She'd get stuck in the hog cranberry vines, and those are slippery. She'd have to get towed out. Once, leaving the post office, she hit Duarte's cement wall.

"I would always tell my mother 'The Hoppers are back.' I knew when they came back because the post office would reek of mothballs. You could always tell when the Hoppers had picked up their mail."

Betty explained that every year, before closing the house, Edward and Josephine would scatter mothballs throughout the big room. In the spring, they'd sweep them into a corner. When they left at the end of the summer, they'd spread them around again. Betty said that once Josephine had offered her a sweet from the cookie jar, but the cookie tasted like menthol. She said she would never accept cookies from Jo Hopper unless she was certain the lid had been tightly screwed onto the jar.

Edward Hopper and Josephine painted during their summers in Truro.

Hopper did paintings of one of the Worthington houses, he made famous the red gas pumps on Route 6, and the high row of shacks on the ridge at Corn Hill. But Betty knew the Hoppers as "ordinary people."

At seventy years old, Betty is a lively and astute research analyst of everything that happens "east of Eastham." Since the sixties, Betty has been clipping newspaper stories about significant events and conflicts that surface in Truro, Provincetown, and Wellfleet. She clips articles, following the arc of each story, its twists and turns, day by day, until its final resolution or its last gasp and fizzle when it can't earn any more print.

Her living room is wall-to-wall bookshelves holding three-ring binders. Each phone book–size binder is filled with clippings that are dated, numbered, and carefully sealed in Avery Diamond Clear plastic sheet protectors. She has pulled her stories from only local papers: the *Cape Cod Times* (circulation: fifty-three thousand); the *Provincetown Advocate;* the *Cape Codder;* the *Provincetown Banner;* and the *Boston Globe.*

In the electronic age, there's a nineteenth-century aura in her household, and something yesteryearish about her amateur archives. Snugged on a shelf beside her binders, one expects to see the fifteen-hundred-page Sears catalog, or "Wish Book" coveted by turn-of-the-century families in remote towns without department stores. Amassing clippings from small-time, fifth-rate newspapers seems quaint, maybe frivolous or unimportant. But Betty Groom's library is the best example I've seen of the adage that the human grain is best illuminated by an accretion of small details, homely examples and simple gestures documented. Great endeavors are accomplished in mouse steps.

Because our Internet culture has devalued paper records, these books of small-town newspaper clippings are rare and exotic Americana. Betty started to collect clips in boxes, but when her husband died in 1982, and her kids were grown, she had the time to organize news stories in distinct books. She recently made a new index and at present she has 160 books, each book has almost 100 pages, double-sided. Her book headings are diverse, idiosyncratic to our seaside town and its shifting, sometimes wacky, lifestyles. There are several books of memos from Town Hall, but other titles are specific: books on P-town Fires; Sharks; the Whydah Shipwreck; Ted Williams; Wind Power in Nantucket Sound; the S-4 Sub

Sinking in P-town Harbor (rescuers could hear the men tapping but couldn't save anyone); Lyme Disease; Deadly Accidents; the Monument; Tony Costa; Aquaculture; Linda Silva; Al Gore in Truro; "Rear Window"; Junger and *The Perfect Storm;* Stop & Shop Debate; Cape Cod Confidential; Worthington (two books). These are only a handful of her books in which thousands of clipped items are collected, paginated, and sealed in plastic sleeves.

Nosy neighbors, librarians, journalists, and town administrators often come to Betty to research a buried fact, or to find an article. A young woman in Provincetown turned to Betty to discover the oddball graftings on her family tree. If there's a missing thread, one was sure to find it in Betty's stacks.

But as if to distract you, competing for space with her binders in her tiny living room are three massive sideboards and china closets crammed with two thousand sets of novelty salt and pepper shakers. The collection was started by Betty's mother early last century, with 750 sets, but Betty has since added more than a 1,000 pairs. One cupboard, which displays her mother's most precious specimens, was a gift from Edmund Wilson. The deep cherry cabinet had belonged to a Victorian spinster, Betsy Freeman, who had lived in the Wellfleet house for ninety-seven years before "Bunny" Wilson moved into the house with Mary McCarthy. McCarthy went on to write about her experiences in that house in her novel, *A Charmed Life,* a book thinly veiled as fiction. McCarthy's portrait of Land's End society, its lifestyles and its problems, seems hardly different from our Cape Tip community as it is today. She describes the same fringe personnel who loiter at the library or come and go from Susan Baker's doorstep: "The ex-lawyer who ran a duck farm, the oysterman who had gone to Harvard, the former Washington hostess who now took paying guests . . ." McCarthy wrote that everyone "had a name that rang a bell somewhere, far, far away; you felt you should have heard of him even if you hadn't." She takes jabs at the rural life here, at the inefficiencies of the marketplace and people's stubbornness. The checkout line at the supermarket "looks like a fortune tellers' convention," and "there was something sinister . . . in the fact that you could not get anything repaired. There was nobody to fix the clock . . . the local laundry service could not clean a suit without tearing and discoloring it." She bemoans the sorry fate of the social drinker here. She wrote that the martini was no longer a hopeful refreshment enjoyed in a moment of repose at "six o'clock," but that the martini was a "fall from grace. The joy of drinking was gone. The slender brimming glass had taken on an aspect of fatality."

Betty explains that Wilson and McCarthy had given Betty's mother the pretty china closet, but of her many salt shaker sets, her mom's favorites were given to her by Josephine Hopper. Betty's family's connections to major figures in twentieth-century literature and art are representative of the relationships of many other year-round residents. These local families don't merely rub elbows with but they are in fact the elbow grease— carpenters, cooks, gardeners, seamstresses, even studio assistants—for famous summer folk who come here from Parnassus or from the ivory towers of New York.

Wilson and Hopper couldn't compete with Betty's adoring stories about her own father. Betty said that every autumn, to brush up before hunting season, her father teased her mother. He told her he was taking some of her trinkets outside for target practice. He threatened to line them up across the fence. "I'll shoot just enough to sharpen my aim, maybe that little one right there, is that your favorite?"

Sitting at Betty's table, surrounded by diminutive twin sets of just about everything—animals, vegetables, birds, teddy bears, baby carriages—so many tiny figurines, I felt I'd been captured by Lilliputians. There's even a salt and pepper set of JFK and Jackie. JFK and Caroline. Disney pups. Disney ducks and mice. But more interesting are the old-timey miniatures of everyday items: little toasters, kettles, pots and pans, coffeepots.

The thing to note here is that no one tries to use salt shakers on Cape Cod. They don't work. Forget family heirlooms, those tiny, cut-glass, silver-capped salt cellars. On Cape Cod, these tableware treasures are filled rock solid, like cement pill bottles. Perpetual sea mists clog the little pinprick holes, and they won't pour out, no matter how hard you pound them with the heel of your hand. In Truro, salt is served in a lidded bowl where you reach in, break its crust, and spoon it out.

After Christa Worthington's murder, newspersons, with insider information who had learned about her, contacted Betty Groom to see if she had clipped something they had missed. They asked her about local gossip and wanted to hear about any new dollops of oil spilled on the fire.

Of course, Betty had started a new book. And before long she had two clipping books marked "Worthington." When I first visited Betty, I asked her to tell me what she felt was the most exciting event to have ever happened in our town. I expected her to tell me about "The Woman in the Dunes," or Tony Costa's garden, or maybe Christa's recent murder. I was surprised when Betty said that the most exciting event was the night that the South Truro Meeting House had burned to the ground in 1941.

"We watched it blazing from our upstairs window. This is before the forests grew up, when everything was still empty dunes; we could look directly across the Pamet and see South Truro. The hills were bare—that's why Thoreau had said it looked so pitiful—but that night the flames were high. My father kept saying he wasn't sure we were right, it might have been a barn on fire. But the next morning we looked out our upstairs window and the Meeting House was gone." In fact, the Truro Meeting House had been located right behind Tony Costa's future garden.

There are a lot of ghosts along Old County Road. Betty is someone who believes some of the dead just don't want to leave Cape Cod. She says she knows when her father is in the house, "because I smell his Philip Morris cigarettes. I smell his cigarette smoke and I know he's still around. He made a big ruckus the night my mother died. He was waiting for her and wanted her to hurry up."

Betty works at the Truro Historical Museum, with Diana Worthington; she's on the Disabilities Committee, the Recycling Committee, the Building Committee, Truro Treasures Committee, but her greatest service to our town is her commitment to her clipping books, preserving a record of document, a tome of readable, sometimes all too colloquial, news features, narratives, and editorials. Her books chronicle local events, the movable feast, the aftermaths of conflicts and the afterglow of good deeds. She understands which stories pulse with unresolved tensions, what stories matter, and of course she also collects nostalgic fluff. Nostalgia tempers caustic historical fact; it's a spoonful of sugar with the cod liver oil.

Betty's Worthington clips include stories by Ellen Barry of the *Boston*

Globe, Marilyn Miller of the *Cape Codder*, Hamilton Kahn and Kaimi Rose Lum of the *Provincetown Banner*, and the trio at the *Cape Cod Times*, Karen Jeffreys, Eric Williams, and of course Emily Dooley.

With the Worthington murder, Dooley cut her baby teeth on Cape Cod gothic. Entangled whales or not, her beat suddenly became a high-profile corridor of evil. For filler, Dooley adds a puff story about Jan Worthington's TV movie deal. Describing the "Christa movie," TV producer Joan Barnett said, "It's a story about watching a woman spiral downward . . . there is probably a cautionary tale to be told."

At her table, Betty Groom sharpens her scissors. As soon as she gets her newspaper—from a bucket clipped to a pulley that's rigged to a post on Truro Center Road—she clips and preserves the hard-won harvest, the sometimes overripe cornucopia of murder lore. Emily and Betty have an almost symbiotic relationship.

Betty also keeps copies of town reports from 1888 to the present. Most of these memos relate to financial squabbles and forestalled decisions about where to spend town money, with all the redundant language inherent in long-winded, bureaucratic gabbles.

Article 32. Voted (as amended) to raise and appropriate the sum of $10,300.00 to be used in conjunction with funds donated for the restoration of the steeple, the weathervane, the clock, and the exterior of Town Hall . . . in the following order of priority: 1./ steeple 2./ weathervane   3./ clock   4./ exterior.

Betty shows me another notation on the same page of minutes, dated 1982. The sheet is typed on an old typewriter, maybe it was even a manual typewriter with its ghosted lettering and uneven caps where the shift bar lifts the keys in irregular, lurching patterns. The excerpt says: "The Board of Selectmen shall continue to make every effort to seek ways to keep Truro the Garden of Eden of Massachusetts."

"The Garden of Eden of Massachusetts," Betty says in a voice of mock authority. She chuckles like Mrs. Claus, as if she thinks it's a hoot.

I ask her, "Oh, you don't think it's paradise? But you've got that bird of paradise right outside under your porch. So why not?"

"I guess it's all the changes. The trophy homes. The land getting eaten up. And, you know, you look around and there's nowhere to hide from people. No Eden, not here."

The selectmen's oath seems proof that the town has finally forgotten the most notorious garden ever to be tilled in Truro—Tony Costa's marijuana plot where the killer had planted four girls.

EURODISNEY

Christa often traveled from Paris to international glamour hot spots to chronicle lifestyles of the leisure class for *W*'s famous "City Style" stories. Fairchild had specific ideas about what places were fascinating, had allure, were colorful, and "in vogue" at any current instant in a particular season. Fairchild understood that taste is "mood." Locale begets mood, and mood is a catalyst of fashion. Christa might be sent to Lake Como, to Baden-Baden, or to Mykonos. In these settings, she explored the city's geographical allure, its climate, cuisine, and nightlife, but, most importantly, she went there because it was a trendy watering hole for the wealthiest of the wealthy, both the aristocracy and Nouvelles, celebrity couples and trophy hounds. Christa was expected to drop names, sending ripples that might radiate delicately, like petals dribbled on a lake, or names that caused major rip currents as they collided.

On her trip to Gstaad, Switzerland, a winter resort for the golden-heeled of European society, the icy air gave her sinus headaches. Or, more likely, her headaches were caused by the noxious "*l'air du temps*" of the rich and famous. She told friends that the work before her was "odious"; she tried to chronicle extravagances and luxuries that were so over the top and never-ending that she felt trapped on a rhinestone hamster wheel. She wrote, "Nicknamed 'Gstaadopolos,' for all the Greek shipping tycoons who have made their holiday homes here, Gstaad offers all the village coziness, Heidiesque charm and powder snow that money—lots of money—can buy.

"Its main street has more *banks* than churches. When a princess dropped her glove at the base of a ski lift, it was promptly helicoptered up the mountain to her." She describes life in Gstaad with Valentino, Plácido Domingo, David Bowie, John Travolta, and a peaked and wobbly Audrey

Hepburn. " 'Gstaad is like England thirty years ago,' says yacht broker George Nicholson. 'It's a service-oriented village. Everything is delivered.' "

She describes the Palace Hotel in Gstaad as "a bit of Hollywood in the Alps where non-skiing snow bunnies make their presence felt in pink lynx furs and gold lamé boots, children aim their remote-controlled toy Ferraris at the concierge's feet, and by nightfall lounge-lizard playboys like Sebastian Taylor have moved into the most visible leather-covered chairs. A 1930s Rolls-Royce ferries guests up from the station, and any service can be arranged, from bridge lessons to flying home by hot-air balloon as one Italian magnate chose during a transit strike."

Her regular junkets put her on a dizzy glamour carousel, but on a *W* ramble to Marrakesh, Morocco, Christa looked forward to a tryst with a lover who promised to meet her there. His wife had entered a spa for two weeks, not exactly a rehab hospital, but he was certain they wouldn't let her out until she was tiptop. "They bury them in mud," he told Christa.

She had last seen him one afternoon when he took her to an amusement park outside of Paris that was very antiquated and charming. In a miniature train, favored by little children, she sat crowded onto his lap as it slowly circled the track. He fucked her silently, with imperceptible hitches of his hips. Her hand-me-down Yves Saint Laurent poncho afforded enough privacy for a battalion. But other times, he had missed their connection. It had been hit or miss. But she believed that this once, his wife up to her neck in mud, he wouldn't beg off. He would show up in Marrakesh.

First, she endured the typical luxe hardships as she followed her itinerary, visiting a baroness, then dropping in on Yves Saint Laurent. In her story, she describes the pin dot as a place "governed by the elemental seesaw of heat and cool, light and shadow." She introduces the local peasants as they flee the midday sun: "You see them begin to scatter—the workers on bicycles, old men on their donkeys, the veiled women on foot with baskets on their heads and babies wrapped into bundles on their backs; even the wiry, sly faced children."

In her few jots about the working world, the underprivileged, one senses Christa's conflicted feelings as she moves from the hardscrabble boundaries into the paradise of her regular clan: "Yves Saint Laurent describes the effect of the town as 'spellbinding.' Pleasure becomes absolutely paramount. It's the slow sensual world of life in the shade. 'I do absolutely nothing here,' exults Saint Laurent's business partner, Pierre Berge."

Christa dribbles more names, and quotes Countess Boul de Breteuil: " 'This is the last acceptable paradise.' " And Marie-Hélène de Rothschild says, " 'If you go for four days, it's as relaxing as ten.' "

But her UEA and Vassar influence fights its way to the surface when she writes, "The succession of smells—the indolent perfume of bougainvillea, the crisp aromas of mint and oranges, all mingling, suddenly and unexpectedly, with the stench of mule dung—are entrapped and magnified in the heat of the day, suggesting a world in which the sublime and the earthy are always in balance." And Fairchild encouraged Christa's uncanny ability to concoct a delicious roux of opposing details: light and shadow, mint and dung; wealth and the "normal poor." But as she wrote notes about Marrakesh and sponged up the little spills of glamour and sunshine, she fantasized about meeting her lover that night. She thought of his kiss, the taste of his lips, the sticky down on his testicles, the low vibrato of his joyful release.

But she still had to visit the villa and gardens of Countess Boul de Breteuil, a setting that had "real Arab opulence."

" 'I never move,' says the countess, although she is known occasionally to go ballooning with Malcolm Forbes. 'Here I live in a luxury I could find nowhere else. Life is calm and quiet.' " Christa noted that the countess had nine servants and two pet dogs, Miss Love and Mr. Lost.

Next, Christa popped into Saint Laurent's new digs, "a house surrounded by the spectacular Jardins Majorelles—lush public gardens. . . . When rumors began to fly that the gardens were being sold to make way for urban apartment complexes, Berge arranged to purchase them."

She was told to drop in on other expatriates like "transplanted Parisian Jacqueline Fossiac" who pretends to live like the peasants. "She's taken the traditional peasant clay or mud house . . . but inside it's another story. One finds polished roseate walls—rubbed to a high sheen by *twelve* artisans. . . . The accommodations are spare but hardly Spartan."

Back at her hotel room, the big Marrakesh sun sets outside her windows like a melting Caramello. She reads the message from her paramour, penned by the concierge in tight, unnatural handwriting. It says: "Christabel, can't make it. Oops."

She soaks a washcloth under the cold-water tap and wrings it out. She reclines in bed, folds the wet cloth in a neat square and presses it over her eyes.

Here she was—alone—in North Africa, without even a pet dog like the royal mutts Miss Love and Mr. Lost. She thought these names were silly but they evoked a pinching afterthought. Christa was Miss Love, but *where* is Mr. Lost?

Each time another man surprises her with an unexpected round of emptiness, she wants to go home. The words of the countess had a scratchy echo, like a phonograph needle bouncing across a 78 record. "*The last acceptable paradise.*" Of the many exotic detours Christa navigates, and no matter how many weekends or fortnights she spends in Africa, Greece, or Sweden, for Christa, Truro is always the "last acceptable paradise." Her desire to be on Depot Road is always a nagging ache—to hell with palm trees, volcanic sands, and bougainvillea; she wants to see the raggedy Scotch broom, wild strawberries, blueberries, and roses that grow unattended along the Pamet.

She has brought a book along, although she rarely gets a chance to read once she gets off the plane and has to show up for teas and parties. But this night she's reading one of her favorite "tortured female writers," Edna O'Brien. Christa reads a story called "Violets," about a single woman preparing for a tryst. "Married men are lunchtime callers," O'Brien writes. Christa savors the lyric story, halting on its astringent last lines:

> I wonder if someone has to enter the gates of paradise, even the tiniest adulterous paradise, in order to find it, in order to lose it, in order to re-find it, in perpetuity. And, wondering I float into the first bewildered kiss.

She reads until she can't stay awake. She turns out the bedside lamp and pulls the sheet up to her chin. Scuttling across its hem is a creature of nightmare genius, a scorpion or centipede at least six inches long. Its hard shell makes a percussive rattle. She jumps to her feet. With the light on, she hunts for the desert crustacean but it's disappeared. She tears the bedding off the mattress. She lifts the dust ruffle, first on one side, then the other. She doesn't telephone the desk, unsure of what she actually saw. Maybe she had imagined it. She worries that the hideous creature might have been an apparition, the embodiment of her internal demons. Then, it shoots from beneath the bed and trundles with lightning speed into the opposite corner of the room. She grabs a shoe and pounds the centipede, but her sandal is dainty and doesn't seem to harm it. The pest is as tough as a lobster. Next, she takes a heavy soapstone wine bucket she had secured in preparation for her evening with her lover. She drops the empty wine bucket on the creature.

Unable to sleep, she sits down in the rattan chair, curling her legs under her. She opens her book. She reads the same story, "Violets."

I was brought up to believe in Hell and I was brought up to believe that men are masterful and fickle.

During her years in Paris, Christa had often dated married men. She was "entertained" in fabulous nooks and crannies around the map, she cuddled up in hotels, minor palaces, and grand apartments in posh corners of Milan, Paris, Amsterdam, where her assignments left her in the lap of luxury, and in the jaws of wolves who circle the fashion world. One of these men had a winery and lived in a "castle." The place would have been a perfect retreat where she could hang her giant mirror. But it wasn't to be. After a grinding schedule, where she tried to organize time for her romance, commuting to his winery in the midst of the fall season, the relationship broke down. She had another abortion.

On the rebound, she met a young painter. She was entranced when he had showed her how to draw a horse on a table napkin. "It's got three circles," he said. "Its cheek, its shoulder, its rump." He sketched the three circles and from the template finished his drawing with a few brisk strokes. There it was—a stallion—galloping across the napkin, flying in midstride across the white square, like a kind of Pegasus. She told him about a riding camp in the United States called Mon Ami le Cheval, and she later called him by that name when talking about him to her friends. With "three circles" he had beguiled her. He taught her other simplistic rubrics about sex. He told her that he believed that women should have pleasure in fiery multiples of five. Five, he said, or he was a failure.

"He was a loser," one friend said. "He was a no-talent, he was using her." "Her choice in men!" was the echo from her lifelong pals. Belinda, in England, said, "Christa chose men who were not up to snuff to avoid intimacy or commitment. She would always go for a guy with some kind of problem so she wouldn't have to raise up any higher. It shows that she didn't have confidence in herself."

But five was a magic number. And for many months, she was on and off with the painter. Their relationship was carnal, fiery, and sometimes violent. Once they had tussled on a stairwell and she had tumbled over the railing. Radz said that Christa would call him in New York to tell him about her problems with boyfriends. Often she joked, inventing disparaging names for her ex-Romeos. There was "Mon Ami le Cheval," and after her disappointment in Marrakesh with the man who had seduced her on an amusement park mini-train, she referred to that cad as "Eurodisney." But sometimes she didn't joke, she was angry, or disgusted, and sometimes she was frightened. Radz said, "I'd hear, 'We just broke up.' Or 'We broke up four times.' Her affairs in Europe were always problematic. The story I never got from Christa was: 'I'm madly in love and things are great!' "

Christa's evenings were tied up at parties, and her travel assignments for *W* took her out of town, her time at home was fractured, her personal life compartmentalized. She was always trekking somewhere for her job. But some friends say she didn't want a domestic arrangement with a man. Belinda said, "She kept herself isolated. By choosing married men, or like every place she had, Gramercy Park, her Paris apartment, and the flat she had in London, everything was so tiny, too small for anyone to move in with her. Maybe it was an 'only child syndrome.' "

Barbara Holloway said, "One of the best parties I ever went to in my whole life was in Paris when I went as Christa's guest. It was the film director Bertrand Tavernier's birthday, at his home, and Christa had just interviewed him, probably for *W.* Elia Kazan served us chocolate cake; several of the most glamorous French movie stars were there; in fact, we were the only people at the party who weren't famous. After we left, we headed for La Coupole, a favorite late-night hangout where Harvey Keitel and a stunningly handsome Argentinean director, both of whom had been at the party, tried to pick us up. Christa didn't want anything to do with them. They'd be too high maintenance. I'm not sure I ever quite forgave her."

In 1986, Christa came home to Hingham to visit her mother, who had had a minor procedure for a detached retina. When her mom was feeling well enough, Christa drove Gloria to New Hampshire to visit Christa's high school friend Gail Motlin. Motlin was a little miffed that Christa hadn't come to her wedding, nor had she mailed a gift, or returned the RSVP. It was as if Christa was jealous that her old friend had hooked up and had won a lifetime commitment from someone. Gail said that during that trip home, Christa met a man on the South Shore and got pregnant again. "She was the most 'fertile Myrtle.' She just looked at a guy and got pregnant." Christa went back to Paris, and Gail said that she didn't know what Christa was planning to do. Perhaps the next time she saw Christa she'd have a child in tow. "But there wasn't a child. Christa took care of it. That's her third abortion."

Christa met an Englishman named Peter at a party in Paris. Gail Motlin called him "that dreary, cigarette-smoking British guy." He was a friend of her EAU classmates Barbara and Belinda. "He shouldn't be confused with the 'antiques dealer' she had dated in London." Peter was very handsome, but a rather dry and haughty academic. Belinda said, "He was very attractive, intelligent, quintessentially British. Think Hugh Grant."

"Very Hugh Grant," Barbara said.

One sees poor Christa in a Hollywood freeze-frame with a fifth-rate Cary Grant. Belinda went on to say that this was Christa's famous "Chunnel" relationship. Christa had gone back and forth from Paris to London to see her academic "prof" even before the Chunnel was christened. She took commuter jets out of Orly. The Englishman was not merely handsome, he was the epitome of the Anglo breeding and high-brow WASPisms that her Worthington aunts and cousins would find an excellent extension of their ilk, if she were ever to bring him home to Truro. She thought that with his little sniffs and shrugs, his ability to quote Auden or Keats with the immediacy of a whippoorwill, he'd fit right into the royal mythology of the Worthingtons at Pamet.

Some of her friends say that Peter was "love of her life Number 2." When she visited him in London, they spent time reading poems out loud. He'd sometimes ask her to memorize specific couplets and quatrains, and he expected her to recite lines to him when she next visited. Christa thought he was wonderful. It was a romantic fantasy to have poetry books lost in the bedcovers. But sometimes she was too busy at *W* or she procrastinated, and she didn't memorize her homework until she was on the airplane, soaring over the Channel. She'd turn to her seatmate and ask the stranger to prompt her as she tried to recite Philip Larkin, or Baudelaire's "A Hemisphere in Your Hair," from *Paris Spleen*, or her new favorite, William Blake's "The Clod & the Pebble":

"Love seeketh not Itself to please,
Nor for itself hath any care,
But for another gives its ease,
And builds a Heaven in Hell's despair."

So sang a little Clod of Clay,
Trodden with the cattle's feet,
But a Pebble of the brook,
Warbled out these metres meet:

"Love seeketh only Self to please,
To bind another to Its delight,
Joys in another's loss of ease,
And builds a Hell in Heaven's despite."

Although he offered her a foothold in a more literary circle, rekindling a point of view she'd left behind at her English seminars at Vassar, her new attraction had a drinking problem, and it made the relationship combative.

During his weekend binges, when he overindulged in what he glibly called "restoratives," or "neck oil," she wasted hours watching BBC reruns of American TV shows as he recuperated. Sometimes he never got up off the floor. When he eventually resurfaced at the end of her visit, it was time for her to go back to Paris. They'd get into rows. She called him names, mimicking London's East End slang just to annoy him: "You eff-ing booze artist," "You eff-ing bottle baby." He'd answer in turn. They would have a contest to see who could better deconstruct or disembowel the mother tongue. She'd have to race to the airport. But she would return in a week or two.

She came back with a book called *Living with Addiction* that she hoped would help her learn useful strategies of intervention and support for her lover. The book seemed applicable to both her boyfriend and her father. She also picked up the Al-Anon manual, *The Dilemma of the Alcoholic Marriage*. She read a chapter that described the dynamics of many of her relationships in a breakdown of typical archetypes: "The Doubter," "The Demander," "The Punisher," "The Martyr."

After having little success, she showed up one weekend with a different approach. She had been reading Dr. Edward Bach's *Flower Remedies*. The book instructs the reader to utilize flowers to cure personality disorders. For instance, "Mustard dispels black depression, melancholia, gloom," and "Gentian fights doubt, depression, discouragement." "Chestnut Bud addresses the failure to learn from experience. This is the remedy for people who tend to make mistakes over and over again."

Peter was resistant to trying the capsules or teas she bought at the health food store. He called her an idiot to have paid so much money for "essence of gorse" or "Hornbeam caplets." He browbeat her and once during an argument he had called her mother "an Italian cow," a rude insult suggesting that Christa wasn't really Anglo. Her friend, the novelist Eli Gottlieb, said, "Christa consciously placed herself in the role of victim. It goes hand in hand with refined perception. When the perception is very refined, you have less talent to act. There's something subversive there; she was like a perverted Madonna—not the singer, *the* Madonna."

Despite her British boyfriend's alcohol abuse, Tim Arnold claims that the professor in London was Christa's longest relationship. "It lasted more than a year."

A year doesn't seem very long, but it was twice her typical endurance test, until she met Tony Jackett, and their frail bond was stretched, entangled in Ava.

In 1987, Ben Brantley left *WWD* to write for *Vanity Fair* and then for the *New York Times*. Christa was appointed to his vacated position as acting bureau chief, a job she thought would become her permanent slot.

But at *WWD* the "boys club" atmosphere prevailed, and Christa warred, at least in her interior thoughts, with her supervisors, especially Patrick McCarthy. McCarthy was "in the picture" but not as powerful as Fairchild. When McCarthy eventually took over Fairchild's mantle, he didn't have the fashion authority of a John Fairchild. But Christa did have that kind of authority; she had the knowledge and savoir faire that McCarthy lacked. A *WWD* writer, who assumed Christa's position as fashion reporter, said, "In the fashion world, if you're a woman and very smart they don't really want that. Things don't add up for you. Christa was very smart, a very talented writer, and people got nervous. People are very territorial, trying to hang on to their jobs even when they aren't good enough. Because of her strengths, she was a threat to them. Fairchild encouraged his female protégées to have a point of view—up to a point."

On the elevator one afternoon, Christa bumped into Fairchild and Dennis Thim, an advertising and promotions executive at *M* magazine, a short-lived Fairchild enterprise. Christa thought of Thim as one of "the suits," and not a creative force like John Fairchild, or like she was herself. The elevator doors pinched shut and the cable reversed. As the compartment dropped, Fairchild turned to Dennis Thim and introduced Christa with more formality than Christa had expected. Of course, she had already met Dennis Thim. Fairchild praised Christa and told Thim that Christa would be Thim's number-one gal; Thim could depend on her. Christa was confused by the possessive more than she was annoyed by the sexist colloquialism "gal."

Then Fairchild told Christa, "You know Dennis, right? He's replacing you." This was how Fairchild drop-kicked Christa from her prominent perch as "acting bureau chief." She didn't get the job. After eight years at

Fairchild Publishing, Christa had been passed over in that one claustro-phobic and frozen instant of an elevator ride.

When the men got off the lift, she remained in the compartment and rode it back up to her office. She went to her desk, took a few things, and got back on the elevator. She never returned to the office.

Patrick McCarthy explained it differently. He said that Christa didn't like being bureau chief, it had too many administrative headaches. She wasn't an "organized" individual. "She just didn't want anyone else to be bureau chief."

Belinda said, "It was very hard when she was passed over at *WWD*. We had talked about the deadlines, the horrible procrastinations, the tidying of the kitchen before sitting down to write. She could get stuck. She had this inertia and would get paralyzed. But, still, she did well in Paris. She was close to senior management and it really hurt her, it affected her professional confidence."

Christa crated her mirror and left Paris. She moved to London, her tail between her legs, and fell into the arms of her Hugh Grant boozer prof for consolation, whether he was ready for her arrival in England or not. She moved into yet another teensy apartment upstairs from Barbara Holloway. Barbara said, "Like every other apartment she ever lived in, it was a tiny place, too small to welcome any but the most intimate of guests. But she spent a lot of time hanging out at my place. It was big enough for group gatherings." In London, Christa connected with another dear friend from Vassar, Carol Ostrow, who had successfully juggled professional work and family. Ostrow had understood that one has to make personal sacrifices to build a real life. Ostrow's elegant example was one trigger for Christa's urge to have a baby. But her relationship with the prof, without the foamy chop of the English Channel as a buffer between them, seemed to get more difficult and bleak.

She was writing freelance pieces for the *London Independent,* the *New York Times,* and for American fashion glossies. Even without the *W* masthead, she still had her Rolodex from God, and she wrote freelance updates on designers' collections, style trends, and celebrities. But she also started writing about "decor," perhaps a bit of a tumble down from her high perch at the prow of haute couture. But she liked the "physical wardrobe" of a house. She visited the salons of sophisticated furniture designers, but she liked better her junkets to pawnshops and flea markets, where she collected treasures. Her interest in these cast-off items seemed to come from her desperation to piece together meanings, hints of family, remnants of belonging.

She was thinking about returning to the States, but couldn't make up her mind. Her friends describe Christa's indecision as a self-perpetuating disorder. One ex-boyfriend said, "She was always betwixt and between." And Radz said, "You know the saying, 'When there's a fork in the road, take it'? For Christa, it was always, 'Take it and wish you had taken the other fork.' " Eli Gottlieb, who has lived in Rome for many years, said, "I don't miss the States, but Christa was always conflicted. She missed the U.S.A. when in Europe, and vice versa. Wherever she lived she felt she was there because she had made a mistake. She second-guessed everything. She seemed to believe that one needs to nourish regret to be a thinking person; regretting meant she was keeping alert."

Christa was in London in the late summer of 1989 when she received a phone call from her tenant at Gramercy Park, Deb Kirk. A steam pipe explosion had killed three people at her building and released a thirty-story geyser of scalding steam and mud. The *New York Times* reported it to be "the worst accident involving the steam system in memory." The victims were two Con Ed workers and one resident, who had been taking a nap in her bedroom. Several others were injured. Christa's tenant was unharmed but the building was condemned due to damage from the blast and asbestos contamination. She told Christa that she had to move out.

Con Ed provided housing for residents at hotels and short-term leases at apartment buildings around Manhattan. The earliest that any residents could reoccupy would be in six months. Apartment owners began a class action suit against Con Ed, seeking retribution for "devaluation of property value." Asbestos was a threat throughout the city; it was pre-anthrax and pre–West Nile virus, but it was a source of widespread anxiety. It would be hard to sell their units. The Con Ed debacle was Christa's first indoctrination into litigious schemes and the ambulance-chasing habits she would increasingly become embroiled in.

Deb Kirk, an editor who had worked with Christa on magazine pieces at *Elle* magazine and at *Harper's Bazaar*, said, "I lived in Christa's apartment for only one month. Then the explosion. I had to move to a hotel. I didn't know Christa well, but I knew her as a writer. Her prose was so polished. At *Elle* she did stories about design. This was before *Elle Decor*. She wrote beautifully—even if it was about furniture. I was impressed by her attentiveness to the edit. She requested to see galleys, to see what fact-checkers might have done to her piece. She was extremely careful about everything that went out with her name on it. Later, at *Bazaar*, when I saw her personal essay about wanting artificial insemination, I was surprised that someone who had always been so careful could make these startling admissions, so heartfelt, so sincere. There was a great sadness in her story."

In January 1990, residents who lived in the top ten floors were allowed to move back into 32 Gramercy Park South. But the remaining floors were still under renovation and not yet inhabitable. During these months, workers had been arrested for pilfering tenants' belongings. Nothing had been stolen from Christa's apartment; it was empty.

But it wasn't vacant for long. One afternoon, movers pushed a dolly off the elevator, careful to tip its formidable crate so it would clear the doorway. Christa's mirror had arrived, shipped across the Atlantic at some expense. Christa was coming home to New York.

THE SEA FOX

Tony Jackett might be one of the more celebrated fisherman heart throbs in Provincetown, but he has a colorful predecessor. To better understand Tony, it's helpful to remember Manuel Zora, a Portuguese captain in Provincetown during the twenties—the tense decade of speakeasies, flappers, and rumrunners. Zora was fishing in Provincetown when the Eighteenth Amendment provided him with a whole new raison d'être. Zora was the *original* Casanova and outlaw in Provincetown. His exploits were fiercely successful and his reputation as a smuggler during the Prohibition Era outclassed Tony's measly fifteen minutes. Zora, which means "fox" in Portuguese, was so elusive that the coast guard gave him the nickname the Sea Fox. Although Tony's father had known Manny Zora, Tony had never met him, but in some ways, Tony is a cookie-cutter version of Zora's blithe and dramatic figure.

Zora left Portugal at a young age as a cabin boy on the *Cabo Verde*, a ship that "smuggled" men out of Portugal so they could avoid the army. On his first voyage, Manny learned the trade of the "contrabandista," watching his captain evade the coastal patrol in the Gulf of Cádiz. His captain told him that he would smuggle matches, silk, men, and tobacco but he would never carry dope. He told Manny there was a difference between operating "outside the law" and being a real criminal.

His time on the *Cabo Verde* schooled Zora for his new life in Provincetown, where he was captain of the *Mary Ellen*. A fishing boat out of Provincetown, the *Mary Ellen* had another connection. She was in business with the most notorious fleet to ever sail the waters from Maine to Florida. After the Eighteenth Amendment, a motley armada of distinctive vessels—schooners, steamers, barks, and freighters—assembled along the Atlantic Coast. These shaggy vessels were the outlaw supply ships navigating "Rum Row." While the ships of the rum fleet remained a few miles offshore, out of jurisdiction of the coast guard, local captains of smaller boats made more risky trips back and forth to collect their precious cargo. Zora regularly sailed out to these "mother ships" to pick up cases of rum and other spirits, and he brought the jeweled bottles ashore, always dodging the coast guard.

Tony Jackett's botched attempt to land his bales of marijuana is quite similar to so many of Manny Zora's colorful rum-running legends. Maybe when Skip Albanese decided to sink his boatload of weed outside Wellfleet Harbor, he was remembering the Sea Fox method. Zora would sink his bottles in cloth sacks in the Pamet River or in Provincetown Harbor. Later, he had only to go back and haul them up like lobster traps.

And similar to the tale of Tony's camouflaged drug boat from Colombia, with its false name *Divino Criador* painted on its stern, there's a corresponding story of how Manny Zora had puttied and painted the stern of *his* boat. To cover up bullet holes after the coast guard had marked him as he fled the scene of a rum connection, Zora opened his locker and took out his paintbrush. Before he tied up at the pier, where authorities waited to nab him, he had camouflaged the evidence that he had captained the boat they had fired at. These tales sort of blend together into one uproarious local mythology.

Another reason that Tony and Zora seem fraternal is that like Tony, Zora had a fascination with artists and hankered after the bohemian lifestyle of the intellectuals who flocked to Provincetown. It was one way to meet louche and easy egghead girls. Playwright Eugene O'Neill had befriended Zora after buying booze from him, and he invited Manny into the elite social circle of the renowned Provincetown Players. Zora attended their soirees and watched their performances. Zora was the first of very few Portuguese fishermen to be invited into the notorious men's club known as the Beachcombers, a bohemian circle of discerning artists and writers, "the summer intellectuals," who met each week to cook for one another and to drink. The Beachcombers didn't permit women, but Zora liked socializing with the artists because they'd later hook up with pretty girls. Yet Zora was never the type to settle down with just one. When I asked Tony about Manny Zora, he told me, with a chilly voice, that his father had told him what had happened to Zora. Zora had returned to Portugal, where he had died penniless and alone. And writer Scott Corbett described Zora's resistance to having a domestic situation when he wrote, "He was not temperamentally suited to live a proper and exemplary home life. He would never manage to do so with any woman, even though he had tried often enough."

Tony Jackett, after all of his troubles, might also seem to be "not temperamentally suited to live a proper and exemplary home life" but he had got lucky. Tony had Susan.

Tony Jackett had been a basketball star on the Provincetown High School team called the Fishermen. Susan Soults was four years older than Tony, but her younger sister, Cheryl, had been a cheerleader for the team and she knew Tony a little better than Susan did.

Just out of high school, Susan worked at Turner's Candy Store. She was dating Alan Avellar, who was in the coast guard, stationed in Groton, Connecticut. He came back to Provincetown weekends whenever he got leave. But some weekends Susan had nothing to do. Cheryl wanted to date a young man but their mother insisted that she could see him only if Susan went along to chaperone. Cheryl asked Susan if she would "double date" with a buddy of her boyfriend.

"I didn't want to do it," Susan said, "but my sister told me, 'I'll give you that sweater you have always liked—' "

Susan agreed to go on the double date with her sister "just once." To everyone's surprise, Susan soon married her blind date, Jimmy. They moved to Oskaloosa, Iowa, where her new husband was enrolled at William Penn College.

"All I wanted was to get married and have five kids. But Jimmy couldn't have kids," Susan said. "I was grief-stricken. Then we found out about the Florence Crittendon Home in Sioux City. We adopted two Sioux Indian babies, one right after the other. I was happy. I liked Iowa. But Jimmy wanted to move back to Provincetown. When we got back to town, he took a job as a golf pro at Highland Links. But for us, it was the beginning of the end. To think it all started with a sweater—"

Waiting for her divorce, Susan lived in a small apartment at Young's Court with her toddler kids, Kim and Shelby. One evening, when she was at her mother's house, her mom was talking to her sister about Tony Jackett. "My mother always loved Tony. She says, 'Cheryl, he's so cute—you should get a date with him.'

"But my sister says, 'He's too young.'

"I say, 'Yeah, he's a baby.' Little did I know I was going to marry him."

Susan said that the next week she and her mother went to see her aunt, who lived near Tony's house on Pleasant Street. The women were going to make the traditional Portuguese Christmas pastries, fancy turnovers called *trutas*. These crescents of whiskey-infused dough, stuffed with sweet-potato filling, drenched in brandy and lemon, are then fried in lard. Real Portuguese recipes always say, "Do not use vegetable shortening!"

Susan said, "We arrive at my aunt's house and as we're getting out of the car my mother sees Tony in the street. She calls to him, 'Come over here and have a cup of coffee with us!' But I'm thinking, He's twenty-one, I'm twenty-five, what's she doing?"

Tony told them he was going to the movies. Then he noticed Susan. No man in Provincetown would ever decline an invitation to get within arm's reach of Susan Soults. Tall and blond, shapely, not fat nor thin, with skin like porcelain. She looked like an unsuspecting angel transposed on a feverish Jayne Mansfield. Tony came over like a puppy and sat down in the living room.

The house was full of women. "Tony was always comfortable with women. He was only twenty-one, real chatty, acting like a pal, but then he would look at you. It was something wonderful behind that look, something sizzling, not just the *trutas*." Susan didn't help her mother and aunt make the sweets, but stayed on the sofa beside Tony. She had seen Tony at his summer job at the Dairy Queen, but now he was working on the *Plymouth Belle*, fishing with his father. Maybe he wasn't so much of a kid anymore. His face was chiseled and had lost its baby fat. He was wind-burned like a real highliner captain. His knuckles were scraped from working on deck. He was a baby "Manny Zora" in every way, but already he had started to develop his own suave style with women. He saw her looking at his raw, deckhand fingers and was embarrassed. He worried that she wouldn't want him to touch her with such calloused mitts. "Chains just bite you," he said.

The next week, at Young's Court, Susan had put the kids to bed when she heard a knock at her door. It was Tony. Susan said, "He explained to me, 'I called your dad and he told me where you live.' He said he had thought about me all week. I can't say I had thought about him all week."

Susan said that they sat down to talk. They talked for a long time and Tony was very polite. Then, when she walked him to the door to say good night, he kissed her. "That first kiss lasted three hours," she said. "No kidding, we necked for three hours! I thought I really liked this guy despite the fact that he's so young. He's a wonderful kisser. My face was red from his whiskers. He came over every day after that. He was good with my kids. He was fishing with his father, but in winter they didn't always steam out. We'd go for rides with the kids in the backseat."

Tony said, "That night we met, I was going to a movie. It was *The Summer of '42*. Then Susan's mom, Mary, sees me—Mary loved me—she says, come over and have something with us. Susan and I sat on the sofa. It was the first time I felt foolish for a woman. Usually they came after me—ones I didn't want. With Susan, I felt I had to go after her. I went up there to Young's Court and knocked on the door, and it was beautiful. It changed all my values and everything I wanted to do. I forgot about being a town playboy and got serious about fishing, so we could get married. I had to make a decision. I might never feel this way about a woman again."

Tony's mother wasn't happy about his attraction to Susan, an older girl with two children—and these kids were almost foreign, coming from an Indian reservation. When Susan became pregnant with Braunwyn, and she and Tony were married that fall, Tony's mother attended the wedding, but she looked stricken. Her favorite boy was stolen away, and what made it worse, her husband, Anthony Sr., had left her only five weeks before. Her whole world was caving in. "I was in the middle," Tony said.

Susan said, "I always got the feeling that Tony's mom thought I was stealing her baby. Her husband had left her, I was marrying Tony. She didn't want him to love anyone more than he loved her. I was a good wife, a great mother, but I was always lacking, according to Tony's mom."

Susan stood beside Tony when he bought the *Jo G.* and she faced all the hardships of being a fisherman's wife. She had four of his babies. "I could have had a baby once a year with Tony. Even with a diaphragm I got pregnant. I had all my babies in that little house we bought on Highland Avenue in Truro. Beau was eight months old when Tony got the

Josephine. I was so happy with the kids, that's all I ever wanted. I didn't want to be a career girl."

Tony said, "I had left the *Plymouth Belle* because my father was getting under my skin. Maybe if he hadn't left my mom I would have stayed on. Susan had just had a new baby. I had to make a change, at least for a while. I went to an interview at the Royal Coachman, to be an overseer for the property. I drove down there in my Capri—it was the first one on the Cape. I saw an ad for it in *Playboy*. The ad says, 'Sexy European,' and I had the Capri for ten years. But when I get to the Coachman, I say, 'What am I doing? I can't do this job,' and I went back home. Vic Pasolini called me. His son was quitting and I could get a site on the *Charlotte G.* So I went out with Vic. I was in her foc'sle and was thinking, 'What am I doing on this boat?' After leaving my father it was a setback in a way. I knew I wouldn't stay with Vic. I had to get my own boat. Six months later I buy the *Jo G.* My father seems hurt. He says, 'You want everything too young, too goddamn quick.' But I felt so lucky. I had my boat. I had Susan.

"I knew I had it good compared to some guys. For instance, my friend started a romance with this woman. She moves into his house in Truro, and she puts her own money in it. He had burlap bags for curtains, so she buys new stuff, gets rid of the old stuff.

"Well, she starts drinking. He tells her, 'There's only room for one drunk in this house and that's me.' She says, 'If it wasn't for me you wouldn't have these new curtains.' So he takes the curtains off the windows and throws them in the fire. He takes her new coat, which he had bought her for Christmas, and throws it in the fire. He throws her out. The next day he goes fishing.

"While he's gone, she has a yard sale and sells everything. When he comes back, there's only one chair. A month later he takes her back. They start all over again."

Susan never acted so erratic. She was happy. Tony said, "I told her, 'Darling, you've got your house, your kids, everything you want.' "

But in the mid-eighties Tony had trouble paying notes for both the boat and the house. He faced tedious scrutiny and negotiations with the IRS, and unlike Manny Zora, the Sea Fox, Tony hadn't been able to slip through that DEA ambush. He went back and forth to Boston for the grand jury investigation after the boondoggle with the *Divino Criador*.

And his boat needed work all the time. The *Josephine* was becoming a sinkhole. Susan said, "Seamen's Bank kept reorganizing papers for us, but finally we lost the place where I raised my six kids."

Yet, when Susan remembers how she first connected with Tony, more than thirty years ago, she smiles. She sees them sitting together on the sofa at her aunt's. The kitchen is crowded with women, but the women have left them alone to get acquainted.

She can hear the *trutas* splattering in the kitchen. She smells the fried dough, the rich sweet-potato filling with its splash of whiskey and aromatic brandy. These crescent puffs were a Christmas tradition, and like that simple and joyous routine, Susan says, "A good marriage will stand up to the test of time."

CHIC SIMPLE

In New York, Christa started at *Elle* magazine as "Marion McEvoy's hire." *Elle*'s offices were in a landmark building on Fifth Avenue, a Beaux Arts treasure with an inlaid sunburst on the lobby floor. The magazine was run by three women—McEvoy, Rona Berg, and Gina Alhadeff. The three editors shared one corner office, their desks meeting at three corners.

McEvoy had brought Christa to *Elle* to pump up its culture and fashion writing. It was at *Elle* that Christa first met her friend Eli Gottlieb. Gottlieb said that he was a young writer at *Elle* when "this new arrival was rumored to come in, a hot new ticket, with formidable credentials. Christa had a certain air, a certain hauteur. She was refined but could bust out laughing."

It was an era of intellectual liberty at *Elle*. Susan Sontag and Christopher Hitchens were contributing editors. It was not just about ladies' underwear, and Christa's writing was of a higher level and in keeping with a more elevated format. But Christa did a lot of writing about architecture, style hiccups in housewares and furniture, and she even came up with a novel column idea for the magazine, "Eco Watch," where she wrote about cultural events within a growing society of conservation buffs and nonprofit organizations. She reported on soirees and shindigs out on Long Island or in Manhattan, where wealthy bird-watchers, weekend naturalists, and environmental hobbyists mingled with real zoologists and Sierra Club masterminds, who encouraged guests to write checks for nature preserves, wetlands, and bird sanctuaries. Of course, movie stars often appeared at these parties to pad their do-gooder profiles.

Eli Gottlieb, author of the novel *The Boy Who Went Away*, said that Christa's writing wasn't dry or too intellectual, but highly literate. He said she could have written a novel, but never seemed ready to begin. He said, "At first, Christa worked in a cubicle like the other staff writers, but soon she got an office with a door. The rest of us were in an open floor, but she was the prized exotic, the lemur brought over from Madagascar."

At *Elle*, some of her colleagues bristled at Christa's sometimes solipsistic manner. Eli said, "She was so enclosed in a hurricane of self. One of the staffers was so furious about Christa's dithering, she announced, 'I want to bend her thumbs back until they touch her wrists.'"

But Christa was also the object of a certain kind of loving ridicule. Just as the Scituate Art Association had been protective and tolerant of Christa's mother, Gloria, Christa became a little pet, in part because her annoying habits were so pathetic. A research assistant said, "She made us feel protective. She had this high voice, sort of babyish or childlike, and this really innocent face. She evoked our sisterly or maternal instincts."

Her coworkers said that Christa was helpless; she made a style of it—there was something very deliberate about it. Gottlieb said, "You could smell it was a way of life and some people lost sympathy. She was indignant all the time, outraged, that was her mode, but to her credit she directed a lot of her humor against herself. Her misfortune with men became a running joke. I'd say, 'Christa, this is your masterpiece.' She had one fuckup after another."

Christa seemed most comfortable with a persona of "victim as heroine." She'd often talk about the Worthington curse or the Worthington jinx. But she had a sense of humor when she told her friends stories about her family. Her grandmother Tiny had once told Christa, "The real problem with marriage is that men never learn how to perform cunnilingus. In my time we didn't have sex manuals." Other stories involved her aunt Diana. Christa came to the office one day and announced that her aunt Diana had unknowingly rented an apartment to serial killer Hadden Clark in Wellfleet. Hadden Clark had just been arrested.

And Christa talked about her aunt Lucinda. Lucinda had a stormy marriage; having had tumultuous affairs with a movie star and with local fishermen, she had divorced and remarried the same man three times. Christa said, "You have to give her credit. At least she tried to do better each time, but it didn't work out."

Wherever Christa worked, and whomever she met, she seemed to carry with her a steamer trunk of family baggage that was both a millstone around her neck and a sort of pedestal for her perch in life. Eli said he had seen her family's toxic effect firsthand when he went to Cape Cod. But he also saw how different Christa appeared when she was at home in Truro, where they had briefly dated. He said, "At *Elle*, Christa was annealed in a Parisian mannerism, but on the Cape, I remember opening my door and seeing this solar Heidi with her hair undone. The sun had brought out her freckling. In shorts and sandals, it was a much simpler version of Christa. Our friendship deepened." Christa gave him the keys to her beach hut, "the dream tryst cottage." It was there she would later meet Tony.

Writer Tatyana Mishel met Christa at *Elle* before they were both laid off in '91. Tatyana was the woman whose bustline Christa had complimented in an amazing non sequitur. Mishel described Christa's carriage around the office as "floaty." She said that she didn't mean that Christa was "spacey," but that she seemed sort of removed and ethereal. She seemed lost in her own secrets, her own private celestial navigation, and Christa didn't sit around like the other editors and writers talking about "the hot new thing."

After they had both left *Elle*, Tatyana and Christa often met to play tennis. Tatyana said that these tennis games were an outlet for Christa, and she could never shut up about her romantic problems with "this Vanderbilt guy. He was this fabulous society stud, the son of Gloria Vanderbilt. I remember she seemed so impressed by the connection." As Christa returned each serve or as she bounced the ball on her racket before she slammed it, she told Mishel about her troubles with married men. Mishel said, "I started to see how Christa made a lot of wrong choices."

Mishel had a friend who lived in the apartment next door to Christa at 32 Gramercy Park South. Her friend was a musician, and Christa complained about his music. The walls were thin. They had a long, ongoing battle about it. Once, Mishel visited Christa after leaving her friend's apartment. She said that Christa's place had seemed very curious to her. It was like "where a sultan might keep his harem, lush with fabric and pillows. And there was this giant mirror—"

In the early nineties, Christa wrote the text for three fashion guides for Chic Simple, a specialty imprint of Alfred A. Knopf at Random House. In the front pages of each volume is a mission statement: "Chic Simple is a primer for living well but sensibly in the 1990s."

Christa worked with editors Kim Johnson Gross and Jeff Stone on three little jewel-box books. Each opened to reveal sparkly color photographs accompanied by Christa's bright, highly charged and lyric text. She made three lively contributions to the Chic Simple list: *Clothes; Scarves; Accessories.*

The guides explored style expectations, options, dos and don'ts, how-tos, niblets of fashion history, and notable quotations. After her years with Fairchild, Christa knew every truism and how to bend it. "From the cycles of trends, classics evolve"; "Access not excess"; "Pattern is an emotional Morse code."

She peppered her texts with excerpts from poets and philosophers and bons mots from models and designers:

"A suit looks good when the woman who wears it seems to have nothing on underneath."—Coco Chanel

"Beware of all enterprises that require new clothes."—Henry David Thoreau

"If you have a choice between two things and can't decide, take both."—Gregory Corso

"A sweet disorder in the dress/kindles in clothes a wantonness." —Robert Herrick

Without a workaday job, Christa was doing mostly freelance writing for different magazines and newspapers. When she signed on to do her first book for Chic Simple, she liked having an office to come to. Vassar had taught her that a woman should have a place outside the home "to hang her hat."

Her editor, Jeff Stone, said, "There was a slightly Holly Golightly aspect to Christa, not in the party-girl way but in the small town girl comes to New

York idea. The way she dressed—she could have chopsticks in her hair, but not in an East Village 'look at me' pretension, but probably, 'Where did I put the chopsticks?' She wasn't dramatic. Except in her writing."

Kim Johnson said, "She'd come in under deadline and sit at a desk and write. It's one A.M. and she would be there with us, with her cup of tea. I guess she didn't have anyone waiting at home. She didn't seem to have a guy in her life. She never seemed that tight with anyone."

Jeff said, "She put up barriers. She wore many layers. Literally. She wasn't fashiony, but wore lots of loose tops and sweaters as a kind of barrier." It was Jeff Stone who had tried to evoke a portrait of Christa as someone who was innocent, like a baby animal, when he said, "She'd sit at her desk and unbutton her sweaters, peel them off, and make a kind of nest for herself."

But Christa's voice, in her three Chic Simple guides, is sophisticated and fiery with a carnal edge. Even as she describes hats or gloves, the text resonates with sex. She writes about both the bondage and the pleasure derived from a closet full of unexpected erotica. "Tulle—is barely there. It holds all the sexual dynamite of the veil, signaling the control of chastity . . . and its imminent release."

"Delightfully feminine details—a spindly shape, a sparkling surface, a colorful sheen—convert the plainest of sheaths into a sensation."

"Footwear is the libido of the wardrobe. It embraces fundamentals: life force; sex drive; whether you intend to run or walk." And she writes about the head scarf: "It reveals as it conceals . . . the louder the 'go away' message, the more audible the 'come hither.' "

In such lines—"whether you intend to run or walk," and "go away" or "come hither"—one sees many instances of her interior demons seeping into the pages of these offbeat little books.

But in her Chic Simple volume *Scarves,* Christa reveals an almost antifashion sentiment when she describes how scarves are used in many cultures both as diapers and as slings to carry babies, wrapped tightly against their mothers' bodies. In a fashion guide, such a reference seems out of context, a digression from chic ideology into domestic instinct and maternal longing. "Whether used to carry babies, or berries, displaying crown jewels, or doing a belly dance, the scarf is a sartorial tool." These four references describe everything important to Christa: babies, berries, riches, sex.

"Christa was a fashion anthropologist," Jeff Stone said. "She could write about fancy or frivolous stuff and turn it into approachable elements, instead of getting it all chromed-up. She might be writing about mules; it was just these fluffy mules at the end of the day, but she would go further, she would get 'the magic' of mules."

He said that Christa had invited him to her fortieth birthday party at the Grolier Club, a "writers club." Kim couldn't attend, but Jeff decided to go. He had been at Rizzoli's bookstore, and when he left the store to start out for the party, the weather was an event in itself. It was a snowstorm. The taxis had disappeared. It was a whiteout, but Jeff went on foot. "I like walking in blizzards," he said, "but it was like a scene from an O'Henry story. When I finally get there, I'm already very late. I wipe the ice off my glasses and I follow this guy dressed in a tux into a room where a fire is roaring and three other guys are holding silver trays of hors d'oeuvres. There's Christa in a black velvet gown with her hair done up in a chignon, she really looked like a Sargent painting sitting in a chair there. She was *all alone*. No one had come. There's a full bar, and these three awkward guys holding trays of canapés for two hours, with some sixties rock 'n' roll in the background. I say, 'Christa!'

"She laughs. Someone else would have been sobbing. She says, 'Isn't it amazing? I throw my own party and no one comes—' "

Jeff said it was the longest fifteen minutes, and he didn't know what to say. "It was one of those moments when you feel like you want to ask her, 'Hey, do you want to get married?' "

Then other guests began to arrive. By the time Jeff left the party, the place was packed. He said that her guests weren't fashionistas, but ordinary folk, artists, down-to-earth modern souls, and of course a few down-and-out wannabes living in lofts rented by dad. The shabby chic without any pretensions. He said that no one seemed to be trying too hard. It was refreshing.

During this time, Christa was still battling the "love of her life Number 3," the Vanderbilt scion she had complained to Tatyana about. Stan

Stokowski was the son of the renowned conductor Leopold Stokowski, considered a maestro of the "great golden age" of conductors. A contemporary of Toscanini, Stokowski was famous for conducting without a baton, waving his expressive hands, for his wacky speeches to audiences, and for once hiding the orchestra behind a curtain. His musical collaboration with Walt Disney, for the film score of *Fantasia,* made him a household name. Leopold Stokowski was mysterious and volatile; he had had a notorious affair with Greta Garbo. But just as celebrated was Stan's mother, millionaire heiress Gloria Vanderbilt, direct descendant of Commodore Cornelius Vanderbilt and the sole beneficiary of her father's fortune at only fifteen months old. Shuffled around and raised primarily by a nanny, the press had called her the "poor little rich girl," as she had received kidnapping threats simultaneously with the murder of Lindbergh's toddler son. Gloria Vanderbilt was sent to her aunt's compound on Long Island, where she was to spend her childhood with girl cousins, just as Christa had gone to Truro and had shared her youth with her Worthington cousins. When Gloria Vanderbilt married Stokowski, she was forty years his junior. He would drink himself to death shortly thereafter.

In Stan, Christa recognized a familiar struggle to her own entrapment in the Worthington clan, a society that was half blood kin, half myth. Stan was an outcast, a misfit. He had a very prominent childhood and chose to drop out. Like her, he was the unhappy progeny of difficult parents. Yet Christa was impressed by the conductor's fame, and she also recognized the glamour connection. Gloria Vanderbilt was not only a force in American Old Guard society, she had become a principal player in fashion when, in the eighties, she launched her successful line of designer jeans and a perfume; its eye-catching bottle was decorated with the Vanderbilt swan. John Fairchild said that Gloria Vanderbilt entered the business when it became acceptable for a society princess to be an entrepreneur. "Fashion as a profession was at last becoming respectable in this country." He said, "Gloria Vanderbilt needed lots of money to support her luxurious lifestyle and, as a result, she besieged fashion with a vengeance, traveling the length and breadth of America."

Christa teased Stan, asking him when he would introduce his mother, Gloria Vanderbilt, to her mother, Gloria Worthington. She told a friend that if there were to be a wedding, she hoped it would be in the Vanderbilt digs out on Long Island's "real money North Shore." This was a premature daydream. Stan had just disposed of a former girlfriend, and wasn't looking to settle down. But Stan was extremely handsome and had credentials that brought him close to her ideal: "a WASP with a sail bag." In fact, Stan was a dabbling boat-builder. He made sailboats with his bare hands. She wanted to bring him to Truro to repair a Worthington sloop. She spent wonderful halcyon days with Stan on Long Island, and told her friends what it was like to spend the night in the family mansion. But Stokowski, recently loosed from a previous relationship, didn't want to get his feet wet again. He preferred to stand on shore and skip stones, watching them skitter and sink.

During their romance, Stokowski came to Truro with Christa and they stayed in Tiny's Hut. One afternoon, when Stan was in the shower, she ransacked his suitcase. She had the feverish curiosity of a love-struck teenager who wants to fondle her beloved's personals, his cashmere socks, his collar stays, even the waxy styptic pencil and icy clippers in his Dopp kit. In a side pocket of the valise, Christa was surprised to find something unexpected. She plucked an elegant leather ring box from its hiding spot. She felt an involuntary throat spasm and had a momentary coughing fit, as if she had inhaled gold dust. A ring box!

She felt an instant woozy delirium. She was all mops-and-brooms and "higgledy-piggledy" to use a word that, surprisingly, had been defined in the Houghton Mifflin *American Heritage Dictionary,* third edition, with the quotation: "There is something delightfully and liberatingly ludicrous about parading higgledy-piggledy in a line of walkers of all shapes and sizes (Christa Worthington)."

The well-heeled dreamboat Stan Stokowski was going to ask her for her hand.

She was certain to be a Vanderbilt bride and no longer a Worthington spinster. She held the hinged box in her palm, thumbing its silky kidskin leather. She was dying to peek at the diamond, but she didn't want to cheat herself out of the romantic instant when he would present it to her. Stan was still in the shower. If he didn't get out soon, he was going to run out of hot water. She only had a moment to make up her mind. If she looked at the ring, it would destroy the virgin transaction, and she didn't want to cheat. But this was Christa's weakness. She wanted control. She wanted to orchestrate every drama, to put her marks on every blueprint, to be in the driver's seat, even now, cupping her secret dreamscape in the palm of one hand.

She flipped open the box.

It wasn't a brilliant De Beers diamond. It was a travel alarm clock.

She looked at the expensive little clock. She twisted its winding spring until it was tight and wouldn't turn further. She cranked it again, until she heard a muted "snap." She had broken it.

Her face was still hot, her tears rolling down both cheeks when Stan walked into the room scrubbing his back with a towel. Christa burst into laughter, that deep, abdominal laughter that many friends have described as Christa's most beguiling feature. Christa laughed at herself at the drop of a hat.

"What's so funny?" Stan said.

What a joke she had played on herself, she was thinking. But then again, why shouldn't she have imagined the clock was a ring? Later on, in her relationship with Tony Jackett, Christa would sometimes have the same daydream, a blueprint composed of the "white picket fence—happy ever after" ideal. Even Tim Arnold, who hated to recognize Christa's fancy for Jackett, said, "At one point, if Jackett had asked her to marry him, she would have done it in a minute." Her friend Gail Motlin said, "It might not have lasted, but she'd have married John Wotjacinski or Stan, or Tony. But no one ever asked her."

When Stokowski sensed Christa had expectations, their faux honeymoon was over. Christa tried to hold on, but Stan became involved with another woman, an old girlfriend he hadn't completely abandoned.

This crossroads was the catalyst for the episode some friends have called Christa's "fatal attraction" period.

Christa's friend Eli said, "Stokowski was a creep. He was the perfect invented man to destroy her because he was very attractive, a bona fide WASP. He had no real fiber. He's the offspring of two great families and he's a do-nothing. I hear he's working in a florist shop. Christa was gaga for him." He said that Christa was always setting herself up. She was too available, too accessible. "There was never a step to get over to get to her. She was there for the taking. A doormat."

Eli's mom, Esther Gottlieb, had met Christa on several occasions, and because of Esther's instantaneous warmth and her unflappable common sense, Christa had opened up to her. Esther said, "She was in a great deal of stress when she was in a romance with Vanderbilt's son. She talked to me about it. Her skin was exposed to every bit of breeze and bad weather. She was so sensitive you could almost see her reacting to the tiniest change in air temperature. In her work she was very focused; she was all business. She had a great deal of refinement, her face, her carriage—a societal finesse that goes back to a certain Victorian quality—but then her personal life was full of throbbing pain. She was so lonely."

Christa didn't accept Stan's rejection. She followed him back out to Long Island and tried to attend parties, clambakes, polo matches, wherever she thought he'd show up with his new bride-to-be. She "stalked" him.

She saw him shopping in a fruit store with his pretty girlfriend. The girl was pinching tomatoes and the shopkeeper barked at her. Christa was pleased, and she decided not to confront her former lover; it was enough to watch his embarrassment from a distance. As she walked outside, she was surprised to see loose strawberries tossed across the sidewalk. Someone had dropped a carton, or a shopping bag had split open, tumbling little crimson pillows left and right. For some reason, the spilled fruit seemed heartbreaking to her. Christa waited for Stan to leave the store. He marched right through the little minefield without stopping, leaving smeared dollops on the sidewalk, which seemed only to underscore his brutal mind-set.

The next day, she followed him into a wine shop. When Stokowski saw her, his face was stone. She recognized her father's frozen veneer, when he didn't want to talk. So she turned and went to the cashier. She purchased a mini-bottle of something that was displayed on the counter, a dollhouse size "magnum" of champagne, which seemed like a mean joke about her childish dreams for a life with Stan Stokowski.

Her oldest pal from UEA said, "I warned Christa that Stokowski didn't want a permanent relationship with her, but she was of no mind to recognize this. She was living a fantasy version of her life, a *Great Gatsby* version with the expectations of a patrician upbringing. She was looking for that fantasy balloon to drift away on. Her tendency was to want something to happen that would change her life."

Another friend said, "Christa was always being used and abandoned. Always in disarray. You'd look at Christa, and it would be high on the Fujita Scale. Someone should step in to clean up the debris. She was like the human equivalent of an 'Adopt a Highway.' "

SUNSET DRIVE

Years after her Stokowski trauma, during her secret life with Tony, Christa sometimes reverted to her stalker habits. She would climb into her car and find herself driving up 6A in North Truro, looking for the cottage on Sunset Drive where Tony lived with Susan.

Sunset Drive is in a shambly section of North Truro, in a cluster of modest homes built across a low meadow. The sunken spot has the feeling of a West Virginia "holler" in its remoteness and front-yard litter, except in Tony's Appalachia, the debris wasn't defunct washing machines, junkers, or tractor parts, but fishing gear and lobster traps. Christa knew she'd be conspicuous if she cruised back and forth before Susan Jackett's house. It was a dirt road and she'd have to drive slowly in and out of ruts, her suspension squawking, but she was dying to see the place.

The yard had nets and Styrofoam buoys tossed about. You couldn't miss it. But the windows were shaded behind big pines and she couldn't get a glimpse of Tony's better half at the kitchen sink, or in an upstairs window. She pictured Susan sitting before the TV watching *Martha Stewart Living* with the blinds down, but it looked as if no one was home.

Christa let the car idle at the front walk. She thought, I must be kidding myself. The address wasn't the idyllic Pamet Estuary, nor was it Gramercy Park. It wasn't Paris. Tony's modest home was almost like a trailer park. But sometimes Christa believed that Susan Jackett had everything.

Once, at the A&P in Provincetown, she saw Susan choosing ears of corn, before a sign that said BUTTER & SUGAR, 12 FOR $2.99. Pulling the husks back from the tip ends to examine the kernels for worms, Susan didn't hurry as she carefully sorted the good ears from the wormy pieces. Christa imagined Tony buttering an ear of corn. She walked up to the table beside Susan. She started to peel corn, elbow to elbow with Tony's bride, tossing bad ears into a common reject pile. Susan grumbled when she found another bad ear, and Christa chimed in with her commiserations. It wasn't a good batch. The A&P was in decline. Susan finally went off with her cache, pushing her shopping cart. Christa left her heap of picked-over corn in a jumble of disheveled husks, and left the supermarket.

The Truro Transfer Station has a little modular building nicknamed the "swap shack" where people donate unwanted items. Cleaning out their summer homes, or emptying closets to get rid of unstylish clothes and bric-a-brac they no longer need, residents dump garbage bags full of gizmos, bad art, and dime novels in the doorway, and volunteers organize and shelve the never-ending stream of domestica. The place is a cramped "living museum," an urgent and revolving display of oddball furnishings, small appliances, "worst" wedding gifts, and reject Christmas offerings. There were items of utterly no worthwhile use mixed up with little treasures, real finds in the crumbs-from-the-table donations from wealthy summer folk. Christa liked to browse through the china, tableware, and books. One afternoon she saw Susan Jackett at the swap shack inspecting a wool throw rug. Susan spread the rug over the table, rubbing the heel of her hand over its uneven pile, worn smooth in high-traffic places, but otherwise still plush. Christa didn't need a "new" rug, but she suddenly wanted that one. When Susan turned away for a moment to talk to a friend across the table, Christa tugged the rug to the floor, rolled it up and left. She told her friend Gail, "I just didn't want that bitch to have it."

Christa's obsessive curiosity about Tony's wife was a universal side effect of a woman's flirtations and random sex with a married man. "Married men are lunchtime callers," Edna O'Brien wrote. Women complain about their brief interludes with married men, their "hot lunches" and "coffee breaks," their splash in the golden gutter after 5:00 P.M. It's an unhappy condition that a mistress can never avoid, when "dial-up dates," prostitutes, and contract kettys are immune. Amateurs can lose their minds.

When Christa had found out she was pregnant, she had told Tony, "You don't have to tell your wife. It's our secret. She doesn't have to know." Christa found the secret empowering. Tony said, "At first, Christa didn't want Susan butting in. She wanted to run her own pregnancy." But all of that would change.

Christa drove up Route 6. Route Sex was the running joke across Cape Cod, but it didn't have the little pinch of comic pleasure it used to have. Christa saw Susan's car parked at the mini-mart, and she pulled into a space beside it. She went into the store and strolled the aisles until she was side by side with Tony's blonde siren. She wanted Susan to notice her belly, but she wasn't even showing yet. A friend had told Christa that she was "glowing," but Susan didn't pay any attention to her.

NOTICE OF REJECTION

n July, I wanted to talk to Beth Porter, but she was in Nashua Street jail. Beth regularly received Toppy as a visitor, but I was told that if I wanted to talk to Beth, she would have to telephone me collect. I was advised that I should send her my telephone number. I wrote her a note asking her if she would be willing to call me. Within the week, Nashua Street returned my correspondence with a form letter, although nothing had been checked off on the following list.

NOTICE OF REJECTION
OF NON PRIVILEGED CORRESPONDENCE:

- ☐ Threats of black mail or extortion;
- ☐ Plans to escape;
- ☐ Plans for sending contraband in or out of the facility;
- ☐ Coded messages which are not easily decipherable to reader;
- ☐ Description of the making of any weapon, explosive, poison or destructive device;
- ☐ Sexually explicit material, graphic presentations of sexual behavior which may advocate prohibited sexual activity.

I didn't get a chance to speak to Beth before she was released from Nashua Street jail the second week of July. I was certain Toppy had warned her not to speak to me. But I reached Robert McLaughlin, a private attorney who had recently represented Beth. He was probably contracted by Toppy, but he said he couldn't divulge that information. "I can't say how I was retained," he said. But he told me that Beth was in jail again. "I was trying to get the three courts, Quincy, Dorchester, and Roxbury to let her go into a treatment program. Her only crime was possession of heroin, it wasn't a question of her committing crimes to support her habit. It helped that she was pregnant at the time. That was the device we used."

"She was pregnant?"

"Yes, that was the strategy to get her into a treatment setting."

"Is she keeping this baby?" I asked.

"I don't know. But the judge said that the program was appropriate for her. It's more helpful to get her into a program rather than creating more state expense."

"So she's in rehab?"

"Was. She walked. She left the program and was arrested again. She probably went to South Bay. That will be a year, I think. But I no longer represent her."

I was surprised to hear that Beth was pregnant. It might be Toppy's kid or maybe it had been Ed Hall's little gleam, from a moment they had shared when he wasn't pinned on heroin. I wondered if Beth was going to have her baby in prison. I could hear Goody Hallett and Hester Prynne cackling from the bell towers in hell. But when I talked to Trooper James Massari, one of the state police investigators working on the case, he said, "She's not pregnant. She's not at South Bay."

"So she's not having the baby?" I asked. "Is she in Weymouth with Toppy?"

"If she's with Toppy, you know he won't let her talk to you anyway."

Tim Arnold knew Christopher Worthington when he was dating Christa. He said that Toppy was a control freak and was sometimes very overbearing. He spoke of when he and Toppy had once taken a bike trip together. They had stopped at a roadside stand to buy muffins. Tim said, "He was very intimidating, almost vulgar, when he spoke to the shop girls. It made me very uncomfortable."

Tim also described one time when he had watched Toppy "force-feed" bologna slices to his house cat. "The cat didn't want to eat the lunch meat. It resisted. But Chris just crammed it down its throat. He was force-feeding it. It was some kind of 'control thing,' and not a happy moment for the tabby cat."

THE FLYING PLUMBERS

The same week that I spoke to Beth Porter's lawyer, Tim Arnold telephoned me, his voice shaky with an odd mix of comic grit and full-tilt resentment. Two state police officers had come back to visit him. They had "dragged him over the coals." He said, "The unit consisted of the alpha cop and his brutal sidekick. They had it ratcheted up to the kill mode."

He told me that they went down a checklist, starting with money matters. Tim said, "I didn't know about Christa's will. That money she left to me, well, I would never get it unless both Toppy and Ava passed away first. I think it was just a blank line on the page and Christa had to put a third name in."

"Maybe she was appreciative for those months you helped with the baby."

"They were going over my story about finding Christa. They said the flashlight was a ruse. They asked me if I ever peeped in her windows, unzipped, and masturbated. They had this hot revenge in their questioning and said I treated Christa badly in the relationship. Christa and I had some loud arguments. She had saved her message tapes; I have some angry arguments on those. But if you can scream about little things, you can avoid the serious things. But why are they starting this up again?"

I told him, "O'Keefe says that they go back to the beginning and start again as if they haven't done the investigation. If they don't start from scratch, they can't see what they might have missed."

Tim said, "The officers told me that everything I said was a fabrication. My story was rehearsed. But originally they said I had passed the lie detector test 'with flying colors.' "

"What did they ask you at that test?"

"They asked me to state my name. Then they asked, 'Did you kill Christa Worthington in her house?' "

When investigators go from *A* to *Z* like this, it sometimes knocks a subject off his feet.

Tim said, "I waited in the hall while they tallied my score. Waiting there, in the hall, I felt like a bad kid in school. But they came out and said I had passed. I went home very relieved."

Yet a recent government report on routine security screenings, written by a panel of experts at the National Academy of Sciences, had stated that "lie detectors lie" and "were likely to produce many false results."

Tim said, "This new cop was like a football captain. He was calling me 'a jerk,' and he said, 'You're full of shit. You're lying.' He was really pouring it on."

The officers told Tim that they knew he had been harassing Christa and that he couldn't accept her dismissal of him. They said that Tim went over to her house and looked in the windows. He left notes for her. He was obsessed. "They're saying I was really hanging on, and that I treated her badly. They're trying to make me this jealous person who—like—kills her. They asked me who fixed her roof, who did her plumbing—"

I tried to imagine Tim as the "jealous type," someone who bristled when workers came into the house. "Who did her plumbing?" I asked.

"Flying Plumbers."

This operation is a couple of beloved local tradesmen who also fly bi-planes after snaking your drain or fixing your water heater, but the offbeat company name had a superhero allure to it.

I said, "So she didn't fool around with the Flying Plumbers or the boys from Longpoint Electric or anybody who worked at the house?"

Tim said, "No. She didn't flirt with the plumbers. I might have looked in her windows, but not like a peeping Tom. In the meantime, they took my computer and a couple of notebooks. The computer is broken, but they'll copy the hard drive. I haven't used it since before Christmas."

Earlier in the investigation, the state police had decided to announce that Tim wasn't considered to be a "possible." They had told Amyra Chase that Tim wasn't physically capable of doing the crime with his "condition."

Tim said, "They came over to the house, looked me in the eye, and told me I had been cleared." The *Boston Globe* spoke to Tim and he had told them what the troopers had said, that he "was cleared."

Tim told me, "When I spoke to the *Globe,* the police went ballistic. They didn't like me saying I was cleared. They were angry. I just wonder, was it just a tactic for them to come and say I was cleared? Were they looking for my reaction? Because now they come back and they say I was a prick to her. The football goon says, 'I don't care how many lie detector tests you had, I think you were involved.' I tried to refute it. By the end, my voice was raised.

"It sounds so much like they think I did it. Is that what they want me to think? Do they expect me to say, 'Oh, yeah, I'm the one you want'?

"I miss her," Tim said. "I always have an urge to call her up."

We were driving up Route 6 one Saturday afternoon looking for some place to eat lunch. "Not here," he said. "Not where people know me."

I took him farther up-Cape, over to Chatham Bars Inn, an old Victorian inn on Shore Road near the lighthouse. It was a tourist trap for WASP day-trippers down from Boston. Its cavernous dining room looks over the Atlantic, the menu is pricey—but it's a cloth napkin dive.

We sat down in a corner and Tim ordered a beer and a scallop roll. He wasn't feeling topnotch. "I feel like shit," he said. "They've got to find somebody. If they think they're on my trail, they're really out there."

He pressed his hand against his face. When the waitress came back to fill our water glasses he put his hand in his lap. As the waitress walked away, again he covered one eye.

His hand up, he said, "They talked to me about Keith Amato. They said he was a 'red herring,' but do they want me to think they're after him to trick me? I have this irrational fear that they're going to come get me."

He told me that at least he was seeing Ava on a regular schedule. "For a while, Ava would say, 'Mommy's coming back, right?' to see if we would say yes. She's not asking that anymore. I can't stop myself from remembering when I found the baby beside Christa. Ava said, 'I had to have nursies,' like she knew it wasn't right to breast-feed—with Christa like that. Now, when I see Ava, she tells me, 'You used to come to my house when you and Mommy were best friends.' "

He was wrenched by Ava's statement, by her acknowledgment of his importance to Christa, when everyone else believed him to be, at worst, a killer or, at the least, an annoyance to her. Of our many meetings, this time Tim seemed more macabre than usual. More unsettled and distressed. Once self-assured in his devotion, he was losing his confidence. I started to wonder if his nervousness was a somatic response to his ordeal or if it was guilt chewing through his mild-mannered veneer. And what kind of guilt was it? That of the contrite ex-boyfriend, or the cornered killer? The first seemed more likely, but I have learned from O'Keefe that nothing is settled until it is settled. Underlying doubts accrue like a papery termite colony, but real evidence hardens like mortar.

The waitress brought a sample dessert tray with petrified slices of cakes and cups of mousse and sorbet, like tubs of solid concrete. I always think these "dessert trays" are in poor taste. But Tim chose a wedge of lemon pie. At least his appetite was intact.

He ate his dessert and asked me, "Has anyone you've talked to told you if Christa loved me?"

It's sad he would have to ask an outsider this crucial question. I told him, yes, of course, someone had said Christa loved him. Yet most of Christa's friends had told me otherwise. Her friend Kim Gibson said that Christa had told her that she was getting spooked by Tim. He would often walk into the house uninvited. Once she had found him in the kitchen. When I asked Tim about it, he said, "Christa and I had argued and I left. Then I came back into the kitchen to continue the debate. That's the 'unauthorized entry to the kitchen' story."

Christa's friend Gail Motlin told me that Christa's struggles with Tim might have been partly her own doing. She said, "When I heard from a friend in P-town that someone named 'Crystal' had been murdered, I just knew that it was *Christa*. When I learned she was dead, I wasn't completely surprised, because she could piss you off with her arrogance. Once, as kids, we were talking and she turned her back and said, 'Oh, shut up!' She could dismiss you. It was so hurtful."

But Kim Gibson insisted that it was Tim who had a temper. Christa had telephoned her after Tim had smashed the kitchen crockery.

I asked Tim, "Did you throw a dish at Christa?"

"Who told you that?" he said.

"Look, I've thrown things. It's no big deal."

"I didn't throw a dish," he said.

"Once I threw half a watermelon against the wall; it exploded and stained the wainscoting."

He smiled as he arranged his pie fork across his plate. "Throwing a dish isn't the same as stabbing someone in the chest. But I didn't throw a dish."

"Okay, okay," I said.

As if to offer proof of his temperate and nonviolent nature, he said, "I've met a woman. She's from Vermont. I'll be going up there."

"You're getting off the Cape?"

"I have a residency at the Vermont Studio School."

"That's a great place. So you're going up there to paint?"

"In September. My father's driving me."

I said that his father was a good egg. He told me that Christa had said that, too, but that her own father had not earned her respect.

Tim said, "She was very harsh to Toppy. She used to say that he wasn't a big success. 'You aren't good enough,' she implied. Toppy didn't buy into that patrician ideology of the Worthingtons. She felt like she and Toppy were on the outside looking in. You know, that's how she felt in Paris, and maybe in New York, too. One time, she refused to go to the movies with me to see *The Talented Mr. Ripley* because she had heard that the film was about a pretender, someone aspiring to wealth, someone on the outside looking in."

"She blames Toppy for what? Her in-between status?"

"The hardest thing for Christa was knowing that her mother married Toppy because she was pregnant. She felt responsible for forcing them together."

Christa had only Tiny Worthington, her grandmother, as a good example. Tim said, "Even Diana had destructive relationships with men, especially that hippie boyfriend she met at the flea market. But Diana is hoping that the trust will hang on to the house. It would be a healing opportunity for relatives to stay there and cleanse the place from being a murder scene."

"I guess. She's been over there already, getting rid of all of Christa's things."

That evening I picked up the ringing telephone. It was Tim. His voice sounded as if he had urgent information. He said, "I remember what happened with that dish. I threw that dish at my mom. You know, it's a balancing act to live with your parents, right? I threw a dish at them when they were sitting on the sofa."

FALLING OUT OF FASHION

In Christa's last years in New York, her increasingly extreme behavior in her personal relationships reflected a certain stasis or even a downslide in her career. A friend said that Christa was "floating in her professional life." She had worked at *Elle;* she knocked off the Chic Simple titles; and she was still freelancing for the *London Independent* and the *New York Times*. But these were frivolous stories about collectibles, military memorabilia, celebrity profiles; she covered Christie's auctions of vintage clothing or map collections, retro lawn and garden decor.

Although written with Christa's lucidity and wit, they were still fifth-rate assignments. Her onetime editor Deb Kirk said, "Christa didn't publish a lot. She wasn't that prominent."

She did accept an assignment to write an article that seemed, in hindsight, a tragic mirror or harbinger of what was to befall her a few years later. For the *London Independent*, Christa wrote a cheeky piece about Court TV and the O. J. Simpson trial.

The piece included a quiz for readers. Its questions have unsettling echoes:

"Describe the alleged murder weapon."

"Answer: 15-inch serrated knife."

In the satirical piece, Christa offers a compendium of "catchphrases" often heard on Court TV: "pool of blood," "trail of blood," and "the plaintive wail (made by Nicole's Akita)." She writes about O.J.'s kids with the same poignant information reporters would relate about Ava's situation in the aftermath of Christa's killing. "Child psychologists join the panels of experts to discuss how the crime might affect the young and impressionable." Uncharacteristically, Christa editorializes about America's new cultural obsession with crime scene voyeurism "that blurs the distinction between entertainment and reality." Christa warns, "Maybe you should turn off the TV."

In the same period in which Christa wrote her O.J. story, she churned out another article for the *Independent* about domestic diva Martha Stewart. In it, she quotes Camille Paglia: "Martha Stewart is one of the most important forces at a time of crisis in America for the female sex role." In this story, a gleeful romp through Martha-land, there's a wistfulness in Christa's description of Stewart's powerful hold on American women. The "image of haute bourgeois perfection," which she says Stewart presents, isn't just a joke to Christa, and between the lines one senses Christa's secret hopes to find happiness in hearth and home. Martha offers "inspiration and information," and "casual elegance, simple yet complex." Perhaps, if Christa herself could perfect the technique of making chocolate curls without letting them melt, she might win herself a perfect man.

Her writing life seemed to be unraveling rather than weaving together into a sturdy safety net. Her friends encouraged her to write something "serious," to try that novel or a nonfiction book about her crazy years in Paris. Christa told a friend that she already had the title for a memoir about her Paris career. She said she might call it *Falling Out of Fashion*. But she didn't begin a memoir or scribble notes for a novel.

Instead, Christa took a position in a notorious rat's nest of garmentos when she signed on to be head writer at J. Crew Group, Inc. Famous for its clean-cut, freckle-faced models in pastel T-shirts and khakis, the J. Crew catalog can be found on Westchester coffee tables, stuffed in college mailboxes, hidden in desk drawers at Charles Schwab, and tossed across lounge chairs and beach towels from New Jersey to California. The mail-order catalog position offered Christa a walloping $125,000 salary, which helped her ignore the company's homogenized ethos and its 100 percent cotton mission statement, its repugnant marketing campaigns with memos that said "Polyester begone!" and "Dress preppy, live preppy."

Her friend and old boss at Chic Simple, Jeff Stone, asked her how she managed the deadening corporate atmosphere. He said, "When I asked her, 'How can you do this?' she just giggled and rolled her eyes. She was like, 'I don't give a damn.' "

But Christa had immediate trouble with the founder and cantankerous head cheese of the J. Crew empire, Arthur Cinader, and with his
daughter Emily Cinader Woods, who ran the company. Christa told her
friends that Cinader senior was "the grand evil power. A total despot. He's
worse than anyone at *WWD*."

Cinader couldn't keep staff for long. Some of his top people left to create their own catalog, Tweeds. Christa tried to endure the pressure-
cooker atmosphere, but copy written for the catalog had to be up to a
standard that only Cinader had the key to. Once, Cinader had read copy
that began "This fall's kicky colors . . ." and he screamed at Christa, "Why
do you say 'kicky' and not 'bouncy'? Isn't it obvious that it should say
'bouncy'!"

After six months, Christa started to skip work. She went to London for
a birthday party, a weekend trip that dribbled into a two-week hiatus.
Thinking she was sick, Cinader was angry to learn she'd been jet-setting
instead of nursing the flu as she had related in her phone message. It's uncertain if Christa was dismissed from J. Crew or if she gave notice. Some
of her friends thought that Christa was insane to give up such a good
salary, but others thought that when she dumped J. Crew it showed her
typical panache and high standards. She wasn't a mail-order maven or
prep-wear queen. That wasn't Christa.

Instead, she made an appointment with Amy Spindler, fashion editor
at the *New York Times*, who interviewed Christa for a prized position
as head writer for the "Patterns" column in the "Fashion of the Times"
pages. Spindler said, "I interviewed Christa more than once, but I didn't
get a good impression. I thought she was so destroyed. Professionally, she
didn't seem hungry enough. So I didn't assign her."

Christa was miffed when she was turned down to write the "Patterns"
column for the *Times*. Over forty years old, she wondered if her age had
been a factor. Youth mattered. She saw a lot of Gen-Xers getting top spots.
Her rejection only fed her growing obsession to escape career for family.
She started to invent confabulations, dream goals, about a home somewhere "with a little one." Finding a man to share it with seemed more and
more out of reach. But she couldn't have a baby without a little collaboration, no matter how temporary the liaison.

THE AMAZING TARQUIN

I n late summer, Emily Dooley and I received a progression of heated e-mails from T. C. Churchwell, a man Christa had met in New York and with whom she had had a short-lived romance in 1996. He is known to her friends as "the magician," and they all felt Christa's interlude with Churchwell had signaled a turning point in her life. Soon after her affair with Churchwell, Christa wanted to leave Manhattan.

When I sat across from Churchwell to talk about Christa, I remembered what Janet Malcolm had once written. In her book *The Journalist and the Murderer*, she described the reporter's desire to connect with a subject who is a prismatic character worthy of a novel, whose portrait creates new mayhem for the reader and whose interest never evaporates. Malcolm writes of the serendipity of finding "a protagonist" with a "certain rare, exhibitionistic, self-fabulizing nature who presents himself as a ready-made literary figure." Meet T. C. Churchwell.

In his late thirties, Churchwell had been performing his magic act in New York City for a few years when he bumped, literally, into Christa at a crowded nightclub called the Barfly, across the street from her pad at Gramercy Park. When he was a kid in New Hampshire, Churchwell went to the library and borrowed every magic book he could find. He started writing his own tricks. Coin tricks were his specialty. He says that when he came to New York, he saw musicians with guitar cases opened on the sidewalk. He saw empty hats, violin cases, even someone's boot was displayed as the unshod genius juggled tennis balls or oranges. Churchwell watched these receptacles fill up with cash. One man pretended to be a robot, moving in ratcheted motions, as he earned a whole bucket of coin. Churchwell had a "brainstorm," and when he came back to the city, he set up a table in Washington Square Park. He started earning. He was amazed how people can't resist someone doing "sidewalk magic." He said, "Most of the magicians on the street are plastic, but I love doing it. I love messing up people's heads. I do in-depth tricks. People fall under the spell."

Soon he was performing in minor theaters and strip clubs, using his stage name "The Amazing Tarquin." Blond and handsome, Christa had once said he could earn cash as a body double for Nick Nolte. She knew several wannabe actors who earned money in the film industry, blocking scenes and standing on marks for cinematographers. Filmmakers try to get look-alikes with similar coloring and matched complexions to figure out the correct lighting for scenes, but the stars themselves didn't show up until the shoot. She wasn't teasing him. She thought he was handsome. Her relationship with T.C. was sometimes sweet, sometimes comic, but always tumultuous. A friend said, "I worried about this one."

Not an official figure in "the orbit of opportunity," the magician was in the larger mural of Christa's downward spiral. When the Massachusetts state police went to New York City and started to nose around his neighborhood on Twenty-second Street, Churchwell sent Emily Dooley and me accelerating messages, e-mails he copied to the Massachusetts staties and to numerous armchair crime geeks who follow Christa's murder case on the Internet chat slab *CrimeNews2000*. Churchwell's e-mail subject lines were incendiary, sensational, and always wacky.

Subject: The Mass State Police harassed my family

The Mass. State Police are calling my family members trying to get information about where I live. This is total harassment. . . . Instead of wasting time chatting with me or my family they should go arrest the killer.

Subject: The Mass State Police crashed my apt.

Today, at 4:30 the Mass. Police shoved their way into my apartment, threatened me with the arrest for the murder of Christa if I didn't take their DNA swab and answer their questions. One of the four claimed to be NYPD and said there was a bench warrant for me downtown (which is impossible) and threatened to take me to the station naked (except for a robe). I succumbed [sic] to the test after I told them I couldn't go outside because of my mental condition and they said they knew about it and asked me what medication I was taking. They said they were not leaving until I answered their questions. I told them I needed to call my lawyer but one cop stood in front of my phone. . . .

You may post this e-mail if you think it will help. TC

To: mspdetectives@capecod.net
Subject: Thanks a lot

. . . There's only one reason why you are asking all these questions. It's because you blew the investigation. You have no clue, you basically screwed up and now you are drowning and reaching for anything. If you think I would get a taxi or car or limo or whatever I needed . . . um, a bus or plane or a train, go all the way up to Cape Cod, kill someone I hadn't seen or been in touch with for years, well you are as stupid as I think you are . . . thanks a lot for screwing up my night. You will pay for this.

I have lunch with O'Keefe. We sit at a picnic table at a little roadside stand on 6A, swatting yellow jackets. I ask O'Keefe, "So what's happening in New York? Churchwell has been e-mailing me ten times an hour. Did you send the boys down there?"

"They went down in a cruiser."

"Five hours on I-95?"

"Our budget isn't first-class. Then, you know what happens? They're sitting in traffic in Manhattan, and their engine explodes. It's fried. But NYPD comes over, they take the boys to a hotel, get them cozy, and then they tow the cruiser to the garage. They rebuild the engine overnight. The works. It's all new."

"No kidding? They rebuilt the engine? Who pays for that, Massachusetts?"

He shakes his head.

"You mean it's a freebie from New York? On Mayor Bloomberg's tab?"

He explains that there is a code of honor. Local police always bail out an out-of-town crew. In the old days, they would have provided fresh horses.

I say, "T.C. claims that they barged into his place. Is that right? He told me that they probably came down on a paid vacation to see the Trade Center hole, it gives them a hard-on, he says, so why are they bothering him? So tell me, what are they doing down there?"

"They're detecting." He bites into his roll-up sandwich.

"They're detecting?" I'm always amused by the comic force of O'Keefe's one-word answers. It's so Don Rickles.

I say, "But why take Churchwell's DNA now, it's been six months?"

"Look. They know *what* they do and *when* they do it. An investigation is a methodical process. That magician is an egomaniac. They went down there to do a lot of things, not just visit him and hold his hand. We're talking to lots of people. We need to find out who she was screwing."

Whoever it is, he's disappeared into the woodwork.

O'Keefe says, "Someone is going to open his mouth and put his foot in it."

He says that, with a little patience, it will materialize. A person rats out someone or a killer starts crowing. O'Keefe says that's how it will happen, "unless we get a 'cold hit' with CODIS, you know, the FBI's Combined DNA Index System. Either way, it could be some years."

I ask him, "Tarquin's DNA—is that a shot in the dark?"

"We'll see."

"T.C.'s DNA stands for 'Definitive New Antihero.' Will he also get a polygraph?"

"We won't bother. When it's a nutcase, a polygraph is never accurate."

At her local watering hole, the Barfly, across from her apartment at Gramercy Park, Christa had sometimes met friends for a drink. The girls sat in a booth and waited for something interesting to happen.

Like clockwork, after midnight, when he had finished his act at a topless bar or at a strip club like Stringfellow's, or maybe after doing tricks at Canastel's, a favorite feedbag for celebrities, fashionistas, and glitter Nazis, "The Amazing Tarquin" breezed into the Barfly.

The Amazing Tarquin, aka T. C. Churchwell, was no longer a rising star but was more like a disabled satellite orbiting the same seedy wee-hour solar system, night after night. He told me that at Canastel's he had once sat down at a table with O.J. and Nicole Simpson. He made $1,000 a night with tips from patrons. He even got tipped by the girls at strip joints who were happy to have a break in their routine. He had been popular and was invited to perform at private parties for Aerosmith and David Lee Roth. He made $5,000 at the Aerosmith gig. He was doing all right, having his fifteen minutes of fame. T.C. says that he and his roommate, Chappy Brazil, were the reigning nightclub magicians. But in 1998, Brazil was killed when a Las Vegas police cruiser crossed the center line and hit his motorcycle head-on. At Brazil's memorial service at Caesar's Palace, Master Magician Lance Burton broke a gold wand in half, symbolizing "the futility of magic without the life of the magician." Brazil was most famous for stealing watches from hapless audience members. T.C. studied Brazil's technique and became proficient at performing the trick himself.

And T.C. boasts that the millennium's newest phenomenon, TV star magician David Blaine, had once been his young apprentice. Churchwell insists that he himself had written most of Blaine's tricks and, for proof, he says he had published them in a magic book called *Apocalypse*, co-authored by Harry Lorraine. He says that the book is a rare find at magic shops. But then he says, "I also work for the Institute of Community Living. I have a degree in psychology." T. C. seems to understand his glory days as a magician might be finished, his perch knocked out from under him by Blaine.

Although T.C. had once introduced Christa to megastar magician Doug Henning, Tarquin had worked mostly at strip clubs, doing magic between the girl acts, then after work he'd unwind at the Barfly. He was a regular there, and its patrons knew by word of mouth that after midnight "the magician shows up." The bartenders gave T.C. free beers if he'd stick around and do some tricks table to table. Fans would buy him rounds. "I wasn't under pressure to perform. I'd fool around and try out new material." T.C. has tattoos on his forearms, a top hat and a wand, the tools of the trade. T.C.'s tattoos are statements similar to Tony Jackett's inked forearms. Tony has tattoos of a cross, an anchor, and a Portuguese *figura* of a fist that wards off evil. Both men prize their graphic IDs, in hopes they can live up to these images. And Churchwell always showed up at the Barfly dressed in a 1920s jacket with a high collar and long thin tails. People would ask him, "Hey, are you getting married?"

T.C. roamed tables, performing standard routines that always made an impression, and he would begin to accrue some tips. He asked someone to remove a card from the deck without showing it to him. He asked the innocent to return the card to the deck and shuffle. T.C. would then choose the exact card from the reshuffled stack. Or he would ask someone to "think" of a card, and then ask them to remove a card from the deck. It would be the card they had secretly visualized. He could fold up a ten-dollar bill and unfold a fifty. While doing a trick he could remove a person's Timex from one wrist and buckle it on his opposite hand. T.C. would light a cigarette and tap its ashes into his hand, but the ashes would magically smudge the palm of a girl sitting across the table. He was cheeky and entertaining. He teased tourists, and flattered Gramercy Park residents. There were a lot of actors and dancers. Once, when a ballerina got off her stool at his request to demonstrate a dainty curtsy, he asked her what it was called. She said, "It's a plié, of course. Pronounced plee-ay."

T.C. said, "In New York, we call them 'plays.' "

He had set her up for his joke. She punched his arm.

One night, Christa was sitting with some women. The women loved T.C.'s ritual and asked him to join them at the table and do a little magic for them. As he performed a few card tricks, he noticed that Christa didn't watch his hands; she missed everything he was doing. She kept her eyes on his face: "She just looked at me, it was weird."

The next night, when T.C. arrived at the Barfly, she was sitting all alone. "She has her hair in a raggedy bun. She's dressed in some Woodstock outfit. A big loose dress. Later I find out she has nothing on underneath it." They sat together and the bartender got annoyed that Tarquin wasn't mingling with customers, keeping them happy. Christa ordered wine but didn't drink any. T.C. said, "She hated drinking because her dad was an alcoholic and she had had to take care of him."

He said, "The table began to feel cramped because she used big words."

But that night they left the Barfly together. "We got grope-y, but we didn't go to bed together." On the third day, they met again at the Barfly at midafternoon. "She wants to have a discussion about my sexual interests. I thought that was a kind of clinical come-on." They went to her apartment and got into bed. The first time he made love to her, she started to weep. He told her, "This is not a good time to cry. Not a good time for laughing either." She explained to him it was a way of letting go of her old boyfriend. She didn't tell him whom she was mourning, but most likely it was Stan Stokowski. "Whoever," T.C. said, "she had a coupon book full of them. This guy was some kind of royalty or a rich guy with a title, 'the Count of Mounting Christa,' or someone. She said that one boyfriend had beat her up and threw her over a banister. That might have been the one she called Mon Ami Le Cheval.

"She talked about that one all the time," T.C. said. "She liked combat. I didn't take the bait. When I met her father, he was a block of ice. He came to New York with two different women. Not with Christa's mother."

One night when Churchwell came home drunk to her, he told her, "I guess you finally got what you wanted, some old drunk man to take care of like your father."

She scolded him until he covered his ears with her sofa pillows.

"But then she was sympathetic, so caring. I'm slurring all over the place. She put me to bed on the couch. She had this giant mirror right over the couch. It was really annoying. I'd have to look at myself.

"Most girls liked me because I'm a magician, but Christa wasn't interested in that. She liked that I was a computer geek, and an artist. I can even paint flowers." He said that he currently had some paintings up at the Colgate-Palmolive Building.

But because he had worked at topless clubs, Christa was jealous, and she started showing up during his act. "She would stand outside the door, crying. She wanted me to stop my act and come outside. She'd say, 'I brought your asthma medicine. The cigarette smoke is so bad in there.' She'd be standing there holding my Primatene."

He said that at the time Christa was writing magazine articles and pawning her Chic Simple books. "We went to events in the Hamptons when she was pushing an *Elle* article or something. Everyone knew her. That PR diva Lizzie Grubman was starting out and Christa was invited to these glamorous launch parties. One night she says, 'I have to go to the Puffy Combs party.' I thought 'Puffy Combs' was some kind of hair spray or something she was writing ads for.

"But then she wasn't into the fashion scene anymore. She was going on this talk show about single women having babies with frozen spunk. She wanted the baby thing. I told her that I already have a daughter in New

Hampshire. She didn't listen. I'd look at her face and her eyes were like a slot machine with my x and y chromosomes popping up."

Then Christa began working on the AOL Web site *What2Wear*, answering wardrobe questions. In the spring, she packed up her computer and she and Tarquin moved out to Orient Point, Long Island, where she sometimes rented a house. She bought T.C. some new magic gear. She told him that she wanted to start up a business together doing children's parties in prosperous Long Island. Baby boomers would stop at nothing to have gala birthday parties for their kids. They rented ponies with bone-white unicorn prostheses glued to their foreheads; they hired actors to play Mutant Ninja Turtles, but some parents still wanted traditional live clowns and magicians.

She brought T.C. to a pet store where they bought a rabbit for the kiddie parties they planned to book.

Christa printed up some fliers. She paid for advertisements in a weekly, but they didn't get any offers.

They had long, open days. They fucked a lot. T.C. said that Christa would sit at her keyboard to work on *What2Wear* queries. He said, "Once she was sitting on my lap as she worked. She had an IBM ThinkPad and instead of a mouse it had a TrackPoint, a rubbery button like a clit. I said, 'I'm going to watch you move your finger on the ThinkPad and I'll move *my* finger on *your* ThinkPad.' We didn't fuck but I brought her off touching her ThinkPad."

Churchwell said Christa was a "jungle cat. She liked to fuck a lot. Think of that movie *Angel Heart*. My nickname for Christa was 'Muffin' because that's what we called her 'ThinkPad.' It was her electric muffin."

He later told me that they had also named the rabbit "Muffin."

But Christa had had more sophisticated nicknames. Tim Arnold had said friends had named her "Christabel," after a character in A. S. Byatt's novel *Possession*. Or maybe it was after Samuel Taylor Coleridge's long-winded epic poem of the same title.

Is the night chilly and dark?
The night is chilly, but not dark.
The thin gray cloud is spread on high,
It covers but not hides the sky.

The moon is behind, and at the full
And yet she looks both small and dull . . .
The lovely lady Christabel
Whom her father loves so well,
What makes her in the woods so late,
A furlong from the castle gate?

Looking at the poem now, one imagines Christa's dangers when she was isolated in the Truro moors the night of the murder.

T.C. began to understand why he and Christa spent a lot of time in bed. "One day I come out of the bathroom after we did the horizontal mambo, and she's lying there with her legs in the air. Like a human funnel. She tells me if she had a kid, I wouldn't have to take care of it. She says, 'Let's just try it, okay?'

"Again, I tell her I already have a daughter in New Hampshire. But every ten minutes she'd nag me. I'm stuck out there on Long Island and she'd say, Now!—or maybe an hour later—Now!"

Churchwell said that they tried to "play house," and she set up rigid dinner hours. She wanted him to go bike riding with her like the other happy couples zigzagging down the village streets. She rented two bicycles. She'd see women riding bicycles that pulled little baby prams. The baby carts had bobbing poles beribboned with warning flags. She'd see these flags and her eyes got all swimmy. Once T.C. took a hike by himself, and she rode her bike to find him. "I was walking back from the docks with my head down, so I didn't see her pedaling toward me. I didn't see her so I didn't say hi. She got really mad that I didn't greet her. She jumped off her bike and threw the bike at me. Sometimes she wanted that violence. Other times we were a good couple. It wasn't a façade, but most nights we argued. I'd sleep in the other room. Once, I put the chair against the door, but she kicks the door down. I know she wants to do the mommy and daddy dance again. Two doors got demolished that night."

When he threatened to go back to the city, she bought him a new computer with Windows 98, so he could make computer art.

But T.C. finally did go back to New York. He brainstormed to find a foolproof kiss-off and asked an old girlfriend to telephone Christa and leave erotic messages for him on the answering machine. The ex used her husky voice and said, "T.C., I really want to do you."

Christa didn't appreciate his crass brush-off. She wasn't going to let him go without a hissyfit. She trailed him all over the city. "She was the walking wounded," he said. "Christa was so childlike. Frightened and clingy. It was like the times when her father came down to the city with two different women. I could see the bad pull he had on these women and on Christa. Christa seemed so 'tiny' in front of her father. When I dumped her, I felt bad. I just remembered her standing there with my Primatene. You could see the little girl in there. She'd put on that little-girl face."

When they parted, Christa asked T.C. if she could keep the rabbit.

Her friends heard a different tale. Christa had given Tarquin his walking papers, not the other way around. When it was really over, Churchwell tried to reclaim some items from the Gramercy Park apartment. Christa didn't allow him to come up to the seventh floor without a police escort. When he finally arrived to get his things, she threw everything into the hall.

"The next thing I know, she opens the apartment door and throws a Bible at me. My Bible. Christa didn't own one. She throws the King James and it hits me in the head and it tears in half."

T.C. often finds ways to link dramatic events to his disappointments in life. He says that he and Christa broke up the "same week of Flight 800," and he claims that his wife had died on the same day that Christa McAuliffe was killed on the *Challenger*. He said, "Then I later meet the 'other Christa.' Maybe that's a stretch, but I think it's significant." He told Emily Dooley that he counseled 9/11 victims as a staff member of the Institute for Community Living, a psychiatric help center in Lower Manhattan. The *Portsmouth Herald* ran a story about Churchwell, a native of Portsmouth, New Hampshire. The reporter explained Churchwell's volunteer role after the tragedy. "Armed with compassion, Churchwell is taking hold of others and pulling them to emotional safety. He said, 'I've got to help these people. . . . It seemed like one of those Japanese horror movies . . . like a Michael Jackson video.' Churchwell became part of a human chain to unload trucks arriving on site. It was not until the task was nearly complete that he realized he was handling body parts."

But when Dooley spoke with the director of the Institute for Community Living, she was informed that T.C. wasn't a *staff* member at their organization.

O'Keefe understands that Tarquin is a volatile character, but that doesn't mean he's a killer. O'Keefe gives his nonspecific opinion of Tarquin with his typical bone-dry locution. He's at once dismissive and mysterious: "Churchwell? He's a colorful guy."

Christa's debacle with the magician gave her the confidence to give up trying to find a man to father her baby. A study by Yale and Harvard researchers, Neil Bennet and David Bloom, had reported that a forty-year-old woman was more likely to be shot by terrorists than to find a marriage partner. Christa decided that she didn't need to find the full embodiment of a man—that is, the ambulatory creature itself. She just needed the seed packet for her "flowerpot." She decided to turn to the busy avenues of ART, "assisted reproductive technology."

She understood the challenges ahead; she had followed the news stories about other women with "high altitude careers" who decided to have children later in life. They might start with donor sperm, then if unsuccessful have to graduate to IVF (in vitro fertilization) or GIFT (gamete intrafallopian transfer) and then the next step might be donor eggs, finding an egg broker or a surrogate mom. But these options were expensive, with unpredictable, escalating costs. Christa quickly learned the new diction and a world of acronyms that exists within the baby quest culture. Most of these acronyms represented infertility procedures, or perhaps the pitfalls of these procedures, like VLBW (very low birth weight), and this reminded Christa of other emotionally overwrought acronyms, like IOU and DOA and SOS.

Soon after her breakup with T.C., Christa wrote her infamous essay for *Harper's Bazaar* about choosing single motherhood. She wrote, "At the far end of my child-bearing years, choice, the feminist banner I waved in the '70s, is painted in very different colors." She quotes psychologist Jane Mattes, "Two good parents is the ideal. One good parent is good enough."

Christa attended Single Mothers by Choice meetings, and she agreed to represent that organization on a national syndicated TV program, *The Leeza Gibbons Show*. Friends can't agree about why she would put her personal struggle on the take-out menu of a sleaze-fest TV talk show. One friend said that Christa had joked that she hoped a "white knight" might watch the show, and her appearance on *The Leeza Gibbons Show* was like making a dating service videotape. Others said that Christa had a strong social consciousness and she believed she could be a spokesperson for women facing the same challenges that she was up against.

Christa visited a fertility center to discuss artificial insemination. She was told to postpone IVF hormone treatment because of its inherent risk of "Super Twins Syndrome," and the probability of multiple births with VLBW infants. There was also a risk of "late onset" ovarian cancer. She should begin her campaign with the least invasive procedure. It would be performed with something quite like a turkey baster.

Christa brought home profiles of available sperm donors and their corresponding voice recordings. In her *Harper's Bazaar* essay, she explains how women can fall in love with someone's "smooth baritone" only to "wince when the voice makes a grammatical slip." Christa not only noticed poor grammar, she could also discern soul errors in someone's statements that revealed his falsehoods and his jerry-rigged persona. But she found one tape and listened to it ad nauseam. This was *the* "voice she could listen to for a lifetime." When she decided that this "voice" was the right candidate for her, she discovered that all the frozen vials, all of the "product," was "sold out."

In the meantime, her periods had become irregular, as if her own body was "holding its nose in the air" in protest to her single mom pursuits. She went to the doctor again. After tests to check her hormone levels, she was told she might be perimenopausal, and the likelihood that she would ever become pregnant wasn't promising.

She called her friends in a weepy, soggy state. Billy Kimball recalls his surprise. He hadn't spoken to her for months and here she was pouring her heart out about such a personal matter. "She had an extreme edge in her personality, always ready to share bad news at a moment's notice— but this time she was more desperate. She wasn't making a joke of it."

After she had attended her twentieth reunion at Vassar, her vision of herself had never been so shattered. Christa's Vassar tribe seemed split up into two groups, the haves and have-nots, the women Didion had called "the yearners and regretters." There were mommies and nonmommies. Of the professionals, celebrated or quietly successful, the smallest, most envied group were the mommies who had had both vaulted careers and happy-hearth family arrangements at home with the kids.

But soon Christa was momentarily sidetracked from her mommy quest when she received a phone call from Hingham. Her mother was sick.

PART THREE

DOWN BY THE HARBOR

Truro harbormaster Warren Roderick, although twenty years younger, is like a bookend historian to Betty Groom. Betty chronicles the town's ups and downs with clippings, but Roderick is a raconteur, a storyteller. He knows everyone. He grew up on the same street in Provincetown with Tony Jackett. He kept Tony's books for the *Josephine G.* and helped haul her up when she foundered in the Pamet. And Warren knows the Worthingtons pretty well, having been harbormaster at the Pamet for the past ten years. The harbormaster job is sometimes like being a waterfront valet, ship steward, or concierge, and part-time stevedore. But Warren was also a summer therapist and confidant to many, especially Christa. And it was Warren who introduced Christa to Tony.

The Pamet harbor is the most idyllic spot in town. The harbor is on the west bank of the Pamet River, facing the green estuary and rolling slope of Corn Hill with Provincetown beyond. A favorite meeting place for Truro year-rounders and old-timers, many show up with their cocktails at sunset to debrief and gossip. The mouth of the river is always percolating at the ebb tide, its sparkling water like a wagging glass tongue.

The harbor must be periodically dredged or it goes back to its original state as a sandy bowl, not deep enough for most craft but perfect for launching little day boats. It was once a peaceful picnicking spot for Victorian ladies. The Worthingtons remember it that way. Now it has a few too many moorings, finger piers, and docks that have made it a little too busy in summer. Sometimes the water smells of gasoline, but one visiting New Yorker said, "This is nothing. You should see what it's like under the Whitestone Bridge in Queens."

"Tiny's Hut" is the family nickname for Ada Worthington's little cottage at Pamet harbor, nestled at the left of the parking lot, catty-corner to the harbormaster's shack. The place is small, tight, but summer winds flow through its windows like silk. Shorebirds, warblers, and red wings make orchestrations dawn to dusk. The Pamet is like Radio City for bird-watchers, with the terns' creaky chorales or the precocious virtuosos of goldfinches and mockingbirds. A worse racket happens when people launch boats in the predawn quiet. There are always sails slapping, mast poles clanging, the whine of cables and winches, the glugging tones of in-board engines, and the familiar "hornet buzzing in a coffee can" of little outboards.

The summer of '97, Christa was staying in Tiny's Hut until the paying tenants left the Little House and then she'd move up the street. When Christa was at Tiny's Hut right on the river, she often walked over to the harbormaster's shack to complain to Warren Roderick about the ruckus each morning. She didn't like it when men were too boisterous as they backed boat trailers onto the ramp to unload their Whalers and skiffs for a day of fishing. She couldn't get their attention the way she could typi-cally halt obnoxious loudmouths in restaurants or before takeoff restric-tions on U.S. Air or the Delta Shuttle, when, as they punched their cell phones, she'd start reading a book out loud in tandem.

Tourists hauling boat trailers and local residents who rent moorings year-round don't think the harbor should be a dome of silence. It's supposed to be busy. A lot of local men steam out to go fishing before heading to their day jobs. Like Kenny Hnis, who goes out early to pull his traps. He starts his day on the water, then comes ashore to work as a surveyor for local banks and mortgage companies.

Christa liked to visit Warren with a list of demands. She didn't want boaters to launch before sunrise. She didn't like it when someone came ashore in front of her house and left his gear on her property, or when people rowed dinghies back and forth to moorings and left their "ten-ders" in her yard.

Each season the town rents two Porta-Potties for Pamet harbor from Sandcastles portable rest room company. Christa insisted that the toilet tycoons come back and move the rest rooms to the other side of the park-ing lot, away from Tiny's Hut. Christa was a Brunhilde, a Princess Busybody, the Eva Perón of the harbor. But Warren didn't mind too much. He felt a little sorry for her. Her big family was difficult, and she didn't seem welcomed into the fold.

He said, "Her cousins didn't like Christa. They were always nasty. Like she was a born 'Scarlet,' like they were thinking of that old saying, 'She was a whore in her mother's stomach.' But when they saw her face-to-face, they cooed 'Oh, hi, Christa.' "

She'd wander around looking lost. She was a "lostaholic." Warren didn't mind if she stopped into the shack for a little chat.

That summer, when Christa left the city before coming to the Cape, she visited Gloria in Hingham. Her mother's initial treatments for colon cancer weren't encouraging. Gloria's illness might have sparked a renewed connection between mother and daughter. For more than two decades, Christa hadn't been very accessible. She was churlish when giving her reasons not to visit her parents, and she refused to come home unless it was on her own terms. Kim Gibson said, "When Christa was in Paris or New York, she never came home. I'd see Gloria and she'd tell me 'Christa hasn't called me,' and she'd be sad. When Gloria got sick, Christa felt guilty, I think, and she wanted to come home to nurse her." But another friend said, "If I hear one more time that Christa came back to take care of her sick mother—oh, please. She always came back when she was out of funds and out of luck. She wanted that Crow Point house." Yet when Christa visited her mom this time, both women were at a crossroads with dangerous transitions ahead.

They began to reknit their threadbare bonds, the frail flyaway strands of love and sisterhood that a mother and daughter are supposed to weave over a lifetime. These ties, if still frayed or broken, should be mended before it's too late.

Gloria and Toppy were worse than usual. They had dipped into a marital crevasse. Her parents were so icy, Christa told a friend, "I can see my breath in that house, like in those ghost movies." Her father's aloofness and regular disappearing acts seemed twice as harmful now that her mother was sick. But Gloria sometimes seemed bemused. "Look at these shoes," Gloria said, showing Christa the shiny loafers, the Nikes with tissue still stuffed into the toes, and oxfords in their shiny boxes. Toppy had brought home all these new pairs from the shoe store where he had met Beth Porter.

"He has to pretend to buy something if he hangs around her shop," Christa said. She wondered how long Beth Porter would hold on to her retail job, now that she had Toppy's "shoe size."

Christa still had the rabbit she had purchased with T.C. for kiddie shows. For some reason, she hadn't been able to abandon it in Manhattan. She thought it might cheer up Gloria. She had planned to build a hutch for it. It was a comic companion in the house at Crow Point. Gloria had a soft spot for fluffy creatures and would probably adopt every furball brought into the place. But her mother was too sick.

So when Christa came to the Cape she had the rabbit, but it seemed a sorry reminder of the silly steps she had made in her romance with the magician. And, worse, the rabbit reminded her of Long Island, where she and T.C. had tried to set up their magic-act business. She couldn't think about Long Island without thinking about Stan Stokowski and her stabbing humiliation when he rejected her.

The rabbit had to go.

She found a lesbian couple who wanted to adopt it.

Christa was still dismayed after being denied the "Patterns" column at the *New York Times.* She had hoped it would be her next anchor in Manhattan, even when critics demeaned the style pages and called them the "Girl's Sports Section." Even having often decried her career in the fashion industry, she had secretly fantasized about one day being the "It Girl," like Anna Wintour. She never reached the pinnacle of the fashion world; she had never climbed to top place on that mountain of slippery tulle. Rejections. Mistakes. Missteps. Her mother's sickness put some of these ills into perspective, but Christa still marched around Pamet harbor with a bee in her bonnet.

She was sitting with Warren in the shack, still the "lostaholic," but at least she looked a little better than when she had first arrived. Her skin was golden; a little too much sun had brought her freckles out. She was talking with Warren when Tony Jackett, who was working as assistant harbormaster that summer, charged into the shack to make change for someone who wanted to launch a boat. The fee was under $10, but the boater gave Tony a Benjamin Franklin. Tony rummaged around. "We don't have it in the cash box," Tony told Warren.

Christa said, "Oh, I might have it."

The men looked at her. She was wearing a skimpy tank top and shorts. She couldn't have that much cash on her.

Warren told the boater he could pay later. He didn't want Christa to step into the awkward role of "Pamet harbor treasurer." But Tony was smiling.

Warren said that Christa's first face-off with Tony came soon after that. One afternoon, Christa stormed up to them. She was holding the diagram of a new pier to be built on the river in front of her house. Her father, as an abutter, had opposed the new pier for years, but it was finally going to be constructed. Christa held up the plans and asked Warren, "Is this what it's going to look like? Aren't these pilings too high?"

Warren said, "So they won't loosen in an ice flow."

"But they're much too high," she said. "Aren't they going to cut them off?"

Warren said that the pilings really were too tall, the *Andrea Doria* could tie up, but the pilings were going to stay.

Seeing that her protests were hopeless, Christa said, "Oh, God. Well, you know what I'm going to have to do? I'm going to have to pretend I'm in Venice."

Warren said, "That was typical Christa. Pretend it's Venice. But Tony shoots me a look like, 'Where'd you dig this one up?' and he says to her, 'Venice? I don't get it.' Now Christa was one of those ladies who won't suffer fools gladly. She's trying to decide if he is giving her the business or is he just bone stupid? She gives him a look of daggers and marches off.

"But Tony feigns being dumb when it suits him. He has made a career of playing dumb. For instance, if something breaks at the house, a toilet seat, a faucet leaks, Tony will tell Susan, 'Oh, you better get your father over here. I don't know how to fix that.' Well, he knows how to fix it, he's been a dragger captain and he has jury-rigged everything. But he says he can't remember fixing a toilet, so Susan better get her father to do it. It's not really a lie. Tony doesn't put the effort into creating a lie. What he does isn't lying, but he puts the past into a fog. He can't remember fixing that toilet. He doesn't lie per se, he makes the past into something he ends up believing."

Warren seems to be saying that laziness can be like a religion. Wastrels are believers.

But after their first run-in, Christa started bumping into Tony. She told Tony, "Thanks for moving that Sunfish yesterday. It was there almost a week."

He told her, "It was a rental from Flyer's. Remember last weekend, there was heavy chop? They chickened out and never sailed it back to the yard. I guess they left town."

"They lost their deposit?"

"I guess."

"Too bad. So sad."

"In a few weeks, the summer pests will all be gone," Tony said. Year-rounders start the countdown the second week of August. In September, they climb onto any overpass on Route 6 waving to westbound travelers with signs that say DON'T GO AWAY MAD, JUST GO AWAY and IT'S BEEN GREEN, and BYE! SEE YOU NEXT YEAR. BRING YOUR WALLET.

Christa liked to hear the men talk about the harbor. Warren sometimes teased Tony about *Josephine*. At first, Christa didn't understand that *Jo* was a dragger and not the name of Tony's wife. *Josephine* was RIP, not Susan. Warren was Tony's boyhood friend, and he used to keep Tony's books for the *Jo G.*, a sorry occupation, indeed. But Christa liked that Tony wasn't "the WASP with a sail bag," but had been a real seaman, a dragger captain—despite Warren's ridicule.

Christa had planned to return to Gramercy Park before fall, but she started thinking she might hold on. There was no hurry to leave, at least not until the weather turned cold and the pipes in Tiny's Hut would have to be flushed. For the first time, she felt no pressing need to be in Manhattan in time for the grand parties during Fashion Week. In September, the tenants would be out of the Little House at 50 Pamet. Maybe she'd move in and stay until cranberry picking.

The next weeks she watched the parking lot, looking for the assistant harbormaster to show up. He worked half-time, usually noon to six, but his hours weren't regular. Sometimes she heard his voice outside her windows. He was helping a woman tie up. He was dragging a dinghy onto the beach, for a woman. He was rowing out to someone's boat, bringing them a bright red plastic gas tank. Another woman. He was always talking to girls. Once, she saw him talking to Molly Benjamin, a compact woman with an eye patch. Molly's an independent character, a fishing colleague who writes a fishing column for the *Cape Cod Times*. She lost her eye after she walked into a gaff on board a dragger. Her tub of oyster stew is the first to disappear at the Wellfleet Oysterfest. She's salty, all right, in fact, she looks a little like "Long John Silver" and wasn't competition.

Next, Tony was scolding two kids who were wading at low tide. The boys were throwing muck at one another until they were black head to toe. "It's a playground to you," Tony said, "it's a nursery to some. You're waking up the baby clams." He warned them that they might get "the Pamet crud," a rash some people suffer after spending too much time digging in the muck.

He made little impression on the brats, but his fatherly reprimand charmed Christa. She went outside to ask him "something," she didn't know what, but he had moved onto a finger pier. He was grabbing the boys by the waistbands of their muddy shorts and tossing them into deep water. The boys squealed and scampered back to be thrown from his arms again.

In September, she closed up the shack and moved into the Little House. To escape the busy harbor traffic, she went swimming on the back side at Ballston Beach. By August, bay water would get too warm, sometimes like a bathtub, but the Atlantic side was still refreshing, its waters Coke-bottle green.

Tony told Warren, "Where's my little hippie?" when he didn't see Christa around. Tony had not yet found the right vernacular for Christa's bohemian charms, and "hippie," of course, was dismissive. He felt her dangerous pull on him, and he tried to fight it with the demeaning nickname.

"She's at Ballston," Warren told him.

The next day Tony showed up with a new pair of Rollerblade boots. Warren told him, "You're fifty years old. You must be nuts."

Tony said, "I want to learn. Maybe I'll go down to the Ballston Beach parking lot. It's got that flat straightaway."

"You can fall on your ass right here, in this parking lot," Warren said. He knew that Christa was at Ballston Beach, and Tony was going down there to "practice" his skating in front of her. Warren figured that Tony would fall on his ass pretty good before the summer was out.

She saw him at Ballston Beach. He was bare-chested, wearing cutoffs. His bronzed complexion, muscled physique, his head of glorious black ringlets were very pleasing, but she was amused to see Tony slicing back and forth across the narrow strip of asphalt on Rollerblades. He circled the macadam, skating in graceful figure eights, first in one direction and then reversing. He charged forward with long strides, before gliding in a half-moon.

Christa thought that he looked like that really hot ice-skating champion Elvis Stojko.

Tony turned around when he saw her, sunk down on his heels, gliding backward. He was pretty good, she thought. Once or twice he hit a patch of gravel and almost had a pratfall, but he tiptoed out of the loose pebbles and sailed smoothly into a turn. She knew he was showing off a little, maybe for her sake.

She walked over to talk to him. She told him, "Nice booties." He was sweating, and the breeze chilled his copper skin, making his nipples erect. His eyes were deep and liquid, although a little cloud edged one cornea. Fishermen often get cataracts after years caught between the blinding sun and its blazing serrations reflected off the water. One day he'd have to take care of it.

Christa said, "Grown men look silly on Rollerblades."

He told her, "I'm just learning."

She told him he looked pretty good for an amateur.

He thought the way she said "amateur" sounded like a challenge, an innuendo. He said, "You know, you think I might come up to the house sometime?"

She said, "You'll have to call first. My line is busy because I've got a modem. Keep trying."

Keep trying was another innuendo.

A week later, Tony was sitting in his Jeep at the harbor parking lot at sunset. He was watching the day end, still hoping something might happen next. He had stayed to drink a beer someone had handed to him when Christa's black Honda pulled up beside him. She smiled at him from the driver's seat, then threw her car in reverse, backed up, and left the parking lot.

He waited a few minutes, then cranked his starter and drove after her.

At the Little House, she changed out of her tank top and shorts. She untangled a wraparound skirt from a hanger. She draped its silky panels around her hips, pulling its sash tight. This was an item a man might easily peel off, spinning her like a top. She decided not to wear it and kicked it away. She tore another dress from the closet, a tight string bean shift that she had trouble zipping up. She felt a little twinge in her abdomen. It was a familiar, purring ache, what doctors had called "middlesmirtz," a tenderness that accompanies ovulation. Even infertile women can have the condition.

Tony was at the door. He was wearing his scuffed work boots. Work boots "with no socks" is gay couture in Provincetown, but Tony's version was blue collar and hetero. She felt a wallop in her diaphragm.

He said, "Your driveway winds around like a seashell. This is a sweet place. Can't see it from the road. It's a secret."

He was talking like Nick Brown, swooning like a real estate agent. He came into the kitchen. She thought she would show him the view from the living room, but he didn't seem interested in sunset views, ten-mile vistas, sweeping horizon lines. He was a fisherman, after all, he'd seen the wide open ad nauseam.

He was staring at her.

She leaned back against the kitchen sink and crossed her arms, feigning a little snobbery. She had once written in a Chic Simple guide, "The louder the 'go away' message, the more audible the 'come hither.'" She knew he was married and she analyzed that detail—for a moment. Then she tipped her face and looked up at him from under an avalanche of hair.

He stepped up to her. She was tiny. He tugged her closer, lifting her onto her shoe tips until their hips notched. He kissed her. His stubble had a subtle hint of that morning's shaving cream. A delicious soapy taste mingled with harbor salt.

She thought his kiss was more than a simple "American" kiss. Not Latin exactly, but deeper, with that distinctive Brazilian heat she had dreamed about.

Christa pulled his arm and led him to her bedroom.

They sat down on the same edge of the bed, sitting side by side, as if they waited for a bus. Tony plowed the heel of his hand up her spine and reversed direction, tugging her irritable zipper down. He lifted her shift away. He scrolled his fingertips across her bare belly, and shoved her onto the bed. He kissed her collarbone and carefully, in slo-mo, nipped her breasts. He rode his fingertip hipbone to hipbone. He knew her body. He navigated an exact map of fiery landmarks, some completely fresh to her until she felt each trigger.

She thought of him skating in the parking lot, rolling and dipping, tacking back and forth with smooth momentum. He glided into her, through her. This man knew everything.

He stopped at the Little House a few more times before Christa had to leave for New York, although he was careful to avoid her tearful good-bye. He said, "She knew how to keep me coming back. She was industrious." Christa had told him about the "European ideal—using one another in bed—no strings." She pampered him with a lot of oral sex and extra attentions he wasn't seeing at home, not since their son Kim had died, and Susan had been taking Prozac. While taking the antidepressant, her sex drive wasn't the same. His first go-round with Christa was a brief, whirlwind sexfest. Nothing more. He told Warren, "I can't believe it. She likes sex. She likes sex as much as we do!"

Tony talked about his first tryst with Christa. "It wasn't like *Fatal Attraction*. We didn't knock chairs over, or crash into the kitchen counters. But it happened fast. We kissed, right by the butcher block.

"I'd never heard of the Worthingtons, not until that summer. Then I got the lowdown. The Worthington history at the Pamet. The Worthington problems. Who owns this or who owns that? She bitched about her family. Jan owed her money. Christa had this energy. Energy is infectious.

"Christa was the antithesis of my wife; she had this unkempt, bohemian charm. It was refreshing. She'd lost a job at the *New York Times* and she was mad about it. But I could make her laugh. You know, if I saw her at the A&P I wouldn't have thought twice. But there were things about her I really liked. She says, 'We can use each other. For sex. That's how it is in Europe. Americans are too repressed.' "

Tony says he believes she told him about her European married lovers to make him feel comfortable about having an affair with her. He said that "she was careful not to spook me so she never said she loved me. But I knew she liked me. She was a loner. She didn't know how to be happy. I never worried about finding someone there when I stopped by. I'd walk in. She'd light up."

Christa went back to Manhattan that October. She worried about her parents' arctic home life. She told friends, "I walk into that house. My nose hairs freeze." She was feeling guilty about leaving her mother with Toppy. Her off-and-on therapist in Manhattan told her that she should visit her mother more often, but she shouldn't feel responsible for her parents' unhappiness. The therapist gave Christa a new prescription for a different antidepressant, Wellbutrin.

When Christa twisted the cap off the little bottle, she stared at the purple pills. The pills had happy faces imprinted on them. The pharmaceutical company had designed the trademark lettering in a crescent, and above the grin, its milligram dosage and the acronym "SR" (sustained released) were stamped like two eye dots and a nose, to make the familiar smiley-face symbol.

The next week, when she mentioned the smiley face pills to her therapist, the doctor tipped her head and looked at Christa, as if poor Christa was really grasping at straws.

Christa was writing for the Arts and Leisure section at the *New York Times,* usually assignments on decor, home fashions, and antiques. She wrote about collectors' stockpiles, everything ranging from pug dog art to military knickknacks. It wasn't the same pressure nor the same excitement as haute couture, and she could write these slight features with one hand tied behind her back. But these pieces revealed the same wit and elegance that Christa had earlier brought to her more glamorous assignments.

Writing about familiar household gadgets with her typical bemusement and alacrity, she made them simmer. "For more than 300 years, inventors have tried to come up with the perfect corkscrew. . . . 'Corkscrews are as diverse as snowflakes,' says one ardent collector . . . a descendant of the gun worm, the corkscrew might have been improvised by thirsty hunters in the field trying to get into a bottle."

And in a story about popular "pug dog art" she writes, "The pug's special status dates to Imperial China. Among the lap dogs bred by the eunuchs of the Imperial Palace, pugs were revered for the way the folds of their brow formed the Chinese character for the word 'prince.' . . . Pugs became pets of the middle class in Britain only at the time of Queen Victoria, a dog lover, who banned the practice of cropping pugs' ears. . . . Today a pair of small Meissen ceramic pugs—male and female—costs $18,000."

Christa's relentless intellectual curiosity is a constant; it's tangible even in her most breezy, frivolous cast-offs. A reader senses her hunger for making connections with her subjects. She wasn't a renowned art critic, or a theater guru like Ben Brantley; her beat was on the fringes of the fine arts. But her stories showed her fascination for how the human touch transforms the material world, and how man creates the physical embodiment of cultural ideals and notions. She was an "anthropologist," interested not only in the craftsmanship, but also in the emotional baggage of antiques, domestic artifacts, twentieth-century textiles and tidbits.

Her writing in these pieces shows a tenderness for her subject, not merely an urge to deconstruct it. With everything in her personal life raggedy and unraveling, Christa's writing remained bighearted.

She continued visiting old haunts with friends, but her Gramercy Park apartment was shrinking. She felt almost breathless from its hornet-cell confinement. She talked to a realtor to see what price she might get if she decided to put it on the market. She thought of the airy rooms of the family house at Crow Point, where Gloria was waiting. She pictured herself one day being "lady of the house," in Hingham, but more often she imagined going back to Truro. When Tony Jackett had never stopped in to say good-bye to her, although he had known her departure date, she didn't want to believe it was a brush-off. She took it as a sign of his casual nature, and that their little fling wasn't over; it was in suspended animation. She had left the furnace on in the Little House and didn't drain the pipes or winterize it. She planned to go up to see Tony.

In a *Times* piece about marine gizmos, she wrote about chronometers, brass sextants, and eighteenth-century octants crafted in ebony and ivory: "The sextant, which measures one-sixth of a circle, has remained the most accurate manual instrument for charting by the stars since its invention in 1775, by John Bird, an English instrument maker. 'It's part of the tradition and feeling of the sea to be able to use the sky,' said Don Tregworgy, associate director of the Mystic Seaport Museum in Connecticut, who teaches celestial navigation. He had begun collecting outmoded instruments of radio and satellite navigation for the museum—though his heart is elsewhere."

Christa recognized the expert's melancholy, because she, too, felt her "heart was elsewhere." If only a sextant or antique octant could be of use to her. Celestial navigation and wishing on stars was all too often a hokey metaphor for being lost in life, as one searches for homeport. In New York, most nights she couldn't see the stars at all because of too much man-made light. But in Truro, stars surfaced every night like a fiery canopy. When she thought of night skies in Truro, that glittering tent, she imagined Tony Jackett. Tony Jackett in bed with his wife.

She made the effort to drive up to the Cape every other weekend. Sometimes she went the extra leg to Hingham, but usually she shot due east on 195 through Fall River, New Bedford, and straight to the canal bridge. Warren said, "Tony knew when she was back because he'd see the lights on in the Little House. You know, you come over the hill on Depot Road, and see it blazing up there by its lonesome. Tony would drive over to the harbor just to look. Sometimes, if I saw the lights, I'd let him know."

Because Christa was keeping the oil burner running all winter, a major demographic of Truro field mice had moved into the snug little house. She called Warren to ask him what to do about all the mice she was finding. She wanted to rent a vacuum with a HEPA filter to vacuum up all the mouse droppings. She had moved a lot of her furnishings and possessions from Gramercy Park to the Truro house and she wondered if the mice would chew books, or burrow into upholstery. Warren told her, "Set traps."

She squirmed. "Oh, I can't use traps. Then I'd have to do the forensics and the removal of bodies."

"Just throw them into a garbage bag," he told her.

Sometimes, in bed with Tony, a mouse would shoot up the door frame and scramble along the molding. Christa would squeak, then explode in giggles. How could she fear a little mouse when she was in Tony's arms. He said, "Red squirrels are worse."

"Red squirrels?" She didn't know if he was teasing her, maybe he was talking about her auburn hair.

After her trysts with Tony, she'd come back to Manhattan under a black cloud. She didn't want to be in the city. Christa's friend Jay Mulvaney said, "That last year in New York, I had tried to bring Christa in on a couple of projects. I was with the Council of Fashion Designers of America, and I brought her in to try to package something. She wanted the money, but she wasn't happy about the fashion world industry. She had burned too many bridges. It was a time when Christa and I had started to reject the New York life that at one time we had both really wanted. I was getting out of town and going to western Massachusetts a lot. Christa wanted to be in Hingham or Truro. Christa was beginning to question herself: 'Do I have the chops for New York or not?' and then realizing, 'Do I really want to have the chops?' "

In her essay "Goodbye to All That," Joan Didion wrote of her New York experience: "I cannot lay my finger upon the moment it ended, can never cut through the ambiguities and second starts and broken resolves to the exact place on the page where the heroine is no longer as optimistic as she once was."

Christa sold her Gramercy Park apartment for an undisclosed figure. But friends say that she didn't think she got a good price and was disappointed. In May of '98, she returned to Truro and moved into the Little House.

She swept up mouse droppings.

She emptied closets and washed all the linens. As she did the laundry, she remembered the story of Harry Kemp, Provincetown's beloved "poet of the dunes," who yearly gathered local residents to organize reenactments of the Pilgrim women's "First Monday Wash Day." In the forties, Kemp wore his poet's cape and borrowed Manny Zora's dory to reenact the Pilgrim's First Landing. Christa was thinking about these Pilgrim women as she aired blankets on the porch railing. She plumped sofa cushions and "sunned" them. The sea air would purify everything, providing a fresh start, and this was how she reclaimed her role as mistress at 50 Depot Road.

Then she was down at the harbor pestering Warren. "Is Tony working?" she said. He told her that Tony was on the clam flats west of the Provincetown Inn.

Christa drove out to the breakwater. It was a minus tide and the sand flats were glistening. She didn't have her sunglasses, but she made a visor with her hands. She saw him a half-mile out. He was wearing his white Errol Flynn tunic, its bleached shirtfront like a surrender flag. Soon the tide would turn, and she hurried to get to him.

The breakwater's huge granite stepping stones take your full concentration or you can twist your ankle. She tried to maneuver the rocks, but teetering once too often, she jumped into the knee-deep water and sloshed over the flats.

As she neared him, she was already scolding him. "Are you trying to dump me? You know I'm back, where've you been?"

She looked beautiful, sun-drenched. Her bare legs were still pale as alabaster, but her hair was already highlighted with natural golden ribbons. Like her friend Eli had said, once she's on Cape Cod, Christa becomes a kind of "solar Heidi."

She ran over to him and stood right under his nose, looking up into his eyes. She tried to corner him. On the flats, Tony never felt cornered. In any direction he turned there was the "wide open," and a steady horizon line, everywhere he looked. But he didn't see much reason to ignore her.

She was standing barefoot like him, in a foot of water.

It was May, the plankton was blooming and the sea was so perfumed, so floral, it smelled like a garden.

His mother had died the previous fall, and this made him want to clean up his act. He imagined his mother's ghost looking down at him.

His mother hovering above town might help him behave himself. But Christa was back, ready to start it up again.

They walked over to the breakwater. It was deserted at lunch hour and there wasn't anyone nearby. She kneeled at his feet and tugged his jeans down. Tony later told Warren, "She's blowing me, and a hundred feet away I see the water is crazy. It's a bluefish blitz. Fish are thrashing, jumping and snapping their jaws, making a ruckus. She doesn't stop. It's a huge blitz happening, but they don't distract her—"

Warren liked to tease Tony about getting a blow job in front of those bluefish. "Thar' she blows!"

Tony tried to defend himself and reminded Warren, "She likes sex as much as we do!"

Tony stopped by the Little House a few times a week. "I'd be driving down Depot Road saying to myself, 'Go home, go home,' but I'd just hang a right."

Tony said, "I never stayed long. Driving in and out of there it was so easy to be seen. But I was *never* seen. I think now it would have been better if I had been outed early on."

Susan later said that she had always sent Tony off to work with one warning: "Tony, *think* before you *act*. Think: 'If God looks down at me, and sees what I'm doing, would he smile?' "

Christa let the fur fly when real estate guru Nick Brown called to inform her that Toppy had put the Little House on the market. Nick explained that the Worthingtons have a long history of heated real estate transactions. "John Worthington lost a house in a card game. He was a compulsive gambler and lost the cottage in a game down on Longnook. But Lucinda married him three times, anyway. Other Worthingtons had sometimes borrowed money from friends, and when they couldn't pay a debt the 'friend' got the land. It was like the old 'tax taking' scheme, but on the other foot. But there's so many Worthingtons and there's little land left to go around."

Christa had lent money to her cousin Jan. Jan didn't mention the transaction in her brief essay in memoriam to Christa published in *Provincetown Arts*. In the essay, Jan tells how important her cousin Christa had been to her: "She once recommended a hairdresser to me . . . and I walked away with by far the best haircut of my life."

After Christa's confrontation with Toppy about the bungalow, friends say Christa began to worry about the house in Hingham. Some have said that when she visited her mom there, she wasn't paying a sympathy call so much as she was putting her paw prints on the Crow Point house. She was squatting. Christa wanted security and proof of her stakes in particular family properties. She was also concerned about her mother's homestead in Naples, Florida. And Christa's impulse to land Stan Stokowski was in part because of her idealized vision of all the pricey Vanderbilt real estate.

Tony heard some of Christa's tirades about landholdings when he visited her. But she was in a wholly different ballpark from him. He had been a home owner only during the years he'd been fishing. Susan said, "I was so happy then. I had all four of his kids in that house in North Truro." But they lost the house when Tony couldn't meet payments on the *Josephine.* Tony said, "At the beginning, Christa seemed to have this sophisticated outlook about us. I never gave her the impression I would leave my wife, and she said, 'The fact that you're married keeps me from being emotionally attached.' "

But Christa was falling for him.

That summer she went to art openings at local galleries in Provincetown and to poetry readings at the Fine Arts Work Center. She knew that Tony was often at art openings. She'd see him in a corner talking to the artist, or standing with his friend Chris Busa, the editor of *Provincetown Arts* magazine. Chris Busa's assistant editor was a pretty blonde named Jennifer Liese, who went on to be an editor at *Artforum.* Christa was furious that Tony was spending so much time talking with Chris and the young blonde. She never tried to talk to Tony in public. Her aunt Diana might notice. But Christa charged up to their intimate circle and talked to Chris Busa. She told Busa that she was interested in starting an arts magazine out on Long Island. She talked business, but it was a way to warn Tony that she didn't like to see him talking to other girls.

Tony and Busa had been friends since high school. Busa's father was the painter Peter Busa who had had a studio in Provincetown. Busa said that Tony's interest in a writer like Christa wasn't unusual. "There's historical tension between the artists and fishermen in Provincetown. It's like *Lady Chatterley's Lover.* Lots of Worthington women hooked up with fishermen. Her aunt Lucinda had dated a Portuguese fisherman, and Jan Worthington saw them, and had even married a fisherman. Tony likes artists. I introduced him to Motherwell and brought him to the Beach-combers. In P-town there's a kind of democracy between the fishermen and the intellectuals. A democratic respect and alliance."

But Warren Roderick said that one time when Christa went out to a Friday-night opening in Provincetown with her neighbors Francie Randolph and Tom Watson, she couldn't hide her reaction to seeing Tony with Jennifer Liese again. Christa often socialized with Randolph and Watson, local artists who lived opposite her on Depot Road. The couple invited the public to their "Open Studio" soirees, hoping to sell work, and they showed their work together in group shows such as one called "Inter-sex-tion: Couples in Mixed Media" at the DNA Gallery. These hus-band-and-wife art teams are a dime a dozen at "My Better Half and Me" group shows at summer art bins, but when Christa saw Tony standing beside Jennifer, she stormed out of the place with no explanation to Francie and Tom. Her "European sophistication" had yet another ding in its veneer.

In midsummer, Christa invited a few of her New York friends to come up to the Cape. They sat around the living room and listened to Clinton's speech about Monica Lewinsky.

Adulterous couples across America watched Clinton's ordeal, see-ing their own risks and secrets mirrored. Clinton's philandering didn't seem to directly reflect Christa's adultery with Tony. Jilted wives Hillary Clinton and Susan Jackett had nothing in common. But Christa had a funny gut feeling about Monica Lewinsky. The intern's delusions were embarrassing to Christa. Monica's rose-colored glasses reminded Christa of her own infatuations, especially her obsession with Stan Stokowski.

She told her friends defensively, "When it comes to sex, the woman is always the 'intern.' "

When her New York friends were gone, Christa enrolled in a cooking class at the Green Briar Jam Kitchen in East Sandwich. An antique home-stead with a bright, open kitchen lit by turn-of-the-century skylights and white enamel sinks, Green Briar is like walking backward into the nineteenth century. The kitchen has long rows of gas burners and blue-and-white speckleware kettles hanging suspended from hooks. Christa wanted to make strawberry jam from wild strawberries.

She'd read an ad in the *Cape Cod Times* for Jam Kitchen cooking classes. The lure of it was somehow instinctive and metaphoric; her desire never waned for babies, berries, riches, and sex.

The insurmountable odds didn't arise from the process of cooking the fruit, the difficulty was in the search, in finding the secret fruit. But the volunteer at the Green Briar Jam Kitchen assured her that there were plenty of wild berry patches to be found on Cape Cod. One must be organized in her search and know how to tack back and forth over meadows without tracing the same aprons and wasting time going over the same terrain. Many acres must be searched to find enough berries for an eight-ounce pot of jam. If worse came to worst, she could lengthen her batch with California strawberries. Christa said, "Absolutely not."

After searching the banks and crannies along the Pamet, all the way south to Ballston, she had found less than a cup, and some of these were too green, almost pearly white and she didn't pick them. She drove over to Ducky's pit, where she'd heard there was often a good harvest to be found, if she could avoid the dusty track where teenage boys rode their motorbikes and balloon-tire four-wheelers. The junkyard is an ecosystem of its own, and the teen boys were just part of it. But there, in old growth along the berms, and in every green oasis between massive junk heaps and open deserts of sand, she found almost a pint of tiny, deep-red strawberries.

Tony again entered the pale of the Worthington compound, where Christa waited. Tony never telephoned. He materialized. She was ready. She'd be standing in her backlit doorway as he pulled up. Naked. She went around the house in the buff, something that Tony marveled about when he talked to Warren. He loved a woman who scrambled eggs at the stove wearing nothing, not even an apron.

But Warren told Tony, "You can't expect your wife to walk around naked with all those kids in the house. When has Susan not had kids around? She had two kids before she saw your ass."

Tony told Warren how Christa had once charged out of the house, buck naked, and scrambled onto the hood of his car. She wanted to do it right there, on his Jeep. He started to make love to her, but the hood was burning. He had to run inside for a blanket. These free love escapades seemed to enforce Tony's nickname for her, "My little hippie." To Tony, Christa was so "Woodstock" at those instances, he had no other comparison, no literary education in the refinements of Bohemia to find a better pet name.

Christa's unorthodox lifestyle was exotic to him. But he told her, if she always walked around naked, maybe she should worry about peeping Toms. Did she ever worry about prowlers?

Tony said that as the summer advanced, when he stopped by her house, there was no more chitchat, she wanted to "get straight to bed." He said, "She never made dinner. Her refrigerator was empty." Christa knew that if she had made a meal for him, he'd "get spooked." Moms bake. Wives cook. Sex kittens sizzle.

Tony said, "And we never exchanged gifts. I never acknowledged her birthday. We tumbled into bed, that's all."

Clinton's dalliance was an unnerving, familiar episode to many American men. But Tony saw how the president got caught because the girl had talked. Christa promised she wasn't telling anyone about their trysts. He saw her sheets luffing on the clothesline; she wasn't saving them like that famous blue dress. He trusted her.

But in fact she was talking to Warren, and talking to some of her cousins. She was just too smitten not to boast about him.

Eli Gottlieb said, "I heard all about Tony in phone calls when I was in Rome. She was totally in love with Tony. It didn't take that much, she was too available. Too accessible. No step to get over to get to her. She was there for the taking, despite all that 'culture of sophistication.' "

Barbara Holloway had a different reaction to Tony. She said, "Christa chose men who were not up to snuff to avoid intimacy or commitment. Choosing married men is the same excuse. I never thought she was in love."

But Warren Roderick, who was there in person to watch all the carrying on, said that Christa was in deep over her head. He said that she believed that Tony was the misunderstood husband, the discouraged

fisherman, the wounded proletarian poet. She told Warren that she believed that because Tony had married so young, he shouldn't be held ac-
countable for an unhappy marriage. She wanted him to have a second
chance. Warren said, "She once came to ask me why I thought Tony had
been such a financial failure in life. So I told her it's hard to fish with
a small boat, you know, with the weather, things like that. I could have
told her that the only problem with the boat was that it was tied up at
MacMillan Wharf too much. Instead of fishing, Tony always looked for
the big scam. But Christa invented her own scenario. She decided that
Tony never had the right encouragement from Susan or his father, but if
she could get behind him, she might turn it around for him."

Tony's son Beau Jackett published an essay about his father in the
Provincetown Advocate in the spring of 1997 that gives an interesting explanation of his father's unlucky career.

> Through my community and my father I have learned the small-town
> values that will benefit me for the rest of my life. . . . My father is an
> idealist, for whom fishing is more than an occupation. Within my fa-
> ther's code, what passes for failure in the world is, in fact, a kind of vic-
> tory. The traditional definition of "defeat" is not part of my father's
> vernacular; defeat is not defined by catching no fish for several weeks.
> Defeat is relative; it is defined within one's personal code of values—
> my father is so mentally powerful that he rarely experiences personal
> defeat.

This excerpt by Tony's eldest son seems to illustrate Warren's theory
about how Jackett men might put the "past in a fog." When Beau writes,
"My father is so mentally powerful that he rarely experiences personal
defeat," defeat is somehow reborn as victory.

Christa's interest in Tony's career was piqued when she learned about
his smuggling episodes. Warren said, "One day she comes to the shack
and says, 'I know that the *Jo G.* wasn't just used for fishing.' "

Warren hadn't involved himself in Tony's smuggling sprees; Tony had
his mates Buddy Johnson and Joe Lisbon. But Warren was their accoun-
tant. He did their books.

Warren saw how starry-eyed Christa was about stories of Tony's midnight activities; to Christa, he was like Provincetown's legendary rum-runner Manny Zora. "Christa comes to me and says, 'Warren, Tony told me everything. He's a pirate, a buccaneer!' I see she fell for it. Tony had pulled out all the stops. Here's this beautiful, intelligent woman and this Port-uh-gee is giving her a line. She falls for it. I don't tell her that most of those drug scams the *Josephine* pulled, Tony wasn't even aboard. It was Lisbon on the boat."

An old friend said, "Christa had a fantasy version of her life where she finds the White Knight, a poet with a tool belt, a painter in a room with northern light," these were her romantic ideals. But a handsome drug-smuggling pirate and "buccaneer" blew these other dreamboats out of the water.

Yet she would never land any one of them.

Barbara Holloway said, "The other day, I was looking for something Christa once gave me. She had bought it on Bond Street in Mayfair. It was an address book that was so beautiful I never used it. I put it away in a drawer. It was empty. No names or telephone numbers. Nothing. Not even Christa's last address."

WINDOW OF TIME

Christa had discussed with Warren Roderick Tony's history of drug trafficking, his reputation as a playboy, his inability to achieve highliner status with the *Jo G.*, but what bothered Christa most about Tony was Susan. When Tony came to see Christa, he couldn't refrain from talking about his life at home. He'd mindlessly drop Susan's name; he'd talk about the antics of their cat Emerson, or he'd mention that his daughter, Braunwyn, was acting in a play. Or that his boys had waited hours at the Registry of Motor Vehicles. His eldest son, Beau, took a new job at Kinko's in Boston.

He talked about his wife's courtesies and kindnesses without any self-consciousness. If Christa complimented him on a shirt he was wearing, he'd answer "Susan ironed it." If his kisses tasted sweet, he'd say "Susan baked a jelly roll."

Christa saw how deeply rooted he was in his family life, even as he was grinding his hips against hers. She wanted to understand Susan's hold on him and Christa started to peel the onion about her nemesis. What did Susan have in her bag of tricks that Christa was missing? She started to think of Susan not only as her rival but as an ideal.

The woman as wife, the wife as mother, the mother as hub of the family.

Tiny Worthington had been like that, a hub, but since Christa's grandmother had passed away, the Worthington tribe was a splintered wheel. And a wobbly one at that, like Fairchild's tongue-in-cheek label "wobbly WASP."

Once, when Tony had referred to Susan as "the mother of my kids," the designation had so unhinged Christa that she almost punched him. Susan's title seemed a hundred times more glamorous to Christa than the mantle "*New York Times* reporter," or "*Women's Wear Daily* acting bureau chief." She had felt a similar anxiety when she had learned that her first boyfriend, John Wotjacinski, had married Antonia. Antonia had instantly become "Toni Wotjacinski," and with John she had had two beautiful kids. A boy and a girl, like the American dream.

"Toni Wotjacinski" had a beautiful ring to it.

Susan Jackett's dominant role as "awesome matriarch" almost seemed to engender physical changes in Christa. Christa's unspoken jealousy, part envy, part admiration for Susan's uncontested station as "center of the world," seemed to trigger in Christa a subconscious brewing of hormones and an awakening of biochemical receptors. Christa's longing for a child hummed through her. Her body was suddenly commandeered by wanton enzymes and pituitary pipe dreams.

Long before Christa had become involved with Single Mothers by Choice, and its crazy array of wishful acronyms, Christa had learned everything about midcycle strategies. All Vassar girls had read the book *Our Bodies, Ourselves*, a text that was required reading for *Ms.* magazine subscribers and *Whole Earth* apprentices in the 1970s. Being well read, and with several trips to Planned Parenthood under her belt, Christa knew exactly when she ovulated. "She was a fertile Myrtle," Gail Motlin had said. Christa had learned to recognize midcycle changes. After her abortions, she paid attention to her body out of wariness. She knew it was dangerous when she felt the corresponding "pelvic congestion" that sometimes was painful midmonth. The vulva plumps, lips are pinked. Cervical mucus is crystal clear and stringy, like "Chinese glass noodles." Those were the signs that "all systems are go."

Then, of course, fertilization could still be impeded by blocked tubes or scar tissue from pelvic inflammatory disease, or a tipped uterus, what her doctors had said might be underlying factors in a woman's inability to conceive.

Christa had tried to accept what her doctor had told her, it would be "improbable" at her age to get pregnant; she was nearing menopause, her periods were becoming irregular. But when the male doctor had delivered this news, she sensed his dismissive tone. He wasn't supportive of "high altitude" career girls choosing to get pregnant at a late age. He was lumping her in with other pathetic, self-centered women, what the press had named the "breakthrough generation" of women who won't accept cultural or medical taboos about getting pregnant late in life, when it's really their fault that they didn't prioritize having babies before having successful careers. But men at the same age have the privilege to remarry young trophy wives and to have a *second* round of kids.

Christa hoped she might still have a tiny window of time. When she didn't have luck with the magician, she had thought that maybe his sperm count was low, his jockey shorts too tight. She had thought, "Where is his magic now?"

But when she was with Tony, she felt his force, that river of testosterone that seemed almost audible, coursing through him. With a man like him, any woman who can still cloud a mirror would surely become pregnant.

Christa told Tony, "I'm allergic to rubbers." She wasn't fibbing. Latex condoms gave her an itchy rash. And Christa had also reassured him that she had recently had an FSH fertility test to evaluate her body's production of follicle-stimulating hormone and the doctor had said, "Christa, it's highly improbable that you could become pregnant." After having had earlier abortions during a period of high fertility of El Niño proportions, now she was facing a drought of hormones; she was entering a desert landscape where women of a certain age are put out to pasture. She told Tony that, yes, she had believed the doctor's opinion—but in her deepest heart, she hoped it was just an *opinion.* Her reassurances were enough for Tony, and he didn't use protection. He knew that Christa was a sophisticated fashion writer. She went to Vassar College; she was a chic single woman, a globe-trotter who had had affairs for twenty years. She must have family planning know-how. He left her in charge.

Warren said, "When I asked Tony if he was using protection, he got mad at me. He said, 'Do you think Christa's that kind of girl? She doesn't have STDs. And she told me she's infertile.' "

But Tony later said, "I had more sense as a teenager. We didn't use protection and at the time I didn't think about it. But now I remember what she did. She'd lie in bed, totally inert. Once, afterward, I offered her a Kleenex. She shoved it away. She wouldn't get up."

Pulling the sheet to her chin, she tilted her hips as if to circle an invisible Hula-Hoop, or the way a lab technician rotates a dish of agar to gently disperse a growth agent. That's what Tony Jackett believes to be the truth.

"She was three steps ahead of me. She was an operator. I didn't see it coming. I went for a buggy ride."

When her period was late, Christa already had the early pregnancy test in a drawer. She waited two extra days to tear it open.

She didn't rush back and forth to the bathroom to check her panties. She didn't feel any of her usual premenstrual tugging, that weight like a sagging brick in her pelvic-floor muscles. Even before she was late, she had felt different. Lighter. Lifting higher. Her breasts were a little tender, her nipples puffy like meringue caps. She didn't have the same heavy, waterlogged sensation of a typical cycle. This was a heads-up to her.

When the little window panel on the EPT test wand turned blue, Christa walked into the front room. She was numb. She looked out her windows at Cape Cod Bay. Before sunrise, the disc is zinc, then it skims golden. As the sun ascends, the sky deepens with shocking color. The water reflects the sky, bright as bluing. Like a giant blue diaper pail.

Writer Carole Maso, Christa's classmate at Vassar, had a miracle baby one year before Christa had hers. The story goes, Maso met a stranger on an airplane. After touchdown they had a brief tryst. After one tumble, Carole became pregnant.

In her book, *The Room Lit by Roses: A Journal of Pregnancy and Birth*, Maso chronicles her experience as a first-time mother-to-be at the age of forty-two. Carole has a longtime partner, Helen, and was not all alone like Christa. Although happy in her same-sex relationship, Carole had the ache to have a baby for quite a long time. She had classic "High-Achieving Women's Syndrome" or career girl "Baby Hunger." She writes that she felt "that pull, that tone, that hum. The zone of fertility, the buzz of readiness, the surge of absolute ripeness." Carole Maso turned to a stranger on an airplane and got lucky.

Christa's old boyfriend from UEA said that Christa had truly thought she was infertile. So she was thrilled to find out that she had conceived. He said, "She felt nature had passed a sentence and out of the blue the gods had reversed their decision."

Another friend said, "Her whole life, Christa had walked with one foot in the gutter, kicking a tin can, and with the other foot on a pedestal. When she was 'barefoot and pregnant,' it was the first time in her life Christa had both feet on solid ground. It was the greatest opportunity for her."

But when Christa told Tony, he responded with the recoil of a shotgun. To calm him, she said, "Don't freak out yet. I could lose it." But the first weeks of her pregnancy went smoothly. At first, she was walking on eggshells, but soon she was certain that her pregnancy was a miracle. And miracles come to fruition.

Carole Maso catalogs the first weeks of her miracle pregnancy in lyric notations. "By the twenty-first day that black dot is a retina. The foot like a fan . . . On day forty-four twenty milk teeth are embedded in the gum ridges. . . . I have never come close to this much happiness. What is going on?"

Whether Christa snagged her pregnancy from her ex-smuggler fisherman, or if the baby was a complete surprise to her, remains an unsolved question. Of their union, there remains only one primary source, Tony Jackett. Warren Roderick said, "Tony puts the past in a fog. He makes himself believe things happened a certain way, when they really didn't. Now he complains that she didn't use rubbers, but back then, I didn't hear any complaints from him."

Tony had begged Christa to have an abortion. She refused. Instead, she told him that if Susan threw him out of the house, he could move into Tiny's Hut. Warren said, "Kevin Davis promised to give Christa a coal stove for the hut if she paid him to build a chimney. Christa wanted to settle down with Tony. He had told her before that Susan won't sleep with him often enough. He's in a cold marriage. Christa would tell me, 'Look at this man—he's got beautiful kids. Beau is brilliant. Braunwyn is so resourceful against all these adverse conditions.' Like she thought Tony was so great, he deserved someone like her. Whatever Tony had told Christa, she was buying the whole nine yards."

Christa went to Outer Cape Health for a prescription for prenatal vitamins. She was glowing inside and out. Warren said she wasn't just glowing, she was "gloating" at her childless cousin Jan who had always been nasty to her.

Warren said, "Look, I'm a provincial guy, I spent my whole life in this area, but I know it when I see it. You have your fantastic lawyers who don't have their own wills, your fantastic oncologists who die of cancer, and you have your sophisticated women like Christa, who travel the world, but who fall for a Portugee who gives them a line."

Christa really thought that with a baby coming, Tony would choose her over Susan.

Warren said that when Tony learned that Christa was pregnant, he disappeared from Pamet harbor. He evaporated like steam, faster than it takes instant coffee to get cold. "We were going to move moorings for the *Josephine G.* but he never showed up. I got Kevin Davis to help me." Warren said that right before Christmas, his mother-in-law met Christa at a party. Christa had told her she was pregnant, and his mother-in-law asked Warren, "Does that girl have a husband?"

"No, Ma," Warren said.

The next day Christa called Warren to tell him she had met his mother-in-law. He said, "Christa calls me. She says, 'Warren, I'm going to have a baby in May!' She sounded so happy."

Tony came back to Pamet, his tail between his legs. He told Warren, "I hear you know something about me."

Warren said, "Yeah."

Tony said, "I was too ashamed to tell you. I've been puking for two months."

Warren didn't think it was sympathetic morning sickness, but dead-cold fear.

One afternoon at the harbor, Tony was leading a group of fifth graders from Truro Central School on a little tour of the flats. He introduced them to the basic principles of aquaculture, its economics and ethics. He gave them basic pointers, so if these kids wanted to come out and dig clams with their own rakes and buckets, he wouldn't have to worry about his seedbeds. He was explaining, "Any quahog that fits through this little one-inch gauge I have right here has to be thrown back. Its hinge width has to be more than an inch or it's still 'seed.' But if it's over an inch, that's a 'littleneck' and that's a keeper. Soft-shell clams have got to be two inches." He took another gizmo from his pocket, a two-inch ring with which he measured long-neck clams. As he watched the kids measure their little treasures, he wondered what size his little secret was that Christa was carrying—sea monkey, littleneck, cherrystone?

Warren said that although Tony had complained that he was puking for weeks, standing over the toilet bowl with a nervous stomach, fearing Susan's future debriefing, he was still turning into the driveway at 50 Depot Road. Despite her brimming condition, he was having sex with Christa that fall. It was Pepto-Bismol, Mylanta, and Thou.

Christa continued seeing Tony past her first trimester. He didn't show up as often as before, but they continued their relationship, although it was morphing into something forbidding, a wait-and-see game. Tony bought a cell phone so she could call him. They talked about the situation. A lot. Each one feared different scenarios. Christa's immediate fear was her forthcoming amniocentesis. At age twenty-five, a woman has a 1 in 1,250 chance of having a baby with Down's syndrome, but at forty-two she had a 1 in 26 chance.

Tony's number-one fear was that his problem wasn't going to vanish into thin air. With Christa's pregnancy, he didn't feel the "rush" of patriarchal pride he had had when Susan became pregnant with Braunwyn, his firstborn. He didn't even like to imagine the hybrid they had created: fruit of his loins combined with the fidgety traits of a Vassar Miss Deb. But Christa couldn't stop herself from conjuring up the baby with Tony's curly hair, his golden skin, his big dark eyes.

Tony was uncomfortable when Christa talked about the baby because he tried to compartmentalize it, to think of it as a rhetorical problem, a concept he might still defuse or debunk. But Christa was so exalted and dreamy, walking on a cloud, she reminded Tony of the beautiful, undaunted figureheads on display at the New Bedford Whaling Museum. "I couldn't be mad at her," Tony said, "she was so happy. She tells me, 'When the baby comes, I won't bother you. You don't have to tell your wife.'"

Tony knew that Susan would never know what was happening because he wasn't in love with Christa. Jackett said, "I didn't walk around like a love-struck teenager. I wasn't in love. Susan would have known if I was. I never told Susan 'I don't want to be with you, I want to raise my new daughter.' If I had wavered, Susan would have made up my mind for me."

Christa called her friend Gail Motlin to tell her the news. Gail said, "I know that Christa was surprised when she got pregnant. She really didn't believe she could. She didn't want to get the amniocentesis to see if the baby was okay; she was scared, but she finally did it. After the test, she was going to tell Gloria. Gloria had always given Christa mixed messages. Gloria had always worried about losing her looks, she didn't want to grow old, but sometimes she'd go to thrift stores and buy toys for her 'future grandchildren.' She was conflicted." The "amnio" test proved Christa's baby was fine. The happy news was like the first stage of a rocket liftoff, when the ship pushes through gravity's resistant membrane, sails easily into the blue, its used-up burner successfully ejected. She tried to make herself think of Tony that way, as "space junk." He had launched the miracle, now he could burn up on reentry or orbit the planet without her. It was over. But she couldn't let go.

At Christmas, Tony started to drift away. When he didn't come over to the house, she chalked it up to his family obligations. She pictured Tony centering a little tree in a wobbly Christmas-tree stand, screwing the bolts as his sons held its tip-end so it would be level. She envied the little scene as she conjured it. Tony had told Christa that the women in his family got together to make Christmas *trutas,* and Christa pictured Susan putting a plate of the sugary crescents before him. Christa would wait for him to fulfill his family role, but she was certain he'd come over with a little left-over Yuletide cheer just for her. But Tim Arnold said, "She saw him during her early months of pregnancy, then when Tony thought things were getting too hot, he broke it off."

As with her obsession with Stan Stokowski, Christa held out longer for Tony to decide. He'll sort it out for himself, she thought. She was certain he'd make the choice she wanted him to make. Ellen Webb said, "She loved Tony. She was in love with him. When someone abandons you, they become all the more desirable. He was sparkling. Handsome. Carefree. He was all the things she didn't think she was. But then there was no communication from him. Dead silence. He didn't take care of her."

A few days before Christa left Truro to go to Hingham, she drove over to Sunset Drive. She rolled down the sandy lane and idled in front of Tony's house. She cranked her window down and heard hip-hop music. Kyle Jackett was playing CDs or he was listening to "Jammin' 94.5." The radio died, then shifted to an eerie, repetitive beat, the kind of "industrial disco" Christa recognized from her lonely nights in singles' bars in Manhattan. The music drilled, simmered, pulsed in unhappy cycles. She took the plastic wand from her handbag. Its positive reading had stained the tip Bleu. Blau. Blauw. Azúl. She didn't want the souvenir and pitched the little stick onto Tony's scraggly front lawn.

That night, when she was lying still, she felt the first internal wing beat, a fluttering. It felt like a Mexican jumping bean, a brimming seed weighted to turn end over end. The baby was tumbling. Never before had Christa felt someone so near, so with her. It was the two of them. Christa and her Mexican jumping bean.

Carole Maso writes about her pregnancy: "Are people from unhappy or broken families constantly trying to remake, retrieve, make whole, complete?"

Christa drove up to Hingham to tell her mother about the baby. Gloria was propped up in bed; her water glass was dry. Her Kleenex box empty. A bowl of congealed chicken noodle soup looked like a science experiment. Gloria seemed much worse, and Toppy was nowhere to be seen. Later that evening, Toppy crept in, trying to avoid his daughter's greetings or grimaces, but she trailed him room to room, until he turned around to face her.

Gail Motlin said, "Finally, Christa is pregnant. Her mother is dying, and her father says, 'Meet my girlfriend.' Now that's kind of a mess. Tony had finally dumped her. And Christa started to worry about how much money Beth Porter was getting from Toppy, but she asked for money, too. Toppy once told Christa, 'Between you and Beth, I might as well just get rid of it all.' "

Christa decided to stay at the Crow Point house with Gloria. She would nurse her mother and she could have the baby at South Shore Hospital. Cape Cod Hospital was much too parochial anyway, and if she was living in Hingham, the address would be reflected on the baby's birth certificate and her claim on the house would seem more valid. Despite these material tensions, Gail Motlin said that when she visited Christa and Gloria, they had seemed to be working out their differences. They had formed a united front. Before Gloria was too weak to leave her bed, she got down on the carpet with Gail's two children and seemed much more motherly than she had seemed when Gail and Christa were little. "It was a genuine love of children," Gail said, "and I hadn't seen that before."

Christa fell into a routine of caring for her mother. She cooked or reheated small portions of food that her mother might eat, and she was careful that every new six-ounce can of Ensure was chilled. There's nothing worse than a room-temperature protein milkshake. These deathbed fortified drinks are unappetizing whether hot or cold, merely because of their sad nuance, being so similar yet so opposite to baby formula. Christa dabbed her mother's face with cold cream and patted it dry. She changed Gloria's soiled bedding, sometimes twice a day. Christa sorted and washed all the laundry, including Toppy's suspect trousers that always reeked of Porter's cigarette smoke. She brushed Gloria's thinning, flyaway hair, and sometimes Gloria grabbed the brush and tried to return the favor. Christa's hair was thick. Her mother warned her that it would be normal if she lost some of that "mare mane" after the baby arrived. It had to do with hormones cresting and subsiding after she "foaled." They cackled at Gloria's crazy horse analogy, enjoying the word *foaled,* which seemed so cartoonish it was easy to visualize. Christa climbed into bed beside her mother. For several afternoons, they watched television together, like two children in "The Land of Counterpane." When the baby thumped, Christa squealed and tugged her mother's hand to her stomach so she could feel it kick. Sometimes they just got silly. When Christa found a love note in Toppy's shirt pocket, she read it out loud to her mother. Porter had written to Toppy, "I'll love you 'till you die,'" but that was crossed out, and Porter had reworded her oath, "I'll love you until you get old."

Gloria and Christa laughed, flailing and flopping around the bedroom, until Christa bumped a juice glass and she had to find a towel to mop it up. They didn't always get along; Christa still felt she had a love-hate relationship with her mother, but psychologists say that a love-hate relationship is the strongest kind of bond. Love-hate is full-spectrum color, surround sound; it cranks up the juice, throwing circuits wide open on the cross-currents of emotion.

But as Christa's pregnancy advanced, Gloria's condition seemed to worsen in sync. It was difficult for both women to be in such an awkward situation, hitched up to one cart, but harnessed nose-to-tail in opposite directions. Eli Gottlieb said that Christa knew how absurd it was to find herself in that dramatic triangle. "We called it 'Christa's masterpiece,' waiting to give birth to a married man's child as her mother was in an oxygen tent. It almost seemed like a logical conclusion to the ongoing saga of her vivid victimization."

Gail Motlin said that Christa never mentioned any physical complaints related to her pregnancy; she never bitched about the typical backache, fatigue, or the list of accompanying ills that most women seek attention for and groan about when they become blimps. "She never dramatized the birth ordeal, because she really wanted the baby." There were moments when her father seemed interested in Christa's well-being. He never knew what to say except to question her about her choice of obstetricians, but he was trying a little bit to build a bridge. Yet, because her father was seeing a girl forty years younger than he was, and he was talking about selling the house as her mother was dying, with Gloria in the next room sometimes curled up in a fetal position, Christa couldn't relax with him. Gail Motlin said, "You know, when we were kids, Toppy threw the grandest birthday parties for Christa. Her birthday was just three days before Christmas. I remember one time he piled us into his tiny car. He was so handsome, so debonair. We were sitting on each other's laps, stacked in, and he drives us all the way to Boston to see *Mary Poppins*. But now you think, poor Toppy, he just wanted to get laid."

Christa often called Warren Roderick to give him an update of her progress. "I'm getting really big. Huge." She told him what the doctor might have said at her checkup, or she'd describe, in detail, items she had purchased for the baby's layette. "These little 'onesies' are so cute, they have teeny little snaps, and the baby face cloths, they come rolled up in little tubes like men's handkerchiefs." Her years as assessories editor at *WWD*, where she had learned to be adept at noticing the tiniest details, gave her great pleasure now. She told Warren, "You should see these cute little socks, they're so tiny—like little finger puppets."

Warren said, "I started to feel a little funny—Christ, I wasn't the father, you know?"

And it was Warren Christa called when she had had a little scare. She was bleeding and she had to go into South Shore Hospital. It wasn't serious, but she wanted Tony to know what she was going through. She knew that Warren would tell him. Warren said, "Her situation was a nightmare. She's eight months pregnant, her mother is dying, and her father is carrying on with a trampy addict. I ask her, 'How do you get along?' and she says, 'I'm all right,' but I know that in the back of her mind she kept thinking Tony was going to call her."

Jan Worthington and Pam Worthington tried to give Christa a little support. Gail Motlin said, "All she wanted was her cousins' approval, but even her aunt Lucinda never talked to her."

During that winter and into the spring of '99, hospice volunteers often arrived to help out with Gloria, and sometimes Christa left for the afternoon to go out with Amyra Chase. They shopped for maternity clothes. Christa had read about the trendy new Mommy Chic line by Angela Chew with $550 "Napa leather maternity pants," but she settled for Lucy Ricardo trapeze tops, matronly smocks, and tent dresses. Today, it's become trendy to wear tight-fitting maternity clothes, but Nancy Samalin, a New York child psychologist, told the *New York Times* that "Mommy Chic" says, " 'Look at me.' That kind of behavior projects a narcissistic image. It's about the mother, not the child." Christa veered away from the new VIP (very important pregnancy) haute couture, and admired Amyra's natural style as she ferried her children back and forth to school. Christa liked hearing from Amyra about the small events and little problems she faced on the winding road through motherhood. With four kids, Amyra had learned to navigate every little detour or switchback with confidence, and she was a model to Christa. Christa didn't think of Gloria as the example. It was hard to remember her mother with the strength and elegance she once had had; she couldn't even butter a roll.

As Christa neared full term, her due date seemed to have a whole new gravity. Gloria wanted to see her grandchild, and Christa tried to encourage her mother to hold on. But Christa's obstetrician said, "You've dropped," when the baby's head had become engaged lower in her pelvis. "It won't be long now."

The approaching events—a birth, a death—presented an eerie synchronicity that Christa tried to accept. Christa's "window of time" had a wholly different resonance now. Giving everything over to both her mother and to her unborn baby was a human test few people face. Christa felt as if she were spinning two plates on separate sticks, but which plate would crash to the floor first? At this volatile crossroads, real estate agents kept arriving at the door. Toppy had put the house on the market and they wanted to know when they might show it.

Amyra Chase was ready to accompany Christa to South Shore Hospital. One night, Christa had felt the famous and quite uncomfortable Braxton Hicks contractions that many first-time moms confuse for the onslaught of real labor. But after one false alarm, Christa waited for legitimate signs.

During these final days, Christa sensed a tangible, almost sensate opposition within the Crow Point household. The grim loiterer skulked in one corner of her mother's room, while above the roof, a cherub waited to descend like a bubble from heaven.

Century 21 and ReMax intruders were clueless to the drama going on, and they buzzed at all hours.

Ava was born on May 10. Family members said, "Like ships passing in the night," Gloria had missed her chance to meet her granddaughter by a little more than a week. Christa was still pregnant when Gloria passed away. Fatigued, and heavy on her feet, at full term, she stood in the doorway to watch her mother's body carried out of the house. Christa thought of a prized toy she had had as a little girl, it was hand-carved in the Ukraine and mass-produced for sentimental Americans: wooden nesting dolls in graduated sizes. One doll fits inside the next, and the next, until at its center is a tiny baby. With Gloria gone, Christa had lost the outermost doll, the protective figure that had contained them all, her mother. Now it was just Christa and the little one inside her.

Christa went into labor in shell-shocked mourning for her mother. Her cousin Pam and her aunt Diana had come to South Shore Hospital. Amyra was beside her. Her labor progressed without a hitch. Because Christa had wanted her baby so much, because it had become her sole quest and singular pledge in all of her human experience, she showed none of the typical churlishness and accusatory outbursts that laboring moms inflict on witnesses and innocent bystanders in birthing rooms. She was a model primipara, praised by the nurses and hospital staff, one and all.

Christa held Ava to her breast the minute she was born, and snugged her in her arms. Their bond was instant. She had given her daughter a name that echoed her beloved grandmother Tiny's name, "Ada" Worthington. Christa thought the name "Ava" was a slight improvement; it had a richer, more velvet sound.

No father was listed on the birth certificate.

The birth went unacknowledged in the community. It was a private event, celebrated by Christa's closest friends.

It was a miracle.

Hester Prynne and Goody Hallett weren't so lucky. *Cape Cod Pilot* explained, "The poor Goody Hallett asked only that she be allowed to die, and while the town fathers were inclined to oblige her in this, a little writhing at the whipping post first might serve as a valuable warning to others."

Warren Roderick said, "Christa called me. She says, 'Warren, I did it! Warren, I have this beautiful baby girl. She's in my arms. Warren, she's so cute!' I got teary-eyed. But I felt funny because I'm not the goddamn father."

Warren said that he had teased her. "I told her, 'You're going to be the biggest pain-in-the-ass mother.'" He joked that her kid would know five languages before first grade and that he wouldn't want to be the poor schoolteacher. No teacher would be good enough for Christa's kid. But these comic predictions should have been coming from the father, not him.

Warren said, "She wanted me to tell Tony everything. I had told Tony when she went to the hospital with false alarms, but Tony didn't want to hear anything about it. He said to me, 'Look, when it's born, it's born.' "

Shortly after Ava had arrived, Christa made arrangements for her mother's memorial service. Warren said, "She wanted me to come to her mom's memorial service in Hingham and to bring Tony with me. She was proud of her mother's work, and she had Gloria's paintings all laid out."

John Cornachio, Gloria's friend from the Scituate Art Association, said, "Gloria had already been cremated. There was no coffin, but lots of photographs from the past, and a big display of her art. Christa was there with the new baby. Gloria had been looking forward to the baby. It was so sad she had missed her chance."

A waterfront property in Hingham is a real estate find, and Christa and her father sold the Downer Avenue house with lightning speed, for $200,000 more than their asking price. Tim Arnold says there's a family rumor that when they sold the Crow Point house, Toppy had purposefully left Gloria's urn behind in the attic.

In midsummer, Christa was making plans to return to Truro with Ava, and Toppy had moved into a little ranch house on a busy street in Weymouth, where Porter was seen coming and going.

Gail Motlin said, "Christa told me that the first time she went over to Toppy's Weymouth place, she couldn't believe it. Christa saw Beth Porter's stuff scattered everywhere. And, worse, Toppy had all these scented 'love candles' arranged on the bedside tables. It really upset her to think of her father like that."

Christa called Warren a few weeks later to tell him she had finally talked to Tony. He had agreed to come up to Hingham that afternoon to see his daughter for the first time. Warren said Christa had sounded very excited. She was still optimistic. But at midday, Warren saw Tony down at Pamet harbor with Susan and her sister Cheryl. They'd been drinking.

Warren said, "So I see Tony's not going anywhere. Poor Christa is waiting for him, Christ. So I get Tony away for a minute, without Susan listening. I say, 'Why didn't you go up to see Christa?' and Tony tells me, 'She's savage.' Like he's a victim or something. I smell the booze on him."

Warren was eyewitness to the disaster unfolding, but he couldn't do anything. It was like the S-4 submarine that foundered in Provincetown Harbor. They could hear the men tapping, but local fishermen were told to wait for the navy. Many dragger captains believed they could have hauled her up with their nets and saved thirty-eight lives. The town felt helpless, watching those men perish.

Warren said, "This was the pattern: Tony refuses to acknowledge what has happened, and Christa still hopes she'll get Tony to convince himself that he's in love with her.

"This girl had to be shaken out of her daydreams."

SUTTON PLACE EAST

The 2002 summer season wound down with typical wacky high-lights. Emily Dooley tried to find distractions from her predictable routine at the *Cape Cod Times*. Tired of whales gone AWOL and of Town Hall skirmishes, she was ready to jump off the treadmill and try something different. So when some Hollywood scouts arrived in Provincetown to audition contestants for the syndicated NBC game show, *Weakest Link,* she decided to write a story about their efforts to find some improbable Einsteins in Nowheresville. Then, on second thought, she herself signed up to try out for the show.

The show's producer, Sarajane Smollon said that she sent scouts to the Outer Cape "to take advantage of a popular summer resort where tourists from all over the country congregate." But Emily got the feeling they were hoping to find more than "wise, witty personalities who come to life on television," and that they might have been hoping that Norman Mailer, or filmmaker and summer resident John Waters might want to show up to audition. They'd settle for a brainy transvestite. Auditions were held at the Crown and Anchor Inn, Provincetown's premier drag bar, with two shows a night. They were certain to get their pick.

Emily said she was a little nervous and her initial tongue-tied answers had flopped, but soon she relaxed. She made the first cut. She would be informed later by telephone if she would be asked to go to the next level of auditions. There are many bright lights on Commercial Street, mile-a-minute raconteurs, verbose divas, and old salts who might make it to the game show podium. In her *Times* story, Dooley quotes tourism director Patricia Fitzpatrick, who said, "No one here has a weak link. They might have some missing links, but no weak links."

Soon after Hollywood scouts swarmed into town, there was another invasion with biblical proportions. Every few years, the Outer Cape suffers from a natural disaster that closes down businesses. Motels must give refunds as angry tourists pack their cars to head elsewhere, and restaurants stop serving. It's not quite the seven-year locust plague that some places endure; here it's an explosion of midges. The "midge" has a diminutive, cute ring to its name, but the swarm is a calamity for local folk. This year it's fierce. Tiny little bugs, mosquito-size flies but without the stinging proboscis, hatch in the millions at Pilgrim Lake, a system that the Cape Cod National Seashore is trying to restore to a tidal lagoon. Once known as East Harbor, the inlet was filled in for the railroad dike in 1868, creating a man-made lake where the water is brackish. The little flies like it low-salt, and have set up housekeeping. Once they have hatched, clouds of midges swoop en masse over Route 6, straight into Beach Point, in North Truro, a string of waterfront motels, restaurants, and an active cottage colony.

The first sign of an invasion begins with pixel dots on bedroom walls, in kitchens, on screen doors. Then, before long, the buggy decor grows in density. It becomes a squirming tapestry of teensy bugs, then a twitching shag carpet of bugs. Skylights are veiled, windows are obscured. People try to swat them away from their faces, afraid they might bite, but these flies exist on honeydew. They don't sting. But they utilize landing strips wherever they find them, backs, arms, legs, faces. Car windshields. TV screens.

Local resort manager Patricia Dumas, who oversees Sutton Place East, a cluster of antique cottages at Beach Point, said it's the worst outbreak in years. She had never seen it like this, she said. Her tenants complained when the swarms got through screens. She said, "If someone walked outside, they'd get a mouthful. There were cyclones of them. They moved in clouds."

Day's Market had to shut early each night when the midges, attracted to light, came through the doors and coated the ceiling. The popular Beach Point restaurant Paparazzi's bought a blower and installed it over the door, to keep the bugs from entering with customers. Some tenants couldn't adapt to the "natural setting" and screamed at motel managers. Dumas said, "Some New Yorkers just don't want to be this close to nature. During a recent bluefish blitz out in the bay, one tenant complained that 'the sea breeze smelled too fishy.' " At the Shoreline Motel, a tenant pestered by the swarm became abusive, making threats to the manager.

Patricia Dumas said, "When they die, they leave a pile of brown, fuzzy dust on the windowstill three to four inches thick."

The midges have accelerated the Seashore's plans to open the tidal gates that would return Pilgrim Lake to a saltwater harbor and estuary, as Myles Standish had originally discovered it in 1620. When the sea sluices through, the midges will go.

The Worthington murder began to lose its contrast, its edges, as the summer advanced. The burning sun, the busy season, cash registers purring, helped local residents forget. It was business as usual. Michael O'Keefe flew out to Nantucket, not on holiday, but to investigate an embarrassing case brought against a Nantucket summer police officer. The officer is alleged to have molested a twenty-year-old woman when he was on guard duty at Nantucket Cottage Hospital. The woman was under police custody after she had attempted suicide. The victim told police that she "awoke to find the man using his hand to violate her."

The summer police officer resigned. O'Keefe scheduled a pretrial conference for October.

One morning all of Truro Center was evacuated when the postmistress at Truro post office discovered a "chirping package." The bomb squad came in. The post office was cleared, neighboring Duarte Real Estate logged off and left their offices, and patrons were told to leave Jams specialty shop before they could buy their Danish and coffees. When the street was roped off, the authorities went to work.

The little beeping package provided enough oddball information to kindle serious interest by police. Their knee-jerk terrorist training kicked in when they saw the return address on the Express Mail package. The handwritten return address said, "A. Dove, Washington, D.C."

"A *Dove*" originating from Washington, D.C., seemed to have a foreboding political resonance they shouldn't ignore. The Unabomber was nicked, but another wacko wordsmith might be making an ironic statement, sending a bomb with a peacenik return address like this one.

When the package was X-rayed, it was found to contain a small, harmless travel alarm clock. A local girl had left the clock behind when she visited her boyfriend the week before in Washington. When he mailed it to her, he had forgotten to remove the battery. Interviewed by the *Provincetown Banner*, the boyfriend, Andy Dove, said, "I'm upset that a name would raise such suspicion. At one point in time, 'a dove' was probably considered romantic."

One evening that week, the wind picked up. It was a typical spook night out here in no-man's-land. The house creaking. I was surprised to find a drop of blood on my windowsill. I blotted it with my fingertip. When I walked into another room, I found another blob of red beside my telephone console, and, again, in the most unexpected place, beside my water glass.

I picked up my cat and examined its paws. It looked at me with its typical arch expression, as I spread his toes to look for an injury. With autumn approaching, Cape Cod begins its familiar rotation of Indian summer days and blustery gothic nights. Climbing roses drop their blooms and circle like briers. Headstones, in so many sunken cemeteries in Truro, shift and tilt and rise up from nowhere with the first frost heaves. Or blood appears without explanation. These jewel spots remind us of Christa.

CAMPAIGN STRATEGIES

I f I want to talk to O'Keefe, he tells me I have to meet him early, before he gets going. I leave Truro at 7:00 to get to the DA's office at 8:00 A.M. Heading up Route 6, I'm following a raucous shawl of black-backed gulls, but they're crossing over to Chatham. I keep going west.

At Barnstable, O'Keefe hasn't poked his head in yet, so I sit down in the anteroom to wait. I leaf through the one and only magazine they've had on their coffee table for the last six months. *Architectural Digest.* In the DA's shabby complex it seems a little out of place, like a comic book at the morgue, or a stroke book at the rectory.

After some time, a youthful lawyer dressed for a TV courtroom, a fresh-faced novice assistant DA, comes in to ask me if I'm waiting for O'Keefe. I say that I am, and he tells me that his boss is outside.

"He's outside?"

The foppish youngster nods at me and smiles. Like "Hey, the mountain isn't going to come to you."

I walk out and find O'Keefe in his Taurus, and it's purring. He pushes the door open. I sit down beside him, a little alarmed to see that he isn't dressed for work. He's wearing pajamas. No, I guess it's his jogging togs, or weight-lifting sweats. He's been exercising. He drives across the street and orders a coffee to go. I tell him I've had plenty of coffee already. He gets back behind the wheel and we're on the road.

His routine of driving off with me is getting predictable. I say, "Are you taking me to your place to see the video?"

He says, "I've got to shower and get dressed." Every in-between minute is accounted for. If you want to talk to O'Keefe, you have to take him as he is.

"Okay, at your house we can watch that tape."

"The Worthington tape isn't any different from the photographs you already saw."

"Every window is helpful."

"Did you see *The Blair Witch Project*? You don't need to see the tape."

"*The Blair Witch Project*?"

He's deadpan. He loves twiddling with me. He torments people with his empty mug. In the grist mill of murder, he knows the wheat from the chaff. I'm an outsider, still sorting it grain by grain. He's tolerant of me, but I see that maybe it's just his dismissiveness.

We walk into his big, empty house. He breezes out the kitchen slider leaving me standing at his breakfast table. As I start to follow him outside, I hear him start the outdoor shower. I sit down to wait for him.

The first assistant district attorney showering just outside the slider means I've been graduated or I've been demoted to being just "one of the boys." I analyze, for an instant, the campaign strategy behind this.

And then I recall how Keith Amato was under suspicion for using Christa's outdoor shower.

The outdoor shower.

A modest structure, part altar, part privacy enclosure, it's a precious enclave found at most Cape Cod properties. Both practical and nostalgic, the outdoor shower is usually a narrow stall of cedar planking or pressure-treated slats, sometimes embellished with climbing hydrangeas or roses, or a carpet of mint that releases a soothing spicy scent when trampled underfoot.

But with Christa's murder, the outdoor shower resonates with implications; the outdoor shower has suddenly become a secret grotto of carnal impulse and subversive intent.

I hear O'Keefe crank the shower off. He walks into the kitchen barechested; his upper body is tan, muscled, bulked-up. He wears only a white towel snugged around his hips. He sits down across from me and tears the lid off his coffee-to-go.

Sitting there, half naked, he has a lot of confidence in *my* confidence.

I don't eyeball him and never drift below his Adam's apple. We talk Debbie Smith. DNA. The killer's saliva on Christa's breasts. None of this is new to me. It's a rerun. But something about sitting across from O'Keefe, in his wraparound terry, reminds me of sitting beside Tony Jackett in his

Jeep. These two distinct professionals are knee-deep in the same primal river. They're not going to push me in, but they wouldn't mind if I fell in. I wonder if men see something about us, about women like me. We're standing on the edge, on the lip, in perpetuity. As Christa had once written, "Pain addicts are the real fans of *Wuthering Heights*, preferring the fix of unrequited love."

I walk into the living room, O'Keefe's sleeping porch since his breakup with his wife, Joan. I sort through a pile of videotapes stacked in a Frank Lloyd Wright construction site beside the TV. I look for *The Blair Witch Project*, maybe it's here.

O'Keefe climbs the stairs to get dressed. He talks to me from the second floor, searching for his collar stays with little asides, hints, and immediate retractions of these hints. I exit the kitchen slider to look at the pool, smooth as Saran. I picture the first assistant district attorney, the candidate, doing his morning laps in his altogether, or maybe treading water in the moonlight. When I turn to come back inside, I'm surprised to see that his outdoor shower has no enclosure at all. It's wide open. I could have followed him outside without warning and seen everything. But I didn't live up to the expectation.

O'Keefe comes downstairs transformed, dressed in a deep blue suit, starched white shirt, and gorgeous tie. "Look at this," he tells me. He hands me a golf tally slip, something I'm not familiar with. I look at the score card as if it's a Chinese menu. He says, "I won four hundred fifty at the Ridge Club."

I'm impressed by the dollar amount. "How many bumper stickers is that?" He says his wagering doesn't have any connection to campaign funds. It's crazy money.

Next, he's telling me a news tidbit about Tiger Woods. Whenever O'Keefe starts talking golf, he's through with me, veering off his campaign trail—for the meanwhile.

MOMMY CHIC

Warren Roderick said, "Christa told me that her father had wanted to move Beth into the Crow Point house. Christa wasn't going to give up the house and all her mother's stuff so easily. I told her to come down here. Forget about it. But she was always worried about material stuff. Then, they decided to sell the place. It sold overnight. She got half the house price, half the stocks."

Warren's little bit of encouragement was hardly necessary and Christa moved back to the Little House in late summer 1999. Truro was sunny and the roses were blooming. Truro might be called "the tailpipe of the nation," and air quality was sure to get worse if the EPA relaxed restrictions, but the sea breeze still smelled sweet. When Christa settled in, she discovered the place a mess. She didn't have the energy to do a "reenactment of the Pilgrim Women's First Monday Wash Day." She was happy if she had a clean fork, or a towel that wasn't damp. She didn't worry about her appearance, or bother with keeping her own clothes neat, but she delighted in dressing Ava. She washed Ava's nightgowns and footie one-piece suits in a mild detergent called Dreft that sifted in a pink stream from its pink box, like granulated cotton candy. When washing Ava's things, she was careful to use two rinse cycles. If the ruffles on a cotton bonnet looked dingy, she washed the bonnet by hand in the bathroom sink and pinned it to the clothesline by its ribbons. The delicious pink tones of having a baby in her life, like finding Ava's bonnets on the clothesline—the same clothesline that was a symbol of Christa's loneliness in childhood—seemed miraculous to her now.

Her first week in Truro, she visited Warren at the harbormaster's shack and introduced him to Ava. Warren asked her if he could hold the baby. She let him take Ava for a moment, but she never let go of her booty. It was as if they were sewn together by an invisible silk. If Warren dipped right or left holding the baby, Christa mimed his movements. She was never more than a few inches apart from Ava. She took Ava back into her arms and looked at Warren, eye to eye. She said, "Warren, will you tell Tony to come over to see his daughter."

But Tony had already enlisted Warren in a scheme that, today, Warren says, "I feel really bad about it."

Warren explained, "That fall, I did things I'm ashamed of. I shouldn't have listened to Tony. When Christa started putting pressure on Tony, Tony asked me to lie and make up stories. He wanted me to tell Christa that he was seeing other girls. To get her off his back. He tells me, 'You're going to tell her what a bum I am.' "

Warren hated to watch her face crumple each time he would spin a new story. He thought it was probably for the best that she give up on Tony, but it caused her so much unhappiness.

But Christa exulted in Ava. Christa stopped before the big mirror and held Ava up to study their magnificent reflection. She snuggled Ava cheek to cheek, or held her baby tucked under her chin, totem-pole style. Seeing them mirrored together gave Christa the little extra push she needed to tackle the heavy chores of caring for a new baby all alone. She'd sit down to pee and sometimes she couldn't grab the toilet paper before having to hop up and tend to Ava. Her aunt Diana was helpful. Her cousins came and went to ogle the baby, but they didn't pitch in.

Being a single mother was more than a single job. Only an octopod or perhaps someone like Shiva could wash dishes, brush tangled hair, answer the phone, fold laundry, and hold the baby all at the same time, but Christa couldn't do more than maybe three things at once. Before the baby, her friend Eli had said that her "natural tendency to be a slob meant she had trouble finding a perimeter," but with Ava, who needs a perimeter? Her whole world was confined in her arms. Her "perimeter" was the tight radius within earshot of Ava's gurgles and whimpers.

At only three and a half months, Ava was sometimes fussy. Infants at that age are intellectually more advanced than their corresponding motor ability. A baby might see something she wants to touch, but she doesn't have the motor control yet, and that makes her irritable. She shrieks with frustration. Uninformed doctors used to call this "colic." In the *New York Times*, there was a recent article about a behavioral scientist who invented Velcro gloves for infants, so that impatient babies can pick up toys much sooner with "sticky mittens."

Christa didn't have these Velcro baby mitts, so if Ava was fussy, Christa sat down and nursed her. Her nipples weren't sore anymore. She heard one of her cousins say, "That baby is never off her breast!"

When her family saw that Christa needed some help with household chores, word went around that there might be a baby-sitting job. One afternoon, a car drove up to the house. Christa went to the window to see who it might be. It was a big car, an old Ford Galaxy with real chrome bumpers and not the cheap fiberglass trim seen on new cars today. The car was souped up and altered, what they call a "muscle car." A large woman got out of the driver's seat. She was very heavy, perhaps topping three hundred pounds. Christa went to meet her before she climbed the stoop, worried that the old porch planking might give way and crack.

The woman told Christa that she'd heard she was looking for a baby-sitter. Christa invited her into the house to find out where she had heard this. She asked the woman to sit down. The woman looked around the place, at the little Hitchcock chair Christa had offered. She told Christa that if she was hired, she would bring her own reinforced chair and leave it at the house. She had broken a few chairs in the past, and she didn't want to be responsible for someone's heirloom antiques.

When the woman had left, Christa telephoned the busybody who had set up the impromptu interview. She wasn't going to hire a baby-sitter who needed a special chair. The woman had upset her. Christa was in the throes of a mild postpartum depression and she suffered a common symptom, something called "catastrophic imagination" or "morbific thinking." After she met the baby-sitter prospect, she had terrible visions of Ava being crushed by the fat stranger. It might merely have been Christa's postpartum hormone imbalance, a condition that causes some women to go so far as to nail their windows shut.

In September, Christa interviewed another woman for a nanny position. Ellen Webb, a petite and pretty blonde with a teenage son, had been working at the Mustard Seed Kitchen. She'd been caring for a hundred-year-old couple, but the novelty had worn off. She was ready for a change.

She said, "I didn't think Christa could afford me, but at the interview, she hired me! Christa was overwhelmed. She hadn't been eating right. I started right away making her 'comfort foods,' you know, meat loaf, shepherd's pie. I would have to force her to let me hold the baby so Christa had a chance to wash her hair."

Ellen said that Christa had no one but her aunt Diana. "Tony had left her when she was six months pregnant. There was no communication with him. Dead silence. There she was, all alone. And you know how dark it is in Truro at night."

But with Ellen's help, Christa settled into her routine as a new mother. Ava was her sole purpose. Ellen said, "Magazines occasionally asked her to write an article, but she said no. She tried once or twice to lock herself in her office, but she couldn't resist Ava. Christa had no luxury in her life but the luxury of time. And she coveted it."

Ellen said that Christa had taught her a great deal about mothering. Ellen admitted that she might have been too strict with her own son, but Christa was totally permissive. Christa never said no to Ava. "When Ava started standing up in her high chair, Christa's solution was to stop using the high chair altogether. My solution would have been different. And this is after Christa had assembled the high chair herself. She would always just read the instructions on car seats and everything and put them together, like a wiz. But she never made Ava do anything Ava didn't want to do."

Earlier that summer, Gail Motlin had seen the same thread. "She was still living at her dad's house when Christa came to visit me with Ava. Ava never came out of a blanket. She was on her mom's breast the whole time. I saw that Ava had terrible cradle cap, down to her ears. Christa told me that the pediatrician had told her she didn't have to wash Ava's hair, if the baby didn't like it. Of course, babies don't like to get water in their eyes. They'll cry at first when you plop them in a bath. Those first weeks, Christa never washed Ava's hair. She was literally smothering the kid."

Although very protective of Ava—for instance, she wouldn't let Ellen drive Ava in her tiny little Festiva—Christa started to find a more even plane. Christa never refused Ava, but Ellen Webb said, "I learned that there isn't one way of being a parent. Ava was turning out to be a spectacular little kid. I believe Ava was meant to be. The whole thing was predestined—the whole timing—right after Christa's mother died. Ava is an old soul. She came out with the lights on."

When Ellen told Tim Arnold about Christa—"There's this fashion writer who lives right behind you"—Tim said he had waited two months to call Christa. Ellen said, "Oh, Christ, he didn't wait that long. He was over there in an instant."

Winter in Truro can cause people to suffer from "light deprivation disorder," when the sun sets at 3:30 in the afternoon. As the burning glob sinks into the bay, you want to yell, "Wait, wait, don't leave! What did I do to offend you?"

So Christa was pleased when Tim showed up to take walks with her, because he would come back to the house with her just as the winter twilight made her feel most vulnerable. Expecting Tim to show up was just the little push she needed to pull herself together and "spritz herself up." She looked in her closet, then decided, oh, what the hell, this will have to do. When she was pregnant with Ava, she hadn't been impressed by trendy maternity clothes. And now that Ava was born, she wasn't going to suddenly try to be like one of those L. L. Bean or Tweeds catalog fashionista soccer moms. She had always thought that L. L. Bean and "fashion" was an oxymoron. Tim would have to take her as she was, in lumpy cords and baggy sweaters. But, like Gloria, she always remembered to put on her designer sunglasses at the last minute.

Later, making tea, she looked for a clean mug. If Ellen had come, her mugs were lined up on the white shelves, gleaming. If Ellen had the day off, she'd find one clean mug for Tim and rinse out a dirty cup for herself. Christa was candid about her situation. She told Tim that she was very uncomfortable keeping Tony's secret for him. She had a father like that, and she didn't want to do it for Tony. But when Christa saw that the conversation might be tipping toward something too heavy, she told Tim stories about the Worthingtons. Tim said, "One of the first things we talked about was her grandmother Tiny's affair with Paul Robeson." Robeson was a pretty impressive name to find in one's little black book. Then Christa told him about some of her past liaisons.

"She told me about a few men. She tended to—I think this came from her mother—have this attraction to glamour. Any relationship that put her in a better light, she would tell me about. Stan Stokowski. The London professor. Her friend Eli Gottlieb, who was ghostwriting a book from a yacht somewhere. She had known the children of several celebrities. But she never talked about the magician."

Tim said, "Her mother was a first-generation Italian immigrant and was driven by that whole American myth about rising to stardom. She was competitive and climbing, and as a painter she had a lot more talent than she was given the opportunity for. Christa had that characteristic, too, of never really achieving the highest goal."

Christa couldn't believe how easily she spilled her feelings to Tim. He was so receptive and he seemed to refrain from jumping to conclusions. He was good with Ava. He said he missed his own two kids, and she told him that she'd like to meet them. Eli Gottlieb said, "Christa sent me a photo of Ava, and on the back of the snapshot she wrote, 'I've met the most wonderful man!' "

Tony Jackett had vanished from Land's End.

He was staying miles away from Christa and his unacknowledged newborn. Warren told her that Tony said he hoped Christa might go back to her brethren in New York, and return to her desk at the fashion rags or perhaps find a new worldly occupation she couldn't possibly conduct from Nowheresville, Cape Cod. In other words, he hoped she'd just disappear. He wanted her to dry up and blow away before word leaked out to Susan, who was living only a couple of miles down the road. Susan Jackett was in a fog. For the time being, Susan was living with Jackett as if behind a storefront window sprayed with artificial snow during secret renovations.

Christa didn't see Tony down at the harbor. He avoided Warren's shack, and if he worked for Warren, he made sure to stay out in the estuary. She stopped watching for his car. When she was pregnant with Ava, she had read an old Buck-a-Book copy of a paperback called *How to Fall Out of Love*. It said to fall out of love you must stop addictive habits— stop looking for your ex's car in parking lots, stop choosing name brands that were his favorites, stop watching TV shows that you assume he is watching at the very same instant—these patterns must stop!

Tim was a helpful distraction.

She invited him to move in with her in the spring of 2000. "She knew I had family coming to stay at the house, and how chafing that was, so she asked me if I wanted to come live with her and Ava. I couldn't sleep in the same bed with her, so that made it weird. She was very tense. There wasn't enough psychological room to share the same bed. She never got enough sleep. So I went upstairs. But then she complained if she heard me walking around up there."

Some nights she did invite him into her room. He climbed into the sheets beside her, with the silver mirror pulsing at the foot of the bed. Ava was never more than an arm's length away, but Tim was experienced with babies, having had two kids. Sex can't be postponed just because your babes are snoozing in the nearby. A couple must retreat to the boudoir even as they attend to the nursery. Life has to go on as man and wife. Of course, they were not a married couple, but Christa seemed happy to have Tim plugged into the daddy role. And when Tim made love to her, she showed him her paces, and for a little while she could forget she was Ava's mommy.

When Ava was beginning to creep, then crawl, and pull herself up on furniture, Tim helped Christa childproof the little house, finding more and more hazards room by room. He was so helpful, sometimes Christa found it in her heart to thank him with furious emphasis. Other times, she scolded him for not doing chores the way she wanted them done.

Tim said, "She was spare with her praises," and "There's a kind of 'Worthington trait' where she wanted to be the only one shining. I think she liked men who weren't her intellectual equal. It never worked out if her men were too talented. She'd date actors, artists, and writers, for instance, the gold standard—Eli Gottlieb—who had won the Prix de Rome. Romances never lasted very long, yet Eli remained a cherished friend."

Tim showed her his new paintings, and she couldn't refrain from a churlish remark or warning. His work was a little "too decorative" or "too romantic." She grilled him about his influences. "Who are your favorite painters?" He thought that was like asking him, "What are your favorite colors?" He told her he liked Vermeer, Cézanne, Paul Klee. He admired local painter Jim Peters, who paints nude figures, relentless portraits of backsides, expressly those of his wife's haunches. "That 'male gaze,' he's got that in spades," Tim said.

Christa had her own opinions about art, and her own paralysis. Christa's friend Steve Radlauer said that he had been encouraging Christa to write a novel. "She had this very particular palette as a writer, if she should ever choose to use it." But Tim said Christa was in a battle between her "materialistic and artistic self. Most of all, she wanted the social status." She had told Tim, "My word is gold in New York."

Her interest in Tony Jackett seemed like a rejection of those expectations—status, art. Tony's reference points were so simple. Tony couldn't be judged from the same high bar that was first set at Vassar, and set again in New York and in Paris. With Tony, she didn't have to be a "High-Achieving Woman" with a "High Altitude" career. She could lounge around at sea level. Maybe she wanted to be like Susan Jackett. She saw the little house with the picket fence, the widow's walk, and Tony coming home from successful fishing trips. Tim said, "She had this naïve hope Tony would provide all that mindless security. No interior life, what a relief."

Christa was attracted to Tony's perch in life because it couldn't be intellectualized ad nauseam. It was real life.

On Mother's Day, Tim arrived at the house with a gift for Christa, a robust "Jackmanii" clematis. Tim had wandered up and down rows of little pots set in Nazi-exact lines at Bayberry Gardens looking at plants that had been forced to explode with early blooms. He thought he had got the pick of them all. That afternoon, with Christa as the peanut gallery, he looked for a sunny spot to plant the vine. He read the directions on the tag, a place with "protection from full midafternoon sun."

It became a running joke. "Protection from full midafternoon sun" seemed like good advice for a frazzled couple.

On Father's Day, Christa presented Tim with a different climber. A clematis called "Nelly Moser." They planted the new vine near Christa's. The two "his and hers" clematis were supposed to cement their bond, as if the temperamental plants could provide their relationship with literal "roots." But by midsummer the vines had no more blooms and looked unwilling to produce. It was probably the normal cycle for these finicky specimens, but Christa's life with Tim seemed to wither in tandem, growing more arid and strained.

Ava was toddling around and they had a few arguments about her daily routine and care. Tim said, "Christa was cautious about making Ava do anything. She was hypersensitive about that." Once, when Tim's two kids were visiting, his son Andy happened to be standing beside Ava in the kitchen when Ava turned her Tippee Cup upside down, letting sticky orange juice spill across the floor. Christa snapped at the boy, "Why are you just standing there!" She thought Tim's son was "so stupid" not to have intervened in the little disaster. But Tim believed that Ava had conducted her Tippee Cup experiment quite willfully.

Christa's impatience with his kids made Tim bristle. She was always too quick to dismiss them. Tim said, "My kids didn't like her." Gail Motlin said that she, too, had felt the same intolerance from Christa when she visited with her two children. Gail said, "Christa acted like Ava was a princess, and my kids were wacky and destructive." Gail went shopping with Christa and Ava. Gail said, "Christa went into the Gap Kids store and asked some poor teen clerk 'What are the best shoes for Ava?' She's there forever and the clerk is trying to help, but Christa leaves without buying any shoes. Then, when I gave Christa my kid's 'Cozy Coupe,' and we were trying to put it in a friend's car, someone who was willing to deliver it for her, Christa says, 'Wait a minute. Ava wants to ride it.' We had to stand there in the driveway while Ava pedaled back and forth. Christa just never put her foot down with Ava. I guess Ava was just such a miracle to her, she wasn't going to edit anything out."

Tim and Christa, walking down at the harbor, saw a merganser duck chasing away one of its own brood because the duckling was entangled in a plastic six-pack holder. While the other ducklings paddled freely, the mother bird attacked the stricken baby duck until it no longer surfaced. Christa was very distressed by the scene. She discussed it for several days.

It seemed to be quite an overreaction, and Tim understood that all of Christa's overprotective responses to Ava came from her own tormented childhood.

Like Ellen Webb, Tim had to admit that Christa's method of mothering had been successful. He said, "Ava is a fantastic, well-adjusted kid. Christa knew what she was doing. Rules, regulations, manners were never first. She didn't try to introduce this forest of rules for Ava, or have 'time-outs' that are bewildering to a kid."

It was Tim who sometimes felt that he had been put into time-out when Christa asked him to watch Ava and she went off God-knows-where.

Warren said, "I saw this guy Arnold, she called him Uncle Tim, I think. Anyway, I see him with Christa driving somewhere in her car, but he's sitting in the backseat with the baby! What kind of man sits back there? It didn't look right to me." But Warren said that at least Christa had started to believe his fibs about Tony. She was angry at Tony now. "She came down to the shack and would scream at me, 'Who does he think he is!' "

She sometimes spoke the same way about Toppy, lumping her father into the same category, although Toppy drove all the way to Truro to visit his granddaughter. Christa never told Ava to call him "Grandpa." He was familiar to the toddler, but Christa had not yet decided how to integrate Toppy into her plans for Ava.

Because she was so angry at Toppy and Tony Jackett, she'd sometimes vent her ire upon handymen and landscapers who came to the house. Warren said that Christa refused to pay painters who had restored the old white columns on her front porch. She wanted Warren to inspect the columns after the painters had hired a lawyer when she reneged on their contract. She wanted Warren to examine their work and give his opinion. "Is it a slipshod job?" she asked Warren. He told her, "These old columns are hard to sand down. But they look great to me. I think they did a pretty good job." Warren thought she was looking for someone to bark at; it was Christa blowing off steam, and not her typical penny-pinching when she wanted to get the job done for free.

Tim said, "She would criticize everything. She had this superrefined criterion that she used to her advantage when examining clothes or art for her magazine writing, but when she did it with people, seeing more and more faults in them, it made it hard to be with her. She'd get really perturbed about things, right out of left field. She had twenty years living by herself. She didn't know how to give and take."

Christa's irritation with him increased. "I'm in a bad mood," she'd tell him. "Mood spelled backward is 'doom,'" she informed him, threatening he-didn't-know-what. Tim absorbed her assaults, even if he felt he didn't deserve them. Still nursing Ava, Christa wasn't taking any mood-elevating meds when perhaps some antidepressants might have helped. Gail Motlin said, "I have this wonderful image of Christa holding my adopted son and looking so happy. She was on Prozac at that time. Prozac was working wonders for her. I want to remember her like that."

Tim and Christa had increasing rows, including a heated argument about Christa's old UEA boyfriend. Tim said, "I like him, he's an interesting guy, a journalist. Once, when he was in Turkey, he got his brake lines cut. He leads this exciting life, but he thinks he's so clever. He had called the house and was very obnoxious and rude to me, and Christa and I had a big argument about him." Christa's New York friends often made Tim feel like a hick.

But Tim had lived in New York. He had Yankee roots. "I'm the one who has a Bradford in my family background," he said.

After their argument, he stormed out of the house. She warned him, "If you leave this time, don't bother coming back."

Tim answered, "Well, that sounds good to me."

Christa locked all the doors. Later, she was startled to find Tim standing in the kitchen unannounced. How long he had been loitering there, hiding out, she didn't know. He had barged into the bungalow uninvited. She told him if he had a key, she wanted it back. But they ended up having "make-up sex" and a few more weeks passed before Tim finally moved out.

Christa told friends on Depot Road about the incident, and after the murder, it was dredged up again. It became part of the map of events, a landmark notation on the legend: "The time Tim Arnold broke into Christa's kitchen." It was linked to everyone's vision of the crime scene. The kitchen hall, right beside the butcher block, was the murder location.

Whenever he is asked about his alleged home invasion, Tim says, "I came back into the house to finish our argument. But I never threw a dish at Christa."

Christa's British friends, Barbara and Belinda, said that Christa had told them she was uncertain about her future with Tim, his inertia was exasperating, he was becoming a millstone, and sometimes he would fly off the handle. Barbara said Christa had told her, "Tim was getting to be a liability. Christa had been so isolated with Ava, that's why she let him into her life in the first place. But then she told us, 'Oh, my God, what have I done?'" Belinda said, "Long before Tim had surgery, she knew there was something not quite right about him. He didn't have a real job, for one thing."

Stateside, her friend Gail Motlin, a pharmacist herself, said, "I'd like to know what meds he's on." Tim's up-and-down behavior exhibited common symptoms of depression.

By midsummer, Tim's relationship with Christa had been teetering already when Tim's AVM condition suddenly worsened. He was having dizzy spells and losing his balance. And even before tests would show that he had had a "new bleed," and physicians at Mass General Hospital would suggest that Tim have surgery, Christa didn't want him to be near Ava in his condition. She said it was time for him to leave.

"It made Christa very nervous," he said. "When I was dizzy, she thought I might fall with Ava." Tim had become a threat to Ava's safety. Christa couldn't childproof a circle around him. They discussed her concerns, and Tim agreed to move out.

"I had kept wondering if I would become more desirable to her, because I knew I had money and career issues, things that I'm still working on, that for her were sort of prohibitive. But then my health took a turn for the worse. She worried I would be disabled. She didn't want to end up taking care of someone. She said, 'I don't want Ava to get used to you if you might die in a couple of years.'"

After their living arrangements had failed, Tim said, "We got together out of proximity." If he hadn't lived directly behind Christa's house, he didn't think Ellen Webb would have introduced them to one another.

"When I moved back to my father's place, part of me wanted to go back and fix it up with Christa. It staggered on for a little while. We were still sleeping together for a few months. Then that was it."

Ellen Webb said, "When they broke up, I think Tim still wanted to work it out. He was in love with her. Christa knew it and she didn't want the responsibility, so she would say, 'I think he loves Ava better than me.' Ava called him 'Tim-Mom.' "

Tim said, "Ava was the hub of our relationship." State police didn't think the baby was what brought Tim back to the house again and again. Christa allowed him to come over, but it sometimes caused tension. She was careful not to take advantage of him as a baby-sitter, but sometimes he felt used that way. He'd come over, anxious to see Christa, but in five minutes she'd be in her car, and he'd be left sitting beside Ava, in front of a French-language cartoon.

MEET THE JACKETTS

I t's working," Christa told Amyra. Christa had lost three pounds her first month attending Weight Watchers. She had signed on at the famous American institution for fatties, and had joined the lines of women queued up for the weekly Health O Meter weigh-in. The scene at one of these meetings was the antithesis of what Christa had watched on the runways in Milan and Paris. But Christa was getting results. She was working on that little pudge of fat that she had had trouble losing since her pregnancy.

She had also started to see a therapist at Psychiatric Collaborative at Conwell Commons in Provincetown. She was fighting bouts of depression and, worse, she occasionally had panic attacks with their grueling "fight or flight response" that left her feeling wrung out. She visited the therapist until at one appointment he made the mistake of calling her "Christi." Christa had always hated when people altered the end vowel of her name to make it sound sugary and singsong. She told Tim, "I spent hours with him and he can't remember my name?" Christa didn't go back.

Ellen Webb said, "Every now and then, when it was really dark, she'd fantasize about Paris, not about New York." In fact, Christa took Ava to Paris for a short visit. Ellen said, "The trip went very well." Being able to travel with Ava made Christa believe she still had some control, she could reenter some of the arteries of her previous life, even with a baby in tow.

She came back from Paris with a resolution to slim down, read a serious book, maybe enroll in a writing workshop. She had started to read *Le Divorce* by Diane Johnson on the plane, but she was distracted. It wasn't Ava's occasional squirming during the long, transatlantic flight that interrupted her concentration, but Christa had immersed herself in her new plans about Tony Jackett. She had decided it was time for them to talk turkey.

Since she had come back to Truro with Ava, Tony had pulled in his horns and avoided her. At first he was AWOL from his job at Pamet harbor, but he couldn't goldbrick forever and he had returned. Yet he had had nothing to do with her except when he enlisted Warren to tell her tall tales. If she pushed the baby stroller to Pamet harbor, as soon as Tony saw her he would duck away. You'd think he was the Amazing Tarquin; it was like a magic act, an illusion. One minute Tony's standing there next to Warren. The next instant he had vanished.

It wasn't until Ava was eighteen months old that Tony met his daughter face-to-face. He had just walked out of Warren's shack and there was Christa pushing Ava in her stroller. He was cornered. Christa waited as Tony bent down to take a real look at their baby. He tried to manage his feelings; his fractured grin lifted and fell in explosive transitions, until his face looked like the gouged and broken marble of a Greco-Roman ruin. He spoke to his daughter in baby talk clichés. Ava could already talk circles around that. But she smiled at her daddy and seemed mesmerized by his warring features.

Christa wanted to shove him away. He didn't deserve to be in Ava's presence, after months of abandonment and rejection, but here he was making goo-goo faces at her, as if he had carte blanche. Christa's feelings of propriety were her defense against a rumbling surge of danger signals. Tony still had a chemical effect on her. All of her triggers were primed: anger, tenderness, that slicing ache and radiant tingle in her center of gravity—that hunger for sex. How could she still feel that, after everything he had done to her?

The next week, Christa had an appointment with an estate lawyer. When the attorney learned about her situation as a single mother, she didn't lump her in with Hester Prynne but talked about Tony as a "deadbeat dad." She told Christa that she would handle everything.

Tony said, "She wanted to put Ava on my health insurance. Christa was pushed into all of this by the lawyer." Although he wasn't named on Ava's birth certificate, Tony made arrangements for Christa to receive health insurance benefits for Ava. Susan was going to learn about this sooner or later.

Then Christa told Tony, "You have until Ava's second birthday to tell Susan." Ava's birthday was in May, less than five months away. He had his ultimatum, the line in the sand, the date for the *Challenger* liftoff. He told the TV reporter on *48 Hours,* "Suddenly, I'm standing before a firing squad."

He said, "Christa was seeing the likeness in the baby. Ava looks like me. She worried Ava might start asking 'Who is my daddy?' "

In March, Susan Jackett went to Florida, and Tony decided that when she returned, he would tell her about Ava. He thought that Susan would need to lean on someone, and maybe Braunwyn would be able to help. Tony said, "Braunwyn always worried I would run off with a young, pretty girl. She'd say, 'Make sure she's ten years older than me.' " When Tony told Braunwyn about Christa, she said, "My first reaction was, 'There goes the family.' "

Braunwyn drove over to the bungalow unannounced and found Christa in the kitchen. The mythology seems to be that all of Christa's visitors charged into her kitchen unexpectedly, including her killer. But Tony said that Christa "was very cool about the whole thing." She greeted Braunwyn, welcomed her into the house. Braunwyn was weepy. Sometimes her shaky voice was accusatory, but she said that she just wanted to see Christa for herself, and meet her half-sister. Maybe then, she could believe it. Christa was glad to see the secret was open. Braunwyn had pierced the membrane. A new stage of reconciliation would emerge from the sloppy afterbirth of letting the truth out. Maybe then Tony would be able to choose her.

After having told her father, "She better not be younger than me!" when Braunwyn finally met Christa, she wasn't very impressed. She told Tony, "She's kind of a frump."

He said, "You know, if she was in the A&P I wouldn't have noticed her." Tony repeatedly uses the A&P scenario as proof of his innocence. At the harbor, Christa had put a spell on him, but at the A&P, away from the Worthington Kingdom, he would have been immune.

Braunwyn said, "Is this your final spree? Are you all done now?"

"I'm done," Tony said.

But Tony had yet to tell Susan. He said that for weeks he had tried to test the waters, inventing infractions that he might tell Susan to gauge her tolerance. He explained his experiment. "I tried telling her different things, in theory. 'What if I did this, what if I did that, could you do another hurdle with me?' She'd say, 'If you do something like that, you'll take a hike,' and it was never anything as bad as what I had to tell her."

When Susan had returned from Florida, Tony told his friend Chris Busa that it was time for him to face his wife. Busa said, "He looked white." Busa knew that Tony was serious.

Tony said, "I rode down Shore Road and right past my house. I got onto 6 and kept going to Wellfleet. Then I turned around and drove all the way back Route 6 to Herring Cove, to the suicide parking lot. Then I drove to Wellfleet again. Back and forth for a couple hours."

He finally turned onto Sunset Drive. He tried to think of the baby's face. His baby. "She's innocent," he said. He knew his wife so well; for her, the baby would be the counterbalance—like those sixty-ton weights rigged to the interior grids of skyscrapers or suspension bridges for counterbalance, to keep them stable in high winds. Tony hoped Susan's soft spot for children, her worry for Ava, would keep his marriage from toppling.

He walked into the house. He found Susan in the kitchen cleaning the refrigerator. He said, "I've got to talk to you."

Susan said, "What is it?" She turned around and looked at him. She put the sponge down—its pink wedge looked heartbreaking to Tony. Here was his wife, going about her routine. Keeping his home for him.

"I'm in some trouble," he said.

"You're in trouble? What kind of trouble, IRS?"

"No, worse," he said.

"Worse, really? You mean police?" Susan said.

"No, worse than that."

She squinted at him through her long, blond bangs. "Worse than police?"

"I had an affair a couple years ago. There was a child."

Tony said, "When I saw the anguish on her face, it was agonizing to me. I was so cruel to someone who didn't deserve it. She asked me, 'Were there others?' and I said, 'Yes.' "

Susan had a second job cleaning cottages to earn money to pay their car insurance. She told reporter Vanessa Grigoriadis, "There I am working a second job, and pressing his shirts before he goes up to Pamet, and little do I know what he's doing when he gets there."

Tony said, "When I was with Christa, I wasn't in love, I wasn't in a 'trance,' so Susan never picked up on anything."

The night Tony confessed to Susan, she went over to her father's house in tears. She explained to her father what Tony had said, and he told her, "Is that all? You say the fling is over? So get on with your life." She left her father's house and got back into her car where she screamed at both men. But she reexamined the facts. When Tony had confessed, he didn't say that he wanted to be with Christa. He didn't tell Susan, "I'm leaving. I want to raise my new daughter with the new love of my life." (Both Tony and Susan said this, as if in a united front.)

She went home and slept on the sofa.

Susan said, "The next day Cindy Worthington called me. She said, 'Susan, don't let this destroy your marriage.' " Cindy Worthington had divorced her husband twice just to turn around and remarry him each time.

Susan tried to calibrate facts and falsehoods. She remembered making lists of pros and cons when they were buying their house. "New roof. Needs new septic."

Despite a few problems, the structure was sound. Susan said, "Our marriage was strong. We've had too many years together. Tony is a good man. People make mistakes. I don't want to feel this anger in me."

Within the month, Susan invited Christa and Ava for dinner, gathering the whole family at the house. In the crowded kitchen, Christa was welcomed by Luc, Kyle, and Keith Amato, who was closer in age to Christa than the Jackett children. Braunwyn let Ava play with some of her daughter Etel's toys, although Etel was a little wary-eyed. Susan said that Christa had told her, "Thank you, thank you," and at one moment alone in the kitchen she had said, "Susan, I'm sorry."

Susan said, "It didn't sound very convincing."

When everyone was introduced, trying to settle into their new roles,

Susan took Christa aside and asked her, "What do you want? What do you really want?"

Christa said, "I don't know. I really don't know."

Susan said, "I told her, 'If you want our family to embrace the baby, they will, they're good kids.' Of course we fell madly in love with Ava."

Her daughter Braunwyn and her three sons rallied around Susan. "My mother is a hero," Kyle Jackett said.

Christa bought a car seat for Tony's Jeep. He took Ava for short visits, but Christa didn't tell Ava that Tony was her "daddy." She made Tony and Susan promise to keep the secret. Susan said, "Christa told Ava we were just 'friends.' Christa would die, literally, before telling her daughter that Tony was her father."

Susan insisted that Tony start getting therapy. Christa agreed with Susan. He went to see renowned hipster and Freudian guru "Sol" in P-town. Christa wanted Tony to come to a therapy session with her in Orleans, to talk to a counselor named Anne-Marie Miller. But Tony said he wasn't going to do it. "Not me and you without Susan," he said.

Susan said, "I saw the therapist four times and then when I had finally met Christa, I told the therapist I didn't want to come back. She says, 'What happened?' I told her that now that I have met Christa, I'm not going to have that anger in my heart. I want my marriage to work. We've been together for thirty years. I know Tony better than he knows himself. He could have continued to see Christa or visited the baby behind my back—that would have been a betrayal. But he never wanted to leave me. He told me that he never loved anyone but me."

But when news stories and TV shows had identified Christa and Tony as "lovers" Susan said, "They were not lovers! That makes me so mad. He never took her anywhere. He never gave her presents. She got what she asked for: 'European-style sex.' Look at her, at forty-six years old, she had never made a real commitment to anyone.

"We embraced her in our family but she got cold feet when she couldn't find a weakness there. She expected Tony to roll his eyes behind my back and flirt with her, but I was the mother of his kids. We raised six kids. She thought of me as the competition. Christa told me, 'Every time he was with me, Tony talked about you, Susan.' "

Tony said that Braunwyn's estranged husband, Keith Amato, and Christa were alike. "Keith's got a sense of entitlement. His family is well off. They had places in Gramercy Park and the Upper East Side. He's in theater."

The summer after Tony's secret was out, Keith and his daughter Etel sometimes stopped by Christa's bungalow after swimming to use the outdoor shower. Sometimes Keith came alone.

Christa was surprised to see him, but it was never an issue, really. Warren Roderick said, "The cops asked me about Keith. Did he use her shower? I said that Keith was susceptible to the Pamet Crud, so he would want to have a shower. He'd walk through the woods from Margaret Worthington's to get there. I asked the cops why would Christa be involved with Keith? They said, 'For revenge. To get back at Tony.' "

Some nights, Christa had a mysterious feeling that someone watched her. She felt an icy ribbon climb up her back. A prowler was outside. And once she had heard a distinctive, percussive racket. It sounded as if the "prowler" was scraping a stick across the shingling ridges as he walked the length of the house.

Whatever was making the noise, it was too meditated, almost too intimate, to be the typical wildlife intruders that sometimes made a ruckus. It wasn't the resident fox with its gorgeous "brush" that floats in a horizontal plume behind him. Once, she walked outside to find the fox pawing the lid from an overturned trash can. But foxes and coyotes don't tap the wall or shoulder the house. They tiptoe around.

She heard the wall thump again.

When she went outside to look around, there was nothing.

Sometimes, she'd meet Tim halfway between his house and the bungalow. He'd say that he was just on his way over to the house to see her. Tim said that Christa often ambushed people in her yard, before they could reach the door. She wanted to be in control. People couldn't just show up. She was watchful and protective of her boundaries. It was her privilege, not a visitor's, to decide if and when she wanted company. She might invite you inside or chase you away. It was Christa's choice.

AT FREEDOM HALL

With only a few weeks to go before the November election, the local press was bearing down on the candidates for Cape and Islands district attorney. *Boston Globe* writer Brian McGory wrote, "Michael O'Keefe is a no-nonsense, 20-year prosecutor with a conviction record of 19 and 0 in murder cases. Kevin Callahan is a small-town lawyer who defends two-bit suspects, manages a staff of zero, and who failed the bar exam the first ten times that he tried. Who in their right mind would support Callahan?"

Kevin Callahan had been Ted Kennedy's driver and advance man. "In the Kennedy orbit, loyalty trumps all else." It is well known that a driver is privy to a public man's most private moments. At the end of the night, it's the driver who gets the last dance. Of course, Teddy is going to have to acknowledge Callahan's faithful service to him. But the DA race shouldn't be decided on Kennedy's simple nostalgia for Callahan's years "Driving Miss Daisy."

The *Boston Globe* was behind O'Keefe, but of course Boston constituents don't vote in Cape and Islands contests. One question directed at O'Keefe by a local paper sparked a mini–chain reaction on the Outer Cape. The *Cape Codder* asked, "Mr. O'Keefe, why can't you solve the Worthington case?"

O'Keefe explained that inadequate funding had impeded his efforts. " 'We ran out of funds from February to July . . . it's a lot of overtime pay to put a group of state police on a murder investigation on a weekend. Second, we have to have a crime lab that operates in the twenty-first century, that's able to turn evidence around in six months.' " In the interview, O'Keefe described the budget crunch, but he also said, " 'This case will be solved. . . . We're now in possession of very significant evidence.' O'Keefe refused to detail this 'significant evidence,' explaining that to do so would hinder the arrest of the murderer."

In the following days, the community reacted to O'Keefe's teaser. Off Cape news outlets, amateur sleuths, and Truro residents were phoning the local newspapers, the DA's office, the state police barracks, and logging on to *CrimeNews2000*, the notorious "small town on-line" forum that hosted "Worthington Wednesday." People wanted to know more about this "significant evidence." To some, it seemed too convenient for O'Keefe to be so nonspecific. One resident said, "Hey, people, if you believe this, your shit detector is busted." Another on-line critic said, "I find this totally unethical and disgusting. O'Keefe is using a dead woman's DNA for his campaign."

The Worthington question aside, the candidates were interviewed about their vision of the job. Callahan said, "Do you feel as safe today as you did yesterday?" and "I'll be tough on crime."

But O'Keefe answered, "I believe that the district attorney must appreciate the difference between genuine evil and human frailty and have the courage to act accordingly."

The Freedom Hall in Cotuit is a drafty old white clapboard meetinghouse on Main Street. Main Street in Cotuit isn't well lighted, and the winding road seems dead asleep, even a little spooky. It looks like the perfect Amityville for O'Keefe's "genuine evil" idea, until I see two lines of campaign supporters holding bright O'Keefe placards on either side of the street. Volunteers do these "standouts" at rotaries and street corners, but in the eerie dark they look suddenly comic, like the anthropomorphic playing cards in *Alice in Wonderland*. O'Keefe's red-and-blue signs outnumber his opponent's Shamrock-green boards.

The format at the Freedom Hall forum isn't a strict debate; instead, the candidates are asked to give five-minute statements and then take questions from the audience. Like a fifth grader hunched over his seatwork, Callahan speaks from his chair behind a Formica table onstage. He has the annoying mannerism of referring to himself in the third person. He reads a list of abstractions he seems to have chosen for their alliteration: "Prevention. Protection. Prosecution." He looks down at his notes, as if he can't remember these multisyllabic words on his own.

When O'Keefe speaks, he stands up from his chair and walks around the table to face the audience. He looks as confident as an MC at a Friars Club roast. His brief speech is razor sharp and wholly informed. O'Keefe doesn't speak in abstractions, but describes the job he knows from first-hand experience. He says, "The DA's office, with twenty attorneys, is the largest law office on Cape Cod." He seems to know there are at least a few size queens in attendance who are impressed by these numbers.

No one asks about the Worthington case.

The following day, the candidates meet face-to-face on a live radio show aired on a local National Public Radio station, WCAI. That night, there's one final debate on a local-access cable TV station but my system doesn't get the channel. O'Keefe's powerhouse assistant, Stephanie, tells me to drive up-Cape to a bar in West Yarmouth where a crowd of young district attorneys from the Barnstable office are meeting to watch their boss on TV.

The tavern has several TVs bolted high on the wall like in an airport or a hospital. I'm sitting here at the bar with a cup of black coffee, in a tight cluster of GOP lawyers, cops, and O'Keefe'd coeds, all because of Christa.

As the debate starts, from the get-go Callahan is exceptionally hostile, yet his attacks are weak. He says, "There are two important reasons . . ." and he holds up *three* fingers before the camera. Callahan circles the same empty cul-de-sacs, but O'Keefe responds with a litany of tangibles and galvanized facts. O'Keefe killed.

After the debate, O'Keefe arrives at the bar with DA Rollins to begin the unwinding process. They are ferried along by a sparky twenty-something blonde, a young assistant district attorney at the Barnstable office. She's like a Kojak Clara Barton, or a female Fairchild "walker" for the law bosses. She steers them by their elbows, one after the other. She brings Rollins his usual, she doesn't have to ask. I'm surprised to see that Rollins's favorite poison is a glass of Chablis that comes delivered with an identical glass of ice. He plops ice cubes into his wineglass, careful not to splash me. It's a strange little two-fisted mannerism—but then I see O'Keefe taking a slug of Tropicana. It's plain OJ or something even more electric-orange, like Tang, the 1960s breakfast mix "preferred by astronauts." Tonight, both seasoned district attorneys follow a refreshment code that seems to challenge the "Real Men Don't Eat Quiche" rule. But it's paramount to O'Keefe to remain fine-tuned and sober the final week of the campaign.

Before he passes the torch to O'Keefe, I want to ask Rollins about Christa. Rollins has seen it all. In his thirty years as district attorney, he has been criticized for taking some unpopular stances, like the time he dismissed charges against members of the Black Panther party after race riots in New Bedford. Rollins said, "They were insupportable charges. I don't condone criminal behavior but neither do I condone going after people." I want to ask him about the Worthington triangle, but like O'Keefe, Rollins heads me off and shifts our powwow to golf mythology. A young DA is telling Rollins about golf games and sneaking hunting trips into his busy schedule. The kid says he doesn't shoot Canada geese anymore since he learned that they mate for life.

Rollins says, "Not true. You're thinking of swans."

The junior DA says, "Swans? So do you find any time to hunt, Phil?"

Rollins says, "Oh, sure. I nab any opportunity to go hunting. I keep my shotgun in my golf bag." For someone who has been standing over dead bodies for thirty years, Phil's face is impish, pink as a cherub in a Renaissance painting, a Botticelli baby floating over a bloody religious massacre. But for Phil, it's the tousled remains of hair stylist Cheryl Tavares, found in the trunk of her car in the Bourne commuter lot. Her killer confessed to police that he "had strangled her at the beach on Buttermilk Bay." A murder at "Buttermilk Bay" is oxymoronic and suggests the distinct challenge of being the DA on Cape Cod. Investigating murders on the Cape takes more than the typical reconnoitering. It requires a bit of "water off a duck's back" indifference, a weary immunity to seeing blood smeared in sailboat galleys, blood spattered on oyster shell driveways, and never any double takes or disbelief about finding dead bodies in paradise.

Despite the breakneck pace of his campaign, O'Keefe takes time to have lunch with me. We walk into the Dolphin, a popular eatery and watering trough on Main Street, across from the DA's office and the Barnstable County courthouse. Weekdays it fills up with lawyers, judges, paralegals, and a good sprinkling of resident oldsters. O'Keefe introduces me to a silver-topped retired colonel from World War II as we poke along the bar rail on our way to a table. A reporter from Channel 4/Boston greets Mike and tells him that he had wanted to buy him lunch, but when he had called the office, O'Keefe's secretary had said he had just left with me. The TV reporter gives me the up-and-down to see if I have an angle or if I'm just a bimbo.

O'Keefe tells the reporter, "Next time call ahead. She made the date weeks ago, back when she was a teenager."

Eating lunch, I ask him about the tumult after his misunderstood statement in the newspapers about progress in the Worthington case.

He says, "We still need to find out who was banging her."

I had recently learned that another local Truro resident had been "swabbed." He was a painter in Christa's circle of friends on Depot Road. A married man.

I know the painter only slightly, but O'Keefe asks me, "What do you think? Is he someone who'd do her?"

His colloquial talk, "Who's banging her?" "Who'd do her?" reminds me of the time he asked me, "What do you think, did Arnold croak her?" O'Keefe pretends to "include me in," trying to jump-start something in my imagination. But it's police work. They're hoping to use me to agitate people in the circle of opportunity. They want me to spill my conversations with O'Keefe to Tim and others, so they can monitor a fever of reactions.

He asks me about the latest swabee, would the fellow be likely to visit Christa? I tell him, "If she sends a certain kind of invitation, any man will RSVP in person, right?"

State police investigators can't spray luminol on fleeting *nuances;* they can't fingerprint a woman's bedroom eyes, her flirty signals, and pouty-lipped come-ons. These are transient and intangible.

O'Keefe tells me that the police are widening the circle, getting DNA samples from local residents that they had not approached until now. I picture the hapless police going through the phone book, highlighting Truro's "349" exchanges. In Truro, Chief Popcorn didn't sound optimistic, when he recently told the newspaper, "Because there is no clear motive, [the investigation] is like a dog chasing a ball in a swimming pool."

I ask O'Keefe, "So where are they now? What are Troopers Plath and Massari doing in their investigation?"

"Investigating." He grins.

"Can't you give me an example of their daily drill?"

"Read the police manual," he says.

With election day nearing, he's careful to keep Worthington info close to his breast. He won't swagger or admit that the case is stalled. A high-profile investigation during an election is a tightrope for him.

Along with all these Worthington obstacles, I ask him what has been the hardest part of the campaign.

He says, "No golf."

He doesn't say no booze, no sex, no sleep. I have learned that he often uses golf talk as a sort of mask. O'Keefe as everyman—golfer—normal guy, like when he had said his job was no different from being a plumber.

He says, "We've got a tournament set up for eight A.M. November sixth."

"That's the morning after the election? But that's going to be a long night, with all the partying. You think you will want to play golf?"

"If I can sober up by then."

"Just don't go to bed at all."

"That's your motto, not mine."

Ouch. But he won't let me pay for my lunch. He says, "The campaign is flush." He gives the waitress a card, but she comes back to tell him that our lunch is covered. It's been financed by the WWII colonel.

The Committee to Elect O'Keefe and Mike's supporters gather at the Cape Codder Resort Hotel in Hyannis to follow the returns on election night. With the Frankie Spellman Band, a cash bar, and plenty of free hors d'oeuvres the crowd is three deep at the watering trough, humming like a hydroelectric turbine. Numbers look good for O'Keefe; he's trouncing Callahan.

Early in the evening, O'Keefe wins Falmouth, Callahan's hometown.

But the Outer Cape doesn't vote for O'Keefe. The Silva and Worthington murders are still unsolved. P-town and Truro are noted along with only a trickle of villages on the Cape and Islands who went for Callahan.

Rollins gets up to a microphone holding twin Chablis glasses, one in each hand. With O'Keefe winning 58 percent of the vote, Rollins says, "Like some females here tonight, those figures aren't bad! With such a margin, he might think he's God."

During the campaign, O'Keefe had been chided by the press for his dourness, his bone-dry locution, and his clipped remarks. The *Globe* had reported, "Forensic scientists could comb his psyche and fail to find an ounce of charm." But there's magic in O'Keefe's stony authority. I felt it when he snapped the elastic loop on the "Christa Worthington" accordion file, making me jump out of my skin, and when he smoothed his campaign sticker on my bare leg.

O'Keefe stands beside Rollins and graciously acknowledges his mentor and supporters. He smiles. His empty mug runneth over. He says, "Reports of my lack of charm have been greatly exaggerated."

The morning after the election, a nor'easter chugs across the coastline with drilling rain and forty-mile-per-hour wind gusts. The rain slices across the peninsula in horizontal curtains. O'Keefe's tee-off is postponed. The new Cape and Islands district attorney sleeps on his living room sofa with the TV set on, the Golf Channel burning through the empty gloom.

In Truro, we vote by paper ballot at the grammar school gymnasium. Voters sign in at a table on the right, and sign out at another table on the opposite wall on their way out. An oldster feeds each pleated ballot into a machine that he cranks with one hand, like a meat grinder.

On election day, when I went into the school to vote, I was surprised to see a sign taped on the main entrance door. The sign had been created on the school's I-Mac, with a colorful illustration. It wasn't a cheerful reminder about "getting out the vote" or a seasonal Thanksgiving graphic. The sign was a little shock to my system. It said, "Absolutely no strawberries permitted in this building."

There must be a child with an allergy, perhaps one of those children who must carry an epinephrine kit in her backpack, so she can be injected immediately before going into anaphylactic shock.

"Absolutely no strawberries permitted in this building." I thought of the broken jelly jar outside O'Keefe's office, and of parking lots where strawberries tumble across the concrete willy-nilly. The ruby blood dots on my windowsill. Christa—picking wild strawberries in secret patches along the Pamet and wandering like a sylph across the fruited hummocks at Ducky Noons' junk pit.

PROFESSIONALS

ony and Susan took Ava for visits, and Christa welcomed having a
little more freedom. She enrolled in the playwriting workshop in
the summer program at Castle Hill Center for the Arts in Truro. Christa's
classmates included Tony Perkins' widow, Berry Berenson, and a woman
named Ding Watson, a beloved Truro resident, known for her louche
but colorful history chasing down local men. Christa loved being with
these intense and lively women. But at summer's end, Berry was killed
on a flight to L.A. on 9/11, and Ding died in a head-on as she merged onto
Route 6 from Depot Road.

Christa was very disturbed by the deaths of her classmates. Berry
Berenson had promised to remain in touch with Christa, and they had
planned to get together to critique one another's work. In the weeks following the terrorist disaster, Christa attended another playwriting workshop at the School House Center in Provincetown. She had been writing
in a notebook. It was a stream-of-consciousness account of her mother's
death coinciding with Ava's birth. She brought pages of the rambling
memoir to Sinan Unel's playwriting class. Playwright Jim Dalglish was a
class member in the workshop. He recalls Christa as someone who had at
first appeared "very under the radar."

He said, "Christa was hard to read at first, very quiet. She read from a
notebook, handwritten pages, memoir-ish recollections of her mother
abandoning her, of her mother being competitive. It was some kind of
dream sequence where her mother comes back from the dead to meet
her daughter. But it wasn't a play yet, and she didn't seem interested in
advice. When Sinan told her, 'If you want this to be a play, this is what
you should do to it . . .' she would just respond with a blank face. Her approach was a complete inner monologue. A stream of consciousness *me-*

ness. Very emotional. It was like the spoiled little rich girl with a mommy fixation."

Dalglish said that her quietness gave her a position of power. He said, "Her confidence was understated, but women in the class found it annoying. But I liked it, and I asked her to read the lead part in my play, *Professionals.* It's about a strong-willed businesswoman in New York who won't stop a marketing meeting, although outside the office windows the Towers are falling. Then she finds out that her husband is in Tower One. Christa really nailed it. She understood the passive-aggressive character, the control freakishness, the surface calm and the desperation underneath. I wanted her to play the part when it was produced. She was very flattered I had asked her, but I don't know if she would have wanted to act in the play. The woman who ended up in the role, although a very good actress, never sounded exactly right after Christa's razory interpretation. I'll always hear Christa's voice in those lines."

Dalglish said that he also knew Braunwyn and Keith Amato from their involvement in local theater troupes. Dalglish talked about having an "eerie feeling" after Christa was murdered. He remembered a time when he had watched Keith Amato rehearsing his role in a play Dalglish had written for a production called *Art Brut.* Keith's role required that he "beat up a woman." The director had hired a "fight coach" to teach Keith "about control, balance, speed, and how to grab someone without hurting them or ripping their clothing."

Dalglish said, "It was chilling to watch Keith. He was so realistic. He would just explode. It was incredibly real, and you know, it gave me the spookiest feeling."

Having had this gut feeling, Dalglish might not have been surprised then to note an entry in the *Cape Cod Times* on December 4, 2002: "Man Assaulted Pregnant Wife in Truro."

The crime log states, "A man, who was questioned by state police in the Christa Worthington murder investigation was arraigned on a charge of aggravated assault and battery. . . . Keith Amato, 38, of Harm's Way, Eastham, pleaded innocent to the charge." Amato was alleged to have attacked his estranged wife, Braunwyn Jackett, "the daughter of Tony Jackett and the half-sister of Ava Worthington." Braunwyn isn't carrying Amato's baby, it's another man's child.

The *Cape Cod Times* reports, "The seriousness of the charge stems from the fact that Amato's estranged wife is pregnant." Keith Amato was arrested at Braunwyn's residence after an argument regarding child custody. Braunwyn refused to let him take his daughter Etel for an unplanned visit. Amato shoved Braunwyn against a wall, despite the fact that she is a whopping "seven months pregnant," according to the other local paper, the *Cape Codder*. The paper reminds its readers: "Amato was among those who were asked to give DNA samples" in the Worthington investigation.

My neighbor for the last ten years, Truro police officer Kyle Takakjian, was the arresting officer who had responded to the 911 call from Braunwyn's residence. He went out to Old County Road with Chief Popcorn.

Having a Truro police officer as a neighbor has had its simple rewards—Kyle parks his glossy cruiser on the street and bothersome door-to-door solicitors, JWs, and Halloween vandals avoid our neighborhood. But it can sometimes be awkward to know local cops. A few years back, it was Kyle who met me with a Wellfleet officer at the Truro town line. After a domestic argument at a local clam shack, I had started walking home, but it was a new moon and Route 6 was pitch black. Worse, I would have had to walk past Helen Miranda Wilson's house and risk a face-to-face. I didn't want to explain. So I had accepted a lift from a Wellfleet officer, but by protocol the Wellfleet cop could drive me only to the town line, where we waited for a Truro cherry-top to ferry me the rest of the way home. That's where I hitched up with Officer Kyle Takakjian and piled into his cruiser. In small-town life, one's personal crossroads are sometimes wide open for inspection. Kyle had to adhere to the police handbook and was forced to ask rote questions in a bare-bones domestic violence intervention. He asked me, "Did he physically assault you?"

I said, "Oh, God. Of course not. But the mouth on him."

When I asked Kyle about Keith Amato, he said, "Massachusetts has recently made assault on a pregnant woman a felony offense. It's worse than simple assault and battery charges. The unborn child is considered a 'helpless victim.' The trouble is, there's no room in prison. Amato will probably work something out at his pretrial hearing. He'll agree to get counseling or maybe do community service."

Since Keith and Braunwyn had parted company, Keith had been flopping at various locations, but Emily Dooley and I were intrigued by Amato's current address: "Harm's Way."

"Isn't that about right?" Emily said. "But I never knew there was a 'Harm's Way' in Eastham."

"Sometimes that address just follows you around," I said.

Amato's rough stuff with Braunwyn might be de rigueur for their rocky relationship, but Emily and I thought it might rekindle interest by state police investigators. Amato was known to be hotheaded and volatile, but a new arrest for the alleged felony crime of "aggravated assault and battery" against an "unborn child" seemed to add a little paraffin.

"Does this tweak it for investigators?" I asked O'Keefe.

"No."

"It doesn't interest them, why not? Because it's not news to you that Amato's edgy, he's trash on fire?"

"Yeah."

The same week that Keith was arrested, Emily Dooley broke a story in the newspaper about the Worthingtons' efforts to set up a $25,000 reward and to launch a tip line. WORTHINGTON FAMILY WILL POST REWARD IN SEARCH FOR KILLER.

" 'It's almost been a year,' said Janet Worthington, Christa's cousin. 'It's a good time to do something.' "

After Linda Silva's murder in 1996, a $10,000 reward was posted to help in finding her killer. The reward proved to be of no help. "State Police Sgt. James Plath said, 'We have not had a great deal of success with tip lines and rewards.' " Dooley writes in the *Cape Cod Times* that FBI sources have said that paying reward money to tipsters before a trial can cloud credibility. " 'Sometimes these rewards can be a double-edged sword,' Plath said."

A friend of Christa's said, "Double-edged sword? That's not the most sensitive remark for a cop to make after a stabbing."

I asked O'Keefe about the Worthington reward.

"It's not happening," he said.

"No reward?"

"When we decide to do it, we'll let you know. You're on my list."

"But can the family decide to post a reward without your blessings?"

"They can do anything they want to do. I'm not going to get into what some nitwit in that family said to the newspaper. Whoever opened her mouth has been duly chastised. She should have kept her big mouth shut."

O'Keefe eventually did appear at a press conference at his Barnstable offices with Worthington family members and friends of the victim to announce a $25,000 reward for information that leads to an arrest of the killer. A poster with an unflattering picture of Christa was propped up against a bookshelf so that the press could take photos. Christa's flat expression, her slightly doughy complexion, aren't at all pretty or glamorous but merely serviceable as identification. It's probably a recent passport snap, but it looks almost like a mug shot or a "Missing" photo on a milk carton. It was just like her catty cousins to choose an unflattering glossy. At the meeting, police also announced that a twenty-four-hour tip line had been established. "All calls will be kept confidential," O'Keefe said.

O'Keefe rekindled reporters' year-old appetite for juicy information with his first-ever acknowledgment that police were searching for an unnamed lover. He said, "Investigators believe that Christa Worthington was involved in an intimate relationship with a person prior to or relatively contemporaneous with her death. . . . Perhaps someone can illuminate the identity of that person." Someone had already called in to say that the last person to see Christa was a UPS driver, and the driver hadn't been swabbed yet.

O'Keefe said that he did not necessarily consider the man who had had sex with Christa Worthington to be the same person who killed her. Then, he became Mr. Cryptic again, his usual mode, and said, "We certainly have people we are interested in and that we've looked at but there's no point in sharing that information with the public."

Amyra Chase attended the press conference and sat teary-eyed throughout the proceedings. When Amyra was asked about Christa's little girl, all media and law enforcement personnel fell silent. Everyone forgot about

Christa's final sexfest when Amyra said, "Ava is doing well. She's a light in our family."

The 9/11 disaster had made Christa a little fearful for Ava's future. When a country seems perched for war, mothers of young children always feel most helpless. Single mothers feel twice as nervous. Christa had once seen a documentary film that showed little children running around playfully as white ashes rained down all around them. Mothers in Nevada didn't understand the dangers of radioactive fallout from atomic testing sites. They made home movies of their kids cavorting in the little "snow-storms" in midsummer. Some busy moms had even put their kids to bed at night without washing their hair, letting the poison dust seep into their pores.

Perhaps it was a reaction to 9/11 or to Toppy's continued disassociative behavior, but Christa wanted further legal advice about financial planning and changing her testamentary trust to a "living will."

This was when Christa had asked a lawyer about the possibility of having her father declared "legally incompetent," so she might be named to manage his remaining fortune. The lawyer told her that this was a totally subjective observation and assessment on her part, and it would never stand up in court. Toppy was a law-abiding, tax-paying adult. Good grief, he was an ex–assistant attorney general. He could choose to spend his money any way he wanted. The lawyer joked about the hokey bumper stickers often seen on a Winnebago or a Georgie Boy travel home: "We're spending our children's inheritance." Beth Porter was Toppy's "galloping bungalow."

"If it's rocking, don't come knocking."

Because Gloria had died of colon cancer, Christa started to worry that she might face unforeseen health problems. Monthly, Christa performed self-breast-exams, but cancer can't be detected if it begins at the most secret pin dots and darkest culverts of the body.

She made an appointment to have a colonoscopy. The worst part of it, she was told, would be the preparatory purging. Her skittishness wasn't based on any real evidence of failing health, but she was concerned for

Ava. Single mothers can't get sick. Just in case, Christa named Amyra in a codicil to her will, signed November 14, 2001.

When Tony talked to me about Amyra, he said, "Why did Christa go to all the trouble of having my family bond with the baby if she had planned to give Ava away to strangers?"

Tony brings Ava home to Provincetown on Wednesdays. He is often seen with his little girl on highly visible outings around town. Reporter Sally Jacobs described his routine in the *Boston Globe*: "When Tony wheels his daughter down the now-barren boulevards of this tired seaside town, as he does almost every Wednesday afternoon, many do not even bother to avert their stares. 'We try and keep our dignity,' Jackett said."

For months, Tony has been dutifully retrieving his daughter once a week, meeting Amyra at the Dunkin' Donuts at Sagamore Bridge. Yet when Ava was scheduled to begin spending "overnight weekends" with Tony in November, Tony told me, "I don't know how we'll do it, because that's when I'm really busy. Just because we have an agreement doesn't mean we can't arrange it better for me."

Tony described to me his new pressures as Ava's dad. For years, Tony has pedaled his bicycle up and down Commercial Street with aplomb, with his typical Casanova finesse and flourishes when, suddenly, it's as if his bike has been refitted with new derailleurs, irritable spur gears. At his nicely steeped age of fifty-plus, after raising all his kids, with AARP sending him coupons and free magazines, he thought that life should be like coasting down a familiar street. But, with Ava, so much more is expected of him. Now he's bicycling to work, pedaling along Front Street, that straightaway that bisects the breadth of his hometown, and his chain is getting tangled in his pants cuffs and popping off the sprockets.

Tony said, "I put my name in for the new marine superintendent position. Provincetown has this idea to let a corporation take over MacMillan pier and to run it as a business. I suggested they combine my job with the new position. But this new police chief, Meyers, might have another idea about me. You know, my job comes under the jurisdiction of the police chief. Since the murder, he might have been eyeing me funny. But he swung by the house. I jumped in the cruiser and filled him in. He's a good guy. He said, 'I believe in fresh starts.' But as long as this goes unsolved, there's always this perception I did it. I was hoping that O'Keefe, running for office, would solve it three days before people go to the polls. It's hard on my family. My family is a living museum. We should sell tickets."

Yet, in December, Hamilton Kahn, editor of the *Provincetown Banner*, praised Tony in a column called "Best & Worst of 2002."

"For *best* we pick Tony Jackett (Native Son in the News), whose private life was torn open for all to see following the murder of Christa Worthington. . . . Jackett kept his cool, his dignity, and his family intact."

But Tony complains to me over lunch one afternoon. He's feeling a lot like writer Janet Malcolm's subject, whom she had called a "prisoner of publicity."

Tony says, "This past year I've been courted every which way. They want to do a movie about me. What's in it for me? I take the attitude, you know, like when I was a fisherman. I could steam out, and there might be a pile of fish out there, or maybe I should turn around."

IN WINTER

Ellen Webb invited Christa and Ava for Thanksgiving at her house in Wellfleet. It was Ava's first real Thanksgiving. She was old enough to want to try everything on the table, and Christa scooped spoonfuls from each serving dish and tapped them gently onto Ava's plate. A rosette of mashed potatoes, a ruby glob of cranberries, a sliver of breast meat, a little hill of cornbread stuffing.

Christa told Ava stories about the Pilgrims and about Harry Kemp's reenactments of the landing and of the "Pilgrim Women's First Monday Washing Day." Toppy came to the celebration, and Ellen said it was a happy time despite Christa and her father's ongoing war over Beth Porter. Porter was who-knows-where for the holiday. Christa imagined her at a Turkey Day chow line at one of the Roxbury soup kitchens.

Ellen said, "Christa was sparkling. She tried to relax. Ava sat on my lap and on Toppy's. Toppy was good. My kids said, 'He's a cool guy.' " But in the next weeks, when Christa went to New York at Christmas, she told her friend Radz, "He's giving all my money to Beth."

Christa brought Ava to New York, where they attended Ben Brantley's holiday party. She was excited to introduce her daughter to her old friends and colleagues. People saw the pair of them and noticed a sparkling correspondence, a bubbly magic between mother and daughter: the more adorable Ava appeared to be moment to moment, the more radiant Christa became. Christa looked great. She had slimmed down almost to a string bean. She looked as if she could climb onto a runway with the best of them. At Brantley's party, Christa remembered what it was like to rub elbows with glamour tycoons; it was a high-pitched chatter full of annoyances and fiery fun. She was amused to see Woody Allen and Soon Yi were showing their faces again.

Although Christa and Ava were staying with her ancient squeeze from UEA and his large family, she was also invited to dinner with Radz and his wife. Radz said, "She was having a great time with Ava, my daughter, and me. I thought she was a little overprotective of Ava because she had brought a car seat for Ava when she came up here in a taxi. It was only ten blocks! But she insisted on the car seat." But Christa's friends saw how enraptured she was by her daughter. For the most part, it seemed a healthy immersion. At a dinner party in the Village, Ava danced for everyone. Christa said, "I can't stand it! She's too adorable—" Christa couldn't wait for Christmas, and in the middle of the party she opened a shopping bag and took out a present for Ava—a pink tulle tutu. She helped Ava get dressed in the ballerina gear and the party came to a standstill as everyone watched Ava spin around.

When police asked friends if Christa had connected with any old boyfriends in Manhattan, Radz said that he didn't know her exact itinerary, nor could he pin down her whereabouts every minute. He thought he remembered that his wife had arranged to get a baby-sitter for Ava so Christa could go somewhere.

Radz said, "Christa would have likely spilled the beans at any time, if she had been dating a man here."

When he was asked if Christa was someone "who might go out cruising? Was she someone who might keep secrets from him?" Radz said, "I don't think so—but maybe we didn't know her anymore. People change. Especially in that part of life."

But Christa was wide open with her friends when discussing her worries about Toppy's relationship with Beth Porter. And she had told Radz about her plans to ask for financial support from Ava's father.

Some friends thought that her interest in getting money from Tony Jackett seemed practical, but others believed that she was trying to be punitive. If Tony didn't love her, she'd make him pay for her hurt. Nothing had yet been drawn up on paper. Her old UEA boyfriend told Emily Dooley, "No one knew why she was doing this. She didn't need the money. It seemed like a destructive path on her part."

Ellen Webb said, "When she outed Tony that April, I was flabbergasted and happy. I thought it showed real growth for Christa. Then, at New Year's, she told me she was going to go after Tony for money."

And Tim Arnold said, "She came back from her trip to New York with a new resolve. The Friday before she was murdered, Christa told me she had planned to talk to Tony that weekend about getting support."

An extremely mild autumn in Truro worried some residents. The "global warming thing" might be accelerating. Tides were cresting higher, the wrack line inching closer. But motel owners and managers at cottage colonies were happy to book rooms deeper into the off-season before boarding up.

It wasn't until the first week of January that Truro had its first cold snap. The sky was overcast; an oppressive low ceiling felt like the heavy lid of a tarnished soup tureen. After the bright lights and cozy restaurants on Second Avenue in New York, Christa didn't look forward to the long, dark haul of another Land's End winter with everything shut up. January, February, March, April. Sometimes even May brings churlish, unforecasted frosts that ruin a gardener's first seedlings. Spring comes late to the Outer Cape because of the peninsula's thermodynamics; Truro is just a finger of land surrounded by icy, boreal currents.

The Squealing Pig is one of only a few bars in P-town with a hetero meatrack. Its clientele might have a cross-section of gay stragglers, but most partygoers at the Pig are straight. Boomers, Gen-Xers, and an important dying breed of "dregsters," the last of the nail-chewing fishing crews from the dwindling fleet of draggers still steaming out from MacMillan Wharf. Add to this evaporating pool of testosterone a few macho drug dealers and beefy shopkeepers.

Some Pig regulars have said that Christa "cruised at the Pig." A recent *Boston Globe* story states that her closest friends refused to acknowledge that Christa might have been seen at the Governor Bradford or at the Pig in the days before her murder, but the *Globe* reports, "Worthington did, in fact, patronize the Pig. She came in every few weeks with a few friends and had several drinks, according to manager Denise McGrenra."

A year after the murder, diehard rumorists hold forth at bar rails. From one redundant monochrome image printed ad nauseam in the *Cape Cod Times* and the *Boston Globe*, people think that they know Christa. Her face is burned into their minds. Her face electrifies both sit-at-home crones and closing-time barflies. In homey breakfast nooks, and at last-call clutches at local taverns, murder geeks and armchair sleuths share a charged intimacy that spawns new colorized scenarios of Christa's last night alive:

"He told her to meet him at the Squealing Pig. . . ."

"She was two ahead at the Pig when she first saw him. . . ."

"He had just tied up after two weeks out at Stellwagon Bank and he had a bankroll in his pocket."

He wasn't a "WASP with a sail bag," or a "poet with a tool belt." He was a "fisherman with a paycheck." He wanted to buy Christa a drink. She accepted a grenadine and ginger ale. "One Shirley, hold the cherry!"

Another Pig regular protested. "No, I saw her with my own eyes. She had a vodka martini."

Christa had just washed her hair. She bent over at the waist to wrap her soaked mane in a towel. She stepped up to her full-length myth mirror to study her face, propping up her heavy, lopsided turban with one hand. In a final survey, she checked for symmetry, smoothing her eyebrows with her fingertip, one delicate arch, then the other. She finished drying off and dusted herself with a powder puff dredged in an expensive Guerlain scent. She cinched a robe tight around her waist. Earlier that day, Christa had called the Jacketts to cancel Ava's visit in order to take Ava to a music lesson. Now Ava was banging the piano with her left fist, and smearing the high keys with her opposite tiny hand. In the midst of Ava's happy racket, Christa thought she heard someone knocking at the kitchen door. She swept through the cluttered hallway to flip the porch light on. She didn't see anyone. Maybe the visitor had given up.

Ava's percussive background music seemed to mock Christa's interior battle, an agitation she had felt since coming back home from New York. It was her desire to connect, to hook up, despite her icy terror of beginning the grind again. Desire, terror, all in one. Christa's mixed-up feelings sometimes made her want to jump out of her skin, or at least to get out of the house.

In Manhattan, Christa had indulged her appetite for impish jaunts and noirish fun. Impulse, impulse, impulse. She had liked the assertive conversations, the decorating coups, food and drink, old friends and new men. In New York, she had suddenly recognized how deprived she had been. She craved a little social life after two dutiful years in Nowheresville. Truro nights were raw, beginning to crackle with cold and promises of sleet and black ice. Staying home in the yawing wind, with the house creaking, could begin to rattle anyone's nerves, even a diehard Yankee. She wanted to go dancing. Barbara Holloway had said, "Christa loved to dance. Christa was poetry in motion."

T. C. Churchwell had said, "Christa was the Twyla Tharp of Horizontal Dancing."

Christa sometimes relied on Francie Randolph and Tom Watson, across the street, to watch Ava. She would promise to return the favor the next day. Francie and Tom could have a Saturday night out, have dinner at the Martin House, or go to the Wellfleet Cinemas. It wasn't out of the ordinary for Christa to sometimes exchange child patrol duties with her neighbors. Their kids had bonded.

But, on occasion, if Christa felt that her good-hearted neighbors were getting too nosy, she still had the phone number of the fat baby-sitter.

I sit down with O'Keefe at the little luncheonette across from the courthouse. He orders the same old same old. A flat doily of steamy egg and spiced sausage. He heads into it with the side of his fork, carving a petite hunk. His mother taught him manners. O'Keefe eats even diner food with his typical gentlemanly elegance tempered and fine-tuned with faux-relaxed body language expected in these casual settings. As I watch him work through his breakfast omelette, I see that attending to his three squares is a time-consuming bother to him; he eats just for maintenance. His law enforcement appetites are stomach-shrinking. His mind is always charging ahead to his next duty on his L. E. itinerary.

We talk about Christa's final day.

Police had noted signs of a scuffle in the sand outside the house; drag marks were still visible beneath a scrim of freezing rain. Forensic investigators might have required a choreographer to map the confusion of steps left behind. Whether the tracks were left by goons from Boston, Beth Porter's Dorchester connection, a New York beau, or a Land's End neighbor, no one on Depot Road had witnessed the melee. The driveway at the Little House winds around like a nautilus. Even in winter, the woods are too dense to see anything but the lights from her second-floor windows, warm toffee squares above the tree line.

As usual, O'Keefe is still tight-lipped and merely pretends to discuss the most probable signatures. He says he wants me to invent the one-acts and propose variants of the dramaturgy:

I say, "She meets a man at the Pig and brings him home with her?"

O'Keefe looks at me and keeps chewing.

"No, not that? Okay, he follows her home from the Pig. He waits for Christa to pay the baby-sitter and put Ava to bed. Then he's at the back door."

The new DA-elect is deadpan, unimpressed. He's like a varsity coach watching me dribble a half-inflated basketball up and down the squeaky parquet.

I say, "She meets him outside at his car, to beg off the obligation, to nip it in the bud. Rebuked, he 'loses it.' She's frightened and she runs into the house. She slams the dead bolt shut. He chases her."

O'Keefe looks over my shoulder as he mops his plate with a triangle of toast.

"Okay. Christa expects him. She greets him willingly; her hair is combed, teeth polished, her breath sweet. She invites him in, she beds him, but she doesn't want him there the next morning. Cold-stunned by her sudden Ice Queen act, he takes off. On second thought, he doubles back. He kicks the door open, breaks the lock, splits its warped fir frame."

"She knows him?"

"She never saw him before."

O'Keefe says that I'm not using my brains. "Think," he says. "Think from the other side of it."

O'Keefe searches my face as if watching a Rube Goldberg machine engaging its sprockets, sun gears, planet gears, levers, compound levers and pulleys that might hatch the correct analysis.

I tell him, "Oh. Wait. It's a third party? *A prowler* watches Christa come home with someone. A stranger. *Another* man."

The peeper sees Christa together with his rival. Standing outside, in the freezing blear, the killer monitors their tryst. He watches him nibble her neck and peel her fawn sweater away from her shoulder, and—

When the visitor is finished, laces his boots, zips his parka, and leaves, the prowler muscles his way into the house to confront her. He kicks the door in.

O'Keefe says, "Now, who do you think that is?"

UNSOLVED LOVE

im Arnold sent me a torn page from Don DeLillo's book *The Body Artist*. In his accompanying note, Tim says, "The writer understands the trauma of a sudden death, the strange hyper-focused reality where time becomes fluid—and the desire! The powerful desire to see that person or hear that person, just for a moment—a desire that can become so strong it might actually alter reality." Tim had highlighted passages from the torn page with a yellow marker:

Why not sink into it. Let death bring you down. Give death its sway.
Why shouldn't the death of a person you love bring you into lurid ruin?

Hearing of Tim's relentless bereavement, I wanted to tell him about the "Karla Faye hug." I described Karla crossing her arms and squeezing her own ribs as if to embrace the beloved who is out of reach behind a Plexiglas window. When grief becomes almost a dismembering feeling, maybe just a practice hug would help. But for Tim there is no Plexiglas partition between past and present, no modern-day Thermopane window or medieval portcullis to protect him from vivid memory.

In Christa's copy of Bach's *Flower Remedies*, Dr. Bach says that the unwillingness to face the truth is a "polite form of suicide." He says, " 'Clematis types' are daydreamers. Clematis folk withdraw into a world of illusion and unreality. It is almost as if they wish to leave this earth, perhaps to join some loved one who is dead, or just because life does not come up to their expectations on this material plane . . . they would rather die with a loved one than remain on earth."

Tim took a spade and followed the path through the woods to Christa's bungalow. Walking in the opposite direction of Antone Costa's overgrown garden, he stopped above Mill Pond to stare at the "killed marsh," and farther, to open water.

Circling the footprint of the empty house, stripped almost bare by Christa's aunt Diana, Tim looked in the windows. Standing on end, laddered into a few remaining boxes, he recognized some of Gloria's paintings. These belonged to Ava now. The kitchen floor was swept and mopped, but he saw its demon mural of crimson fleurs-de-lis.

It was there she was felled at the foot of the butcher block table, with its all-too-convenient knife rack–turned–weapon caddy. He squinted at the Cloroxed crime scene, looking for the secret nick in the flooring, where the knife tip had left a tiny divot. It was invisible.

But he had no trouble finding the Mother's Day clematis he had given Christa. It was still living, although it looked stressed in the parched ground. There had been a long drought that summer and these scraggly keepsakes of his secret bond had gone unattended.

With the spade, he sliced a ring around the dormant flower and lifted its pulpy tangle of roots. He looked at the dirty snarl and remembered Christa's whimsical voice when she had once told him, "You're obsessed with ganglia." Then he thought of what she had told Ellen Webb, "He doesn't know how handsome he is," and when Christa had said to him, "You're better than ten thousand Tony Jacketts."

He started digging a different sandy clump, removing the twin clematis that Christa had awarded to him, in turn. He dropped it in the same pail. He rescued the pair of "His and Her" climbers from the abandoned property, and he would "heal them over" for the winter. A true gardener would say that these separate root balls should have their own troughs and not be allowed to invade one another. He carried the meager bucketful back to his father's place. He knew of only one corner at his wooded property, where the sun glanced the eaves of the house at midday. Finding the spot, he carved into the sandy crust, tore the ground, and tamped the naked vines under.

THE CHILD WITNESS
TO VIOLENCE PROJECT

Ava had spilled Cheerios across the kitchen floor. A mouse was nosing the oaty grit. Resting beside her mother, Ava was at eye level with the mouse as it nibbled the serendipitous table spread. The furry pippin, its whiskers shivering with Disney authenticity, was Ava's only compatriot in the winter gloom. She pushed herself up from her mother's side and reached out to pet its silvery coat. The field mouse froze; its glossy black eyes bulged like droplets of motor oil. Then it scrambled along the baseboard and shot behind the refrigerator.

Her mother was still sleeping. If her mother was very sick, Ava knew that her favorite nurse-doctor, Marcia, the cheery PA at Outer Cape Health, would be able to fix her.

Ava climbed onto the piano bench lugging a heavy jar of strawberry jam. She twisted its cap, but the seal wouldn't budge. She propped the red barrel beside her on the bench and banged the piano with both hands. The white keys smeared pink.

When her mom napped Ava wasn't supposed to bang on the piano.

She wanted her mom to wake up.

Ava went back to Christa's side. She shoved her mom's velour top higher, until it wreathed her throat. As she nursed, Ava walked her fingers over Christa's face, lightly marching her fingertips across Christa's eyelids and down the bridge of her nose. Her mother wasn't playing the game. Usually, when Ava did this, Christa nibbled her hand and kissed her knuckles.

There wasn't any milk letting down. Ava stretched across her mother to find the other nipple.

Children speak to blank-faced dolls in a singsong imitation of an adult's condescending interrogation. Ava asked Christa, "Do you want a drink . . .

Okay . . . Do you want my juice . . . Okay . . . Are you sleepy . . . I know . . .
You're very sleepy."

The floor was icy cold. Ava climbed onto her mother. Her mother's
body was familiar; it had pillowed her at any time Ava was ready to
cuddle. Christa never said no. Ava tucked her head against Christa's collarbone, burrowing in; the little girl's curly-topped crown fit the odd, off-
center tilt of Christa's frozen chin.

Ava closed her eyes and held on.

A death by stabbing is caused by massive hemorrhaging and cessation of
heartbeat. Called exsanguination or "bleeding out," the body can empty
six to eight pints of blood, until the heart can no longer compensate for
such blood loss merely by beating faster. The heart stops. Circulation is
arrested. During these moments of trauma, endorphins are released to
cradle the nervous system, allowing the victim to accept the final conclusion, and to "give up." Physician Sherwin B. Nuland writes in *How We
Die,* "Fear passes . . . injury recedes into a soft cloud of indifference."

The sticky place mat–sized circle of blood beneath Christa's face was
blood she had aspirated, choked on, and vomited in the "agonal phase" of
death. Ava had brought a washcloth from the sink and tried to dab at her
mother's sticky face. Ava's bloody footprints made repetitive fleurs-de-lis
patterns across the plank floor as she walked from Christa to the sink,
from Christa to the TV, or from Christa to the kitchen table. Ava returned
to snuggle at the exact location of Christa's stab wound, transferring the
blood source, mother to child.

After Ava was discovered alone with her mother, "sitting in a blood-
stained setting," local DSS social workers knocked heads about what
might be the consequences for Ava and what plan of action caregivers
should undertake. Nancy Edson, a clinical social worker at Family Con-
tinuity Programs in Hyannis, told the *Cape Cod Times,* "At age two children don't understand what death is, but Ava must have felt some sort of
abandonment. 'Why won't mommy wake up? I'm scared. Why won't
mommy eat? I'm scared.' A child at that age is just beginning to understand how to process anger and sadness. Most researchers agree that
memory doesn't start to form until age three."

Lysette Hurge-Putnam, executive director of Independent House in Hyannis, disagreed. "There's a tremendous sense of loss and displacement. At two and a half, you are pretty aware of who the important people in your life are." The DSS and local clinicians concurred that Ava needed someone to steer her through her horrific experience, whether she remembered it or not.

"The first and most important principle is that we must recognize the power of a nurturing, respectful and caring relationship with an adult to help a child recover," writes Betsy McAlister Groves, founder of the Child Witness to Violence Project at Boston Medical Center. Amyra Chase has been taking Ava to the Boston Medical Center for therapy sessions since Ava lost her mother.

"It's an honor," Amyra told me just weeks after Christa was murdered and Ava had come into Amyra's busy household of four children. Amyra had willingly accepted the sudden obligation of caring for Christa's little girl. Amyra had embraced her duties and promised Ava that she would never again be abandoned. Amyra's commitment to Ava is uncontaminated. Some people believe that in Christa's friend Amyra we might see Christa's finest judgment in people. Amyra's immediate and heartfelt enactment of Christa's (as it turned out to be) final wishes is a reflection of the two women's strong friendship, and of Christa's eerie wisdom and foresight. She knew that Amyra was perfect.

The Child Witness to Violence Project at Boston Medical Center provides treatment for very young children who have experienced brutal events in which family members have been harmed, or worse. Children are encouraged to discuss the traumatic scenes they have witnessed. At therapy sessions, they learn to interpret feelings, and to manage the sometimes very complex symptoms and behavioral patterns that emerge after exposure to violence.

In the introduction to her book, *Children Who See Too Much*, Groves describes a scenario with a two-and-a-half-year-old boy that closely mirrors Ava's story. "This child had been with his mother when she was fatally shot. . . . In a play session with this child, he told me that 'his mom was on the floor' and that she 'didn't talk.' "

Groves describes the boy's difficulty in sleeping and in managing his daily routines. His pediatrician had believed that his young age would protect him from recalling the gruesome images he had seen. Groves writes, "As we at Boston Medical Center gained experience in this area, we saw the myth of young age as a protection from the effects of violence disproved again and again."

"Mommy got into my paints," Ava had told Tim and others. Ava's inventive description of the bloody scene reveals how Ava began to immediately filter information and to create, on her own terms, an acceptable scenario to screen out the violence she witnessed. And even at such a young age, Ava expressed worry and confusion about social propriety when she told Tim, with a tinge of guilt, "I had to have nursies."

Protecting Ava's privacy during the little girl's different phases of recovery and adjustment is a first concern of Amyra's. "It's my gut reaction," she said, "to keep everything about Ava private. But Ava's doing great. She's a member of our big family. I must keep it private. Besides, I haven't even made sense of it myself."

Amyra told me that she and Ava have been going into Boston Medical Center as participants in the Child Witness to Violence Project since the very first weeks after the murder. Amyra said, "We go once a week. We go all the time—we'll probably go forever."

Children receiving treatment there are very young, ages eight and under. Groves writes about medical studies that examine links between trauma and early brain development. She states that there is ongoing research into the "correlation between early exposure to violence and permanent changes in brain chemistry." Researchers are also "addressing the question of whether infants and toddlers can be diagnosed with PTSD, or Post-Traumatic Stress Disorder."

Amyra is learning how to be a "resiliency mentor" for Ava, by modeling for Ava and helping Ava fortify her own buffers. Children who see violent events can become "silent witnesses" and need coaxing to recount events in order to recover from them. PTSD symptoms in children can be masked and confused with slow development or early learning special needs; a child's distraction and disturbances can be misdiagnosed as common hyperactivity disorder. It is important for Amyra to be educated in how to recognize Ava's symptoms of stress, grief, and confusion.

Children who come into the Child Witness to Violence Project are engaged in one-to-one play sessions with therapists, where toys such as drawing materials, a doctor's kit, cars, and dolls are used to help them express their overwhelming feelings. PTSD symptoms can sometimes emerge as a child's reduced involvement in play or, contrary to that, can emerge in a child's reenactment of their trauma through play. Groves describes one boy, "Danquin," who played with a toy truck full of occupants, letting it crash to the floor. "Then Danquin announced, 'They are all dead now.' "

Groves describes how some children must be encouraged to talk about what they have experienced, but others "could not wait to talk about it" and needed help to "stop talking and thinking about it."

In September, Ava was christened in the Catholic Church. Tony and Susan drove up to St. Anthony's in Cohasset to join Amyra and her family at the service. Amyra had asked the Worthingtons if they objected. Christa wasn't religious. She was more of a pantheist herself. Raising her pet spider on the T-bar clothesline was about as prayerful as she would get. And, more recently, Mary Jane Dean, an artist in residence at the Fine Arts Work Center in Provincetown, asked volunteers to submit handwritten messages for a conceptual art idea called the Provincetown Drift Bottle Project. As if for a cornerstone time capsule, these personal notes would be sealed in a big glass keg sealed with waxed twine, the bottle braided in jute, then launched from the deck of an Oceanic Research Vessel steaming out from Woods Hole. The bottle, filled with paper messages, was fitted with thirty pounds of lead ballast and was set adrift in the Gulf Stream. Town residents wrote various submissions: life stories; riddles; vows to God or to loved ones; advance epitaphs; poems and promises. Tim Arnold said that for her submission, Christa had written a pledge to her daughter: "My sole wish is for my daughter's well being and happiness." She made a list of her promises to Ava, and left her submission in the Walker Gallery, where it was collected by the artist and the bottle was launched as scheduled. No one has yet contacted the e-mail address on the "drift bottle," and no one is certain if it is still bobbing in high seas or if its seal broke open above the abyssal plains where the messages might have sank into the deep or dissolved like Kleenex.

But Ava should know of the promises Christa had made. If Ava becomes acquainted with the Church, or not, she'll need help to accept her loss. When her longing emerges in its future manifestations, when as a teenager or as a young woman she struggles to accept her mother's death, the big glass bottle, still adrift or unclaimed, seems to have more sanctity, more hope, in its unmapped route than the more traditional and organized shipping lanes to God.

When I recently asked Tim to tell me what Ava was interested in these days, he said, "She has a lot of Barbies. People have been giving her their old Barbie dolls. They're classics."

I asked Amyra about Ava's Barbies, and she laughed. "Ava has only one Barbie," she said.

Now whom are we to believe? The Barbie argument is a benign example of all the word-of-mouth contradictions that have been bandied about for months.

The "Christa Worthington Forum" on *CrimeNews2000* has been shut down to nonmembers. T. C. Churchwell had recently posted complaints about libelous statements made about him. He wrote, "According to some CN'er my paintings and pictures display a hatred for women . . . click here and see for yourself." A gallery of T.C.'s artwork pops up. Electronic doodled pictures of Britney Spears, models, and girlie busts. He writes that his daughter was in tears because of accusations CN'ers have made about her father. In their daily forum, "Discussion du jour," *CrimeNews2000* doesn't comment.

Yet Churchwell seems to love his new following of crime scene tourists. He continues to e-mail photographs and commentary about his affair with Christa to his fans. Recently, T.C. offered a digital picture tour of his life with Christa, posting photographs of the bar where they had met, and snaps of her apartment building across the street.

Above a photo of a current nightclub called Tens, he writes, "This club, formerly known as 'Stringfellow's' on 21st Street, between Park and Broadway, is where I worked and where Christa stood outside and cried until I came out." With a photo of the interior of Christa's watering hole, the Barfly, across from her Gramercy Park condo, T.C. writes, "There! On the left you see a chair . . . Christa would have been looking right at you. This is where I first touched her on the shoulder and she jumped."

A photo of the doorman at Christa's building is captioned: "Here is the doorman. You have to go through him before entering. This is the location of the fabled 'door kicking' incident."

Our reliable Land's End reporter Emily Dooley is preparing to depart. She writes, "Did I tell you I'm leaving the P-town beat? I was promoted to covering Barnstable. Well, it's a promotion in theory. I'm not sure if Pleasantville stories will be any better. Hopefully I can find some insanity there."

"You want insanity? Why leave?"

She says a little goes a long way. For instance, one of her farewell stories out of Provincetown captures the Land's End penchant for wacky family nicknames. "There once was a town on the tip of the Cape, where people were named because of a trait. A large man was Big He, his wife Big She, the child they bore became Little Big He." She quotes dune poet Harry Kemp, who wrote, "If you have an odd way or fight with your wife, you'll be nicked with a name that will dent you for life! 'Boozy' doesn't touch liquor; 'Wine Drop,' once begin it, can gulp down a quart in the tick of a minute. . . ."

In my research into the debated Barbie count, I have learned that Braunwyn had contributed some of her daughter Etel's dolls to Ava's toy chest. Perhaps Ava has another, distinct, Barbie collection at Tony's house, where she comes each week. Whatever the correct Barbie statistic, Ava will cross the canal, trekking back and forth from Cohasset to Land's End, in an elliptical cycle. Christa, speaking from experience, might want to tell her daughter, "Choose one side, one world to make sense of. A world that is safe."

Paris or London. New York or Truro. Heaven or Nowheresville. Christa can't tell Ava the story about Countess Boul Breteuil's notion that Marrakesh was "the last acceptable Paradise." She can't share with her daughter Edna O'Brien's caveat: "One must enter the gates of paradise in order to find it, in order to lose it, in order to refind it, in perpetuity." Christa had many places to hang her hat, but nowhere was exactly right. The "it" place was still misty, unmapped, a faraway corner where she wanted to take Ava, a remote spa that is both secured and swept away, like the Provincetown Drift Bottle. It was Eden or bust. Eden—or nothing.

EPILOGUE

It's a standing-room-only crowd of more than three hundred people in the main courtroom at Barnstable Superior Court. I received my engraved invitation to O'Keefe's swearing-in, but the reserved seating is gobbled up, packed with the family clans of Barnstable County law enforcement celebrities, O'Keefe and Rollins, and relatives of twenty newbie assistant DAs who are to be sworn in en masse.

I'm on my feet, sandwiched in a line of law enforcement personnel. It's a miscellany of county suits, lawyers, Attorney General Francis Bellotti, U.S. representative, Bill Delahunt, and state police officers, both uniforms and plainclothes. Even Truro Police Chief "Popcorn" is here beside me. But I see no Worthingtons. No Jacketts.

O'Keefe and his mentor, soon to be district attorney emeritus, Phil Rollins, stand at the bench dressed in almost identical red neckties. These men aren't John Fairchild or Christian Lacroix. They didn't think to connect beforehand to discuss their neckwear.

A young girl, Hailey Harris, known as the "Wianno Piper," marches down the aisle with her bladder of pipes, playing a predictable skittish dirge. A Massachusetts state police sergeant–*cum*–Irish tenor, just back from a New Year's Eve memorial at ground zero, delivers a fiery "Star Spangled Banner." He gives it a "Mother Ireland" punch, letting it dip and curdle with brogue flourishes.

O'Keefe's eighty-one-year-old mom, Mary O'Keefe, sits in front, her hair as white as artificial snow. Even with his mother in attendance, O'Keefe's origins seem to be right here, as if he had sprung to life a fully formed prosecutor. He's at home, more comfortable in a courtroom than in his empty castle.

In his brief speech, O'Keefe tells us, "I love this room and what goes on in here—the imperfect but sincere attempt of mortals to do justice." As he speaks, I'm distracted by a blinding gleam above my head. Suspended from the courtroom ceiling is an authentic tin sculpture of a codfish lacquered in silver plate. At least three feet long, the striking cod has been hooked to a frescoed medallion on the high ceiling above the bench since 1827.

I think of Christa's killer. I wonder when he'll sit here to face O'Keefe, beneath the silver codfish.

O'Keefe is saying, "It's been noted, that 'adversity introduces us to ourselves.'" He promises that he will urge lawmakers to provide more funding for crime labs and autopsies. He says, "The autopsy is where the voice of a homicide victim can be heard."

O'Keefe's crime-tone diction slices right through all the pomp and circumstance. The word *autopsy* isn't party talk.

I look at the packed banquette of newly sworn-in DAs. It's like a big restaurant staff, a sort of *Kitchen Confidential* of law enforcement. O'Keefe has told me that Christa's murder case isn't on a back burner; it's simmering, it's curing. It's coming to the table. He said, "In the fullness of time, this case will be solved."

I didn't wait for New Year's and I quit that nasty nicotine gum last October, but O'Keefe is still puffing his Marlboro Lights. I leave him to make his own resolutions. After watching him take the red-tape reins from Rollins, I decide to skip the gala reception at the Ridge Club, O'Keefe's posh golf club tabernacle. Believers who show up at the Ridge Club are expected to have their golf bags, a sprinkling of tees across the dash, or a few loose Titleists rolling around in their backseats. I don't have the pro shop talisman.

There's a parade of cars leaving the courthouse parking lot heading for O'Keefe's soiree, but I turn the opposite way, heading home to Truro. I was amused by Rollins' last words at the bench. Before leaving the courthouse, he took a final jab at Truro when giving partygoers directions to the country club. The indefatigable comedian, Rollins invented the most ridiculous map to O'Keefe's reception. He said, "Just head east. In Truro, take a left." The audience erupted in laughter. Of course, "take a left at

Truro" means that you'd be in the drink. Truro is so "out there," so deeply engulfed in the Nowheresville vernacular, that to Rollins it's the opposite port of call to any sane man's dream destination. Chief Popcorn smiled at the lighthearted slur. Truro can take a joke.

Route 6A snakes for miles, empty. When I get closer to home, the traffic comes to a standstill before a busy spectacle. It's a "Stem to Stern" New Year's Day estate sale. "Stem to Stern" is a beloved operation on Cape Cod that brokers antique houses with all of their contents and miscellany. Week to week, houses are open for inspection with their furnishings tagged, from glorious seventeenth-century Chippendale serpentine chests to the most ratty kitchen utensil. They even have a Web site where seekers can preview the inventory.

The usual "Stem to Stern" trademark is a showy grid of antique chairs arranged across the front lawn. Roped off with velvet ribbon, these lines of rockers, ladderbacks, Windsors, and Hitchcock chairs resemble the empty orchestra section at a Boston Pops concert for ghosts.

Drivers always slow down to survey the treasures, but this time a reveler has traffic at a dead stop. A man has commandeered the thoroughfare to maneuver a dolly down the middle of the tight street. On the hand truck, a giant mirror is secured with bungee cord and clothesline. It looks like Christa's mirror. Maybe Diana Worthington has pawned off the icy artifact to the estate sale tycoons just to be rid of the thing. I think it would be fortunate if Ava never has to stand before its blinding tunnel or search its empty heights. As a child, I had thought that my mother's hand mirror was bewitched, like a trick screen. Its round reflective surface was seductive, sometimes like a wishing well, but more often it was frightful, a smoky vortex and never helpful.

Frozen on the blacktop, I recognize my neighbors locked in the traffic grid as the collector steers his prize toward the opposite sidewalk and into the open doorway of a B&B. As he threads the mirror between cars, one by one we see our faces flash in the silver panel. Captured in its gothic frame, our little town shivers and dissolves. Then we start moving.

AFTERWORD

The plywood sheet hammered across the kitchen entry of Christa Worthington's charming bungalow is a raw blaze across the weathered shingle. The original door, removed for forensic tests, has not yet been returned to its hinges. The house is for sale and remains unoccupied. The first-floor windows are blank, the glass streaked with salt spray. Her garden is weedy and untended. It's a forlorn spot, once an oasis, and now a crime scene suspended in frozen animation season after season. The tiny Victorian has not yet been reclaimed for summer leisure or for cozy winter nights. It's neither crypt nor nest. It's stone cold empty.

Farther up Route 6, in Barnstable Village, another house is on the market. New District Attorney Michael O'Keefe is selling his big suburban three-bedroom on Palomino Drive, an MLS listing with arboretum and swimming pool. The DA's comfortable, modern house is for sale at a third of the cost of the tarnished and heartbreaking homestead in Truro. Christa's place has an asking price of over one million dollars.

I visited O'Keefe's house when he was still on the campaign trail. He had said that with his wife out of the picture, the house was "too big for him." As I looked around, I saw his solitary weight bench on the empty sun porch and it had seemed to illustrate its lonesome aspect. Today, he might be selling the property as a practical belt-tightening, or maybe it's a move up. But whatever his reason for making the transition, it's common knowledge that O'Keefe has had a roller-coaster inaugural year because of the Cape Cod community's response to *Invisible Eden*.

Six months after winning a landslide election in November 2002, O'Keefe faced a barrage of public wrath both from his constituents and the local press because of his candid interviews with me in the preparation of this book. Of course, that has nothing to do with his reasons for selling his house. But O'Keefe had brought me there on more than one occasion. In early summer last year, with his gardens blooming and bumblebees circling rosebuds and lilies, he sat across from me at his kitchen table, in a house that "hadn't seen a woman's touch in a while," to talk about Christa.

It has been two years since Christa Worthington's murder and no arrests have been made. But in early December 2003, a neighbor of Christa's on Depot Road, Ron Singer, discovered a discarded kitchen knife on his property. Singer found the five-inch blade tossed into the underbrush, just steps from the country lane where the killer would have traveled in order to flee the crime scene. But Singer didn't think to connect the knife to the Worthington case. He brought the common utensil home, washed it, and used it "to open packages," until a month later when he finally handed it over to police for forensic tests.

The new discovery of a kitchen knife rekindles the community's imagination about Christa's killer, but for a period of time last summer, public interest shifted from the murderer to curiosity about and ridicule of District Attorney Michael O'Keefe. Six weeks before the publication of this book, manuscript pages obtained by the *Boston Globe* revealed that O'Keefe had been speaking to "a writer" about the investigation while he had remained cryptic with other journalists, deflecting queries from both local and national press. The *Globe* reported, "Maria Flook's book provides ample new material about an investigation that has been closely guarded from the public." The *Globe* printed examples of the new information described in the book: "Worthington had dried semen on her thigh . . . had been felled by blows to the head, probably with a cordless telephone . . . the killer stabbed her once with great force." Known to be perennially tight-lipped with the local press, O'Keefe was criticized for speaking to me, and newspapers questioned our relationship.

Reporters, anxious for details about the Worthington case, seemed just as pleased to have the serendipity of a new story unfolding: the DA and the reporter. The *Globe* wrote that my portrait of O'Keefe in the book "led some to question the nature of their relationship." Insinuations about the DA's love affairs sold a lot of papers. But of course, a writer working on a four-hundred-page book, spending hours one-to-one with O'Keefe, will create a more dimensional portrait of her subject than newsdesk reporters who typically gain audience with O'Keefe only at brief press conferences, usually on the windy steps of the Barnstable courthouse.

Boston newspapers, and especially the smaller Cape Cod papers, were animated to wage attacks on the prosecutor and the writer. The DA's office tried to explain O'Keefe's cooperation with me by asserting that I had been incorporated into the investigation. The *Boston Globe* reported, "Investigators say they hoped information from the book would lead to a break in the case. . . . State Police Sergeant James Plath said they have given Flook's book to investigators to read, and they hoped it could offer new clues, possibly by prompting memories in a witness." But a *Barnstable Patriot* story heading said, "Flook's Worthington Book is Murder on the DA," and the story goes further to assert, "It's logical to assume that Maria Flook had already interviewed the killer."

I had made no written or verbal agreement with O'Keefe other than assuring him that the book wouldn't be published for a full year after the murder. The DA's participation in the book became a summer scandal that seemed to hit the high-water mark of public contempt and local fascination reserved for Ted Kennedy's car accident at Chappaquiddick years ago. The Worthingtons stoked the flames by launching an attack on the DA's office, and Jan Worthington told the *Boston Herald* that O'Keefe's relationship with me was "completely inappropriate." The family issued a statement calling for O'Keefe to be removed from the case.

O'Keefe's portrait in the book revealed that the steely prosecutor had some human traits; not serious faults or lapses, but that he was a more complex person than the stony prosecutor people knew for his monosyllabic statements. In these pages he is sometimes revealed to have flourishes of machismo, never peacock nor wolf, exactly, but a vulnerable "human" quality that contradicted his normally hard-boiled manner. I never felt threatened by his *human* side. He was accused by the Worthington family of being vulgar when he talked about Christa in the vernacular. Referring to her history of sleeping with her girlfriends' husbands, he said, "She was an equal opportunity employer." I still believe that statement to be a more delicate analogy than what he might have come up with.

Augustus Wagner, an attorney who sits on the state's Ethics Commission, a longtime friend of O'Keefe, told the *Cape Cod Times*, "I never heard Mike talk like that about a victim. It's true people talk differently in private than they do in public." He recalled the Nixon tapes. "People were offended by Nixon's use of the F-word. You have to ask yourself does private speech reveal the real character or does public action?" The *L.A. Times* wrote, "O'Keefe apologized to the Worthington family for his remarks but did not deny making them."

My response to the firestorm regarding the district attorney was one of surprise. Eruptions of moralism are always unnerving. I didn't expect that the public would believe that a prosecutor who "stood over every dead body on Cape Cod for the last twenty years" would speak like a choirboy. Of course, it's more likely that O'Keefe uses idioms and language that are a little hard-bitten. Law enforcement personnel are living in a darker, more unrefined landscape of crimes against individuals. It's not a world of rhetorical argument or of philosophical buffers. The DA sees the unspeakable and he sees the absurd—for instance, on the day after a murder at a condominium complex, a panel truck rolls up to the curb with a sign on its cab that says: "Aftermath Cleaning Service." These sights are de rigueur for Mike. In our discussions, he didn't sugarcoat what he told me.

In July, on national TV, in an interview with Barbara Walters on her morning gabfest, the ABC show *The View*, the big, blousy co-host Star Jones scolded me about O'Keefe. Much had been made of a scene in the book when the district attorney takes an outdoor shower before sitting down to talk to me, wrapped only in a towel. I told the panel that O'Keefe wasn't the misogynist that the press was making him out to be. I said that during the months we had worked together, O'Keefe had never crossed a boundary line. Ms. Jones boomed at me incredulously, "Honey, he came out in a towel! Now that was crossing a line!"

Reporters criticized O'Keefe, but they also complained about my portrait of the victim's complex world as a single woman with an illegitimate child. A weird retro moralism emerged in response to details revealed in the book—as if readers didn't think Christa, a single mother, should have wanted to seek new partners nor should she have wanted a sex life. Even *Today* show host Katie Couric, a single mother herself, showed this moralistic streak. But oddly, the nexus of moralism erupted from the Worthington family themselves. Perhaps it was difficult for the Worthington family to read about Christa's darker troubles and to learn what her former lovers have said about her, some who said that Christa had mixed feelings about her relatives in Truro.

Worthington family members and their friends made curious accusations about instances in the book. One example of their ire was a letter to the editor of the *Provincetown Banner* in which a friend complained that the book had stated that their daily croquet game began at the wrong hour.

From the launch of the book and during the summer, the DA and I were in the hot seat, although we each hunkered down at opposite ends of the peninsula. But when some startling new murders on the Cape distracted the public from Christa's story, O'Keefe resumed his work, unruffled.

A man's body was found tied to a tree in Barnstable having been burned alive. The remains were so badly charred a specialist from the Smithsonian Institution and a dentist from the State Medical Lab were needed to make an identification. O'Keefe had little information from the crime scene itself. Nearby, there was a gas container, a half-eaten apple, and a neatly folded pile of men's clothing. It took four months before the body was identified as a man who fled Bosnia and worked in a pizza parlor on Cape Cod. In his difficult months in the United States, he was known to authorities only for having tried to find a bed and three squares by setting fire to a trash can at Logan Airport, begging an officer to arrest him.

In August, another young victim was found stabbed in a boat house in Woods Hole after the boy had partied with a paroled sex offender. The alleged killer's name had not yet appeared on the Massachusetts Sex Offender Registry Board—until it was too late.

And recently a body was found in a closet in a Provincetown condo. At first he was thought to be a victim of autoerotic asphyxia, but then it was discovered that his arm was dissevered. That same week, in a front-page story, *Provincetown Banner* editor Hamilton Kahn wrote, "A tragically ironic aspect of the murder . . . was that his body was found *in a closet*, considering it had taken until he was thirty years old before he was able to *come out of the closet*." A letter followed the next week castigating the lead. This is a good example of the often tasteless parallels that Land's Enders seem to enjoy making when addressing unique events east of the Cape Cod Canal.

Like Christa's murder two years earlier, there is something about the remoteness of Cape Cod that exaggerates the gothic elements of a crime occurring here. Because of our community's deluxe tolerance for subcultures, whether it's Audubon soirees or cliques of transsexual ingénues, no matter their preferences, our open arms invite both the independent and the desperate to our hamlets, up and down the peninsula. It's Eden for endgamers, Eden for the rejected, for lost causes, for last-chancers. Henry Miller wrote, "In their loneliness, in their dream of love or lack of it, the lost are ever drifting to the water's edge."

More news from memorable characters in the book: In a recent dispatch from New York, Christa's ex-boyfriend, the magician, T. C. Churchwell, claims he was arrested for assault. He says that he clobbered a "Christa website" regular, who posted on *CrimeNews2000*. In an e-mail, T.C. explained that the "CN'er threatened to kill me and I beat the hell out of him. I did two months in Rikers."

More important, a suspect has finally been arrested in the Linda Silva murder case after seven years. Now behind bars at Barnstable County Jail, Paul DuBois, a foundations contractor who specialized in cement forms, had been a DSS client of Silva's. Silva had found him to be unfit to raise his children, and custody was awarded to his ex-wife. In the pages of *Invisible Eden*, Massachusetts State Police investigator Trooper John Kotfila tells me he believes the investigation was leading them back to the DSS connection.

John and Nancy Burch, Linda Silva's sister and brother-in-law, who I had visited at the Sea Surf Motel, were very pleased by the apprehension of a suspect after having relentlessly pestered the state police to find her killer. But this week a notice in the *Cape Cod Times* Police Log states: "TRURO— A motel owner and his wife were arrested on charges of drug distribution, drug possession and other related charges. . . ." The *Provincetown Banner* reported, "Truro Police arrested longtime residents of Truro and owners of the Sea Surf Motel on Beach Point, for possession and distribution of cocaine. . . . John Lundborn of the Truro Police Department said that the investigation had gone on for four or five years and that the cocaine they discovered was 'a sizeable amount.' " John and Nancy Burch were also arrested on weapons charges. I remember the gun that John Burch had handed to me in our interview—a big revolver he had claimed he'd purchased from a sketchy source he had thought might be involved in Linda Silva's murder. It's curious that the couple would have doggedly harassed the Massachusetts State Police for seven years about their sister's murder while they were at the same time allegedly involved in "drug distribution." It seems typical of Land's Enders' kooky hubris to work both sides.

And the newest little freshet of law enforcement gossip is a story about Truro Chief of Police John "Popcorn" Thomas. A Truro selectman has accused Chief Thomas of making "intimidating and threatening" remarks to him, saying that they were directed "not only to me but possibly to my friends and family." Selectman Christopher Lucy accused Chief Thomas of saying, "If you want to keep nosing into the police department, you're going to lose. . . . I guarantee you it's going to be a bloodbath." Lucy also described finding "a package containing a small toy police badge in his mailbox at Town Hall."

The *Provincetown Banner* reported that Chief Thomas "would not comment whether it was he who had left the toy police badge in Lucy's mail-box," and he would not discuss the investigation that he accused Lucy of meddling in, except to say that it involved "larceny of a boat." But the chief said he had never used the word *bloodbath*; it isn't in his vocabulary.

Chief Thomas' minor problems, the new Cape Cod murders, the arrest of the "cement forms suspect" in Linda Silva's murder case, and the arrest of that victim's family members for drug trafficking are distracting events in our small community. Yet Christa's killer is still at large.

An unsolved murder in our community has a resonating and telescoping effect. The "unsolved" aspect seems to widen, deepen, as if our town is standing at the lip of a canyon that only seems to get larger. One friend said that having no word about Christa's killer is similar to what families experience when loved ones disappear in wartime, when sons or fathers are identified as victims "missing in action." Earning that tragic label has a heroic aspect that might help some families adjust to their never knowing exactly what happened. War is senseless but romanticized in our culture, but an unsolved murder in a small town seems just plain senseless. Unlike the common military abbreviations and acronyms, there is no word for it.

Some residents still believe that the killer might be a local resident. He could be surfing at Long Nook Beach with the polar bear diehards dressed in neon pink wet suits. You might see him at the town dump or filling up at the Wellfleet Mobil on Route 6. He's standing in line at the Eastham Superette, buying a coffee refill for work, putting his paint-stained thermos under the spout, as he asks the clerk for a five-dollar scratch ticket. He's a regular, a mingler, he gets lost in the crowd and operates side by side with us. He might be within or perhaps outside O'Keefe's original list.

Last week I saw Tim Arnold in front of the Red Balloon toy shop, a high-end boutique where he had often browsed for toys with Christa and Ava. Tim wasn't wearing his eye patch, and I wondered if his vision had improved. Maybe he was doing better. But last summer, on June 23, the day before *Invisible Eden* was released, Tim's father, Bob Arnold, told the *Boston Herald* in a front-page story, that his son had been told by police that *he* is the primary suspect in the unsolved killing. Mr. Arnold said, "He knows that they think he is. We know it. And the whole world knows it."

Tim had told me that the state police had continued to "interview" him several times during the months after the murder. At his lowest point, they had intruded on his intake session at a help center in Hyannis, he said, where he had been taken for treatment for his depression and thoughts of suicide. He claimed that the police had grilled him brutally, probably hoping his anguished mental state might lead to a confession. Tim did not confess. But after his session with the troopers, Tim was so rattled and despondent he was admitted into a hospital program off-Cape for psychiatric treatment and remained there for a period of weeks before returning to Truro.

When I saw Tim last week, he was standing opposite the toy store like an innocent window-shopper. In his love affair with Christa, he *was a window-shopper*, never allowed to actually own the merchandise. He shuffled down the sidewalk in his familiar, cringing gait, always with the aura of a lonely-heart.

Tony Jackett, on the other hand, stands tall at his hallowed estuary, the clam flats east of the breakwater in P-town, still a beloved figure in that community. The shellfish constable is upbeat, always willing to have a chin-wag with fishermen and with high school kids. At low tide, he works on the flats and greets newcomers who must pay fees in order to get their tickets punched for a week of clamming privileges. They can rake for clams until they fill their buckets. They are allowed to harvest up to ten quarts per week.

Tony is the subject of a recent newspaper story called "Buried Treasure," about the first day of the clamming season. "Buried Treasure" is an awkward title if you remember Tony's trouble as a smuggler, when he tried to bury bales of marijuana in a sand dune to elude police. But the article says, "Pleased with the results of his propagation efforts, [Jackett] pronounced it 'a great year.'"

Breeding mollusks is not the only thing Tony is famous for; he'll always be known as the father of Christa Worthington's out-of-wedlock baby. But this seaside tri-town area rolls with the punches, and all seems forgiven. Tony has attained regular visiting privileges with Ava and has bonded with the little girl. He's a father figure in many residents' eyes, a gentleman, who works the clam parcels with the local high school science teacher, giving lessons to students. But dressed in tight blue jeans and his signature black leather jacket, he still looks like a ladies' man who just won't die.

Although they had at first been vocal and very aggressive with the investigating officers, the Worthington family today wants to be left alone. John Worthington, Christa's uncle and the patriarch of the clan, recently told a local newspaper, "We really are shutting down on this. . . . We're trying to move on with our lives." In the same story, First Assistant District Attorney Robert Welch III, a prosecutor assigned to the Worthington case, discussed the still unfruitful investigation. He said, "We are working on it. It hasn't reached the status of a cold case. It's a *work-in-progress*."

The most recent development in the Worthington case is the new involvement of a special prosecutor from the Plymouth DA's office. The prosecutor, Frank Middleton, was brought in after Amyra Chase, Ava's new guardian, and the Worthington family, had asked Attorney General Thomas F. Reilly to remove DA Michael O'Keefe from the case. They believed that O'Keefe disparages Worthington's reputation in this book. The *Banner* states that the book "cast Cape and Islands First District Attorney Michael O'Keefe in a dubious light." Of course, what rattles her family are the details of Christa's life. O'Keefe's comments were never unwarranted or out of context. O'Keefe declined to recuse himself from the case but agreed to have Middleton step in, hoping to calm the Worthington family's jitters. If a killer is eventually brought to trial, O'Keefe would certainly be the brains behind the prosecution's strategy, even if he isn't standing at the bench.

Christa's baby girl, Ava, is five years old and will be starting kindergarten in the fall. Living in Cohasset with Amyra Chase and her new siblings, Ava has a busy family life. She regularly sees her dad, Tony, and visits her "other family" in Provincetown. The beauty of Land's End is part of both Tony's and Christa's heritage, and Ava belongs here as much as she belongs in Cohasset.

Neither Jackett nor Chase can completely erase the bloodied starting place where she'd last seen her mother. I think of the time Christa participated in the "Provincetown Drift Bottle Project," writing her wishes for Ava on a scrap of paper. The container was launched with Christa's love poem to her daughter, and the bottle is still drifting at sea, crisscrossing deep, unnameable canyons. Ava will find her mother in her own way.

Once the plywood is pried off the weathered door frame, and a new door is hung at the little house on Depot Road, someone might want to buy it. But with winter coming, fewer people are house-hunting. The windward cliffs leach from green veils to oat. Hummocks of dune grass are flattened in the heartless easterlies. In one week, the marsh elder flamed red then dropped its fringe. Spikesedge and cordgrass fade to dirty white and the woods behind Christa's bungalow are etched in delicate lines, silver streaked. Nothing stops the cold routine at year's end: the frost heaves, leaf rot, salt winds that scour and burn the tender shoots but not the deeper roothold.

ACKNOWLEDGMENTS

A great many sources have come together to be directly involved in the life of this book. Christa Worthington's friends from childhood and from Vassar College, her editors and colleagues during her twenty years as a fashion writer in New York, London, and Paris, and many others stepped forward to offer a detailed portrait of their friend. Their unedited statements, incandescent memories, and authentic insights about Christa have helped to reveal her in these pages. From these voices and from each precise context, I have accrued facts and meanings to illuminate Christa Worthington's story as a felt life. These sources provided detailed accounts that enabled me to realize particular scenes, both Christa's rewarding moments and the many conflicts she faced. Without the gracious cooperation of these individuals, this book could not have been written.

In addition to the sources mentioned directly throughout the text, I wish to note a number of people whose comments were like bedrock, and whose insights mapped my journey backward to find Christa. My thanks to Eli Gottlieb, Jay Mulvaney, Gail Motlin, Carole Maso, Kim Gibson, John Wotjacinski, Belinda Hayes, Barbara Holloway, and Ellen Webb.

Thanks to Avery Chenoweth, David Brophy, Hugh Cosman, Billy Kimball, Jody Cohen, and Esther Gottlieb.

Local residents and friends in Truro were most helpful, and I am grateful to Susan Baker, Keith Althaus, Betty Groom, Barbara Perry, Warren Roderick, Helen McNeil, Nick Brown, Chris Busa, John and Nancy Burch, and Doris and Alfred Silva.

Several editors and journalists who had worked with Christa during her career were particularly key to my understanding of the world of fashion journalism. My thanks to Jeff Stone and Kim Johnson Gross, Christa's editors at Chic Simple; to Bob Morris, columnist for the *New York Times;* to Kate Betts and Thomas Moran, who shared their experiences as writers at *W* and other Fairchild publications; to magazine editors Mallen DeSantis at *Cosmopolitan* and Deb Kirk at *Elle* and *Harper's Bazaar;* and to Christa's colleagues Karen Brailsford and Tatyana Mishel, who had worked beside her.

My gratitude to Emily Dooley of the *Cape Cod Times*, who was of major importance to me, and to her colleagues K. C. Myers, Eric Williams, Karen Jeffrey. During the writing of this book, I have relied on hundreds of both current and archival newspaper accounts. My appreciation to Robin Johnson, librarian and archivist at the *Cape Cod Times*, who helped me to locate story archives about Cape Cod murders including the still unsolved 1974 case of the "Woman in the Dunes" and stories about serial killer Tony "ChopChop" Costa, among others. I have depended on the reliable roundup and redux by area reporters Ellen Barry, Sally Jacobs, and John Ellement of the *Boston Globe;* Hamilton Kahn and Kaimi Rose Lum of the *Provincetown Banner;* and Marilyn Miller of the *Cape Codder.*

I became immersed in Christa's own essays and columns from the archives of *Women's Wear Daily, W, Elle,* the *New York Times,* the *Independent* of London, *Harper's Bazaar,* and others, discovering in these examples what her editor Jeff Stone had once said, that "Christa was a fashion anthropologist." In her three Chic Simple texts and in all of Christa's writings we find a shining mural of fashion journalism. But sometimes we can glimpse its opposite face as Christa often comments on the human grain that exists beneath the glitter and the polished surfaces.

I am grateful to the law enforcement professionals who have met with me during the first year of the investigation. Thanks to Truro police officers Kyle Takakjian and David Perry, and to Truro Police Chief John Thomas. Thanks to the following members of the murder investigation team of the Massachusetts State Police: Troopers John Kotfila, James Massari, William Burke, Robert Knott, and Trooper James Plath. Thanks to attorneys Edward McLaughlin and Chris Snow.

My deepest gratitude to Massachusetts Cape and Islands District Attorney Michael O'Keefe.

Above all, I am grateful for the sustained candor of principal figures in this story who have talked openly despite the upheaval in their lives. Thanks to Tony Jackett, Susan Jackett, T. C. Churchwell, and Tim Arnold.

To Gail Hochman, Tracy Kidder, Melanie Thernstrom, Nancy Rosenblum, Judith Grossman, Alison Presley, Kristen Bearse, and to Gerry Howard, my personal thanks.

My gratitude and special thanks to Charles Conrad, my editor.

REFERENCES

Arnold, Tim. *The Winter Mittens.* New York: Simon & Schuster, 1988.

Berger, Josef. *Cape Cod Pilot.* Boston: Northeastern University Press, 1985.

Chancellor, Philip M. *Illustrated Handbook of the Bach Flower Remedies.* New York: McGraw-Hill, 1980.

Corbett, Scott. *Sea Fox.* New York: Thomas Crowell, 1956.

Damore, Leo. *In His Garden.* New York: Dell, 1981.

Fairchild, John. *Chic Savages.* New York: Simon & Schuster, 1989.

Groves, Betsy McAlister. *Children Who See Too Much.* Boston: Beacon Press, 2002.

Hewlett, Sylvia Ann. *Creating a Life.* New York: Talk Miramax Books, 2002.

Leahy, Christopher, John Hanson Mitchell, and Thomas Conuel. *The Nature of Massachusetts.* New York: Perseus Publishing, 1996.

Lowry, Beverly. *Crossed Over.* New York: Alfred A. Knopf, 1992.

Malcolm, Janet. *The Journalist and the Murderer.* New York: Alfred A. Knopf, 1990.

Maso, Carole. *The Room Lit by Roses.* Washington, D.C.: Counterpoint, 2000.

Rich, Shebnah. *Landmarks and Sea Marks.* Boston: Charles E. Tuttle, 1988.

Thoreau, Henry David. *Cape Cod.* Eds. Joseph J. Moldenhauer and Elizabeth H. Witherell. Princeton: Princeton University Press, 1988.

Whalen, Richard F. *Truro.* New York: Xlibris, 2002.

Worthington, Christa. *Chic Simple: Accessories.* Eds. Kim Johnson Gross and Jeff Stone. New York: Alfred A. Knopf, 1996.

———. *Chic Simple: Clothes.* Eds. Kim Johnson Gross and Jeff Stone. New York: Alfred A. Knopf, 1993.

———. *Chic Simple: Scarves.* Eds. Kim Johnson Gross and Jeff Stone. New York: Alfred A. Knopf, 1993.